The European Arrest Warrant and *In Absentia* Judgments

The European Arrest Warrant and *In Absentia* Judgments

Kei Hannah Brodersen, Vincent Glerum and André Klip

eleven
international publishing

Published, sold and distributed by Eleven International Publishing
P.O. Box 85576
2508 CG The Hague
The Netherlands
Tel.: +31 70 33 070 33
Fax: +31 70 33 070 30
email: sales@elevenpub.nl
www.elevenpub.com

Sold and distributed in USA and Canada
Independent Publishers Group
814 N. Franklin Street
Chicago, IL 60610, USA
Order Placement: +1 800 888 4741
Fax: +1 312 337 5985
orders@ipgbook.com
www.ipgbook.com

Eleven International Publishing is an imprint of Boom uitgevers Den Haag.

The InAbsentiEAW research project is financed by the European Union's Justice Programme (2014-2020).

ISBN 978-94-6236-985-6
ISBN 978-9460-94-439-0 (e-book)

Table of Contents

Preface

This book is the result of intensive cooperation between several partners (both practitioners and academics) with the aim of tackling problems resulting from *in absentia* judgments in the context of the European Arrest Warrant (EAW). The study was conducted in the years 2018-2019 and involves six Member States: Belgium, Hungary, Ireland, the Netherlands, Poland and Romania. In essence, the research project aims at identifying and solving problems which arise in the application of Article 4a(1) FD 2002/584/JHA in practice. The origin of the project lies in the experiences of the District Court of Amsterdam – one of the many executing judicial authorities across the European Union who are tasked with deciding on the execution of EAWs – in dealing with EAWs concerning decisions *in absentia*. However, it appeared that the problems faced in Amsterdam are Union wide. The European Commission financed the study as an Action Grant.

The reader will find not only the main document, which contains the analysis of the issues at stake, concluded with recommendations, but also a proposal to amend the form concerning Article 4a(1) of Framework Decision 2002/584 on the European Arrest Warrant.

In addition, we provide the reader with a Guide to the case-law of the Court of Justice concerning the EAW and to the case-law of the ECtHR concerning *in absentia* proceedings. Last but not least, the practitioner will be pleased to find a Manual for Filling in and Assessing Section (d) of the form for issuing an EAW.

Kei Hannah Brodersen
Vincent Glerum
André Klip

Note to the Reader

Report

Although the report is based on the national reports produced by the experts participating in the project, the analyses, conclusions and recommendations contained in the report are the work of the three authors.[1]

The manuscript was finalised on 30 August 2019. Relevant developments were taken into account up to that date.

Terminology

Although the project title uses the expression '*in absentia*',[2] the title of the report instead uses the expression "rendered following a trial at which the person concerned did not appear in person".

One of the findings of the report is that Member States have varying interpretations of their respective national notions of a trial '*in absentia*', that these national notions do not necessarily correspond to the Union law notion of a trial '*in absentia*' and that these national notions influence the interpretation and application by the authorities of the Member States of Union law concerning EAWs. That is precisely why the Union legislator deliberately chose not to use the multi-interpretable expression '*in absentia*'.

However, old habits die hard. When interpreting the relevant Union legislation, even the Court of Justice still uses the expression '*in absentia*' to denote situations in which the person concerned did not appear in person at the trial.

In writing the report, the authors did not strive to avoid the use of the expression systematically. If only for stylistic reasons, the shorter expression sometimes is preferable above its somewhat unwieldy alternative of "the person concerned did not appear in person at the trial". The authors trust that the context of any reference to the expression '*in absentia*' is such that the reader will not be left in doubt as to its origin (Union law or national law) or its meaning. Nevertheless, forewarned is forearmed.

---

1 The authors would like to thank the national experts for all their hard work in preparing the national reports and in discussing the Report with the authors. They would also like to extend their gratitude to the members of the Sounding Board for their comments to the Report.

2 *Improving Mutual Recognition of European Arrest Warrants for the Purpose of Executing In Absentia Judgments.*

Part I
The Research Project Report

1 Introduction

1.1 Reasons for the Research Project

The research project *Improving Mutual Recognition of European Arrest Warrants for the Purpose of Executing In Absentia Judgments* concerns the application of Article 4a(1) of Framework Decision 2002/584/JHA on the European Arrest Warrant (FD 2002/584/JHA).[1] This provision was inserted into that Framework Decision by Framework Decision 2009/299/JHA on the mutual recognition of *in absentia* decisions (FD 2009/299/JHA).[2] The latter Framework Decision seeks to "enhance the procedural rights of persons subject to criminal proceedings, to facilitate judicial cooperation in criminal matters and, in particular, to improve mutual recognition of judicial decisions between Member States".[3] Article 4a(1) FD 2002/584/JHA contains an optional ground for refusal to execute a EAW concerning a decision rendered following a trial at which the requested person did not appear in person. In essence, this research project aims at identifying and solving problems which arise in the application of Article 4a(1) FD 2002/584/JHA *in practice* and which detract from the aforementioned objectives of this provision.

The origin of this research project lies in the experiences of the District Court of Amsterdam – one of the many executing judicial authorities across the European Union who are tasked with deciding on the execution of EAWs – in dealing with EAWs concerning decisions *in absentia*. On average, the District Court of Amsterdam deals with about 600 EAWs from other Member States each year. EAWs concerning decisions *in absentia* are a particularly problematic category.

In many cases the application of Article 4a(1) has led in the past – and still leads at present – to numerous practical and legal problems. The main problems are that the issuing authorities:

- do not *fill in section (d)* of the model-EAW (the section which relates to Article 4a(1));
- do not use the *prescribed standard text* of section (d);

1 Council Framework Decision 2002/584/JHA of 13 June 2002 on the European Arrest Warrant and the surrender procedures between Member States (*OJ* 2002, L 190, p. 1).

2 Council Framework Decision 2009/299/JHA of 26 February 2009 amending Framework Decisions 2002/584/JHA, 2005/214/JHA, 2006/783/JHA, 2008/909/JHA and 2008/947/JHA, thereby enhancing the procedural rights of persons and fostering the application of the principle of mutual recognition to decisions rendered in the absence of the person concerned at the trial (*OJ* 2009, L 81, p. 24).

3 Art. 1 FD 2009/299/JHA.

- do not use the *consolidated language versions* of section (d) but instead use (poorly) translated texts; or
- provide *incorrect, unclear, unintelligible, or contradictory information.*

These problems:

- necessitate the executing judicial authority *requesting supplementary information* from the issuing judicial authority (sometimes repeatedly);
- lead to *delays and extra costs* in the issuing and executing Member States;
- can result in some cases in a – sometimes even unjustified – *refusal to execute the EAW* (unjustified in the sense that had the information supplied by the issuing judicial authority been correct, clear, consistent and complete, the EAW would have been executed), thereby creating a risk of impunity of the requested person; and
- can result in a *surrender* which *in hindsight* was *incorrect* (incorrect in the sense that had the information been correct, clear, consistent and complete, the executing judicial authority would have taken another decision).

Clearly, such problems may prevent FD 2009/299/JHA from realising not only its objectives of facilitating judicial cooperation in criminal matters and improving mutual recognition of judicial decisions, but also its objective of enhancing procedural rights. Such problems may even lead to impunity of the requested person.

Moreover, such problems can clearly have a negative effect on the high level of mutual trust that should exist between the (judicial authorities of the) Member States. For example, cases in which the issuing judicial authorities provide incorrect information can affect the confidence of the executing judicial authorities in the correct application of Union legislation by the issuing judicial authorities. Also, asking for information when there is no need for this information may affect the confidence of the issuing judicial authorities in the correct application of Union legislation by the executing judicial authorities. Improving mutual recognition, which is one of the objectives of FD 2009/299/JHA, is dependent on mutual trust between the (judicial authorities) of the Member States.

A statistical analysis of the cases dealt with by the District Court of Amsterdam may illustrate these problems. In 2017, *e.g.*, the District Court of Amsterdam took a decision in 475 EAW-cases, *viz.* 299 prosecution-EAWs and 179 execution-EAWs (Tables 1.1-1.3).

Table 1.1 The total number of EAWs decided by the executing judicial authority in which the requested person did not consent to surrender

Year	Number of cases
2008	Unknown
2009	Unknown
2010	213
2011	571
2012	570
2013	533
2014	550
2015	501
2016	451
2017	475

Table 1.2 The total number of EAWs for the purpose of prosecution

Year	Number of prosecution cases
2008	Unknown
2009	Unknown
2010	141
2011	344
2012	331
2013	299
2014	336
2015	281
2016	288
2017	299

Table 1.3 The total number of EAWs for the purpose of execution of a custodial sentence or detention order

Year	Number of prosecution cases
2008	**Unknown**
2009	Unknown
2010	77
2011	240
2012	260

Year	Number of prosecution cases
2008	**Unknown**
2013	243
2014	224
2015	223
2016	165
2017	179

Both prosecution-EAWs and execution-EAWs show high percentages of cases in which the 60 and 90 days' time limits were not complied with (Table 1.4).

Table 1.4 The total number of cases in which either the 60 days' time limit or the 90 days' time limit could not be observed, broken down into prosecution-EAWs and execution-EAWs

Year	Number of prosecution cases	60 days' limit exceeded	90 days' limit exceeded
2008	Unknown	Unknown	Unknown
2009	Unknown	Unknown	Unknown
2010	141	53 (37.6%)	3 (2.1%)
2011	344	250 (72.7%)	25 (7.3%)
2012	331	173 (52.3%)	12 (3.6%)
2013	299	257 (86.0%)	28 (9.4%)
2014	336	296 (88.1%)	36 (10.7%)
2015	281	184 (65.5%)	22 (7.8%)
2016	288	256 (88.9%)	29 (10.1%)
2017	299	259 (86.6%)	53 (17.7%)

Year	Number of execution cases	60 days' limit exceeded	90 days' limit exceeded
2008	Unknown	Unknown	Unknown
2009	Unknown	Unknown	Unknown
2010	77	17 (22.1%)	1 (1.3%)
2011	240	156 (65%)	6 (2.5%)
2012	260	110 (42.3%)	14 (5.4%)
2013	243	197 (81.1%)	15 (6.2%)
2014	224	188 (83.9%)	24 (10.7%)

Year	Number of execution cases	60 days' limit exceeded	90 days' limit exceeded
2015	223	148 (66.4%)	30 (13.5%)
2016	165	149 (90.3%)	18 (10.9%)
2017	179	148 (82.7%)	22 (12.3%)

When the execution-EAWs are broken down into cases in which Article 4a(1) was not applicable and cases in which that provision was applicable, it emerges that Article 4a(1) was applicable to 121 execution-EAWs (out of a total of 179) (67.5%). In 92 of those 121 cases (76%), supplementary information was requested. In 81.5% of those 92 cases the 60 days' time limit was exceeded and in roughly 15% the 90 days' time limit (Tables 1.5 and 1.6).

Table 1.5 The total number of cases in which Article 15(2) FD 2002/584/JHA was applied because the information in the EAW was insufficient to verify whether the conditions of Article 4a(1) were met

Year	Number of cases in which the court applied Article 15(2)	Number of cases in which the public prosecutor applied Article 15(2)	Unknown[1]
2011[2]	0	61	1
2012	0	131	1
2013	0	63	2
2014	3	71	3
2015	3	87	2
2016	7	57	7
2017[3]	1	91	7

[1] When the court asks questions, this is mentioned in the final judgment, which is digitally accessible. Whether the public prosecutor asked a question, can (in most cases) only be assessed through the case files. The unknown category is, therefore, only applicable to the category 'Amount of cases in which the public prosecutor applied Art. 15(2)'.

[2] From 1 August 2011.

[3] The nine cases in which the Public Prosecutor was declared inadmissible on account of a real risk of inhuman or degrading detention conditions in the issuing Member State are not taken into account for this overview. (Declaring the Public Prosecutor inadmissible is the Dutch equivalent of bringing the surrender procedure to an end (ECJ, judgment of 4 April 2016, *Pál Aranyosi and Robert Căldăraru v. Generalstaatsanwaltschaft Bremen*, C-404/15 and C-659/15 PPU, ECLI:EU:C:2016:198, para. 104).)

Table 1.6 In case of application of Article 15(2) FD 2002/584/JHA because the information in the EAW was insufficient to verify whether the conditions of Article 4a(1) were met: the total number of cases in which either the 60 days' limit or the 90 days' limit could not be observed

Year	Number of cases in which Article 15(2) was applied	60 days' limit exceeded	90 days' limit exceeded
2011[1]	61	32 (52.5%)	1 (1.6%)
2012	131	59 (45.0%)	10 (7.6%)
2013	63	48 (76.2%)	5 (7.9%)
2014	74	65 (87.8%)	14 (18.9%)
2015	90	66 (73.7%)	25 (27.8%)
2016	64	56 (87.5%)	15 (23.4%)
2017[2]	92	75 (81.5%)	15 (16.3%)

[1] From 1 August 2011.

[2] The nine cases in which the Public Prosecutor was declared inadmissible on account of a real risk of inhuman or degrading detention conditions in the issuing Member State are not taken into account for this overview.

In 41 of the total of 121 cases in which Article 4a(1) was applicable, the District Court of Amsterdam refused or partially refused to execute the EAW on the basis of that provision (roughly 34%). Regarding the other 58 execution-EAWs (179-121), the District Court of Amsterdam (partially) refused to execute 7 EAWs (roughly 12%) (Tables 1.7 and 1.8).

Table 1.7 The total number of cases in which the execution of the EAW was refused on the basis of Article 4a(1) FD 2002/584/JHA

Year	Number of execution cases	Requested person absent or partially absent[1]	Refusal based on Article 4a(1)	Partial refusal based on Article 4a(1)[2]
2011[3]	**97**	**34**	**0 (0%)**	**7 (20.6%)**
2012	260	114	12 (10.6%)	14 (12.3%)
2013	243	99	13 (13.1%)	9 (9.1%)
2014	224	109	7 (6.4%)	6 (5.5%)
2015	223	127	15 (11.8%)	12 (9.4%)
2016	165	79	11 (13.9%)	8 (10.1%)
2017	179[4]	121	33 (27.3%)	8 (6.6%)

[1] The percentages are based on the numbers in this column.

[2] 'Partially present' refers to cases in which the EAW is comprised of multiple underlying sentences and in which the requested person appeared in one (or more) proceedings and did not appear in one (or more) other proceedings.

[3] From 1 August 2011.

[4] The nine cases in which the Public Prosecutor was declared inadmissible on account of a real risk of inhuman or degrading detention conditions in the issuing Member State are not taken into account for this overview.

Table 1.8 The total number of execution cases in which the execution of the EAW was refused

Year	Number of execution cases	Refused	Partially refused	Public prosecutor inadmissible (detention conditions)
2008	Unknown	Unknown	Unknown	Unknown
2009	Unknown	Unknown	Unknown	Unknown
2010[1]	77	10 (13.0%)	13 (16.9%)	0 (0%)
2011	240	8 (3.3%)	50 (20.8%)	0 (0%)
2012	260	16 (6.2%)	53 (20.4%)	0 (0%)
2013	243	19 (7.8%)	50 (20.6%)	0 (0%)
2014	224	22 (9.8%)	41 (18.3%)	0 (0%)
2015	223	25 (11.2%)	33 (14.8%)	0 (0%)
2016	165	14 (8.5%)	12 (7.3%)	0 (0%)
2017	179[2]	39 (21.8%)	10 (5.6%)	10 (5.6%)

[1] The figures for 2010 are incomplete. Only the months May (partially) until December were reviewed. Data for the period of January-May 2010 was inaccessible.

[2] In six of those cases the Public Prosecutor was declared inadmissible on account of a real risk of inhuman or degrading detention condition for the requested person.

These figures show that the extent of the problems is significant indeed. In the experience of the District Court of Amsterdam, apart from cases concerning detention conditions[4] or the right to an independent court,[5] only cases involving *in absentia* judgments show such an incidence of requests for supplementary information, of non-compliance with the time limits and of refusals.

The problems encountered by the District Court of Amsterdam may be caused by:

- *non-implementation* of the Framework Decision by the Member States (the Framework Decision contains an *optional* ground for refusal; if the executing Member State has implemented FD 2009/299/JHA, where the issuing Member State has not, the executing judicial authority will expect the issuing authority to apply Article 4a(1) FD

4 ECJ, judgment of 4 April 2016, *Pál Aranyosi and Robert Căldăraru v. Generalstaatsanwaltschaft Bremen*, C-404/15 and C-659/15 PPU, ECLI:EU:C:2016:198.

5 ECJ, judgment of 25 July 2018, *Minister for Justice and Equality (Deficiencies in the system of justice)*, C-216/18 PPU, EU:C:2018:586.

2002/584/JHA, while the issuing judicial authority will not apply this provision, because it has not yet been transposed into the national laws of the issuing Member State);
- *differences concerning the implementation* (including implementation as an optional or mandatory ground for refusal) *and/or the application* of the implementing national legislation by the (judicial authorities of the) Member States; differences concerning the implementation of FD 2009/299/JHA and/or the application of the implementing national legislation may affect:
  - which information is supplied by the issuing judicial authority and/or which information is requested by the executing judicial authority,
  - the way in which the issuing judicial authority interprets a request for information by the executing judicial authority, and
  - the way in which the executing judicial authority interprets the information provided by the issuing judicial authority;
- *incorrect implementation* by the Member States;
- *incorrect application* of legislation adopted to transpose FD 2009/299/JHA by issuing and executing judicial authorities of the Member States;
- the fact that a *refusal* of surrender based on Article 4a(1) *will not have any impact on the validity of the judgment and will not influence the possibility of issuing an EAW with regard to the same judgment*; in case of refusal the requested person is still at risk to be apprehended in and surrendered by another Member State.[6]

It was expected that judicial authorities of other Member States, whether they are issuing or executing judicial authorities, are confronted with similar practical problems – an assumption that was confirmed by the research project.

1.2 Objectives of the Research Project

The research project intended to:
- *identify problems* concerning the application of Article 4a(1) FD 2002/584/JHA by issuing and executing judicial authorities;
- *develop common standards* if practical problems are shown to be the result of divergent interpretations of the relevant European and domestic legislation; and
- *propose practical solutions* to the problems identified.

6 Cf. ECJ, judgment of 25 July 2018, *AY*, C-268/17, ECLI:EU:C:2018:602.

The first intention (to identify problems) is covered by this report, whereas the other two intentions (to develop common standards and propose practical solutions) will be covered by the Manual[7] and the Guide[8] which the research project will deliver.

By developing common standards and proposing practical solutions, the research project contributes to:

- *speeding up the procedure* in issuing and executing Member States;
- *lowering the costs* of the procedure in issuing and executing Member States;
- *reducing* the number of *unjustified refusals*;
- *reducing* the number of *unjustified* cases of *surrender*; and
- *improving mutual understanding* and *communication.*

Once common standards and best practices are applied for filling in part (d) of the EAW and for verifying whether the conditions of Article 4a(1) are met, there will be much less need for supplementary information. Hence, the number of cases in which:

- the executing judicial authority must devote part of its time to formulating questions to and reviewing answers from the issuing judicial authority; and
- the issuing judicial authority must devote part of its time to answering questions from the executing authority,

will necessarily decrease. The number of cases in which the time limits are not complied with will also decrease. In the knowledge that each judicial authority adheres to the same common standards and applies the same best practices, mutual trust between the judicial authorities will increase. All this will result in less costs for the issuing and executing Member States.

Of course, the requested person will also benefit from these results. Once common standards and best practices are applied, it is less likely that the rules which are intended to enhance his/her procedural rights will be disregarded or misconstrued.

1.3 METHODOLOGY

The approach of the research project is primarily a *practice-oriented approach*: practitioners who deal with EAWs almost on a daily basis carried out the research project, thereby ensuring that the outputs and results are adapted to the wants and needs of issuing and executing judicial authorities. They have intimate knowledge of the relevant framework decision, their national legislation and their national case-law and are best placed to:

7 *Manual for filling in and assessing section (d) of the EAW.*
8 *Case-law Guide.*

- identify any *practical* problems;
- pinpoint the *causes* of these problems;
- devise practical *solutions* to these problems;
- develop practice-oriented *common standards and best practices*;
- develop *practice-oriented tools* to help practitioners deal with Article 4a(1);
- formulate *recommendations to remedy any defects in national or Union legislation* (if any).

In addition to the practitioners, some of the participants are eminent legal scholars, thereby ensuring that the implementation of the research project conforms to high scholarly and methodological standards. The experts participating in the research project are:
- Mr Justice John Edwards, judge of the Court of Appeal of Ireland and Adjunct Professor of Law at the University of Limerick (Ireland);
- Mr Jan Van Gaever, advocate general at the Court of Appeal of Brussels (Belgium);
- Prof. Vincent Glerum, legal adviser at the District Court of Amsterdam and professor of International and European Criminal Law at the University of Groningen (the Netherlands);[9]
- Dr Szabolcs Hornyák, judge, National Office for the Judiciary (Hungary);
- Mr Hans Kijlstra, judge in the District Court of Amsterdam (the Netherlands);[10]
- Prof. André Klip, professor of Criminal Law, Criminal Procedure and the Transnational Aspects of Criminal Law at Maastricht University and honorary judge in the Court of Appeal of 's-Hertogenbosch (the Netherlands);
- Dr Mariana Radu, Ministry of Justice, Central Authority for EAWs (Romania);[11]
- Prof. Małgorzata Wąsek-Wiaderek, professor of Criminal Procedure at the Catholic University of Lublin and judge in the Supreme Court (Poland).[12]

The participating Member States represent a mix of 'Western' and 'Eastern' Member States and of Member States with civil law and common law legal systems (Belgium, Hungary,

9 With respect to *issuing* judicial authorities, the research is based on information provided by Sjaak Pouw, public prosecutor, and Maik Lammertink, assistant public prosecutor, both of the Fugitive Active Search Team of the National Office (*Landelijk Parket*) of the Public Prosecution Service (*Openbaar Ministerie*).

10 Mr Hans Kijlstra is advisor to the project.

11 The research was done by Mariana Radu, Mihaela Vasiescu (senior judge in the Court of Appeal of Târgu Mureş), Adriana Ispas (senior judge in the Court of Appeal of Constanţa) and Filimon Florin (senior judge in the Court of Appeal of Oradea).

12 The research (in particular, the analyses of case files; some translations; draft answers to some questions) was done by Adrian Zbiciak (assessor in the District Court in Chełm (VII Criminal Chamber) and PhD student at the Catholic University in Lublin) and Paula Duda (advocate trainee and PhD student at the Catholic University in Lublin).

Ireland, the Netherlands, Poland and Romania). This selection facilitates dissemination of the output and results of the research project.

The research project was led by a management team, consisting of Kei Hannah Brodersen (Maastricht University, project manager), Prof. Vincent Glerum (principal researcher) and Prof. André Klip (project leader).

The research was carried out roughly in three stages. During the *first stage*, a questionnaire was drafted by the management team. This questionnaire was intended as a tool to:

- identify any practical problems issuing judicial authorities and executing judicial authorities may experience when deciding on the issuing or on the execution of EAWs regarding *in absentia* judgments of conviction, and
- identify the roots of these problems.

The questionnaire consists of five parts: 1) preliminary matters, 2) national legislation, 3) actual application of national legislation implementing the framework decisions, 4) statistical data on the actual application of the national legislation transposing the framework decisions and 5) conclusion, opinions, etc.

Part 2.1 concerns *national* rules on service of summons, *in absentia* proceedings and possible recourses against *in absentia* judgments of conviction. These national rules are not covered by FD 2002/584/JHA and FD 2009/299/JHA, as these framework decisions do not seek to harmonise these rules. However, it was deemed necessary to include questions about those rules, because they may have an impact on the application of the rules set out in Article 4a(1) FD 2002/584/JHA.

With regard to Part 3, various methods were used by the national experts. Some experts conducted case file research. Other experts reviewed relevant case-law. A number of experts also referred to personal experiences and discussions with other practitioners as source material for the answers to the questions. In some Member States with a decentralised EAW-jurisdiction, a selection of issuing and executing judicial authorities provided the relevant answers. One expert interviewed judges from a select number of judicial authorities and sent questions to all executing judicial authorities of that Member State.

The objective of Part 4 was to put the answers to the questions in Parts 2 and 3 in their proper context and, if any problems with the application of Article 4a(1) were established, to illustrate the frequency of those problems, the severity of their consequences and the need for common solutions.

The questionnaire was discussed with all the experts at a meeting on 12 March 2018. With some revisions, the questionnaire was adopted.

During the *second stage*, the national experts set out to fill in the questionnaire with regard to their respective Member States. The questionnaires were discussed with all the experts at a meeting on 30 October 2018. As it turned out from the questionnaires, some project Member States do not register data on the execution of EAWs[13] or do not distinguish between prosecution-EAWs and execution-EAWs, let alone EAWs concerning *in absentia* judgments.[14] In other Member States, only case file research managed to unearth the data that was required.[15] As a result, the overall picture was too fragmentary to support firm conclusions. Therefore, it was decided not to subject the available statistical data to analysis and comparison.

During the *third stage*, the project report was drafted by the authors. The first draft was discussed with all the experts at a meeting between 24 and 26 April 2019. On the basis of the revised draft, the members of the Sounding Board advised, *inter alia*, on the relevance of the report and, in particular, on the relevance of the recommendations.[16] Their comments were taken into account. At a further meeting between 26 and 28 August 2019 with all the experts, the authors adopted the revised draft.

1.4 BRIEF OUTLINE OF THE REPORT

In the next chapters, the findings of the research project will be presented, by dealing with some general issues first and then gradually zooming in on Article 4a(1) FD 2002/584/JHA and its components.

Chapter 2 deals with some generalities of the EAW-system. By devoting attention to the issuing and executing judicial authorities, the EAW-form, language regimes, requests for supplementary information and time limits, this chapter paints the essential background against which the research project's findings are presented in Chapters 3-8.

Article 4a(1) contains an optional ground for refusal. All project Member States transposed that provision, either as a mandatory or as an optional ground for refusal. Chapter 3 discusses the system of Article 4a(1) and issues relating to its transposition and application in the legal systems of the project Member States, in particular, issues concerning the optional nature of Article 4a(1).

---

13 *See, e.g.*, BE, report, p. 49 and HU, report, p. 41.
14 IE, report, p. 100.
15 *See, e.g.*, PL, report, pp. 90-91.
16 Members of the Sounding Board:
- Mr Patrice Amar, public prosecutor (France);
- Mr Atanas Atanasov, judge at the Sofia Appellate Court (Bulgaria);
- Mrs Joana Ferreira, prosecutor general (Portugal);
- Mr Per Hedvall, Swedish Prosecution Authority (Sweden);
- Mr Hans-Holger Herrnfeld, Federal Ministry of Justice and Consumer Protection (Germany);
- Dr Salvatore Tesoriero, defence counsel (Italy).

The project Member States use varying definitions of the key notion of the research project, the notion of '*in absentia*'. Therefore, Chapter 4 is dedicated to the meaning of that notion, both as a matter of Union law and as a matter of national law.

With respect to another important concept of Article 4a(1) – the concept of a 'trial resulting in the decision' – the project Member States again use differing definitions. Chapter 5 concerns the autonomous meaning of that pivotal concept.

Chapters 6 and 7 discuss the particular circumstances – enumerated in Article 4a(1)(a)-(d) – in which the executing judicial authority may not refuse to execute the EAW even though the person concerned did not appear in person at the 'trial resulting in the decision' (summons in person; representation by a mandated legal counsellor; the right to a retrial or an appeal).

Chapter 8 deals with the margin of discretion of the executing judicial authority with regard to the decision on the execution of the EAW when none of the circumstances dealt with in the previous two chapters applies.

Chapter 9 concludes the report. This chapter contains a summary of the conclusions drawn in Chapters 4-8 and sets out the recommendations which arise from the findings of the project.

2 Generalities of the EAW-System

2.1 Introduction

This chapter is dedicated to generalities of the EAW-system. The subjects dealt with in this chapter constitute the essential background against which the research project's findings with regard to Article 4a FD 2002/584/JHA are presented in Chapters 3-8. These subjects are: the transposition of FD 2009/299/JHA (Section 2.2), the issuing of EAWs (Section 2.3) and the execution of EAWs (Section 2.4).

2.2 Transposition of Framework Decision 2009/299/JHA

2.2.1 *General Remarks*

Initially, Article 5(1) 1 FD 2002/584/JHA provided for a guarantee given by the issuing Member State to the executing Member State that the requested person may apply for a retrial at which s/he may be present, in case the EAW was issued for the purpose of executing a sentence or a detention order imposed by a decision rendered *in absentia* and if the person concerned had not been summoned in person or otherwise informed of the date and place of the hearing which led to the decision rendered *in absentia*. All project Member States (Belgium, Hungary, Ireland, the Netherlands, Poland, Romania) had transposed Article 5(1) 1 FD 2002/584/JHA.[1]

This provision was later, however, deleted by Article 2 FD 2009/299/JHA, and Article 4a was inserted into FD 2002/584/JHA. While FD 2009/299/JHA should have been fully transposed by 28 March 2011 (Article 8(1) FD 2009/299/JHA), the relevant provisions entered into force in Belgium on 14 May 2014,[2] in Hungary on 1 January 2013,[3] in Ireland on 24 July 2012,[4] in the Netherlands on 1 August 2011,[5] in Poland on 14 November 2011[6] and in Romania within 15 days after publication in the Romanian official journal (which

1 BE, report, p. 17; HU, report, p. 13; IE, report, pp. 26-27; NL, report, p. 47; PL, report, p. 47; RO, report, p. 20.
2 BE, report, p. 17.
3 HU, report, p. 13.
4 IE, report, p. 26.
5 NL, report, p. 47.
6 PL, report, p. 47.

was on 11 December 2013).[7] All project Member States have thus exceeded the time limit for transposition.

FD 2002/584/JHA, FD 2009/299/JHA and the EAW-form as amended by the latter Framework Decision are available in all official languages of the Union (with the exception of Irish). They are published at exactly the same pages in the Official Journal of the European Union in all languages of the Union at the time of adoption of the Framework Decisions (with the exception of Irish): *OJ* 2002, L 190, pp. 1-18, amended as of 28 March 2009 by FD 2009/299/JHA, *OJ* 2009, L 81, pp. 24-36. For those Member States which acceded to the Union after the adoption of FD 2002/584/JHA and/or FD 2009/299/JHA, there are 'Special Editions' of the Official Journal, containing the secondary EU law in force on the date of accession of the given Member State in the official language of that Member State.[8]

2.2.2 *Full Transposition or Deviation?*

Taking into account the relevant case-law of the Court of Justice of the European Union,[9] overall Article 2 FD 2009/299/JHA was fully transposed in all project Member States.[10]

In the Netherlands, apart from some minor terminological points,[11] there is only one notable deviation.[12] Article 4a(1) FD 2002/584/JHA contains an optional ground for refusal, whereas the Dutch transposition of Article 4a(1) – Article 12 Law on Surrender – contains a mandatory ground for refusal.[13]

Similarly, the Irish implementing legislation – which is otherwise copy-pasted from Article 2 (1) FD 2009/299/JHA into national legislation – provides for the words "shall not be surrendered…" unless the warrant "indicates the matters required by points 2, 3 and 4 of point (d)", thus also introducing a mandatory ground for refusal.[14]

Poland transposed Article 4a(1) FD 2002/584/JHA as an optional ground for refusal. The Polish CPC was marginally revised on account of FD 2009/299/JHA, as the legislator held that the purpose of the framework decisions was not to harmonise the national law concerning *in absentia* proceedings or rules on serving summonses in national criminal proceedings (see recital 14 of the FD). In particular, concerning the rules on serving the summons, according to the Polish expert, the Polish law is in line with Article 4a(1) FD

7 RO, report, p. 20.
8 Available at https://eur-lex.europa.eu/eu-enlargement/special.html?locale=en.
9 The judgments *B., Melloni, Dworzecki, Tupikas, Zdziaszek and Ardic.*
10 BE, report, p. 17; HU, report, p. 14; IE, report, p. 26; NL, report, p. 47; PL, report, p. 50; RO, report, p. 20.
11 *E.g.*, 'vonnis' instead of 'beslissing', 'de behandeling ter terechtzitting die tot het vonnis heeft geleid' instead of 'het proces dat tot de beslissing heeft geleid'.
12 See NL, report, pp. 47-48.
13 This matter will be further dealt with in Chapter 3.
14 IE, report, pp. 28-29.

2002/584/JHA.[15] This is the case, even though no requirement of personal summoning of the requested person was included into Article 607r § 3 (a) of the Code of Criminal Procedure (CCP). Additionally, this provision does not require that the requested person be informed of the date of the hearing "in such a manner that it was unequivocally established that he or she was aware of the scheduled trial".[16] Furthermore, the requirement that the defence counsel participating in the trial shall be given a mandate by the requested person who 'was aware of the scheduled trial' is not embodied into Article 607r § 3 (a) of the CCP.[17] However, in order to lower the risk of refusals of Polish EAWs, Article 540b of the CCP was introduced, giving judges an optional ground for re-opening of the proceedings – which is rather not considered as a ground for retrial under Article 4a(1)(d) FD 2002/584/JHA (see also Section 3.6).[18] It should also be pointed out that, in addition to the specific optional ground for refusal concerning judgments *in absentia*, Article 607p § 1 (5) of the CCP contains a general and mandatory ground for refusal concerning human rights violations, such as a violation of the right to a fair trial.

2.3 Issuing of EAWs

2.3.1 *Responsible Authority*

The authority responsible for issuing an EAW must be a *judicial* authority (Article 1(1) and 6(1) FD 2002/584/JHA). In regulating the notion of an 'issuing judicial authority', Article 6(1) does not distinguish between the competence to issue EAWs for the purpose of prosecution and the competence to issue EAWs for the execution of a sentence. The expression 'issuing judicial authority' is an *autonomous* concept of Union law.[19] In accordance with the principle of procedural autonomy of the Member States, the role of the Member States is therefore limited to designating which judicial authority shall have the competence to decide on the issuing of the EAW.[20]

The autonomous concept of an 'issuing judicial authority' does not only encompass courts and judges, but may extend to "more broadly, authorities required to participate in administering justice in the legal system concerned".[21] However, organs of the executive

15 PL, report, p. 48.
16 PL, report, p. 50.
17 PL, report, p. 50. This matter will be further dealt with in Chapter 3.
18 PL, report, p. 48. This matter will be further dealt with in Chapter 7.
19 See Chapter 2 for an extensive discussion of the issue of autonomous concepts of Union law.
20 ECJ, judgment of 10 November 2016, *Openbaar Ministerie v. Ruslanas Kovalkovas*, C-477/16 PPU, ECLI:EU:C:2016:861, para. 31.
21 ECJ, judgment of 10 November 2016, *Openbaar Ministerie v. Ruslanas Kovalkovas*, C-477/16 PPU, ECLI:EU:C:2016:861, para. 34.

of a Member State, such as a Ministry of Justice[22] and the Police[23] cannot be regarded as judicial authorities. The issue of an EAW by such a non-judicial officer does not provide the executing judicial authority with an assurance that the issue of that EAW has undergone judicial review and cannot, therefore, suffice to justify the high level of confidence between the Member States on which the system of the EAW is based.[24]

Authorities which are not judges or courts, such as the public prosecutor's office, but which participate in the administration of criminal justice in the issuing Member State may be regarded as 'judicial authorities', if (1) the national judicial decision meets the 'requirements inherent in judicial protection' (*i.e.* if the national judicial decision is taken by a court or a judge), (2) that authority is "not exposed, when adopting a decision to issue [an EAW], to any risk of being subject, *inter alia*, to an instruction in a specific case from the executive" and (3) "the decision to issue [an EAW] and, *inter alia*, the proportionality of such a decision must be capable of being the subject, in the Member State, of court proceedings which meet in full the requirements inherent in effective judicial protection".[25]

When deciding whether to issue an EAW, the issuing judicial authority must "review, in particular, observance of the conditions necessary for the issuing of the [EAW] and examine whether, in the light of the particular circumstances of each case, it is proportionate to issue that warrant".[26]

There is a great variety in the type of competent authority that Member States designated to be their issuing judicial authority. Likewise, the competence to issue EAWs is fully centralised only in one of the project Member States; in all others, it is shared by several domestic actors.

22 ECJ, judgment of 10 November 2016, *Openbaar Ministerie v. Ruslanas Kovalkovas*, C-477/16 PPU, ECLI:EU:C:2016:861, para. 35.

23 ECJ, judgment of 10 November 2016, *Openbaar Ministerie v. Krzysztof Marek Poltorak*, C-452/16 PPU, ECLI:EU:C:2016:858, para. 35.

24 ECJ, judgment of 10 November 2016, *Openbaar Ministerie v. Ruslanas Kovalkovas*, C-477/16 PPU, ECLI:EU:C:2016:861, para. 45.

25 ECJ, judgment of 27 May 2019, *Minister for Justice and Equality v. OG and PI*, C-508/18 and C-82/19 PPU, ECLI:EU:C:2019:456, paras. 60 and 64-75; ECJ, judgment of 27 May 2019, *Minister for Justice and Equality v. PF*, C-509/18, ECLI:EU:C:2019:457, paras. 39 and 43-53. Both judgments concern prosecution-EAWs. A German court has asked the Court of Justice whether an Austrian public prosecutor who is subject to instructions by the executive can nevertheless be considered an 'issuing judicial authority' when his decision to issue an EAW (in this case, a prosecution-EAW) is subjected to court proceedings *before* the EAW is actually issued (C-489/19 PPU (*NJ* (*Parquet de Vienne*)). Two references by a Dutch court also concern the requirement that the decision to issue a prosecution-EAW and the proportionality of such a decision is capable of being the subject of court proceedings: C-625/19 PPU (*Openbaar Ministerie*) and C-626/19 PPU (*Openbaar Ministerie*). A third reference by the same court involves the relevance of that requirement for an execution-EAW: C-627/19 PPU (*Openbaar Ministerie*).

26 ECJ, judgment of 27 May 2019, *Minister for Justice and Equality v. OG and PI*, C-508/18 and C-82/19 PPU, ECLI:EU:C:2019:456, para. 71; ECJ, judgment of 27 May 2019, *Minister for Justice and Equality v. PF*, C-509/18, ECLI:EU:C:2019:457, para. 49.

In Belgium, the competent investigating judge (when prosecuting an adult defendant) and the competent public prosecutor (when prosecuting a minor or executing a sentence/decision or when an EAW is based on a national arrest warrant issued by a court in the trial phase) are responsible for issuing EAWs.[27]

In Hungary, prior to the filing of an indictment, an EAW is issued by the competent investigating judge. After the final judgment, it is issued by the competent judge responsible for penitentiary affairs.[28]

In Ireland, the judicial authority responsible for the issuing (and executing) of EAWs is the High Court. In practice, an individual High Court judge is designated as the judge in charge of the Extradition and EAW lists and is assigned full time to such work. From time to time, a second judge may be seconded to assist the designated judge, depending on the workload. The High Court is assisted in its work as the issuing (and executing) authority for EAWs by a Central Authority (nominally the Minister for Justice but *de facto* a senior official in the Ministry) whose role is facilitative only.[29]

In the Netherlands, until recently, every public prosecutor (*officier van justitie*) could issue an EAW (Article 44 (old) Law on Surrender). The public prosecutor of the FAST (Fugitive Active Search Team) – formerly TES (*Team Executie Strafzaken*) – of the Public Prosecution Service was tasked with issuing an EAW in cases in which the requested person was sentenced to a final custodial sentence of which at least 120 days remain to be served.[30] Hence, with regard to those cases – and those cases only – the power to issue EAWs was centralised. In light of *Minister for Justice and Equality v. OG and PI*,[31] the Dutch legislator amended the Law on Surrender. As of 13 July 2019, the power to issue EAWs is transferred from every public prosecutor to every examining magistrate (*rechter-commissaris*). The examining magistrate is a judge.

In Poland, all regional courts are competent to issue EAWs. They may be issued *ex officio* (in cases pending before regional courts), upon a motion of the public prosecutor (at the pre-trial stage of the proceedings), or upon the motion of a court before which the case is pending different than regional court.[32]

In Romania, all courts within the Romanian judicial system (local courts, district courts, courts of appeal, the High Court of Cassation and Justice) are competent to issue EAWs.[33]

---

27 BE, report, p. 18.

28 HU, report, p. 14.

29 IE, report, p. 32.

30 NL, report, p. 53.

31 ECJ, judgment of 27 May 2019, *Minister for Justice and Equality v. OG and PI*, C-508/18 and C-82/19 PPU, ECLI:EU:C:2019:456.

32 PL, report, pp. 51-52.

33 RO, report, p. 21.

Thus, in all project countries, except for Ireland, the competence for issuing EAWs is decentralised.

In Hungary, the Netherlands, Poland and Romania only courts or judges are competent to issue EAWs. In Belgium, judges and public prosecutors share responsibility for issuing EAWs.

2.3.2 *The Act of Issuing*

a) Who exactly fills in EAWs within the issuing judicial authority?

In Hungary and Romania, EAWs are filled in by the judge.[34] More precisely, in Romania, that judge is the judge delegated with the enforcement of final judgments within the court competent to issue the EAW.[35] In Poland, it depends on the regional court: in some regional courts, the draft EAWs are filled in by the judge him/herself, in others, it is the assistant of a judge, and in yet others, the EAW is filled in by a clerk of the court who is trained in the field of legal cooperation. However, it is always done under the supervision of a judge who is obliged to sign the EAW in his/her capacity as a competent issuing judicial authority.[36] The same happens in Belgium, where the EAW is filled in by a magistrate (judge or public prosecutor) or by administrative staff under the supervision of a magistrate.[37] In the Netherlands, until recently, EAWs were filled in by an assistant public prosecutor (*parketsecretaris*) or a junior assistant public prosecutor (*junior parketsecretaris*) of FAST and were checked by a public prosecutor before issuing them.[38] Under the current legislation (see Section 2.3.1), a public prosecutor will present the examining magistrate with an EAW filled in by the public prosecutor or by a (junior) assistant public prosecutor, and will ask the examining magistrate to issue it. The examining magistrate will carry out the required checks (see Section 2.3.1) and, if he finds that everything is in order, he will issue the EAW. Similarly, in Ireland, a solicitor in the Chief State Solicitor's office, acting in liaison with Central Authority, and representing the Director of Public Prosecutions, initially completes the EAW-form. After scrutiny of the draft warrant, the High Court judge will sign the warrant in his/her capacity as the issuing judicial authority.[39]

Thus, while in most Member States, the person with the power to issue an EAW (the judge or public prosecutor) is also the person who actually fills in the EAW-form, this is

34 HU, report, p. 14.
35 RO, report, p. 20.
36 PL, report, p. 52.
37 BE, report, p. 18.
38 NL, report, pp. 55-56. While the (junior) assistant public prosecutors of FAST all have legal degrees, unlike public prosecutors, assistant public prosecutors and junior assistant public prosecutors are not a part of the judiciary (see Art. 1(b)(7) of the Law on the Organisation of the Judiciary), but are civil servants.
39 IE, report, p. 32.

not always the case. It appears that in practice, in many instances, the form is filled in by assistants, clerks or even administrative staff of the respective authority or of another authority – albeit under the supervision of a judge or public prosecutor. The Dutch expert makes the point that the *issuing* of an EAW by a non-judicial officer does not provide the executing judicial authority with an assurance that the EAW has undergone judicial approval and cannot, therefore, suffice to justify the high level of confidence between the Member States on which the system of the EAW is based.[40]

b) What are the formalities for issuing an EAW? Does your Member State have form sheets for that?

As is apparent from the answers, most experts interpreted both questions as applying to the use of the EAW-form (see also Section 2.3.3).

In Belgium, Hungary and Romania, courts use the form as provided in the annex to FD 2002/584/JHA, as amended by FD 2009/299/JHA.[41] The Polish form is very similar, although section (d) is differently numbered than the original EAW-form as annexed to the Framework Decisions.[42]

Ireland does not have specific form sheets for issuing an EAW. The form as provided in the annex to FD 2002/584/JHA, as amended by FD 2009/299/JHA, is used with guidance as to how to complete it drawn from Commission Notice C(2017) 6389 final of 28 September 2017 entitled HANDBOOK ON HOW TO ISSUE AND EXECUTE A EUROPEAN ARREST WARRANT.[43]

In the Netherlands, the FAST uses the model form of the EAW available on the website of the European Judicial Network. In any case, the EAW must conform to the model which is annexed to the Law on Surrender and must at least contain the information required by Article 2(2) Law on Surrender.[44] After having been issued by an examining magistrate, the

40 NL, report, p. 56. Cf. ECJ, judgment of 10 November 2016, *Openbaar Ministerie v. Krzysztof Marek Poltorak*, C-452/16 PPU, ECLI:EU:C:2016:858, para. 45.

41 BE, report, p. 18; HU, report, p. 15; RO, report, p. 20.

42 PL, report, p. 52.

43 IE, report, p. 35. The *Handbook* was published in *OJ* 2017 C-335, p. 1.

44
a. the identity and nationality of the requested person;
b. the name, address, telephone and fax numbers and e-mail address of the issuing judicial authority;
c. evidence of an enforceable judgment, an arrest warrant or any other enforceable judicial decision;
d. the nature and legal classification of the offence, particularly in respect of Art. 7(1)(a)(i) Law on Surrender;
e. a description of the circumstances in which the offence was committed, including the time, place and degree of participation in the offence by the requested person;
f. the penalty imposed, if there is a final judgment, or the prescribed scale of penalties for the offence under the law of the issuing Member State;
g. if possible, other consequences of the offence.

EAW is transmitted via the national SIRENE[45] Bureau in the Schengen Information System (SIS).[46]

In Hungary, an EAW can be issued either after the issuance of the national arrest warrant or at the date of its issuance. The EAW is sent to the Ministry of Justice and the International Law Enforcement Cooperation Centre by the court.[47]

c) How does the issuing judicial authority usually fill in section (d) of the EAW-form in case none of the options under point 3 apply?

When filling in section (d) of the EAW-form, the issuing judicial authority is required to indicate whether the requested person has appeared in person at the 'trial resulting in the decision'. In case the issuing authority states that s/he did not, one of the following options can be confirmed by ticking one of the boxes under point 3 of section (d):

- 3.1a. the person was summoned in person, or 3.1b. the person was not summoned in person, but by other means actually received official information of the scheduled date and place of the trial, or
- 3.2. the requested person was aware of the scheduled trial and had mandated a legal counsellor who actually defended him/her at the trial, or
- 3.3. the requested person was served with the decision rendered following a trial at which the requested person did not appear in person and informed about his/her right to a retrial or appeal, but expressly stated that s/he does not contest the decision, or did not request a retrial/appeal, or
- 3.4. the person was not personally served with the decision, but will be after surrender, and will at the same time be informed about his/her rights.

These options are meant as guarantees for the executing judicial authority that the requested person has already had or will still receive a fair trial, while being fully aware of his/her rights. However, it is conceivable that in particular situations, none of these options is ticked by the issuing judicial authority because the situation at hand is not covered by any of these options or the executing judicial authority is of the opinion that none of these options applies.

In those cases, when none of the options under point 3 of section (d) of the EAW-form apply, issuing judicial authorities in Belgium and the Netherlands use the free space under

45 Supplementary Information Request at the National Entries. Each Member State operating the SIS has a national SIRENE Bureau.

46 NL, report, p. 56.

47 HU, report, p. 15.

point 4 of section (d)[48] of the EAW-form to provide additional information about the case at hand.[49] The Romanian and the Irish experts opine that such a situation is impossible.[50]

From the answers to this question, one gets the impression either that the situation where none of the options under point 3 apply is not experienced as a big problem in filling in the EAW, or that the Member States do not know how to proceed when none of the options under point 3 apply.

d) Which information does the issuing judicial authority usually provide under point 4 in section (d) of the EAW-form?

The extent to which information is provided under point 4 in section (d) of the EAW-form annexed to FD 2002/584/JHA, which is intended for providing further clarifying information only when point 3.1b, 3.2 or 3.3 is ticked, seems to vary extensively. While Romanian authorities usually provide a proof of the service of summons or of the power of attorney,[51] the Hungarian authorities explain when and how the summons was received by the defendant and when a legal counsellor was appointed,[52] the Belgian authorities briefly explain the reason why 3.1b, 3.2 or 3.3 was ticked and/or repeat what is already mentioned in those sections without further explanations,[53] authorities in Poland apparently explain the relevant parts of Polish criminal procedure in order to show how the conditions for surrender were met in the Polish proceedings that led up to the EAW.[54] Authorities in the Netherlands, in turn, proceed to explain the whole procedure as it unfolded in the relevant case until the request for surrender.[55] In Ireland, as there are no trials *in absentia* as such, option 1 (the person appeared in person at the trial) is invariably ticked in section (d) of the EAW-form, making it superfluous to provide further information.[56]

2.3.3 Using the Correct EAW-Form

The annex to FD 2002/584/JHA contains the EAW-form. Article 2 FD 2009/299/JHA amends section (d) of that form. The form is designed to simplify and accelerate the surrender procedure in accordance with the time limits laid down by Article 17 FD

48 Point 4 of section (d) is intended for providing further clarifying information only when point 3.1b, 3.2 or 3.3 is ticked.

49 BE, report, p. 19; NL, report, p. 57; PL, report, p. 53. As for the Netherlands, in the past, FAST would have ticked one of the boxes under 3 – the one that would most resemble the situation at hand: NL, report, p. 57.

50 IE, report, pp. 35-36; RO, report, p. 21; in Ireland that is so, as *in absentia* trials as such do not exist.

51 RO, report, p. 21.

52 HU, report, p. 15.

53 BE, report, p. 19.

54 PL, report, pp. 52-53.

55 NL, report, pp. 57-58.

56 IE, report, p. 35.

2002/584/JHA.[57] The issuing judicial authorities are *required* to complete the form, and furnish the specific information requested (Article 8(1) FD 2002/584/JHA).[58] The old EAW-form, which was in use up until FD 2009/299/JHA amended it, is not tailored to the specific requirements of Article 4a(1) FD 2002/584/JHA, and will therefore, when used in *in absentia* cases, most probably not contain the information needed to verify whether the rights of the defence were fully respected.

In Belgium,[59] Hungary,[60] Ireland,[61] the Netherlands,[62] Poland[63] and Romania,[64] the issuing authorities need to use the EAW-form as amended by Article 2 FD 2009/299/JHA (which introduced the new version of section (d) of the form (see also Section 2.3.2 under b)). In the case of Ireland, its transposing legislation requires that an EAW shall, 'in so far as is practicable', be in the form set out in the Annex to the Framework Decision as amended by FD 2009/299/JHA.

Thus, in the project Member States, the use of the new EAW-form is mandatory. This does not mean, however, that issuing authorities of other Member States no longer use the old form at all. The Belgian expert reports that Greek issuing authorities systematically use the old form as Greece has not transposed FD 2009/299/JHA yet.[65] The Dutch expert reports that in 2017, the Dutch executing judicial authority dealt with two EAWs from Italy, which had been issued on 20 April 2017 using the old form, although Italy is reported to have transposed FD 2009/299/JHA on 23 March 2016. Consequently, as of then, its issuing authorities should have been using the new EAW-form that provides for the new text in section (d). In both cases, the Dutch executing judicial authority asked the Italian issuing authority for the correct form, by applying Article 15(2) FD 2002/584/JHA; the Italian issuing authority complied before the surrender hearing in the Netherlands took place.[66]

When the old EAW-form is used, the Irish, Polish and Belgian executing judicial authorities usually ask the issuing judicial authority for additional information that is necessary in order to decide on the requested EAWs.[67] Most of the executing judicial authorities of the project Member States do not require that the issuing judicial authorities

57 ECJ, judgment of 23 January 2018, *Dawid Piotrowski*, C-367/16, EU:C:2018:27, para. 57.
58 ECJ, judgment of 6 December 2018, *IK*, C-551/18 PPU, ECLI:EU:C:2018:991, para. 49.
59 As per Art. 2(4) Act on the EAW: BE, report, p. 20.
60 As the form is part of the Act CLXXX of 2012 on the judicial cooperation in criminal matters with the Member States of the European Union: HU, report, p. 16.
61 IE, report, p. 39.
62 As per Art. 2(2) Law on Surrender: NL, report, p. 60.
63 As the form is attached to the Ministers of Justice Ordinance of 24 February 2012 concerning the form of the EAW (Journal of Laws 2012, item 266): PL, report, p. 52.
64 As per Art. 86 (1) of Law 302/2004: RO, report, p. 22.
65 BE, report, p. 39. However, see Section 3.2.
66 NL, report, p. 96.
67 BE, report, p. 39; IE, report, p. 39; PL, report, p. 76.

resubmit a request using the new form.[68] However, when asking for supplementary information, the Belgian authorities might communicate to the issuing judicial authority that it would be appreciated that they use the new EAW-form.[69]

Consequently, using the old EAW-form does not have any further consequences. The executing judicial authorities will simply ask the issuing authority for the necessary information, as provided for in Article 15(2) FD 2002/584/JHA.[70] While using the old EAW-form is not a reason to refuse the EAW, it does mean additional hassle for both the executing and the issuing judicial authorities.

2.3.4 *Language of the EAW*

According to Article 8(2) FD 2002/584/JHA the EAW "must be translated into the official language or one of the official languages of the executing Member State" (by or on behalf of the issuing Member State). However, a Member State may "state in a declaration deposited with the General Secretariat of the Council that it will accept a translation in one or more other official languages of the Institutions of the European Communities".

Three of the six project Member States[71] have deposited a declaration under Article 8(2) FD 2002/854/JHA, accepting as executing Member State a translation of the EAW in another language. Belgium accepts translations of the EAWs in English, in addition to EAWs in Dutch, French or German.[72] In addition to EAWs in Dutch or English, the Netherlands accepts EAWs in all official languages of the EU, provided that an English translation accompanies the original EAW.[73] Romania accepts EAWs in English or French, in addition to Romanian.[74] Hungary accepts EAWs only in Hungarian. However, with respect to Member States which also accept EAWs or translations thereof in other than their official languages, Hungary accepts EAWs in English, German or French, or a translation in one of those languages.[75]

A Belgian declaration to the effect that EAWs are also accepted in English should have been made to the General Secretariat of the Council; it cannot be found on the website of

68 IE, report, p. 39; PL, report, p. 55. It seems that only the Dutch and the Hungarian authorities might ask for the new form: NL, report, p. 96; HU, report, p. 16.

69 BE, report, p. 39.

70 In essence, this is what the Court of Justice been held in: ECJ, judgment of 10 August 2017, *Openbaar Ministerie v. Sławomir Andrzej Zdziaszek*, C-271/17 PPU, ECLI:EU:C:2017:629, paras. 103-105. NL, report, p. 60; BE, report, p. 20; HU, report, p. 16.

71 HU, report, p. 17; RO, report, p. 24, NL, report, p. 61.

72 The original EAW must be provided together with the translation: BE, report, p. 21.

73 Council document 9002/04, 29 April 2004: NL, report, p. 61.

74 RO, report, p. 23.

75 HU, report, p. 17.

the European Judicial Network (EJN).[76] The Dutch declaration has not been published, but is available on the website of the EJN.[77] The Romanian declaration was also published on the EJN website.[78] The same goes for Hungary.[79] The Dutch, Hungarian and Romanian declarations were sent to the General Secretariat of the Council.

On the basis of Article 34(2) of FD 2002/584/JHA, the General Secretariat must communicate declarations made by Member States in relation to, *inter alia*, Article 8(2) (languages accepted) to the Member States and the Commission, as well as publish them in the Official Journal. None of these declarations have been published in the Official Journal. This raises a question as to the legally binding character of such declarations.

EAWs or translations of EAWs in English seem to be accepted by most Member States which have deposited a declaration accepting EAWs in other than their official languages. Hungary, however, accepts EAWs in other languages than Hungarian only on the basis of reciprocity. In practice, however, EAWs in English are accepted, even when there is no reciprocity.

2.3.4.1 Perspective of the Executing Judicial Authorities

Problems with translations provided by the issuing Member State are reportedly non-existent or minimal in Poland,[80] Hungary[81] and Romania,[82] but do occur in Belgium,[83] Ireland[84] and the Netherlands.[85]

In many cases, from the point of view of executing judicial authorities in Belgium, Ireland and the Netherlands the translations of the EAWs are of poor quality, at times leading to misunderstandings or even plain incomprehensibility. In fact, this does not only concern the content provided by the issuing authority. Some issuing authorities even translate the EAW-form itself, although official versions exist in all official EU-languages (see Section 2.2.1; with the exception of Irish). At times, this translated EAW-form deviates from the original EAW-form, sometimes affecting the substance of the text.[86] For instance, Polish issuing authorities sometimes translate the part of the EAW-form which requires to indicate whether the 'person appeared in person at the trial resulting in the decision' as

76 BE, report, p. 21.
77 NL, report, p. 61.
78 RO, report, p. 23.
79 Council document 8929, 27 April 2004.
80 PL, report, p. 56.
81 HU, report, p. 31.
82 RO, report, p. 39.
83 BE, report, p. 40.
84 IE, report, pp. 45 and 60-62.
85 NL, report, pp. 97-98.
86 This observation was made by the Dutch and Irish experts: IE, report, p. 57; NL, report, pp. 97-98.

'the trial during which the judgment was pronounced'.[87] Problems with translations seem to be solved by the Dutch executing judicial authority in a pragmatic way. Deviations that affect the substance of the matter should lead to a request for additional information in accordance with Article 15(2) FD 2002/584/JHA, unless the matter can be clarified by other means (*e.g.* on the basis of a statement by the requested person).[88] Deviations that do not concern the substance of the matter do not have any consequences, as in such cases it is still possible to verify whether the rights of the defence were fully respected.[89] Irish authorities also try to solve problems pragmatically. The practice of the Irish High Court as executing judicial authority is to construe the translation provided in conjunction with the official original language version of the EAW-form and the official English language version of the EAW-form. Only in cases of irreconcilable difficulty, the Central Authority, which scrutinises all incoming EAWs on a preliminary basis before presenting them to the High Court for endorsement for execution in the Irish jurisdiction, would revert to the issuing judicial authority seeking clarification concerning exactly what meaning was intended before presenting the warrant to the High Court for endorsement.[90]

Similarly, if the translation is not clear, Polish executing judicial authorities might either order a new translation of the original EAW, or ask the issuing judicial authority for supplementary information under Article 15(2) FD 2002/584/JHA.[91] The latter is also the approach of Romanian executing judicial authorities.[92] In cases of EAWs translated into other languages than Hungarian and when the translation is unclear, Hungarian executing judicial authorities would either ask for a Hungarian version of the EAW or translate it themselves.[93] Belgian authorities would provide for a translation of the original EAW into the language of the proceedings in Belgium.[94]

Thus, approaches to poor translations – whether into the official language of the executing judicial authority or into a designated language – are quite different among the project Member States. Either the executing judicial authorities would ask the issuing judicial authorities for another translation of the EAW, or translate the original EAW themselves, or ask the issuing judicial authority for supplementary information under Article 15(2) FD 2002/584/JHA. In any case, in none of the project Member States, do problems with translations seem to lead to a refusal of the EAW. Only the Irish expert states that if ambiguities cannot be resolved with the issuing judicial authorities, poor

87 NL, report, pp. 97-98. This phrasing deviates from the official EAW-form, if the actual trial and the pronouncement of the judgment took place at different hearings.
88 NL, report, pp. 61-62 and 98.
89 NL, report, pp. 61 and 98.
90 IE, report, p. 45.
91 PL, report, p. 56.
92 RO, report, p. 23.
93 HU, report, p. 17.
94 BE, report, p. 40.

translations may also lead to refusing the execution of an EAW.[95] That being said, problems with translations lead to additional hassle and delays in the proceedings.

2.3.4.2 Perspective of the Issuing Judicial Authorities

The Belgian authorities are aware of problems that other Member States have with the translation of EAWs *issued* by Belgium.[96]

None of the other Member States is aware of problems arising from their translations.[97] A possible explanation for this discrepancy between the views of issuing and executing judicial authorities is that executing judicial authorities sometimes try to solve problems with the translation themselves instead of asking the issuing judicial authority for a new and better translation of the EAW. The issuing judicial authorities may, therefore, simply not always be aware of problems concerning the translation of their EAWs.

2.4 EXECUTION OF EAWs

2.4.1 Responsible Authority

The authority responsible for deciding on the execution of an EAW must also be a *judicial* authority (Article 6(2) FD 2002/584/JHA).

The project Member States regulated the responsibility for executing EAWs in a very diverse manner.

In Belgium, in the case that the accused consents to surrender, the public prosecutor is the executing judicial authority, unless the investigative judge refuses surrender on the basis of a mandatory ground for refusal. In all other cases, investigative courts – the council chamber (*raadkamer – chambre du conseil*) and the indictment chamber (*kamer van inbeschuldigingstelling – chambre des mises en accusation*) – are the executing judicial authorities.[98]

In Hungary, the executing judicial authority is the Budapest-Capital Regional Court.[99]

As mentioned earlier, in Ireland, the judicial authority responsible for the issuing and executing of EAWs is the High Court (see Section 2.3.1).

95 IE, report, p. 45.
96 BE, report, p. 40.
97 HU, report, p. 31; IE, report, p. 59; NL, report, p. 98; PL, report, p. 77; RO, report, p. 39.
98 BE, report, p. 18.
99 HU, report, p. 14.

In the Netherlands, the public prosecutor in Amsterdam,[100] the examining magistrate (*rechter-commissaris*) in the District Court of Amsterdam[101] and the District Court of Amsterdam[102] itself are designated as executing judicial authorities.[103]

In Poland, all regional courts are competent to execute EAWs.[104]

In Romania, for first instance cases, executing EAWs is within the competence of the courts of appeal (there are 15 courts of appeal in Romania) and for appeal cases, the High Court of Cassation and Justice is the competent authority.[105]

While in Hungary, Ireland and in the Netherlands, there is one centralised judicial authority for executing EAWs, in Belgium, Poland and Romania, the competence is decentralised and shared among various institutions. In some project Member States, not only are courts and judges competent for executing EAWs. In exceptional circumstances,

100 The public prosecutor in Amsterdam receives all EAWs, issued by judicial authorities of other Member States and sent to the Netherlands. S/he is tasked with the decision whether a requested person who has consented to his/her surrender will be surrendered via the so-called shortened procedure. When it is evident that an EAW cannot lead to surrender, the public prosecutor in Amsterdam may summarily dismiss the EAW. The case is then not brought before the District Court. There is no remedy against such a decision; it is not subject to judicial review. NL, report, pp. 53-54. The public prosecutor in Amsterdam is the competent authority to decide on requests for consent for prosecuting and sentencing the surrendered person for an 'other offence' than the offence for which s/he was surrendered (see Art. 27(3)(g) and (4) FD 2002/584/JHA). A Belgian court has asked the Court of Justice whether the public prosecutor in Amsterdam can be considered an 'executing judicial authority' in the sense of Art. 6(2) and Art. 27(3)(g) and (4) FD 2002/584/JHA (C-510/19 (*Openbaar Ministerie*)).

101 Both the public prosecutor in Amsterdam and the Examining Magistrate in the District Court of Amsterdam have duties regarding the deprivation of liberty of a requested person: NL, report, p. 53.

102 In all cases in which, 1) the public prosecutor has decided that the requested person who has consented to his/her surrender will not be surrendered via the so-called shortened procedure, or 2) the requested person has not consented to his/her surrender and the public prosecutor has not summarily dismissed the EAW, the Extradition Chamber (*Internationale Rechtshulpkamer*), a specialised three-judge panel of the District Court of Amsterdam, will decide whether the requested person will be surrendered. No ordinary legal recourse – appeal or appeal on points of law – lies against a judgment of the District Court of Amsterdam concerning the (non)-execution of an EAW. The *Procurator-General* at the Supreme Court of the Netherlands may lodge an extraordinary appeal on points of law, if the interests of justice so require (*cassatie in het belang der wet*). If the Supreme Court quashes the judgment of the District Court in the interests of justice, this does not have any effect on the disposition of the case. Only in two cases appeal lies from a decision of the District Court of Amsterdam in EAW matters: 1) the public prosecutor can appeal a decision to release the requested person provisionally from remand. If the decision was taken by the Examining Magistrate, the District Court is competent to hear the appeal; if the decision was taken by the District Court, the Court of Appeal is competent to hear the appeal; 2) the public prosecutor and the person concerned can appeal against a decision of the District Court on awarding damages for wrongful detention with the Court of Appeal. NL, report, pp. 53-55.

103 NL, report, p. 53.

104 PL, report, p. 52. To avoid confusion, it should be pointed out that on the website of the European Judicial Network the term 'Sąd Okręgowy' (Regional Court) is translated as 'District Court'. Of all the regional courts, it is the regional court having territorial jurisdiction over the place of residence of the requested person which is competent to issue an EAW against him/her.

105 RO, report, pp. 20-21.

such as when the accused consents to surrender, the public prosecutor may execute an EAW (as, for instance, in Belgium or the Netherlands).

2.4.2 Requesting Supplementary Information

2.4.2.1 Supplementary Information

According to Article 15(2) FD 2002/584/JHA

> if the executing judicial authority finds the information communicated by the issuing Member State to be insufficient to allow it to decide on surrender, it shall request that the necessary supplementary information, in particular with respect to Articles 3 to 5 and Article 8, be furnished as a matter of urgency and may fix a time limit for the receipt thereof, taking into account the need to observe the time limits set in Article 17.

Recourse to requesting supplementary information should be taken

> only as a last resort in exceptional cases in which the executing judicial authority considers that it does not have the official evidence necessary to adopt a decision on surrender as a matter of urgency.[106]

Article 15(2) cannot be used, 'as a matter of course', to request 'general information'.[107]

Concerning the application of Article 4a(1) specifically, the Court of Justice held that the executing judicial authority *must* "apply Article 15(2) of Framework Decision 2002/584, by requesting from the issuing judicial authority the urgent provision of such additional information as it deems necessary before a decision on surrender can be taken", if it is of the opinion that "it does not have sufficient information to enable it to validly decide on the surrender of the requested".[108]

However, if this request does not result in "the necessary assurances as regards the rights of defence of the person concerned during the relevant proceedings", the executing judicial authority is *not obliged* to resort to Article 15(2) *again* and may refuse to execute the EAW. This is so, because the executing judicial authority not only cannot tolerate a

106 ECJ, judgment of 23 January 2018, *Dawid Piotrowski*, C-367/16, ECLI:EU:C:2018:27, para. 61.

107 ECJ, judgment of 25 July 2018, C-220/18, *Generalstaatsanwaltschaft (Conditions of detention in Hungary)*, ECLI:EU:C:2018:589, para. 80.

108 ECJ, judgment of 10 August 2017, *Openbaar Ministerie v. Sławomir Andrzej Zdziaszek*, C-271/17 PPU, ECLI:EU:C:2017:629, para. 103.

breach of fundamental rights, but also must ensure that the time limits laid down in Article 17 FD 2002/584/JHA are observed.[109]

2.4.2.1.1 Perspective of the Executing Judicial Authorities

The country reports seem to indicate that quite a lot of supplementary information is almost systematically requested by executing judicial authorities in the course of the EAW procedure, especially pertaining to *in absentia* issues.

All project reports mention *in absentia* issues among the topics that most frequently require additional information before the respective EAW can be executed. Accordingly, the executing judicial authorities of the project Member States ask, *e.g.*, for general information concerning section (d) of the EAW-form,[110] especially if the old version of the EAW-form was used,[111] information about how the defendant was summoned,[112] or at which hearings s/he was present (whether the merits of the case were dealt with at those hearings),[113] especially in cases of cumulative judgments when section (d) was filled in only as to the cumulative judgment, but not for each underlying criminal procedure,[114] or how many hearings were held,[115] whether the defendant was represented by a legal counsellor,[116] and which possibilities to appeal the judgment the defendant has (and whether these proceedings meet the criteria set out in the *Tupikas* judgment),[117] or his/her rights to a retrial.[118]

Other topics on which supplementary information is requested by executing judicial authorities include: the facts of the case,[119] further information about the underlying national arrest warrant or enforceable judgment (especially the correct date,[120] or, in cases of multiple judgments, which judgment would be enforced after surrender[121]),[122] the purpose

109 ECJ, judgment of 10 August 2017, *Openbaar Ministerie v. Sławomir Andrzej Zdziaszek*, C-271/17 PPU, ECLI:EU:C:2017:629, paras. 104-105.
110 BE, report, p. 47.
111 NL, report, p. 121.
112 HU, report, p. 37.
113 NL, report, p. 121.
114 RO, report, pp. 44-45.
115 HU, report, p. 37.
116 HU, report, p. 37.
117 NL, report, p. 121.
118 PL, report, p. 88.
119 BE, report, p. 47.
120 BE, report, p. 47.
121 PL, report, p. 87.
122 BE, report, p. 47; PL, report, p. 87.

of the EAW (for prosecution or enforcement of a sentence),[123] the nature of the penalty that is about to be enforced[124] or detention conditions.[125]

The Irish expert notes that the need for the Irish *executing* judicial authority to ask for supplementary information is in large measure due to difficulties on the part of common law judges in understanding aspects of civil law procedure with which they are wholly unfamiliar, and which may appear counterintuitive to them against their background of a lifetime of practice in an adversarial common law criminal justice system.[126]

The Dutch expert reports that it is quite common that even after having asked for supplementary information under Article 15(2) FD 2002/584/JHA once, the Dutch executing judicial authority still could not verify whether the rights of the defence were fully observed.[127] The same is the experience in Ireland.[128] The Belgian expert reports that this happens only rarely,[129] and the Hungarian and Romanian experts report that it never happens.[130] The Irish expert reports that there may be limits to the extent to which it is appropriate to seek additional information, particularly in circumstances where it would cause significant consequential delays. The Irish Court of Appeal expressed the view that allowing such to occur "runs counter to the objectives and purpose of the EAW arrangements envisaged by the Framework Decision, and should be avoided".[131]

2.4.2.1.2 *Perspective of the Issuing Judicial Authorities*

The Hungarian expert reports that in the cases which were examined by him, Hungarian issuing judicial authorities are usually not requested to provide for additional information,[132] The Dutch issuing judicial authority reports that requests for supplementary information are rare.[133] The Polish expert reports that multiple requests for supplementary information are directed towards Polish issuing judicial authorities in a number of cases.[134] Most supplementary information is requested from Poland by the Netherlands, the UK,[135] Ireland

123 RO, report, pp. 44-45.
124 RO, report, pp. 44-45.
125 BE, report, p. 47.
126 IE, report, p. 91.
127 NL, report, p. 122.
128 IE, report, p. 92.
129 BE, report, p. 47.
130 HU, report, p. 37; RO, report, p. 45.
131 IE, report, p. 88.
132 HU, report, p. 38.
133 NL, report, p. 122.
134 PL, report, p. 87.
135 The Dutch expert reports that the UK executing judicial authorities have a standard questionnaire for this, where not all questions are relevant for EAWs for the purpose of the execution of a judgment. The questions are:
- whether the person concerned was arrested and heard in the case at hand;
- whether the person concerned confessed to the crime;

and Germany.[136] The Dutch (former) issuing judicial authority notes that the UK almost always asks for additional information.[137]

The topics that are most frequently the subject of supplementary information requests addressed to issuing judicial authorities are also related to *in absentia* EAWs.[138] The examples mentioned are requests for information about:

- whether the summons to the hearing and the copy of the judgment were given directly into the defendant's hands or into the hands of the adult member of the accused's household;[139]
- how it could be 'unequivocally established' that the accused was aware of the trial and the scheduled hearing;[140]
- how the defendant had been informed that a decision could also be taken in his/her absence;[141]
- the presence of the defendant at the trial, or whether s/he was present at all hearings,[142] or at the main hearing;[143]
- cumulative judgments (when section (d) is filled in in respect of a cumulative judgment and the single judgments leading to the cumulative judgment);[144]
- whether the defendant has fled from the proceedings;[145]

- whether the person concerned was present at the hearings (both the hearing at which the merits of the case were dealt with and the hearing at which the judgment was pronounced);
- how the person concerned was informed of the penalty imposed on him/her;
- the duration of remand in custody;
- whether the person concerned appealed;
- whether the person concerned is 'unlawfully at large' and whether the person concerned is aware of the fact that s/he is 'unlawfully at large';
- the reason for the delay between the date on which the judgment became final and the date on which the EAW was issued;
- whether a suspended or conditional sentence was imposed and, if so, under which conditions;
- whether a measure was taken against the person concerned restricting his/her freedom to leave the territory of the Netherlands and, if so, whether the person concerned was aware of that measure;
- whether the person concerned was under the obligation to report any change of address to the authorities and, if so, whether the person concerned was aware of this obligation;
- whether the person concerned is to be considered a 'fugitive': NL, report, p. 123.

136 PL, report, p. 88.

137 NL, report, p. 123.

138 Except for Ireland, as Ireland does not issue EAWs for defendants tried *in absentia*, due to the fact that *in absentia* trials as such do not exist in Ireland: IE, report, p. 90.

139 PL, report, p. 87.

140 PL, report, p. 87; RO, report, p. 45.

141 RO, report, p. 45.

142 RO, report, p. 45.

143 PL, report, p. 87.

144 PL, report, p. 87.

145 RO, report, p. 45.

- the way in which the requested person was informed about the judgment rendered in his/her absence;[146]
- the status of the judgment (whether it was final);[147]
- the way in which the requested person was informed about the right to a retrial or appeal, or whether s/he submitted an appeal against the first instance judgment or declared that s/he would not contest the judgment;[148]
- the right to a retrial, its scope and the opportunity to examine the merits of the case within the framework of re-opened proceedings;[149]
- the impact of legal recourses,[150] or the possibilities to use recourses from abroad;[151]
- how the defendant was informed of the *in absentia* conviction;[152]
- whether the defendant was assisted by a legal counsellor and whether that legal counsellor was appointed *ex officio* by the court or by the defendant him/herself;[153]
- whether the defendant's legal counsellor attended the hearing or was present at the delivery of the judgment;[154]
- the absence or presence of the requested person both at the trial resulting in a suspended prison sentence and in the procedure of revoking that suspension.[155]

Other topics that are the subject of supplementary information requests to issuing judicial authorities are: general information about the Member State's domestic legal system[156] or specific legal provisions,[157] information about the circumstances in which the offence was committed and other facts of the case,[158] information about the possibilities of provisional release,[159] clarification why the court issued the EAW with reference to judgments that were delivered many years earlier,[160] clarification why the requested person was considered 'a fugitive' by the issuing judicial authorities and whether the requested person was aware of his/her status as 'a fugitive'[161] or information about the detention conditions in the issuing Member State and assurances that the requested person will, once surrendered, be

146 PL, report, p. 87; RO, report, p. 45.
147 NL, report, p. 123.
148 PL, report, pp. 87-88; RO, report, p. 45.
149 PL, report, p. 88; RO, report, p. 45.
150 BE, report, p. 47.
151 BE, report, p. 47.
152 RO, report, p. 45.
153 PL, report, p. 87; RO, report, p. 45.
154 RO, report, p. 45.
155 RO, report, p. 45.
156 BE, report, p. 47; NL, report, p. 123.
157 BE, report, p. 47.
158 RO, report, p. 45.
159 BE, report, p. 47.
160 PL, report, p. 88.
161 PL, report, p. 88; NL, report, p. 123.

placed in a detention facility that complies with the European Convention for the Protection of Human Rights and Fundamental Freedoms and European Minimal Principles / Rules on the Treatment of Detainees of 12 February 1987.[162]

It becomes clear that, next to requests for more general information, almost all aspects of Article 4a(1) FD 2009/299/JHA are subject to supplementary information requests, indicating that either section (d) of the EAW-form is not correctly or completely filled in,[163] or that, even when it is, executing judicial authorities have problems understanding the meaning of the information provided and assessing the EAWs compatibility with Article 4a(1) FD 2009/299/JHA.

Indeed, the Belgian expert notes that most requests for supplementary information addressed to Belgian issuing judicial authorities were the result of using the old EAW-form, or omissions when filling in the EAW-form, or even misconceptions on how to fill in the EAW-form, such as not filling in section (d), ticking all points of section (d) or ticking the wrong point.[164]

In the opinion of the Romanian expert, the problems in understanding each other's legal systems with regard to *in absentia* EAWs have in fact "opened the way for requesting and providing additional information".[165]

2.4.2.2 Impact of Supplementary Information Requests

The repercussions of these frequent requests for supplementary information seem to be significant. All experts agree that they have an impact on mutual trust.[166] The Belgian expert explains that the approach "'we will refuse surrender unless you provide us with …' [is] a source for frictions and unease".[167] In the view of the Dutch expert,

> [i]n practice, the issuing judicial authority is apt to view a request for supplementary information as a vote of no confidence, whereas the executing judicial authority may be of the opinion that having to ask for supplementary information – in some cases: yet again – does not exactly inspire confidence in the ability of the issuing judicial authority to adequately fill in section (d) of the EAW.[168]

---

162 RO, report, p. 45.

163 This especially emerges from the answers of the Hungarian expert; see also HU, report, p. 38.

164 BE, report, p. 47.

165 RO, report, p. 50.

166 BE, report, p. 52; HU, report, p. 42; NL, report, p. 156; PL, report, p. 98; RO, report, p. 49. For Ireland, see also the example described: IE, report, pp. 93-97.

167 BE, report, p. 52.

168 NL, report, p. 156.

The Hungarian expert specifically mentions the situation in which the executing judicial authority requests unnecessary information, or information that already is in its possession as negatively impacting mutual trust.[169]

According to the Belgian expert, too short time frames within which the answers must be given, capacity shortages and a very high workload only exacerbate the feeling of unease.[170] He also points out that by now, the EAW has become complicated to the point that young legal practitioners are reluctant to invest the scarce time at their disposal to the study of international cooperation instruments.[171]

The Dutch expert, however, points out that in view of the fact that asking for supplementary information when the information provided in the first place is insufficient to decide on the EAW is actually a duty of the executing judicial authorities,[172] these requests should not imply a lack of trust.[173] According to him, "[i]t would be contrary to the spirit of sincere cooperation to suggest anything other than that either the issuing judicial authority or the executing judicial authority acted sincerely and in good faith."[174] Moreover, he points out that requesting supplementary information provides the issuing judicial authority with – yet another – opportunity to demonstrate that mutual trust is justified indeed. In this way, requesting and providing supplementary information can actually foster mutual trust.[175]

2.4.2.3 Acceptable Supplementary Information Requests

Most experts agree that only information that is absolutely necessary in view of executing the EAW and which is directly relevant to the assessment of the situation at hand in the light of the Court of Justice's case-law[176] (and without, of course, calling into question the merits of the *in absentia* judgment[177]), should be requested.[178] According to the Court of Justice, asking for supplementary information should be the *ultima ratio*.[179] This also must be seen in light of the Court's view that requesting and supplying information should all

169 HU, report, p. 42.

170 BE, report, p. 52.

171 BE, report, p. 52.

172 ECJ, judgment of 10 August 2017, *Openbaar Ministerie v. Sławomir Andrzej Zdziaszek*, C-271/17 PPU, ECLI:EU:C:2017:629, paras. 103-104.

173 The Irish expert is of the same opinion: IE, report, p. 113.

174 NL, report, p. 156.

175 Compare ECJ, judgment of 22 December 2017, *Samet Ardic*, C-571/17 PPU, ECLI:EU:C:2017:1026, paras. 90-91; NL, report, p. 156.

176 Compare ECJ, judgment of 25 July 2018, *Generalstaatsanwaltschaft (Conditions of detention in Hungary)*, C-220/18 PPU, ECLI:EU:C:2018:589, paras. 103-104.

177 See the European Commission's *Handbook on how to issue and execute a European Arrest Warrant, OJ* 2017 C-335, p. 24.

178 BE, report, p. 52; HU, report, p. 42; NL, report, p. 157.

179 Compare ECJ, judgment of 23 January 2018, *Dawid Piotrowski*, C-367/16, ECLI:EU:C:2018:27, para. 61.

serve the purpose of granting the execution of the EAW. Member States' efforts should aim at preventing the refusal of an EAW.

The Belgian expert posits the view that if one or more boxes of section (d) are ticked and the executing judicial authority is of the opinion that more information is needed, it should restrict its request to information which is necessary for assessing whether the *in absentia* judgment should form an obstacle to executing the EAW. In other words, it should not consider such circumstance as a licence to ask questions not pertaining to section (d). If, on the other hand, the issuing judicial authority did not fill in section (d) – or used the old version of section (d) – the issuing judicial authority may and indeed should verify whether Article 4a(1) is applicable and, if so, whether one of the conditions of Article 4a(1)(a)-(d) has been met. In its request, the executing judicial authority could refer to the text of Article 4a(1) and ask the issuing judicial authority to examine if and why one or more of those conditions applies.[180]

The Dutch expert states that executing judicial authorities should ask for concrete information concerning the proceedings against the requested person, *e.g.*, whether the requested person actually received the information about the date and the place of the trial and, if so, when.[181] In addition, the executing judicial authority should not ask open-ended questions, but rather formulate questions which allow for a "clear, correct and comprehensive"[182] answer by the issuing judicial authority. To facilitate such answers, the executing judicial authority should identify specific parts of section (d) of the EAW which in its view are unclear, insufficient, contradictory or obviously incorrect,[183] and indicate what kind of information is needed.[184] Similarly, the Hungarian expert pleads for asking only that type of information which is missing due to incorrectly filling in the EAW-form.[185]

Moreover, the executing judicial authority should not leave its counterpart guessing as to the reason why a certain piece of information is needed. Explaining the reason behind

180 BE, report, p. 52.

181 NL, report, p. 157; similar: PL, report, p. 98; similar to this is also the answer of the Romanian expert. However, she adds a series of further questions: to what extent the lawyer chosen or appointed *ex officio* exercised the rights of the defence; when and where the requested person has been handed down the judgment rendered *in absentia* and in what manner s/he has been informed of the right to a retrial or of any other remedy in which s/he has the right to be present; effectiveness of the right of re-judgment of the case in the presence, according to the law of the issuing state; the existence of inadmissibility in the means of appeal or in the proceedings for the enforcement, which resulted in the conviction of the person concerned being finally pronounced and a decision to convict a custodial sentence or a measure involving deprivation of liberty or the nature or the duration of the custodial sentence or deprivation of liberty: RO, report, p. 49.

182 Compare the European Commission's *Handbook on how to issue and execute a European Arrest Warrant, OJ* 2017 C-335, p. 20: "(...) it is vital that issuing judicial authorities ensure that the information in the EAW is clear, correct and comprehensive".

183 Compare the European Commission's *Handbook on how to issue and execute a European Arrest Warrant, OJ* 2017 C-335, p. 24.

184 NL, report, p. 157.

185 HU, report, p. 42.

the request for supplementary information with reference to relevant case-law of the Court of Justice helps the issuing judicial authority in providing that information and may also provide it with an opportunity to clear up any misunderstandings in the initial assessment of the executing judicial authority.[186]

Against that standard, executing authorities of other EU Member States often request more information than seems to be needed.[187] According to the Belgian expert, the amount and type of information requested depends on the Member State and, in particular, the Member State's approach to proceedings *in absentia*, and whether FD 2009/299/JHA was transposed as a mandatory ground for refusal or not.[188] The Dutch expert mentions the United Kingdom and Germany as notorious in terms of asking for supplementary information.[189]

The British authorities seem to provide the issuing authorities with standard questionnaires in every case that contain general questions on the legal system of the issuing Member State.[190] Answering such questionnaires takes up a lot of valuable time. Furthermore, such questionnaires call into question the principle of mutual trust.[191] The Belgian expert also notes that questions often do not fall within the ambit of section (d) of the EAW-form, but rather concern the proceedings as a whole (date of the facts, nature and description of the facts, fair trial, probable cause, pre-trial proceedings, etc.).[192] The Romanian expert notes that there are specific Member States that ask for too much and redundant information.[193] The Belgian expert adds that some questions asked make no sense in view of the facts of the case, for instance, when point 3.4 of section (d) had been ticked, asking if the defendant has the right to be present at the retrial while this is a condition that has to be met before ticking that point.[194]

2.4.3 *Time Limits*

The final decision on the execution of the EAW must be taken, in principle, within the time limits of Article 17(3) and (4) FD 2002/584/JHA,[195] *i.e.* within 60 or 90 days. Only exceptional circumstances – such as a decision to make a reference to the Court of Justice

186 NL, report, p. 157.
187 BE, report, p. 52.
188 BE, report, p. 52.
189 NL, report, p. 158.
190 See footnote 164.
191 NL, report, p. 158.
192 BE, report, p. 52.
193 RO, report, p. 50.
194 BE, report, p. 52.
195 ECJ, judgment of 16 July 2015, *Minister for Justice and Equality v. Francis Lanigan*, C-237/15 PPU, ECLI:EU:C:2015:474, para. 32.

for a preliminary ruling[196] or a postponement of the execution of the EAW on account of a real risk of inhuman or degrading treatment –[197] can justify non-observance of those time limits (Article 17(7) FD 2002/584/JHA). In that case, Eurojust must be informed, giving the reasons for the delay (Article 17(7) FD 2002/584/JHA).

Perhaps surprisingly, despite the repeated correspondence due to supplementary information requests, exceeding time limits by the executing judicial authorities of the project Member States does not seem to be a major problem.

Lack of information available to the executing judicial authority has not been a reason for exceeding time limits in Romania.[198] In Poland, time limits are only rarely exceeded, and if so, not necessarily because of a lack of information to decide on the EAW.[199]

In Ireland, there seems to be a record of frequently exceeding time limits due to numerous or comprehensive supplementary information requests, the reason being the Irish judges' lack of familiarity with most Member States' (civil law) legal systems.[200]

In the Netherlands, exceeding time limits is not an uncommon occurrence. In such cases, the Dutch executing authority will extend the time limit of 60 days with a further 30 days or will extend the time limit of 90 days for an indefinite period. In the latter case, if the requested person is still in custody, the District Court of Amsterdam *must* at the same time provisionally release him/her and notify the issuing judicial authority thereof, regardless of whether the requested person presents a risk of flight. Being of the opinion that the relevant Dutch provision is incompatible with FD 2002/584/JHA and basing itself on primary and secondary Union law, the District Court of Amsterdam has interpreted the relevant Dutch provision in such a way that the time limit is *suspended* – thereby avoiding that the time limit will exceed the 90 days mark and at the same time avoiding the automatic conditional release envisaged by Dutch Law – if there is a very serious risk of absconding which cannot be reduced to an acceptable level by the imposition of appropriate measures and the District Court: a) decides to make a preliminary reference to the Court of Justice; b) decides to await the outcome of a preliminary reference made

196 ECJ, judgment of 30 May 2013, *Jeremy F. v. Premier ministre*, C-168/13 PPU, ECLI:EU:C:2013:358, para. 65; ECJ, judgment of 12 February 2019, *TC*, C-492/18 PPU, ECLI:EU:C:2019:108, para. 43.

197 ECJ, judgment of 5 April 2016, *Pál Aranyosi and Robert Căldăraru v. Generalstaatsanwaltschaft Bremen*, C-404/15 and C-659/15 PPU, ECLI:EU:C:2016:198, para. 99. Equally, the assessment whether there is a real risk that the requested person will, if surrendered to the issuing judicial authority, suffer a breach of his/her fundamental right to an independent tribunal and, therefore, of the essence of his/her fundamental right to a fair trial (ECJ, judgment of 25 July 2018, *Minister for Justice and Equality (Deficiencies in the system of justice)*, C-216/18 PPU, ECLI:EU:C:2018:586), constitutes such exceptional circumstances: ECJ, judgment of 12 February 2019, *TC*, C-492/18 PPU, ECLI:EU:C:2019:108, para. 43.

198 RO, report, p. 46.

199 PL, report, pp. 88-89.

200 IE, report, pp. 105-106.

by another judicial authority or c) postpones the decision on the execution of the EAW in accordance with the *Aranyosi and Căldăraru*-judgment.[201]

The Court of Justice has since held that the relevant Dutch provision is indeed incompatible with FD 2002/584/JHA, in that it requires a provisional release of the requested person *in all cases* once a period of 90 days from his/her arrest has expired; provisionally releasing a requested person who represents a very serious risk of absconding which cannot be reduced to an acceptable level by the imposition of appropriate measures, merely because the time limit of 90 days has expired, is contrary to the obligations arising under the Framework Decision.[202]

Following that judgment, the Amsterdam Court of Appeal interpreted the Dutch provision in such a way that, if the requested person represents a very serious risk of absconding which cannot be reduced to an acceptable level by the imposition of appropriate measures, the time limit of 90 days may be extended *without provisionally releasing the requested person*.[203] The District Court of Amsterdam abides by this decision.[204]

Although the executing judicial authorities also report dissatisfaction with the additional stress and hassle that the supplementary information requests cause,[205] none of the project Member States report that there has been a refusal of an EAW due to exceeding the time limits.[206]

201 NL, report, pp. 124-125.
202 ECJ, judgment of 12 February 2019, *TC*, C-492/18 PPU, ECLI:EU:C:2019:108, paras. 50 and 63.
203 Court of Appeal of Amsterdam, decision of 5 March 2019, ECLI:NL:GHAMS:2019:729.
204 District Court of Amsterdam, judgment of 31 May 2019, ECLI:NL:RBAMS:2019:3906.
205 See for instance HU, report, p. 38.
206 BE, report, p. 48.

3 General Observations on Article 4a(1) Framework Decision 2002/584/JHA

3.1 Introduction: The System of Article 4a(1) Framework Decision 2002/584/JHA

In itself, the system of Article 4a(1) FD 2002/584/JHA is clear. If the requested person "did not appear in person at the trial resulting in the decision", the executing judicial authority "may (...) refuse to execute the European arrest warrant issued for the purpose of executing a custodial sentence or a detention order", *unless* the issuing judicial authority indicated in the EAW that one or more of four specific situations apply. The power to refuse an EAW is, therefore, dependent on two *cumulative* conditions: 1) the requested person "did not appear in person at the trial resulting in the decision" *and* 2) none of the situations referred to in Article 4a(1)(a) to (d) FD 2002/584/JHA applies. If the first condition is not met, Article 4a(1) does not apply. If only the first condition is met, the executing judicial authority may not rely on Article 4a(1) to refuse the execution of the EAW. If both conditions are met, the executing judicial authority may refuse to execute the EAW on the ground that the requested person "did not appear in person at the trial resulting in the decision".

As is apparent from recital (4) of the preamble to FD 2009/299/JHA, that Framework Decision aims at allowing "the executing judicial authority to execute the decision despite the absence of the person at the trial, while fully respecting the rights of the defence" by harmonising the grounds for refusal in a number of Framework Decisions, among which is FD 2002/584/JHA. Apparently, non-appearance in person at 'the trial resulting in the decision' raises the possibility that the requested person's rights of defence were not fully respected. Conversely, appearance in person at that trial establishes a non-rebuttable presumption that his/her rights were indeed fully respected. After all, in case of personal appearance, Article 4a(1) FD 2002/584/JHA does not apply. The possibility that the requested person's rights of defence were not fully respected is excluded when one or more of the four exceptions apply. In essence, each of these exceptions represents situations in which the execution of the EAW would not entail a breach of the requested person's rights of defence. Article 4a(1)(a) and (b) FD 2002/584/JHA lays down the circumstances in which the requested person must be deemed to have waived, voluntarily and unambiguously, his/her right to be present at his/her trial, whereas Article 4a(1)(c) and (d) FD 2002/584/JHA concerns situations in which the requested person is entitled to a retrial.[1]

Essentially, the system of Article 4a(1) FD 2002/584/JHA is a compromise between Member States that afford a high level of fundamental rights protection and Member States that provide for a lower level of fundamental rights protection. Under the – previous – regime of Article 5(1) FD 2002/584/JHA, the differences among the Member States as regards fundamental rights protection had an adverse effect on the mutual recognition of *in absentia* convictions.[2] The compromise consists of a trade-off. On the one hand, all Member States reached a *consensus* on the level of protection of the procedural rights of persons who were convicted *in absentia*. As the Court of Justice has repeatedly held, this level of protection is a *high* level of protection, in order to allow the executing judicial authority to execute the EAW, while *fully* respecting the rights of the defence.[3] This part of the compromise evidently satisfies the needs of those Member States with a high level of fundamental rights protection. On the other hand, even if none of the exceptions of Article 4a(1)(a) to (d) FD 2002/584/JHA applies, pursuant to the wording of that provision the executing judicial authority is *not obliged* to refuse the execution of the EAW. In deciding whether or not to refuse executing the EAW, it may take into account "other circumstances that enable it to ensure that the surrender of the person concerned does not entail a breach of his rights of defence".[4] The optional nature of the ground for refusal permits the executing judicial authorities of Member States with a high level of fundamental rights protection to refuse the execution of the EAW, once it has established that none of the exceptions applies, *i.e.* that the high level of protection was not complied with, whereas that same optional nature allows the executing judicial authorities of other Member States in such circumstances to be satisfied with a lower level of fundamental rights protection and to refrain from refusing to execute the EAW. However, *Union law* sets limits to the discretion conferred by Article 4a(1) on the executing judicial authority; these limits will be discussed elsewhere (see Section 8.3). Whether *national law* may limit that discretion will be discussed in Section 3.3.

1 ECJ, judgment of 26 February 2013, *Stefano Melloni v. Ministerio Fiscal*, C-399/11, ECLI:EU:C:2013:107, para. 52.

2 ECJ, judgment of 26 February 2013, *Stefano Melloni v. Ministerio Fiscal*, C-399/11, ECLI:EU:C:2013:107, para. 62. See also recital (3) *in fine* of the preamble to FD 2009/299/JHA.

3 ECJ, judgment of 24 May 2016, *Openbaar Ministerie v. Paweł Dworzecki*, C-108/16 PPU, ECLI:EU:C:2016:346, para. 37; ECJ, judgment of 10 August 2017, *Openbaar Ministerie v. Tadas Tupikas*, C-270/17 PPU, ECLI:EU:C:2017:628, para. 58; ECJ, judgment of 22 December 2017, *Samet Ardic*, C-571/17 PPU, ECLI:EU:C:2017:1026, para. 50.

4 ECJ, judgment of 24 May 2016, *Openbaar Ministerie v. Paweł Dworzecki*, C-108/16 PPU, ECLI:EU:C:2016:346, para. 50; ECJ, judgment of 10 August 2017, *Openbaar Ministerie v. Tadas Tupikas*, C-270/17 PPU, ECLI:EU:C:2017:628, para. 96; ECJ, judgment of 10 August 2017, *Openbaar Ministerie v. Sławomir Andrzej Zdziaszek*, C-271/17 PPU, ECLI:EU:C:2017:629, para. 107.

The exceptions to the power to refuse to execute the EAW are *exhaustive*.[5] If one or more of these exceptions apply, the executing judicial authority may not refuse the execution of the EAW on the ground that the requested person did not appear in person at the trial resulting in the decision. It follows that in such circumstances under Article 4a(1) the Member States may not make the execution of the EAW dependent on any other condition than those listed in Article 4a(1), such as the condition that the *in absentia* conviction is open to review in the issuing Member State in order to guarantee the rights of defence of the requested person.[6] None of the six Member States involved in this project has made execution of the EAW dependent on additional conditions.

According to the Court of Justice, the system of Article 4a(1) FD is compatible with the right to an effective judicial remedy and to a fair trial (Article 47 Charter of Fundamental Rights of the European Union; hereafter Charter) and with the rights of the defence (Article 48(2) Charter). The right of the accused to appear in person at his/her trial is an essential component of the right to a fair trial, but that right is not absolute. If the person concerned has voluntarily and unequivocally waived that right, an *in absentia* conviction does not run counter to the right to a fair trial. The same holds true, if the person concerned is entitled to a retrial. Exactly these circumstances are mentioned in Article 4a(1)(a) to (d) FD 2002/584/JHA.[7]

In order for Article 4a(1) FD 2002/584/JHA to reach its twin goals of enhancing procedural rights and facilitating judicial cooperation, the Court of Justice must ensure that Article 4a(1) FD 2002/584/JHA is interpreted and applied in accordance with the requirements of Article 6 ECHR, as interpreted by the ECtHR.[8]

This raises the question of how to square this with the Court of Justice's insistence that Article 4a(1) FD 2002/584/JHA guarantees a "*high* level of protection".[9] After all, this provision simply could not be interpreted in such a way that it guarantees a *lower* level of protection than that of Article 6 ECHR, because Article 52(3) Charter does not allow for such an interpretation. In this respect, it is important to note that some of the exceptions to the rule that the execution of the EAW may be refused in case of non-appearance in person are *more demanding* than the ECtHR's case-law. For example, Article 4a(1)(d)(i)

5 ECJ, judgment of 26 February 2013, *Stefano Melloni v. Ministerio Fiscal*, C-399/11, ECLI:EU:C:2013:107, para. 44.

6 ECJ, judgment of 26 February 2013, *Stefano Melloni v. Ministerio Fiscal*, C-399/11, ECLI:EU:C:2013:107, para. 44.

7 ECJ, judgment of 26 February 2013, *Stefano Melloni v. Ministerio Fiscal*, C-399/11, ECLI:EU:C:2013:107, paras. 49-53.

8 ECJ, judgment of 22 December 2017, *Samet Ardic*, C-571/17 PPU, ECLI:EU:C:2017:1026, paras. 73-74.

9 ECJ, judgment of 24 May 2017, *Openbaar Ministerie v. Paweł Dworzecki*, C-108/16 PPU, ECLI:EU:C:2016:343; ECJ, judgment of 10 August 2017, *Openbaar Ministerie v. Tadas Tupikas*, C-270/17 PPU, ECLI:EU:C:2017:628, para. 58; ECJ, judgment of 22 December 2017, *Samet Ardic*, C-517/17 PPU, ECLI:EU:C:2017:1026, para. 73 (emphasis added).

FD 2002/584/JHA requires either that the defendant received the summons *in person* or that s/he by other means *actually* received the information about the date and the place of the trial. Under Article 6 ECHR, on the other hand, even if the defendant was not summoned in person and did not actually receive the information about the date and the place of the trial, it cannot be ruled out that

> certain established facts might provide an unequivocal indication that the accused is aware of the existence of the criminal proceedings against him and of the nature and the cause of the accusation and does not intend to take part in the trial or wishes to escape prosecution. This may be the case, for example, where the accused states publicly or in writing that he does not intend to respond to summonses of which he has become aware through sources other than the authorities, or succeeds in evading an attempted arrest (…), or when materials are brought to the attention of the authorities which unequivocally show that he is aware of the proceedings pending against him/her and of the charges he faces.[10]

In all of these instances, the person concerned will be considered to have waived his/her right to be present at the trial and to defend him/herself.[11] It is, therefore, entirely possible that the conditions of Article 4a(1)(a)(i) FD 2002/584/JHA are not met in circumstances in which according to the ECtHR's case-law execution of the EAW would not violate Article 6(1) ECHR. Consequently, in this regard Article 4a(1) affords a *higher* level of protection than Article 6 ECHR.[12] Moreover, the exceptions to the rule do not *fully* codify the case-law of the ECtHR: according to that case-law, even if none of those four exceptions apply, a trial *in absentia* need not necessarily constitute a violation of the right to a fair trial. The exceptions do not cover, *e.g.*, flight by the defendant, whereas according to the ECtHR's case-law such a circumstance would entail an implicit waiver of his/her right to be present at the trial.[13] It is safe to conclude, then, that the mere fact that none of the four exceptions applies does not necessarily mean that executing the EAW would entail a breach of the requested person's rights of defence. Finally, Article 4a(1) establishes a common and clear ground for refusal. Compared to the previous regime of Article 5(1) FD 2002/584/JHA – which used the ambiguous term '*in absentia*' and which left the examina-

10 ECtHR, judgment of 1 March 2006, *Sejdovic v. Italy* [GC], ECLI:CE:ECHR:2006:0301JUD005658100, § 99.

11 *See, e.g.*, ECtHR, judgment of 12 June 2018, *M.T.B. v. Turkey*, ECLI:CE:ECHR:2018:0612JUD004708106, § 49.

12 Opinion of Advocate General M. Bobek of 11 May 2016, *Openbaar Ministerie v. Paweł Dworzecki*, C-108/16 PPU, ECLI:EU:C:2016:333, para. 74.

13 ECtHR, judgment of 1 March 2006, *Sejdovic v. Italy* [GC], ECLI:CE:ECHR:2006:0301JUD005658100, § 99.

tion of the adequacy of the guarantee entirely up to the executing judicial authority – Article 4a(1) certainly does afford a *higher* level of protection.

The exhaustively listed exceptions of Article 4a(1)(a) to (d) represent the *consensus* between Member States regarding the extent *under Union law* of the protection of procedural rights enjoyed by persons convicted *in absentia* who are the subject of an EAW.[14] Consequently, when applying national measures implementing Article 4a(1) FD 2002/584/JHA Member States may not provide for *more* national protection of those rights. That is, if one of the exceptions of Article 4a(1)(a) to (d) applies, they may not make the execution of an EAW conditional on any additional assurances or safeguards. In accordance with Article 53 Charter national authorities remain free to apply *national* standards of fundamental rights protection when applying national implementing measures *if and only if* the Charter's level of protection and the primacy, unity and effectiveness of Union law are not thereby compromised.[15]

Providing for *more* national fundamental rights protection would compromise the *primacy* of Union law, because Article 4a(1) does not allow for refusing the execution of the EAW if one of the exhaustive exceptions is applicable.[16] Providing for more protection would also compromise the *unity* and *effectiveness* of Union law, because it would cast doubt on the level of protection agreed upon by *all* Member States (*unity*)[17] and would thereby undermine mutual trust and mutual recognition (*effectiveness*).[18]

Arguably, providing for *less* national fundamental rights protection would compromise not only the *level of protection provided for by the Charter*, as interpreted by the Court, but also – for the same reasons as providing for more protection – the *unity* and *effectiveness* of Union law (see also Section 3.6).

3.2 MANDATORY OR OPTIONAL: TRANSPOSITION

All Member States have transposed FD 2009/299/JHA.[19]

---

14 ECJ, judgment of 26 February 2013, *Stefano Melloni v. Ministerio Fiscal*, C-399/11, ECLI:EU:C:2013:107, para. 62.

15 ECJ, judgment of 26 February 2013, *Stefano Melloni v. Ministerio Fiscal*, C-399/11, ECLI:EU:C:2013:107, para. 60.

16 ECJ, judgment of 26 February 2013, *Stefano Melloni v. Ministerio Fiscal*, C-399/11, ECLI:EU:C:2013:107, para. 61.

17 In this respect, one should remember that FD 2009/299/JHA, as a Framework Decision, was adopted by *unanimity* (Art. 34(2)(b) of the pre-Lisbon Treaty on European Union).

18 ECJ, judgment of 26 February 2013, *Stefano Melloni v. Ministerio Fiscal*, C-399/11, ECLI:EU:C:2013:107, para. 63.

19 See the Table of Implementation on the website of the European Judicial Network (https://www.ejn-crimjust.europa.eu/ejn/EJN_Library_StatusOfImpByCat.aspx?CategoryId=104), last accessed on 5 August 2019.

A majority of the experts are of the opinion that the Member States are under an *obligation* to transpose Article 4a(1) FD 2002/584/JHA.[20] To support this opinion, one expert points out that a Framework Decision must be transposed by the Member States in order for it to have legal effect in their national legal orders. Another expert is of the opinion that transposition is a matter for the Member States,[21] while yet another regards the issue as somewhat academic, as all Member States have transposed Article 4a(1) FD 2002/584/JHA.[22]

3.3 MANDATORY OR OPTIONAL: REFUSAL

When transposing Article 4a(1) FD 2002/584/JHA, may Member States *require* that the executing judicial authority refuses to execute the EAW in cases in which none of the four exceptions applies? In other words, may Member States transpose Article 4a(1) FD 2002/584/JHA as a *mandatory* ground for refusal?

According to recital (15) of the preamble to FD 2009/299/JHA, the ground for refusal of Article 4a(1) is *optional*. However, as recital (15) also makes clear, the discretion for the Member States *when transposing*[23] this ground for refusal is

> particularly governed by the right to a fair trial, while taking into account the overall objective of this Framework Decision to enhance the procedural rights of persons and to facilitate judicial cooperation in criminal matters.

This recital represents a compromise between Austria and the other Member States.[24] Austria wanted a mandatory ground for refusal, because from the viewpoint of protecting fundamental rights the value of an optional ground for refusal would be quite limited.[25] Apparently, from the perspective of Austria the wording of recital (15) steers the Member States towards transposition of Article 4a(1) as a mandatory ground for refusal, whereas from the perspective of other Member States the wording of recital (15) affords them enough leeway to transpose Article 4a(1) as an optional ground for refusal. The case-law

20 BE, report, p. 17; HU, report, p. 14; PL, report, p. 51; RO, report, p. 20.
21 IE, report, p. 31.
22 NL, report, p. 49.
23 In this respect the English, French and German language versions are more clear on this point than the Dutch language version. The wording of the latter language version seems to suggest that recital (15) does not pertain to the Member States' discretion when transposing Art. 4a, but rather to their discretion as to whether to transpose or not.
24 Council document 8074/08, 8 April 2008, p. 13, footnote 12.
25 Council document 7846/08, 26 March 2008, p. 4.

of the Court of Justice seems to favour the position of the other Member States over the Austrian position.

With regard to Article 4(6) FD 2002/584/JHA – another optional ground for refusal – the Court of Justice has held that, when transposing this ground for refusal, Member States must provide their executing judicial authorities with "a margin of discretion as to whether or not it is appropriate to refuse to execute the EAW".[26] In essence, the Court of Justice proffers two arguments to support this ruling. Firstly, as an *exception* to the rule of execution of the EAW Article 4(6) FD 2002/584/JHA must be interpreted *strictly*.[27] In his opinion, Advocate General Bot points out that transposing an optional ground for refusal as a mandatory ground for refusal would turn the *general* rule – execution of the EAW – into the *exception*.[28] Secondly, *the wording itself* of Article 4(6) FD 2002/584/JHA – according to which the "executing judicial authority *may* refuse to execute the [EAW]" – makes it clear that the executing judicial authority must have a margin of discretion.[29,30]

The arguments militating for the Court of Justice's interpretation of Article 4(6) FD 2002/584/JHA seem equally applicable to Article 4a(1) FD 2002/584/JHA. As with Article 4(6), Article 4a(1) is an exception to the rule and must, therefore, be interpreted strictly. Furthermore, the opening sentence of Article 4a(1) closely resembles the opening sentence of Article 4(6) ("The executing judicial authority may also refuse to execute the [EAW] (...)"). The word 'also' clearly refers to Article 4 FD 2002/584/JHA, thus providing an additional argument for applying the Court of Justice's interpretation of Article 4(6) FD 2002/584/JHA to Article 4a(1).

Indeed, in his opinion in the *Tupikas* and *Zdziaszek* cases, Advocate General Bobek argued that a transposition of Article 4a(1) as a mandatory ground for refusal is an incorrect transposition. Such a transposition reverses the logic of Article 4a(1) by transforming the *possibility* of non-execution, unless one of the exceptions applies, into a *requirement* of non-execution. In transposing Article 4a(1) as a mandatory ground for refusal, the four

26 ECJ, judgment of 29 June 2017, *Daniel Adam Popławski*, C-579/15, ECLI:EU:C:2017:503, para. 21; ECJ, judgment of 13 December 2018, *Ministère public v. Marin-Simion Sut*, C-514/17, ECLI:EU:C:2018:1016, para. 33.

27 ECJ, judgment of 29 June 2017, *Daniel Adam Popławski*, C-579/15, ECLI:EU:C:2017:503, para. 19.

28 Opinion of 15 February 2017, *Daniel Adam Popławski*, C-579/15, ECLI:EU:C:2017:116, para. 31.

29 ECJ, judgment of 29 June 2017, *Daniel Adam Popławski*, C-579/15, ECLI:EU:C:2017:503, para. 21; ECJ, judgment of 13 December 2018, *Ministère public v. Marin-Simion Sut*, C-514/17, ECLI:EU:C:2018:1016, para. 33.

30 It should be noted that the Court of Justice does not require a Member State to provide its executing judicial authorities with *full* discretion as to whether to refuse the EAW, but rather that it provides them *a margin* of discretion in that regard. No doubt this is a consequence of the 'certain margin of discretion' of which the Member States 'of necessity' dispose when transposing Art. 4 FD 2002/584/JHA: ECJ, judgment of 6 October 2009, *Dominic Wolzenburg*, C-123/08, ECLI:EU:C:2009:616, para. 61; ECJ, judgment of 5 September 2012, *João Pedro Lopes Da Silva Jorge*, C-42/11, ECLI:EU:C:2012:517, para. 33; ECJ, judgment of 13 December 2018, *Ministère public v. Marin-Simion Sut*, C-514/17, ECLI:EU:C:2018:1016, para. 42.

exceptions listed in Article 4a(1)(a) to (d) thereby become the *only* situations in which the executing judicial authority may execute the EAW. Thus, the executing judicial authority is prevented from taking into account *all* the factual circumstances which might enable it to determine whether the procedural rights of the person concerned were respected. Transposing, by analogy, the Court of Justice's ruling in *Popławski*, the Advocate General concluded that the executing judicial authority must enjoy a margin of discretion as to whether it is appropriate to refuse to execute the EAW on the basis of Article 4a(1).[31]

Ostensibly, in its judgments in the *Tupikas* and *Zdziaszek* cases the Court of Justice did not follow the opinion of Advocate General Bobek. Reiterating what it had said in *Dworzecki* about the optional nature of Article 4a(1) FD 2002/584/JHA, it confined itself to observing that

> Framework Decision 2002/584 does not *prevent* the executing judicial authority from ensuring that the rights of the person concerned are upheld by taking due consideration of all the circumstances characterising the case before it (…).[32]

Saying that FD 2002/584/JHA does not prevent the executing judicial authority from doing something is not quite the same as saying that FD 2002/584/JHA *requires* national law not to prevent the executing judicial authority from doing something. The Court of Justice, therefore, did not rule that Member States, when transposing Article 4a(1) FD, must leave a margin of discretion to its executing judicial authorities.

One can argue that the Court of Justice did not do so out of respect for the compromise between Member States with a high national level of protection and Member States with a lower national level of fundamental rights protection (see Section 3.1). The four exceptions represent a *consensus* between the Member States on the level of protection to be afforded, which is a *high* level of protection; if none of these exceptions applies, those Member States that apply a *high* national level of fundamental rights protection can oblige their executing judicial authorities to refuse to execute the EAW, because the conditions of that high level of protection have not been complied with. Requiring Member States to leave a margin of discretion to their executing judicial authorities and thereby affording them the opportunity to execute the EAW nonetheless would have the potential to upset that compromise.

---

31 Opinion of 26 July 2017, *Openbaar Ministerie v. Tadas Tupikas*, C-270/17 PPU, ECLI:EU:C:2017:609, paras. 75-78; opinion of 26 July 2017, *Openbaar Ministerie v. Sławomir Andrzej Zdziaszek*, C-271/17 PPU, ECLI:EU:C:2017:612, paras. 108-110.

32 ECJ, judgment of 10 August 2017, *Openbaar Ministerie v. Tadas Tupikas*, C-270/17 PPU, ECLI:EU:C:2017:628, paras. 96-97 (emphasis added); ECJ, judgment of 10 August 2017, *Openbaar Ministerie v. Sławomir Andrzej Zdziaszek*, C-271/17 PPU, ECLI:EU:C:2017:629, paras. 106-108.

On the other hand, one can argue that the question whether a Member State may transpose Article 4a(1) FD 2002/584/JHA as a mandatory ground for refusal simply was not at issue in the *Tupikas* and *Zdziaszek* cases. Although the referring court indicated that the mandatory nature of the Dutch transposition of Article 4a(1) was problematic – as it had also done in its referral in the *Dworzecki* case –, it did not ask the Court of Justice to rule on this matter. Moreover, the Court of Justice's conclusion in the *Tupikas* and *Zdziaszek* judgments leaves some room for the Court of Justice to declare, at some later stage, that an executing judicial authority should have a margin of discretion in order for it to be able to take into account "other circumstances that enable it to be assured that the surrender of the person concerned does not mean a breach of his rights of defence".

Three of the six Member States involved in this project transposed Article 4a(1) as an *optional* ground for refusal,[33] the other three as a *mandatory* ground for refusal.[34] In four of the six Member States, the legislative choice for an optional or a mandatory ground for refusal was not debated in Parliament and/or explained in the *travaux préparatoires*.[35]

3.4 Mandatory or Optional: Application proprio motu

There is yet another general problem linked with the issue of transposition of the ground for refusal. When a Member State has chosen to transpose Article 4a(1) FD 2002/584/JHA as an optional ground for refusal, are its executing judicial authorities obliged to examine whether to apply this ground for refusal *proprio motu* or not? If so, they must examine whether the requirements of Article 4(1)(a) to (d) FD 2002/584/JHA are met, regardless of whether the requested person invoked this ground for refusal or not. If not, they are only bound to act in this regard when the requested person objects to the execution of the EAW on the basis of Article 4a(1) FD 2002/584/JHA.

The issue of the duty of *motu proprio* application of an optional ground for refusal is a procedural one. Normally, in the absence of Union rules governing the matter, it is for the Member States, in accordance with the principle of the procedural autonomy, to lay down the detailed procedural rules governing the application of Union law. However, this procedural autonomy is limited by the principles of equivalence and effectiveness.[36]

33 BE, PL and RO.

34 HU, IE and NL.

35 BE, report, p. 17 (no debate); IE, report, p. 31 (unaware of public discourse; nothing relevant in parliamentary debates; unaware of internal governmental debate); NL, report, p. 49 (no debate); PL, report, p. 51 (no debate). According to the Hungarian expert no information was available: HU, report, p. 14. The Romanian expert did not answer the sub-question whether there was any debate on the choice for a mandatory or an optional ground for refusal: RO, report, p. 20.

36 *See, e.g.*, ECJ, judgment of 15 March 2017, *Lucio Cesare Aquino v. Belgische Staat*, C-3/16, ECLI:EU:C:2017:209, para. 48.

A number of possible interpretations present themselves.

According to the first interpretation, FD 2002/584/JHA does contain rules governing the matter. These rules are *inherent* in the nature of optional grounds for refusal. As the executing judicial authority is not obliged to refuse to execute the EAW, it is not obliged to examine *proprio motu* whether to apply the ground for refusal. Moreover, FD 2002/584/JHA affords the requested person ample means and ample opportunity to invoke optional grounds for refusal. When the requested person is arrested, s/he is informed of the EAW and its contents by the executing judicial authority (Article 11(1) FD 2002/584/JHA). An arrested requested person has a right to be assisted by a legal counsellor and by an interpreter (Article 11(2) FD 2002/584/JHA in connection with Article 10 Directive 2013/48/EU).[37] If the requested person chooses not to consent with his/her surrender (see Article 13(1) FD 2002/584/JHA), s/he has a right to be heard by the executing judicial authority (Article 14 FD 2002/584/JHA). An arrested requested person must be informed promptly of his/her rights according to the national law of the executing Member State implementing FD 2002/584/JHA (Article 5(1) Directive 2012/13/EU).[38] Furthermore, the procedural rights conferred by FD 2002/584/JHA and by both Directives are *minimum* rights.[39] In implementing these three instruments, the Member States may choose to afford the requested person even more procedural rights. Against this background, when the requested person or his/her legal counsellor does not invoke an optional ground for refusal, the executing judicial authority is allowed to assume that they do not wish to oppose the execution of the EAW on the grounds of a violation of the rights of defence.[40]

A second possible interpretation is that FD 2002/584/JHA does not contain rules governing the matter. Therefore, it is up to the Member States to determine whether their executing judicial authorities are under any obligation in this regard, provided the Member States abide by the principles of equivalence and effectiveness. With respect to the principle of equivalence, the procedural rules which the Member States lay down must not be less favourable than those governing similar domestic proceedings. In this regard it should be pointed out that, according to well-settled case-law, if national law confers on a court the *discretion* to apply national law *proprio motu*, that court is *obliged* to apply Union law *proprio motu*.[41] With respect to the principle of effectiveness, the national procedural rules must not render impossible in practice or excessively difficult the exercise of Union law.

37 The United Kingdom, Ireland and Denmark are not bound by this Directive: recitals (58) and (59) of the preamble to Directive 2013/48/EU.

38 Denmark is not bound by this Directive: recital (45) of Directive 2012/13/EU.

39 FD 2002/584/JHA: ECJ, judgment of 3 May 2007, *Advocaten voor de Wereld VZW v. Leden van de Ministerraad*, C-303/05, ECLI:EU:C:2007:261, para. 30; Directive 2012/13/EU: recital (40) of the preamble; Directive 2013/48/EU: Art. 1.

40 Cf. ECJ, judgment of 6 December 2018, *IK*, C-551/18 PPU, ECLI:EU:C:2018:991, para. 65.

41 ECJ, judgment of 24 October 1996, *Aannemersbedrijf P.K. Kraaijeveld BV e.a. v. Gedeputeerde Staten van Zuid-Holland*, C-72, 95, ECLI:EU:C:1996:404, paras. 57-58.

Referring to the – minimum – rights of the requested person mentioned earlier, restricting the examination of the applicability of optional grounds for refusal to cases in which the requested person invokes those grounds for refusal does not seem to run afoul of the principle of effectiveness.

Yet a third possible interpretation holds that FD 2002/584/JHA does contain rules governing the matter. As with the first interpretation, according to the third interpretation these rules are *inherent* in FD 2002/584/JHA, but other than the first interpretation the third interpretation holds that these inherent rules *oblige* the executing judicial authority to examine *proprio motu* whether to apply an optional ground for refusal.

The – somewhat involved – reasoning underlying the third interpretation is as follows. The mere fact that a specific ground for refusal is optional and that the executing judicial authority, therefore, has a certain margin of discretion as to whether or not it is appropriate to refuse to execute the EAW does not settle the issue. One should distinguish between examining whether a ground for refusal is applicable and deciding to refuse the execution of the EAW on the basis of that ground for refusal. A margin of discretion as to the decision does not necessarily mean that there is no duty to examine the applicability of the ground for refusal *proprio motu*.

One can argue that a duty of *proprio motu* examination of the applicability of optional grounds for refusal is inherent in the system of that Framework Decision. According to recital (8) of the preamble of that Framework Decision, the decision on the execution of the EAW must be subject to 'sufficient controls' by judicial authorities. Because the entire EAW procedure, from the decision to issue an EAW to the decision to execute that EAW, is under the supervision of judicial authorities, that procedure in itself provides for an effective remedy against possible violations of (fundamental) rights and freedoms guaranteed by Union law, regardless of how Member States transpose FD 2002/584/JHA.[42] Indeed, this Framework Decision is

> founded on the principle that decisions relating to [EAWs] are attended by all the guarantees appropriate for decisions of such a kind, inter alia those resulting from the fundamental rights and fundamental legal principles referred to in Article 1(3) of the Framework Decision.[43]

The words 'controls' and 'supervision' seem to require an *active* stance of the judicial authorities, especially with regard to fundamental rights issues. Furthermore, it is arguable

42 ECJ, judgment of 30 May 2013, *Jeremy F. v. Premier ministre*, C-168/13 PPU, ECLI:EU:C:2013:358, paras. 45-47.

43 ECJ, judgment of 25 July 2018, *Minister for Justice and Equality (Deficiencies in the system of justice)*, C-216/18 PPU, ECLI:EU:C:2018:586, para. 56.

that a duty of *proprio motu* application not only is inherent in the system of the Framework Decision, but also follows from the wording of Article 15(1) FD 2002/584/JHA. According to this provision, the executing judicial authority shall decide, within the time limits and under the conditions defined in this framework decision, whether the person is to be surrendered. Those 'conditions' refer to the grounds for refusal, without differentiating between mandatory and optional grounds for refusal and without requiring invocation of a ground for refusal. The second paragraph of Article 15 FD 2002/584/JHA could be cited in support of this argument:

> If the executing judicial authority finds the information communicated by the issuing Member State to be insufficient to allow it to decide on surrender, it shall request that the necessary supplementary information, in particular with respect to Articles 3 to 5 and Article 8 (...).

Again, this provision does not distinguish between mandatory and optional grounds for refusal. In this interpretation, the executing judicial authority is under a duty to examine the applicability of an optional ground for refusal and to decide whether to refuse the execution of the EAW, irrespective of whether the requested person invoked that optional ground for refusal.

With regard to Article 4a(1) specifically, it should be recalled that the objective of this provision is "to enable the executing judicial authority to allow surrender, despite the absence of the requested person at the trial resulting in their conviction, while fully upholding the rights of defence". Again, the wording seems to require an *active* approach by the executing judicial authority: in order for the executing judicial authority to conclude that it may allow surrender, it must first have examined whether the rights of defence were fully respected. According to the third interpretation, it can only reach that conclusion after having established either that one of the conditions set out in subparagraphs (a), (b), (c) or (d) of Article 4a(1) are met or, if none of those conditions are met, that surrender nonetheless does not entail a breach of the requested person's rights of defence.

Of course, one important argument against a duty of *proprio motu* application of optional grounds for refusal would be that such a duty would run counter to the aims of simplifying and accelerating surrender. It cannot be denied that this argument carries much weight. But even conceding that such an argument could be decisive with regard to optional grounds for refusal in general, according to the third interpretation one can still argue that this argument does not dispose of the issue with regard to Article 4a(1) in particular. What is at stake here is the duty to respect fundamental rights. After all, as the

Court of Justice itself said, the executing judicial authority cannot tolerate a breach of those rights, such as the rights of defence.[44]

As discussed, each of the three interpretations has its pros and cons. They are presented here without taking a definite stand on anyone of them. As of yet, the Court of Justice has not settled the issue of the duty of application *proprio motu* of an optional ground for refusal.

In those project Member States that transposed Article 4a(1) as a mandatory ground for refusal – Hungary, Ireland and the Netherlands –, the executing judicial authorities will – likely – apply their national ground for refusal *proprio motu.*

With regard to the Member States that transposed Article 4a(1) as an optional ground for refusal, the situation is more varied. In Belgium, the executing judicial authority will, in principle, not apply the ground for refusal *proprio motu*, but judges are independent and Belgian law does not exclude applying the ground for refusal *proprio motu*. Normally, the public prosecutor will anticipate any argument based on Article 4a(1) and verify if the information in section (d) of the EAW is sufficient. However, in general, if the person concerned does not invoke this ground for refusal, the Belgian executing judicial authorities will not proceed with an examination on their own initiative.[45] In Romania, the executing judicial authorities will not apply the ground for refusal *proprio motu*.[46] In Poland, the executing judicial authorities examine whether an optional ground for refusal is applicable to the case at hand, as transpires from the decisions on the execution of EAWs which were analysed in the course of the research project.[47] Moreover, the execution of the EAW *must* be refused, if surrendering the person concerned would violate his/her human rights. Therefore, according to the judges who were interviewed in the course of the research project, the question whether the EAW will be executed is answered with due deference to the right to a fair trial of the requested person.[48]

3.5 AUTONOMOUS UNION LAW CONCEPTS OR NATIONAL LAW CONCEPTS?

According to a well-established tenet of Union law, the terms of a provision of Union law which makes no express reference to the law of the Member States for the purpose of determining its meaning and scope must normally be given an autonomous and uniform interpretation throughout the Union, taking into account the wording and the context of

44 ECJ, judgment of 10 August 2017, *Openbaar Ministerie v. Sławomir Andrzej Zdziaszek*, C-271/17 PPU, ECLI:EU:C:2017:629, para. 105.

45 BE, report, pp. 18, 20.

46 RO, report, p. 20.

47 PL, report, p. 51.

48 PL, report, pp. 62 and 71.

the provision and the purpose of the legislation in question. This tenet is based on the need for uniform application of Union law and on the principle of equality.[49] When a provision contains autonomous concepts which must be uniformly interpreted, the meaning of those concepts cannot be left to the discretion of the Member States on the basis of their national law.[50] The meaning of such concepts must be determined, irrespective of national qualifications[51] and independently of national substantive and procedure rules in criminal matters "which by nature diverge in the various Member States".[52]

Article 4a(1) FD 2002/584/JHA contains a reference to the law of the Member States. This reference ("in accordance with further procedural requirements defined in the national law of the issuing Member State") is part of the sentence which serves as an introduction to the four exceptions to the power to refuse to execute the EAW ("unless the European arrest warrant states that the person, in accordance with further procedural requirements defined in the national law of the issuing Member State (...)").

Grammatically speaking, there can be no doubt that the reference to the law of the issuing Member State does not pertain to the concepts of 'personal appearance' and of 'a trial resulting in the decision': these concepts *precede* that reference. Moreover, these concepts are pivotal to the system of Article 4a(1), because the applicability and scope of the ground for refusal hinge on their meaning. Judging from recital (5) of the preamble to FD 2009/299/JHA, apparently the Member States felt that previous regimes concerning *in absentia* decisions left too much latitude to executing judicial authorities, resulting in *uncertainty* as to when the execution would be refused. To remedy this situation, FD 2009/299/JHA *harmonises* the grounds of refusal concerning *in absentia* decisions in a number of Framework Decisions by providing "*clear* and *common* grounds for non-recognition of decisions rendered following a trial at which the person concerned did not appear in person".[53] Those grounds for non-recognition could hardly be called 'clear' and 'common' if their applicability and scope depended solely on the national laws of 28 Member States. Therefore, the concepts of 'personal appearance' and of a 'trial resulting in the decision' must be considered autonomous concepts. As far as the concept of a 'trial resulting in the decision' is concerned, the Court of Justice explicitly confirmed that it is an autonomous concept of Union law.[54]

49 *See, e.g.*, ECJ, judgment of 17 October 2018, *UD*, C-393/18, ECLI:EU:C:2018:835, para. 46.

50 *See, e.g.*, ECJ, judgment of 17 July 2008, *Proceedings concerning the execution of a European arrest warrant issued against Szymon Kozłowski*, C-66/08, ECLI:EU:C:2008:437, para. 41; ECJ, judgment of 16 November 2010, *Gaetano Mantello*, C-261/09, ECLI:EU:C:2010:683, para. 38.

51 ECJ, judgment of 10 August 2017, *Openbaar Ministerie v. Tadas Tupikas*, C-270/17 PPU, ECLI:EU:C:2017:628, para. 67.

52 ECJ, judgment of 22 December 2017, *Samet Ardic*, C-571/17 PPU, ECLI:EU:C:2017:1026, para. 63.

53 Recital (6) of the preamble to FD 2009/299/JHA (emphasis added).

54 ECJ, judgment of 10 August 2017, *Openbaar Ministerie v. Tadas Tupikas*, C-270/17 PPU, ECLI:EU:C:2017:628, paras. 65-67.

The exceptions to the power to refuse the EAW *follow* the reference to the law of the issuing Member State. It must, therefore, be determined whether that reference has the purpose of determining the meaning and scope of the concepts which follow it. In this regard, it should again be recalled that FD 2009/299/JHA aims at enhancing the procedural rights of persons subject to criminal proceedings and facilitating judicial cooperation in criminal matters (Article 1 FD 2009/299/JHA) by establishing *clear* and *common* grounds for non-recognition. Against this background, the reference to the national law of the issuing Member State does not serve the purpose of indicating that the meaning and scope of the concepts which follow that reference are to be determined by the national laws of the Member States. Instead, it seeks to serve as a reminder that FD 2009/299/JHA only seeks to harmonise the grounds for refusal concerning *in absentia* decisions and not the national procedural rules of the Member States concerning *in absentia* proceedings, as is also evident from recital 14 of the preamble to FD 2009/299/JHA

> The Framework Decision is limited to refining the definition of grounds for non-recognition in instruments implementing the principle of mutual recognition. Therefore, provisions such as those relating to the right to a retrial have a scope which is limited to the definition of these grounds for non-recognition. They are not designed to harmonise national legislation. (…).

The word 'further' in the expression 'further procedural rules' clearly establishes that the reference to the national law of the issuing Member State does not pertain to any of the concepts which follow that reference.

In its *Dworzecki* judgment, the Court of Justice confirmed that the expressions 'summoned in person' and "by other means actually received official information of the scheduled date and place of that trial in such a manner that it was unequivocally established that he or she was aware of the scheduled trial", as mentioned in Article 4a(1)(a)(i) FD 2002/584/JHA, are autonomous concepts of Union law. In doing so, the Court of Justice referred to the fact that, although FD 2009/299/JHA contains a number of express references to the national law of the Member States, none of the references concerns the concepts mentioned in Article 4a(1)(a)(i) FD 2002/584/JHA. Further, the Court of Justice referred to the origins of FD 2002/584/JHA and the need to establish clear and common grounds for refusal, as discussed in the previous section.[55]

The Court of Justice's arguments seem readily applicable to other key concepts of Article 4a(1) FD 2002/584/JHA, *e.g.* the concept of 'being served with the decision' (Article 4a(1)(c)) and the concept of a right to a retrial or an appeal (Article 4a(1)(c) and (d)).

55 ECJ, judgment of 24 May 2016, *Openbaar Ministerie v. Paweł Dworzecki*, C-108/16 PPU, ECLI:EU:C:2018:346, paras. 29-31.

Among the experts, no unanimity could be reached on this point. Referring to recital (14) of the preamble to FD 2008/909/JHA, one expert voiced the opinion that these concepts are defined by the national law of the issuing Member State.[56]

At this juncture, it seems useful to underline the distinction between harmonising the grounds for refusal and harmonising national legislation concerning trials *in absentia* and to spell out the consequences of this distinction.

If such concepts as "being served with the decision" and "the right to a retrial or an appeal, in which the person has the right to participate and which allows the merits of the case, including fresh evidence, to be re-examined, and which may lead to the original decision being reversed" (Article 4a(1)(c) FD 2002/584/JHA) are indeed autonomous concepts of Union law, as is posited by the authors of this report, then Article 4a(1) does not oblige the issuing Member State to regulate the service of decisions in such a way that it complies with that provision or to provide for the right to a retrial or an appeal as envisaged by that provision. However, if application of the national rules on service of the decision or on the right to a retrial or an appeal leads to results which are incompatible with Article 4a(1), the issuing Member States run the risk that the execution of its EAWs is regularly refused by other Member States.[57]

When filling in section (d) of the EAW, the issuing judicial authority must be aware that this section contains autonomous concepts of Union law whose meaning does not necessarily correspond to the national law meaning of those concepts. Of course, the same holds true for the executing judicial authority when deciding on the execution of an EAW. Establishing whether a particular exception to the power to refuse the EAW is applicable requires a two-part operation. The issuing judicial authority must first determine what happened in the proceedings that led to the *in absentia* conviction at a factual level. Then it must determine whether its findings as to the facts correspond to one of the exceptions, bearing in mind the autonomous nature of the expressions used and taking into account the relevant case-law of the Court of Justice. In doing so, it must divorce itself of national law notions, in other words it must take off of its national law glasses and put on its Union law glasses. If the facts correspond to one or more of the exceptions, the issuing judicial authority may tick the applicable box in section (d) of the EAW. To use the example of the preceding section: if the decision was not served in accordance with the autonomous meaning of that concept or if, in a given case, the person concerned did not have the right to a retrial or an appeal in the autonomous meaning of that concept, then the issuing judicial authority must not tick box 3.3 of section (d) of the EAW. If its findings correspond to none of the other exceptions, it must not tick any of the boxes belonging to points 3.1-

---

56 BE, report, pp. 30 and 32.

57 See also Section 4.2.1 on the indirect influence of Framework Decision 2009/299/JHA on national procedural law.

3.4 of section (d) of the EAW. In the latter case, it remains open to the issuing judicial authority to mention under point 4 of section (d) any circumstance which in its view supports the conclusion that surrender of the requested person would not entail a breach of his/her rights of defence.[58]

3.6 Minimal Harmonisation or Full Harmonisation?

Although not all experts in the project agree, in Section 3.5 it was concluded that the key concepts of Article 4a(1) are autonomous concepts of Union law. This conclusion raises the question whether the Member States, when transposing Article 4a(1) FD 2002/584/JHA, may deviate from the autonomous meaning of the Union law concepts contained in that provision. This question touches upon the nature of the harmonisation sought by FD 2009/299/JHA. Does this Framework Decision seek to *fully* harmonise the grounds for refusal or does it merely seek *minimal* harmonisation?

In the first instance, Member States may not deviate from the result prescribed by the Framework Decision, while in the latter instance they are free to go beyond that result, provided, of course, that they do not seriously compromise the achievement of the result prescribed by the Framework Decision.[59]

In the context of the stated aims of FD 2009/299/JHA, in case of minimal harmonisation the Member States may provide for rules which at the same time enhance the procedural rights of defendants and facilitate judicial cooperation in criminal matters to a *higher* degree than FD 2009/299/JHA. They are, however, prohibited from adopting rules which enhance procedural rights and facilitate judicial cooperation in criminal matters to a *lesser* degree than envisaged by FD 2009/299/JHA.

The judgment in the *Melloni* case can be cited in favour of the argument that FD 2009/299/JHA seeks to harmonise the grounds for refusal *fully*. In that judgment, the Court of Justice in effect concluded that Spain is precluded from providing *more* protection to the requested person than afforded by Article 4a(1)(a) to (d), *viz.* requiring the guarantee that the *in absentia* conviction is open to review in the issuing Member State even though Article 4(1)(b) applies. In reaching this conclusion, the Court of Justice stressed that the *exhaustive* exceptions to the power to refuse the execution of the EAW laid down in Article 4(1)(a) to (d) FD 2002/584/JHA reflect the *consensus* reached by *all* the Member States

58 ECJ, judgment of 24 May 2016, *Openbaar Ministerie v. Paweł Dworzecki*, C-108/16 PPU, ECLI:EU:C:2016:346, para. 50; ECJ, judgment of 10 August 2017, *Openbaar Ministerie v. Tadas Tupikas*, C-270/17 PPU, ECLI:EU:C:2017:628, para. 96; ECJ, judgment of 10 August 2017, *Openbaar Ministerie v. Sławomir Andrzej Zdziaszek*, C-271/17 PPU, ECLI:EU:C:2017:629, para. 107.

59 *See, e.g.*, ECJ, judgment of 7 July 2016, *Ivo Muladi v. Krajský úřad Moravskoslezského kraj*, C-447/15, ECLI:EU:C:2016:533, para. 43.

regarding the *scope of protection* of the rights of the defence of persons convicted *in absentia* who are the subject of an EAW.[60]

The *JZ* judgment offers an illustrative example of minimal harmonisation provided for by FD 2002/584/JHA. In this judgment, the Court of Justice interpreted the concept of 'detention' as referred to in Article 26(1) FD 2002/584/JHA. This provision requires the issuing Member State to deduct

> all periods of detention arising from the execution of a European arrest warrant from the total period of detention to be served in the issuing Member State as a result of a custodial sentence or detention order being passed.

It is designed to meet the general objective of respecting fundamental rights by preserving the right to liberty of the person concerned and the practical effect of the principle of proportionality.[61] According to the Court of Justice, the concept of 'detention' does not refer to measures that *restrict* liberty, but to measures that *deprive* a person of liberty.[62] However, as Article 26(1) FD 2002/584/JHA "merely imposes a *minimum* level of protection of the fundamental rights of the person subject to the [EAW]", this provision does not prevent the authorities of the issuing Member State from deducting *on the basis of domestic law alone* a period or periods during which the person concerned was subjected in the executing Member State to measures not involving a deprivation of liberty but merely a restriction of liberty.[63] In other words, as there is only *minimal* harmonisation of the level of fundamental rights protection provided for by Article 26(1) Member States are allowed to apply *higher national* standards of fundamental rights protection.[64] Evidently,

60 ECJ, judgment of 26 February 2013, *Stefano Melloni v. Ministerio Fiscal*, C-399/11, ECLI:EU:C:2013:107, para. 62. According to Advocate General Sharpston, Art. 4a(1) harmonises the relevant rule *completely*: opinion of 6 December 2018, *Związek Gmin Zagłębia Miedziowego w Polkowicach*, C-566/17, ECLI:EU:C:2018:995, footnote 112. Advocate General Bobek is also of the opinion that Art. 4a(1) aims at *full* harmonisation: "(t)he rules contained in that provision indeed exhaustively cover an aspect of the EAW procedure, thus precluding autonomous national rules on the same subject matter": opinion of 25 July 2018, *Criminal proceedings against Petar Dzivev and Others*, C-310/16, ECLI:EU:C:2018:623, paras. 73-75.

61 ECJ, judgment of 28 July 2016, *JZ v. Prokuratura Rejonowa Łódź – Śródmieście*, C-294/16 PPU, ECLI:EU:C:2016:610, para. 42.

62 ECJ, judgment of 28 July 2016, *JZ v. Prokuratura Rejonowa Łódź – Śródmieście*, C-294/16 PPU, ECLI:EU:C:2016:610, para. 46.

63 ECJ, judgment of 28 July 2016, *JZ v. Prokuratura Rejonowa Łódź – Śródmieście*, C-294/16 PPU, ECLI:EU:C:2016:610, para. 55 (emphasis added).

64 See also ECJ, judgment of 30 May 2013, *Jeremy F. v. Premier ministre*, C-168/13 PPU, ECLI:EU:C:2013:358. FD 2002/584/JHA does not require Member States to provide for the possibility of bringing an appeal with suspensive effect against a decision to execute an EAW, because the entire surrender procedure already complies with the right to an effective remedy (Art. 47 Charter). Neither does the Framework Decision prevent Member States from providing for the possibility of such an appeal, because of the absence of further detail in the provisions of the Framework Decision and because recital (12) of the preamble states that it

applying higher national standards of fundamental rights protection would not compromise the lower Union level of protection. Nor would it compromise the unity of Union law. After all, in case of minimal harmonisation of the level of fundamental rights protection there is no uniform standard of protection. For the same reason, applying higher national standards of fundamental rights protection would also not compromise the efficacy of Union law. Moreover, it is difficult to see how applying higher national standards by the issuing Member State as regards deducting periods of restriction of liberty after surrender could undermine the principles of mutual trust and mutual recognition or in any other way hamper judicial cooperation between issuing and executing judicial authorities.[65]

None of the project Member States have sought to *increase* the degree of enhancing procedural rights and facilitating judicial cooperation. One Member State, however, may *at first blush* have – inadvertently – *decreased* that degree.

The Polish transposition of Article 4a(1) (Article 607r § 3 of the Polish CCP) deviates in a number of significant ways from Article 4a(1). For example, Article 607r § 3 of the Polish CCP does not contain the requirements that:

- the person concerned was summoned in person (in due time), rather it contents itself with requiring that "the requested person was summoned to appear in the proceedings or otherwise notified of the time and place of the hearing or session of the court";
- the person was informed of the date of the hearing "in such a manner that it was unequivocally established that he or she was aware of the scheduled trial";
- the legal counsellor participating in the hearing was given a mandate by the requested person who "was aware of the scheduled trial".[66]

The Court of Justice has repeatedly held that Article 4a(1) FD 2002/584/JHA seeks

> to guarantee a *high* level of protection and to allow the executing judicial authority to surrender the person concerned despite that person's failure to

---

does not "prevent a Member State from applying its constitutional rules relating inter alia to respect for the right to a fair trial", provided that the application of the Framework Decision is not 'frustrated'.

65 The *Melloni* and *JZ* judgments are distinguishable from the later *M.A.S and M.B.* judgment (also known as *Taricco II*). In the latter judgment the Court of Justice allowed Italy to apply higher national standards of fundamental rights protection (*viz.* to apply the national principle of legality to an extension of limitation periods, whereas under Union law the extension of limitation periods is a matter of *procedural* criminal law, to which that principle therefore does not apply), because at the material time the EU legislator *had not harmonised* the limitation rules applicable to criminal proceedings relating to VAT and Italy was, therefore, free at that time to determine that in the Italian legal order extending limitation periods is a matter of *substantive* criminal law, to which the principle of legality does apply: ECJ, judgment of 5 December 2017, *Criminal proceedings against M.A.S. and M.B.*, C-42/17, ECLI:EU:C:2017:936, paras. 43-45.

66 PL, report, p. 50.

> attend the trial which led to his conviction, while *fully* respecting his rights of defence.[67]

By leaving out the indicated requirements, Poland has left out key components of that high level of protection. As a result, one can argue that, when a Polish executing judicial authority is satisfied with the statement that "the requested person was summoned to appear in the proceedings or otherwise notified of the time and place of the hearing or session of the court", it cannot be sure that the rights of the defence were *fully* respected. Although admitting that the Polish legislation provides for less strict conditions under which the execution of an EAW cannot be refused, the Polish expert is of the opinion that in the final analysis the protection offered by Article 607r § 3 CCP is not lower than the protection offered by Article 4a(1) FD 2002/584/JHA. The Polish expert points out that, after all, the latter provision contains an *optional* ground for refusal:

> the executing authorities are allowed to surrender a requested person even if the judgment was rendered *in absentia*. To the contrary, these authorities are not allowed to refuse execution of EAWs concerning the judgment rendered *in absentia* if the European arrest warrants met the requirements of Article 4a of the FD. Thus, the Polish law which provide for less strict requirements under which the execution of EAWs cannot be refused shall not be assessed as contrary to the FD.[68]

It is true that Article 4a(1) provides for an optional ground for refusal and that the executing judicial authorities may not refuse the execution of an EAW if the requirements of Article 4a(1) are met, but that is precisely the point: under Polish law the requirements are less strict. If Article 4a(1) is indeed intended to *fully* harmonise the ground for refusal, then it is difficult to see how providing for less strict requirements could be compatible with that provision.

Arguably, Poland can point to the *Wolzenburg*-judgment in support of Article 607r § 3 CCP. In that judgment, the Court of Justice held that Member States, when implementing Article 4 FD 2002/584/JHA, have, of necessity, a *certain margin of appreciation* and, may, therefore, choose to "*limit* the situations in which the national executing judicial authority may refuse to surrender a requested person". This is so, because limiting the scope of the ground for refusal *facilitates* surrender in accordance with the principle of

67 ECJ, judgment of 26 May 2016, *Openbaar Ministerie v. Paweł Dworzecki*, C-108/16 PPU, ECLI:EU:C:2016:346, para. 47; ECJ, judgment of 10 August 2017, *Openbaar Ministerie v. Tadas Tupikas*, C-270/17 PPU, ECLI:EU:C:2017:628, para. 58 (emphasis added).

68 PL, report, p. 50.

mutual recognition.[69] By leaving out the aforementioned requirements, the exceptions contained in Article 607r § 3 CCP pose less onerous conditions than those of Article 4a(1) FD 2002/584/JHA. In other words, the conditions of Article 607r § 3 CCP are more easily met than those of Article 4a(1) FD 2002/584/JHA. When the conditions of the exceptions are more easily met, the executing judicial authority may refuse to execute the EAW in less cases. It follows, therefore, that by leaving out the aforementioned requirements, the scope of the ground for refusal is *restricted* and surrender is *facilitated*.

However, one can distinguish implementing one of the grounds of refusal mentioned in Article 4 FD 2002/584/JHA from implementing the ground for refusal contained in Article 4a FD 2002/584/JHA. Apparently, Article 4 FD 2002/584/JHA does not seek to *fully* harmonise the grounds of refusal contained in that provision. Moreover, FD 2009/299/JHA, which inserted Article 4a into FD 2002/584/JHA, has a *dual* purpose: not only to facilitate judicial cooperation in criminal matters (*i.e.* to facilitate surrender), but also to enhance the procedural rights of persons subject to criminal proceedings (Article 1(1) FD 2009/299/JHA). While restricting the scope of Article 4a(1) most certainly facilitates surrender, it most certainly does not enhance procedural rights.

Whether Article 607r § 3 CCP *in itself* is compatible with Article 4a(1) FD 2002/584/JHA or not, it must be pointed out that Article 607p § 1 (5) CCP contains a mandatory ground for refusal concerning violations of human rights of the requested person. On balance, therefore, *when considered together*, Article 607r § 3 and Article 607p § 1 (5) CCP seem to provide for a degree of enhancing procedural rights and facilitating judicial cooperation which does not fall below the degree envisaged by Article 4a(1). Moreover, in practice the Polish judges who were interviewed in the course of the research project do seem to take notice of the discrepancies between Article 607r § 3 CCP and Article 4a(1). They indicated that if a requested person contests, *e.g.*, that s/he was aware of the scheduled trial or that s/he was aware that s/he was defended by a mandated legal counsellor, the executing judicial authority will examine this issue and, if need be, ask for additional information from the issuing judicial authority.[70]

69 ECJ, judgment of 6 October 2009, *Dominic Wolzenburg*, C-123/08, ECLI:EU:C:2009:616, paras. 57-61 (emphasis added). See also ECJ, judgment of 13 December 2018, *Ministère public v. Marin-Simion Sut*, C-514/17, ECLI:EU:C:2018:1016, paras. 42-44.

70 PL, report, pp. 62-65.

4 Meaning of the Expression 'Trial *In Absentia*'

4.1 Introduction

One of the hypotheses of this project is that national rules on *in absentia* trials may influence the transposition of Article 4a(1) FD 2002/584/JHA by the Member States and the application of the national transposing legislation by their judicial authorities. In order to determine whether this hypothesis can be verified or falsified, the questionnaire contains a number of questions directed at establishing whether the Member States provide for *in absentia* trials and, if so, what the meaning of the expression '*in absentia* trial' is under national law and whether the national law meaning differs from the meaning of that expression under Union law.[1]

Of course, in order to compare a meaning under national law of the expression 'trial *in absentia*' with the Union law meaning of that expression, one must first establish that Union law meaning. Section 4.2 is dedicated to achieving that goal. In Section 4.3, the *national* law meaning of the expression 'trial *in absentia*' will be discussed. Possible divergences between the Union law meaning and the national law meaning are the subject of Section 4.4.

4.2 Union Law Meaning

4.2.1 *Union Legislation*

Currently, there are two pieces of Union legislation which are relevant for establishing the Union law meaning of the concept of a 'trial *in absentia*': FD 2009/299/JHA and Directive 2016/343/EU.

FD 2009/299/JHA seeks to harmonise the grounds for refusal in a number of other Framework Decisions regarding a decision taken following a trial at which the person concerned did not appear in person. As is evident from recitals (4) and (14) of the preamble and from the wording of Article 4a(1), this Framework Decision aims at harmonising national rules *concerning mutual recognition* of decisions rendered following a trial

1 Questions 3, 4 and 5 and one of the sub-questions of question 6.

at which the person concerned did not appear in person, not at harmonising national rules *concerning trials at which the person concerned did not appear in person* (see also Section 3.5).[2]

This distinction is borne out by the *travaux préparatoires.* The initiative for FD 2009/299/JHA already contained an embryonic form of recital (14). The Explanatory Memorandum explained that the "initiative bears only upon cross-border cases. No harmonisation or approximation of national law is necessary in respect of domestic cases".[3] During the negotiations, the sentence "This Framework Decision is not designed to regulate the forms and methods, including procedural requirements, that are used to achieve the results specified in this Framework Decision, which are a matter for the national laws of the Member States" was inserted into recital (4) to "better express the relationship between this Framework Decision and national law".[4] The expression "in accordance with further procedural requirements defined in the national law of the issuing Member State" in Article 4a(1) does nothing more than convey the same notion.

The *Dworzecki* judgment perfectly illustrates the distinction between harmonising the ground for refusal and harmonising national (procedural) law. In its judgment, the Court of Justice held that the expression "by other means actually received official information of the scheduled date and place of that trial in such a manner that it was unequivocally established that he or she was aware of the scheduled trial" is an autonomous concept of Union law.[5] Given the words 'by other means', it also held that Article 4a(1)(a)(i) does not constitute an exhaustive list of the means that can be used to achieve the end of that provision (to inform the defendant of the trial in such a way as to allow him/her to organise his/her defence effectively). In referring to recital (4), it reiterated in this respect that FD 2009/299/JHA is not designed to regulate the "forms and methods that are used by the competent authorities in the context of the surrender procedure, including the procedural requirements applicable according to the law of the Member State concerned".[6]

Of course, indirectly FD 2009/299/JHA can be relevant for interpreting and applying national procedural law. EAWs issued for the purpose of executing an *in absentia* judgment of conviction may meet with a refusal of surrender, if application of the national procedural rules of the issuing Member State leads to results which are not in conformity with the requirements of Article 4a(1). Such refusals may force the legislator of the issuing Member

2 Advocate General Bobek interprets FD 2009/299/JHA in the same way: opinion of 11 May 2016, *Openbaar Ministerie v. Paweł Dworzecki*, C-108/16 PPU, ECLI:EU:C:2016:333, para. 34.

3 Council document 5213/08 ADD 1, 30 January 2008, p. 6.

4 Council document 7297/08, p. 5.

5 ECJ, judgment of 24 May 2016, *Openbaar Ministerie v. Paweł Dworzecki*, C-108/16 PPU, ECLI:EU:C:2016:346, para. 32.

6 ECJ, judgment of 24 May 2016, *Openbaar Ministerie v. Paweł Dworzecki*, C-108/16 PPU, ECLI:EU:C:2016:346, paras. 43-44.

State to amend national legislation in order to enhance the procedural rights of persons subject to criminal proceedings and, thus, to facilitate surrender to that Member State.

Harmonising national rules *concerning trials in the absence of the person concerned* is the province of Directive 2016/343/EU. However, this Directive does have a link with mutual recognition of decisions rendered following a trial at which the person concerned did not appear in person. The objectives pursued by Directive 2016/343/EU are to enhance the right to a fair trial,[7] thereby strengthening mutual trust and facilitating mutual recognition of decisions in criminal matters.[8] Therefore, the transposition of Directive 2016/343/EU should have a positive effect on the operation of FD 2009/299/JHA. Moreover, in essence FD 2009/299/JHA pursues the same objectives as the Directive: enhancing the procedural rights of persons subject to criminal proceedings, facilitating judicial cooperation in criminal matters and improving mutual recognition of judicial decisions (Article 1 FD 2009/299/JHA).

It would, therefore, make perfect sense if the Court of Justice were to interpret the provisions of Directive 2016/343/EU on proceedings in the absence of the defendant in conformity with its case-law on Article 4a(1) FD 2002/584/JHA, even though the former provisions do not match the latter.[9] Were the Court of Justice to assign to the provisions of Article 8 (entitled: 'right to be present at the trial') and Article 9 (entitled: 'right to a new trial') of Directive 2016/343/EU a *lower* level of protection compared to that of Article 4a(1), then neither the objectives of Directive 2016/343/EU nor those of FD 2009/299/JHA would be achieved. The legislative history of Directive 2016/343/EU also supports such a conclusion (see Section 4.2.3).

Directive 2016/343/EU does not apply to all Member States. The United Kingdom and Ireland are not bound by the Directive, because they have chosen not to opt in this measure.[10] Neither is Denmark, because this Member State has generally opted out of measures with respect to the Area of Freedom, Security and Justice.[11] The other Member States should have transposed Directive 2016/343/EU by 1 April 2018 (Article 14(1) Directive 2016/343/EU). In Belgium, Hungary and the Netherlands, the Directive will not

7 Recital (9) of the preamble of Directive 2016/343/EU.

8 Recital (10) of the preamble of Directive 2016/343/EU.

9 Compare, *e.g.*, Art. 4a(1)(a)(i) ("summoned in person and thereby informed of the scheduled date and place of the trial which resulted in the decision, or by other means actually received official information of the scheduled date and place of that trial in such a manner that it was unequivocally established that he or she was aware of the scheduled trial") with Art. 8(2)(a) Directive 2016/343/EU ("the suspect or accused person has been informed, in due time, of the trial (...)"). But see also recital (36) of the preamble to the Directive: "(...) informing a suspect or accused person of the trial should be understood to mean summoning him or her in person or, by other means, providing that person with official information about the date and place of the trial in a manner that enables him or her to become aware of the trial. (...)".

10 Recital (50) of the preamble in connection with Arts. 1 and 2 of Protocol No 21 on the position of the United Kingdom and Ireland in respect of the Area of Freedom, Security and Justice. IE, report, p. 25.

11 Recital (51) of the preamble in connection with Arts. 1 and 2 of Protocol No 22 on the position of Denmark.

be transposed, because these Member States consider that their existing national legislation already complies with the Directive.[12] In Romania, the legislation transposing the Directive was adopted by Parliament and is currently pending before the President for promulgation.[13] In Poland, the government has announced a draft law for transposing the Directive, which is presently subject to public consultations.[14]

Neither FD 2009/299/JHA nor Directive 2016/343/EU uses the expression 'trial *in absentia*'.[15]

4.2.2 *FD 2009/299/JHA*

The Framework Decision originated in an initiative of a number of Member States.[16] Initially, that initiative did refer to the expression 'trial *in absentia*'.[17] With regard to FD 2002/584/JHA, a 'decision rendered *in absentia*' was defined as "a custodial sentence or a detention order, when the person did not personally appear in the proceedings resulting in this decision". During the negotiations, however, the definition relating to a 'decision rendered *in absentia*' was deleted and replaced by the expression 'the person did not appear in person at the trial'. The reason for this change was that "the definition continued to cause problems (…), notably since the term 'in absentia' has different legal meanings in the law of the Member States". The replacement for the *technical* term '*in absentia*' described the *factual* situation in question and was thought to enhance legal cooperation. The amended text, without the definition of a 'decision rendered *in absentia*', was thought to produce the same legal effect as the former text with the definition.[18]

Consequently, FD 2009/299/JHA consistently refers to the right "to appear in person at the trial"[19] and to "decisions rendered following a trial at which the person concerned did

12 BE, report, p. 15; HU, report, p. 12; NL, report, p. 45. The Dutch expert disagrees with the view that Dutch law already fully complies with the Directive: NL, report, p. 161.

13 RO, report, p. 19.

14 PL, report, p. 45. On 4 September 2019, after the final draft of this Report was adopted, the new Act of 19 July 2019 amending the CCP was published in the Official Journal. For obvious reasons, these amendments are not discussed in the national report nor in this Report.

15 The concept of a 'decision rendered *in absentia*' is used in Art. 8(1) of the Agreement between the European Union and the Republic of Iceland and the Kingdom of Norway on the surrender procedure between the Member States of the European Union and Iceland and Norway, *OJ* 2006, L 292, p. 2. That provision is an almost exact copy of Art. 5(1) FD 2002/584/JHA, which was replaced by Art. 4a FD 2002/584/JHA. The agreement will enter into force on 1 November 2019: Council document 118081/9, 30 August 2019.

16 Slovenia, the French Republic, the Czech Republic, the Kingdom of Sweden, the Slovak Republic, the United Kingdom and the Federal Republic of Germany.

17 Council document 5213/08, 14 January 2018.

18 Council document 7279/08, 19 March 2018, p. 2.

19 Recitals (1) and (8) of the preamble.

not appear in person".[20] Article 2(2) FD 2009/299/JHA deletes paragraph 1 of Article 5 FD 2002/584/JHA. The latter provision contained a reference to "a decision rendered *in absentia*", without, however, defining the meaning of that expression. Judging from recital (4) of the preamble to FD 2009/299/JHA, it was felt that Article 5(1) FD 2002/584/JHA did not contain a *clear* ground for refusal. No doubt, one of the causes of this lack of clarity was the fact that the provision contained a non-defined technical term, the meaning of which varies from Member State to Member State.[21]

Interestingly, in its case-law on Article 4a(1) FD 2002/584/JHA the Court of Justice frequently uses the term '*in absentia*'. In its *Melloni* judgment, *e.g.* the Court of Justice refers to Article 4a(1) in the following way: "Article 4a(1)(a) and (b) of Framework Decision 2002/584 provides in essence, that, once the person convicted *in absentia* was aware (...)."[22] It is clear that the Court of Justice uses the term '*in absentia*' as a shorthand description of situations in which the person concerned did not appear in person at the trial resulting in the decision.

The Court of Justice has already held that the concept of a 'trial resulting in the decision' must be regarded as an autonomous concept of Union law, because none of the references in FD 2009/299/JHA to the law of the Member States concerns the meaning of that concept (see also Section 3.5).[23] It necessarily follows that the same holds true for the concept of non-appearance in person at that trial.

As we have seen, the concept of a person who did not appear in person at the trial was meant as a *factual* description, in order to avoid any possible confusion over the meaning of the technical term '*in absentia*'. Factually, the person did not appear in person when s/he was not physically present at the trial. Legal fictions, such as that an absent person is considered to be present at the trial by way of his/her legal counsellor, are irrelevant. Moreover, the circumstance that an absent defendant is defended by his/her mandated legal counsellor is an exception to the rule that the executing judicial authority may refuse to execute the EAW when the defendant did not appear in person at the trial (Article 4a(1)(b)). Therefore, according to the internal logic of Article 4a(1) personal appearance cannot be equated with appearance by legal counsellor. Consequently, if the person concerned was not physically present at the trial resulting in the decision, but his/her mandated

20 Recitals (2), (4), (6), (7), (10) of the preamble; Art. 4a.

21 Another cause was the fact that the executing judicial authority could require an assurance of the issuing judicial authority regarding the opportunity to apply for a retrial, the adequacy of which was left to the discretion of the executing judicial authority. See recital (3) of the preamble.

22 ECJ, judgment of 26 February 2013, *Stefano Melloni v. Ministerio Fiscal*, C-399/11, ECLI:EU:C:2013:107, para. 42. See also ECJ, judgment of 10 August 2017, *Openbaar Ministerie v. Tadas Tupikas*, C-270/17 PPU, ECLI:EU:C:2017:628, paras. 56, 81 and 98; ECJ, judgment of 22 December 2017, *Samet Ardic*, C-571/17 PPU, ECLI:EU:C:2017:1026, paras. 72-73.

23 ECJ, judgment of 10 August 2017, *Openbaar Ministerie v. Tadas Tupikas*, C-270/17 PPU, ECLI:EU:C:2017:628, paras. 65-67.

legal counsellor was present, under FD 2009/299/JHA the proceedings must be considered as proceedings '*in absentia*'.[24]

This interpretation is confirmed by the case-law of the ECtHR, which must be taken into account when interpreting and applying FD 2009/299/JHA.[25] According to the preamble to FD 2009/299/JHA, the "right of an accused to appear in person at the trial" is included in Article 6 ECHR, as interpreted by the ECtHR.[26] In its case-law on Article 6 ECHR, the ECtHR uses slightly different words to express the same thing: the object and purpose of Article 6 ECHR as a whole show that "a person 'charged with a criminal offence' is entitled to take part in the hearing"; moreover,

> it is difficult to see how he could exercise [the right to defend himself in person, the right to examine or have examined witnesses and the right to have the free assistance of an interpreter if he cannot understand or speak the language used in court] without being present.[27]

The ECtHR uses the term '*in absentia*' to denote proceedings conducted in the absence of the accused.[28] What the ECtHR means by 'presence' and 'absence' is *personal* presence and *personal* absence. If an absent accused is represented by his/her legal counsellor, under Article 6 ECHR the proceedings are still deemed to be *in absentia*.[29]

In conclusion, under FD 2009/299/JHA proceedings are considered to be '*in absentia*', when the person concerned did not appear in person at the 'trial resulting in the decision', *i.e.* when s/he was not physically present at that trial.

4.2.3 *Directive 2016/343/EU*

The proposal of the European Commission for a directive on the strengthening of certain aspects of the presumption of innocence and of the right to be present at trial in criminal proceedings[30] reproduced the text of Article 4a(1) FD 2002/584/JHA almost word for word. During the discussions of the proposal, it was concluded that, although the rules on trials *in absentia* should be aligned with the rules set out in FD 2009/299/JHA, the requirements

---

24 Although if the mandated legal counsellor defended his/her absent client, the executing judicial authority may not refuse to execute the EAW (Art. 4a(1)(b) FD 2002/584/JHA).

25 Cf. ECJ, judgment of 22 December 2017, *Samet Ardic*, C-571/17 PPU, ECLI:EU:C:2017:1026, para. 74.

26 Recitals (1) and (8).

27 ECtHR, judgment of 1 March 2006, *Sejdovic v. Italy* [GC], ECLI:CE:ECHR:2006:0301JUD005658100, § 81.

28 ECtHR, judgment of 1 March 2006, *Sejdovic v. Italy* [GC], ECLI:CE:ECHR:2006:0301JUD005658100, § 82.

29 ECtHR, judgment of 1 March 2006, *Sejdovic v. Italy* [GC], ECLI:CE:ECHR:2006:0301JUD005658100, § 14 in conjunction with § 105.

30 COM(2013) 821 final.

of the latter Framework Decision were too detailed and too prescriptive to be included in an instrument aimed at setting minimum rules for national criminal procedural law.[31] The 'refined' text of Article 8 of the directive (concerning the right to be present at the trial) was considered to be very much in line with the Commission's proposal, but more clear and readable.[32]

The directive speaks of the right of suspects and accused persons "to be present at their trial" (Article 8(1)) and sets conditions under which a trial that can result in a decision on the guilt or innocence of a suspect or accused person can be held "in his or her absence" (Article 8(2)). Therefore, the wording of Directive 2016/343/EU closely resembles the wording used by the ECtHR in its case-law on Article 6 ECHR. This resemblance, together with the legislative history of the Directive, allows us to conclude that what is meant with presence at the trial is personal appearance at the trial in the sense of FD 2009/299/JHA.

In conclusion, Directive 2016/343/EU is applicable to trials at which the person concerned did not appear in person, *i.e.* to trials at which s/he was not physically present.

4.2.4 *Presence by Videoconference?*

Neither FD 2009/299/JHA nor Directive 2016/343/EU refers to the possibility of an absent defendant participating in the trial via telecommunication, *e.g.* via videoconference. This raises the question whether, as a matter of Union law, proceedings in which the defendant was not physically present at the trial but in which s/he participated via telecommunication can be considered as a trial *in absentia*.

In the context of cross-border cases, Union law explicitly recognises a hearing by videoconference or other audiovisual transmission. Directive 2014/41/EU on the European Investigative Order (EIO)[33] regulates mutual recognition of European Investigative Orders issued, *inter alia*, for the purpose of hearing a suspect or an accused in another Member State by way of videoconference or other audiovisual transmission (Article 24(1)). Such EIOs may be issued "at all stages of criminal proceedings, including the trial phase" (recital (25) of the preamble). It should be stressed that the EIO covers *investigative* measures (Article 3), in this case hearing the suspect or the accused. Hearing a suspect or an accused as an *investigative* measure is not quite the same as affording the suspect or the accused the opportunity to *participate* in the trial.

---

31 Council document 13304/14, 22 September 2014, p. 4.

32 Council document 14585/14, 21 October 2014, p. 3.

33 Directive 2014/41/EU of the European Parliament and of the Council of 3 April 2014 regarding the European Investigation Order in criminal matters, *OJ* 2014, L 130/1. Ireland and Denmark are not bound by this Directive.

The ECtHR's case-law makes it clear that a defendant's participation in the trial by videoconference is not equivalent to his/her physical presence at the trial. The ECtHR has held that the

> physical presence of an accused in the courtroom is highly desirable, but it is not an end in itself; it rather serves the greater goal of securing the fairness of the proceedings, taken as a whole.[34]

Therefore, a defendant's participation in the trial by videoconference is not in itself contrary to the ECHR, but it must be assured in each case that videoconferencing serves a legitimate aim and that its application is compatible with the requirements of respect for due process, as laid down in Article 6 ECHR.[35] The defendant must be

> able to follow the proceedings, to see the persons present and hear what is being said, but also to be seen and heard by the other parties, the judge and witnesses, without technical impediment.[36]

Given the wording of both FD 2009/299/JHA and Directive 2016/343/EU and in light of the ECtHR's case-law, perhaps the safest conclusion is that participating in the trial by telecommunication is not equivalent to appearing at the trial in person.[37,38] As a conse-

34 ECtHR, decision of 9 November 2006, *Golubev v. Russia*, ECLI:CE:ECHR:2006:1109DEC002626002.

35 ECtHR, judgment of 5 October 2006, *Marcello Viola v. Italy*, ECLI:CE:ECHR:2006:1005JUD004510604, § 67.

36 ECtHR, judgment of 16 February 2016, *Yevdokimov e.a. v. Russia*, ECLI:CE:ECHR:2016:0216JUD002723605, § 43.

37 The same conclusion was drawn by the *Oberlandesgericht Karlsruhe*, judgment of 21 April 2017, Ausl 301 AR 35/17. In reaching that conclusion, the *Oberlandesgericht* pointed out that being connected to the trial by videoconference does not constitute, in the words of the applicable provision, personal appearance at the trial, even when the person concerned was able to follow the trial in its entirety, not just his/her interrogation.

38 Within the *Council of Europe*, in the context of *recognition of foreign judgments* the expression 'judgment rendered *in absentia*' refers to "any judgment rendered by a court in a Contracting State after criminal proceedings at the hearing of which the sentenced person was not personally present" (Art. 1(f) and Art. 21(2) of the European Convention on the Validity of Criminal Judgments (ECVCJ)). However, any judgment rendered *in absentia* which has been confirmed or pronounced in the sentencing State after opposition by the person sentenced and any judgment rendered *in absentia* on appeal, provided that the appeal from the judgment of the court of first instance was lodged by the sentenced person, shall be considered as judgments rendered after a hearing of the accused (Art. 21(3) of the ECVCJ). About half of the Member States have not ratified this convention. In the context of *extradition*, the concept of a 'judgment in absentia' refers to a judgment "rendered after a hearing at which the sentenced person was not personally present" as mentioned in Art. 21(2) of the ECVCJ (*Explanatory Report to the Second Additional Protocol to the European Convention on Extradition*, § 21). With the exception of France, Greece and Luxembourg, all Member States have ratified this convention. Because of the exceptions relating to opposition and appeal, the Council of Europe definition

quence, when an absent defendant participates in the trial by videoconference, under Union law the trial is considered to be a trial *in absentia*. Of course, the fact that an absent defendant participated in the trial by videoconference may constitute a circumstance which enables the executing judicial authority to be assured that the surrender of the person concerned does not mean a breach of his/her rights of defence (see also Sections 3.1 and 8.2).[39]

4.3 National Law Meaning

4.3.1 Introduction

The answers to the questions designed to establish whether the national laws of the Member States provide for trials *in absentia* show a great variety of possible positions in this regard. It is not our intention to discuss in detail the various national legal systems with respect to trials *in absentia*. The answers are accessible to all on the website of the project[40] and paint a comprehensive picture of those legal systems. In this paragraph, merely the outlines of the national rules concerning trials *in absentia* are drawn in order to establish whether the national law meaning of the concept of a trial *in absentia* differs from the Union law meaning of that concept.

Of the six project Member States, Ireland has the most extreme position on trials *in absentia*. Generally, trials *in absentia* are not possible except for very minor offences. In the other five Member States trials *in absentia* are not exceptional. The national laws of Belgium, Hungary, the Netherlands, Poland and Romania all provide for the possibility of trials *in absentia* in some form or another.

4.3.2 Belgium

In Belgium there is no legislative definition of the concept of '*in absentia*'. The definition of that concept is determined by case-law. According to that case-law, the nature of the judgment – contradictory or *in absentia* – is not determined by the designation given to that judgment by the court. Rather, the concept of '*in absentia*' denotes the situation in

of '*in absentia*' is more narrow – in other words comprises less situations – than the EU definition of that concept.

39 Cf. ECJ, judgment of 24 May 2016, *Openbaar Ministerie v. Paweł Dworzecki*, C-108/16 PPU, ECLI:EU:C:2016:343, para. 50; ECJ, judgment of 10 August 2017, *Openbaar Ministerie v. Tadas Tupikas*, C-270/17 PPU, ECLI:EU:C:2017:628, para. 96; ECJ, judgment of 10 August 2017, *Openbaar Ministerie v. Sławomir Andrzej Zdziaszek*, C-271/17 PPU, ECLI:EU:C:2017:629, para. 107.

40 www.inabsentieaw.eu/publications/.

which the competent court has been properly seized with a case – the summons, the referral decision or the report is in accordance with the law in substance –, the defendant was summoned in accordance with the law – formal deadlines have been respected – and the defendant, if applicable assisted or represented by a legal counsellor, did not have the opportunity to rebut or comment on the evidence or the charges brought against him/her due to his/her absence in court or by abstention from participation in the discussions before the court.[41]

In one specific instance the court is *obliged* to designate its judgment as contradictory instead of *in absentia*. The following conditions must be met: (i) the defendant or his/her legal counsellor was present at the initial hearing, (ii) the case was postponed, (iii) the court ordered the personal appearance of the defendant at the next hearing or issued an order to bring the defendant to court, (iv) that order was properly served on the defendant or the order to bring the defendant to court could not be executed and (v) at the next hearing both the defendant and his/her legal counsellor remain absent. Designating the judgment as contradictory is aimed at sanctioning the behaviour of the defendant by denying him/her the legal recourse of opposition against the judgment.[42]

The presence of the defendant at the hearing at which the judgment is pronounced has no bearing on the nature of the judgment (contradictory or *in absentia*).[43]

If in the course of the trial several hearings are held and the defendant is present at some but not all of these hearings, the nature of the judgment is determined by what happened at the hearing(s). Should it transpire that the defendant was absent at a hearing or abstained from participating when the evidence was presented, the charges were brought or a debate about the penalty to be imposed was held, the judgment must be considered to be a judgment *in absentia*.[44]

It is not possible to be present at the hearing by telecommunication, be it audio- or videoconference.[45]

---

41 Abstention from participation refers to the situation in which, while being present in the court room at the hearing(s) at which the case against the defendant is dealt with in first instance, the defendant and/or his lawyer refuse(s) to announce his/their presence. Abstention from participation represents a deliberate (tactical) choice not to participate in the trial at that moment while still being able to follow the presentation of the case (*e.g.* by the public prosecutor) and to see what evidence is produced. Abstention from participation does not refer to the situation in which the defendant is present in the court room at the hearing and has announced his presence but refuses to answer questions or refuses to challenge the evidence, *e.g.* by invoking his/her right to remain silent.

42 BE, report, p. 8.

43 BE, report, p. 8.

44 If what happened at the hearing(s) is in dispute, the official report of the hearing(s) is decisive.

45 BE, report, p. 9.

4.3.3 *Hungary*

In Hungary, proceedings *in absentia* may be conducted in three cases: (a) the defendant waives his/her right to attend the hearing, (b) the defendant is at an unknown location and (c) the defendant's place of residence is known but it is abroad.

For a waiver of the right to attend the hearing, it is necessary for the defendant to have a legal counsellor and to have entrusted him/her with the function of receiving official notifications.

If the defendant's place of stay is unknown, all measures shall be taken to locate the defendant. The trial may proceed in the defendant's absence upon the motion of the public prosecutor, if (i) the defendant fled or hid during the proceedings, (ii) his/her place of stay was not located within a reasonable time and (iii) the severity of the crime justifies proceeding with the trial in the defendant's absence. Failing a motion of the public prosecutor, the presiding judge must suspend the proceedings.

If the defendant resides abroad, proceedings in the absence of the defendant may take place, if (i) issuing an EAW is not possible and either the duly summoned defendant fails to attend the trial or s/he is detained abroad, (ii) an international warrant or an EAW was issued, but in the 12 months following the arrest of the defendant neither his/her extradition or surrender nor a transfer of the criminal proceedings took place, (iii) the defendant's extradition or surrender was refused, while the criminal proceedings were not transferred or (iv) the defendant's extradition or surrender was deferred. In all these four cases, the severity of the crime must justify proceeding in the defendant's absence and his/her presence via telecommunication must not be possible.[46]

If the defendant is present at the hearing at which the court pronounces the judgment, the court will repeat the previous procedure, present the evidence and render a judgment under the general rules. Therefore, the proceedings will not be considered to be proceedings *in absentia*.[47]

According to Hungarian law, proceedings are *in absentia* proceedings, when the defendant was not present at any of the hearings.[48]

A defendant who is physically absent at the trial can be present via telecommunication (see earlier). Under Hungarian law, presence via telecommunication is equivalent to presence in person.[49]

46 HU, report, p. 7.
47 HU, report, p. 7.
48 HU, report, p. 8.
49 HU, report, p. 8.

4.3.4 *Ireland*

Irish law does not in general permit trials *in absentia*, except in the case of very minor offences not attracting a custodial sentence. Although the possibility of proceeding in the absence of the accused is acknowledged in Irish law, the common understanding is that, if a custodial sentence is reasonably possible, an accused who fails to appear should not be tried *in absentia*. However, Irish law does allow for trials to be conducted in the absence of the accused, when s/he engages in uncooperative, obstructive or disruptive behaviour in order to frustrate the trial. In such cases, the trial judge may order his/her removal from court to protect the court's process. In Irish law, the expression '*in absentia* proceedings' means proceedings conducted in the absence of the accused. Proceedings are deemed to be conducted in the absence of the accused, when s/he is neither present in person nor legally represented.[50]

The situation that the accused was not present at the trial itself but was present at the hearing at which the court pronounced judgment has never arisen in the Irish courts to the Irish expert's knowledge. Theoretically it might arise in the exceptionally rare instance where an accused has had to be removed from court for being disruptive. Hypothetically, one might take the view that the accused should not be regarded as having been tried *in absentia*, because it could be argued that by his/her behaviour s/he had waived his/her right to be present in person. However, one could not preclude the possibility that persuasive counter-arguments might be advanced against classifying the trial as a trial *in absentia*.[51]

The situation that in the course of the trial several hearings are held and the defendant is present at some but not all of these hearings has rarely arisen in Ireland. Again, it could theoretically arise in the rare situation where an accused is removed from court for being disruptive, or where an accused on bail absconds while the trial is underway. The hypothetical answer given in the previous paragraph is applicable.[52]

It could be argued that it is desirable, given the availability of video link technology, that an accused removed from court for disruptive behaviour should be afforded the facility of remotely viewing and listening to the proceedings occurring in his/her absence. At present, video link technology is only used at pre-trial remand hearings.[53]

50 IE, report, pp. 12-13.
51 IE, report, p. 13.
52 IE, report, pp. 13-14.
53 IE, report, pp. 14-15.

4.3.5 *The Netherlands*

In the Netherlands, the defendant has a right to be present at the trial. S/he is under no duty to appear, but the court may order him/her to appear and may also order that s/he be brought to court, forcibly if need be. The CCP distinguishes between *contradictory* proceedings and proceedings *in absentia*. Once the defendant appeared at one of the hearings, from then on the proceedings are considered to be contradictory proceedings in which the defendant may exercise all the rights of defence.[54] If his/her legal counsellor is also present, the legal counsellor may exercise the same rights. In accordance with the adage 'contradictory proceedings remain contradictory proceedings', the proceedings continue to be contradictory proceedings, if the defendant, after having appeared at a hearing, fails to appear at the next hearing(s). During contradictory proceedings, the legal counsellor of an *absent* defendant may only conduct the defence, if s/he declares that the defendant has explicitly authorised him/her to do so.

If the defendant fails to appear at the first hearing, the court shall order that the defendant be tried *in absentia* and that the trial be continued in his/her absence, *unless*: (a) the summons was not delivered validly to the defendant and the court declares the summons null and void, (b) the court orders that the defendant be brought to court, forcibly if need be, or (c) a legal counsellor declares that the absent defendant has explicitly authorised him/her to conduct the defence. As a consequence of the order that the defendant be tried *in absentia*, the absent defendant cannot exercise any of the rights of defence. The defendant's legal counsellor who is present at the hearing but who is not explicitly authorised to defend his/her client is not entitled to exercise any of those rights on behalf of the defendant. As a rule,[55] a non-mandated legal counsellor is only entitled (i) to explain the defendant's absence and (ii) to request an adjournment of the hearing in order either to give the defendant the opportunity to exercise his/her right to be tried in his/her presence or to give the legal counsellor the opportunity to obtain the defendant's explicit authorisation to defend him/her.

The court must revoke the order to try the defendant *in absentia*, if (i) the defendant appears after all or, in case of an adjournment, appears at a next hearing or (ii) has him/herself defended in his/her absence by an explicitly authorised legal counsellor after all. In both cases, the examination of the merits of the case will start afresh and the proceedings will henceforth be conducted as contradictory proceedings, although the court may order that specific investigative acts will not be conducted again.[56]

54 This rule only applies to proceedings within one instance. To clarify, presence at one of the first instance hearings does not make the proceedings on appeal contradictory proceedings.

55 It is not excluded that, in exceptional circumstances, the right to a fair trial might require deviating from that rule.

56 NL, report, pp. 21-22.

The mere fact that the defendant was present at the pronouncement of the judgment is irrelevant for determining whether the proceedings resulting in that judgment are proceedings *in absentia* or not.[57]

As mentioned earlier, once the defendant is present at one of the hearings, from then on the proceedings are considered to be contradictory proceedings. Therefore, if the defendant is absent at the next hearing(s), the proceedings are still considered to be contradictory proceedings. Consequently, what transpired at the hearing(s) at which the defendant was present is irrelevant for determining whether the proceedings are contradictory or not.[58]

If the defendant is present at the hearing, the court will *question* him/her. *Questioning* an absent defendant can also take place by way of videoconferencing. The relevant provision only refers to questioning the defendant, not to his/her presence at the hearing. However, on the basis of the relevant legislative history it is clear that it was intended that an absent defendant could be present at the hearing by videoconference. Nevertheless, according to the relevant legislation, videoconferencing will not be used at the hearing at which the merits of the case are dealt with, unless the defendant and his/her legal counsellor give their consent.[59]

4.3.6 *Poland*

In Poland, for common criminal offences there are no separate *in absentia* proceedings (*i.e. in absentia* proceedings in the sense that the proceedings are conducted despite the fact that the accused is not aware of them). Such special proceedings are only possible with regard to fiscal offences, petty fiscal offences regulated in the Penal Fiscal Code and petty offences provided for in the Code of Petty Offences.

Although the CCP – with a few exceptions – does not use the term 'proceedings *in absentia*', this does not mean that proceedings cannot be conducted in the absence of the accused.

As of 1 July 2015,[60] the CCP expresses the principle that the presence of the accused is *not mandatory*. Polish criminal procedural law is based on the principle that the accused has a right to be present during the trial. Provided that the accused was properly summoned, his/her absence does not stop the trial and does not prevent rendering a judgment.

57 NL, report, p. 23.
58 NL, report, p. 23.
59 NL, report, p. 24.
60 In recent years, Polish criminal procedural law was amended significantly a number of times. The description of the situation in Poland as regards trials *in absentia* is based on *current* legislation. For a discussion of previous legal regimes see the Questionnaire.

There are two *exceptions* to the principle that the accused is not obliged to be present during the trial: (1) in each case the presiding judge or the court may decide that the presence of the accused at the hearing is mandatory and (2) the presence of the accused at the hearing is mandatory in cases concerning felonies, *i.e.* the most severe offences,[61] but only at the first stage of the hearing. The first stage of the hearing comprises the following procedural activities: presentation of the charges to the accused, instruction of the accused about his/her rights, receiving the statement of the accused as to whether s/he pleads guilty and whether s/he wishes to provide explanations and, if so, what explanations. After these procedural activities, the presence of the accused at the hearing, also in case of felonies, becomes his/her right, unless the presiding judge or the court decides otherwise.

In cases other than felonies, if the accused, duly summoned, does not appear in person at the hearing, the presiding judge or the court does not decide that his/her presence is mandatory and there is no clear statement of the accused as to his/her personal will to take part in the proceedings, it is assumed that the accused voluntarily waived his/her right to participate in the hearing.

Indirectly, the CCP defines a concept of proceedings *in absentia* in order to designate the conditions for re-opening judicial proceedings when the judgment was rendered after a hearing conducted in the absence of the defendant. The relevant provision (Article 540b CCP) was introduced in order to implement FD 2009/299/JHA. The proceedings may be re-opened at the request of the defendant submitted within one month from the date at which s/he learned of the judgment. Proceedings are only deemed *in absentia* proceedings if: (1) the defendant did not participate in them and was not represented by a legal counsellor, (2) the defendant was not notified about the date of the trial at all or was notified in a different way than in person and (3) the defendant proves that s/he did not know about the possibility of delivering a judgment in his/her absence and did not know the date of the trial.

As a rule, it is up to the accused to decide on participation in the hearing; s/he may choose to appear only at the hearing at which the judgment is to be pronounced. His/her presence at only that hearing does not make the proceedings *in absentia* proceedings as referred to in Article 540b CCP. When the accused is present at the hearing at which the judgment was pronounced but s/he was not present at the earlier hearings due to lack of proper notification of the dates of these hearings, the situation is doubtful. In such a case it would be very difficult to prove that s/he did not know of the date of the trial. Moreover, it is not possible to re-open the proceedings if the accused was represented by a legal counsellor who participated in the trial.

The judgment may be pronounced in the absence of the accused. Even if the accused's presence at the hearing is mandatory, s/he does not have to be present at the hearing at

61 Felonies are criminal offences subject to a minimum penalty of imprisonment not less than three years.

which the judgment is pronounced. The pronouncement of the judgment takes place at the hearing (or at a session) of the court,[62] but can be adjourned for up to 14 days to a later hearing (or session). Only those parties who are present at the hearing at which the court proceedings were closed are informed of the adjourned date of the pronouncement of the judgment. The accused who was not present at the last hearing is not notified of the date of the pronouncement of the judgment. His/her appearance at a hearing at which only the pronouncement of the judgment takes place cannot retrospectively validate the incorrect notification of the dates of the hearings at which the case was examined. Therefore, the hearing at which only the pronouncement of the judgment takes place is not a hearing on which 'the case was examined'.[63]

In practice, in many cases a trial consists of several hearings and the proceedings can last several years. If an accused whose presence was not mandatory was properly notified of the date, then his/her failure to attend certain hearings, while s/he was present at other hearings, is irrelevant for assessing whether the proceedings were conducted *in absentia* in the sense of Article 540b CCP.[64]

The possibility for an absent accused to be present via telecommunication is expressly provided for.[65]

4.3.7 Romania

In Romania, the rule is that court proceedings take place in the presence of the accused. If the accused is detained, s/he must be brought to court. However, court proceedings may take place in the absence of the accused, if (a) s/he is missing, (b) flees justice, (c) changed his/her address without informing the court and, following a check, his/her address remains unknown or (d) even though the summons was lawfully served on him/her, s/he provides no justification for his/her absence. Throughout the court proceedings, the accused, whether s/he is deprived of his/her liberty or not, may request, in writing, to be tried in his/her absence and to be represented by a chosen or *ex officio* appointed legal counsellor.[66]

A convicted person who was not present during the court proceedings shall be deemed to be tried *in absentia*, if (i) s/he was not summoned to appear in court and had not been informed of the trial in *any other official manner* or (ii) even though s/he was aware of the court proceedings, s/he was justifiably absent from the court proceedings and was unable

62 A judgment is delivered at a hearing or, occasionally, at a session of the court. A hearing takes place in order to conduct evidentiary proceedings in an adversarial manner. If there is no need to conduct evidentiary proceedings, *e.g.* due to plea bargaining, a judgment may delivered at a session: PL, report, p. 5.

63 PL, report, p. 28.

64 PL, report, p. 28.

65 PL, report, p. 29.

66 RO, report, p. 9.

to inform the court thereof. A convicted person who appointed a chosen legal counsellor or representative shall *not* be deemed to be tried *in absentia*, if that legal counsellor or representative appeared at any time during the court proceedings. Neither shall the convicted person be considered as having been tried *in absentia* who, following the notification of the judgment of conviction, did not file an appeal, waived filing an appeal or withdrew the appeal. An accused who formally requested to be tried in his/her absence is not considered to be tried *in absentia*.[67] Whether or not a person was tried *in absentia* determines whether that person may ask for a re-opening of the proceedings in case of a final conviction. If the proceedings are considered to be *in absentia* s/he may request a re-opening, in the alternative s/he may not.

Romanian law distinguishes the following procedural stages of the court proceedings: court inquiry, debate, deliberation and pronouncement of the judgment. The object of a court inquiry is the re-administration and verification of all the evidence gathered during the pre-trial stage and the administration of any other evidence. During the court inquiry the first voice to be heard is that of the accused person, if present, while at the stage of the debates the accused has the last word. Court inquiry and debates can take place on the same day or at different dates depending on the circumstances or complexity of the case. Deliberation and pronouncement of the judgment shall take place on the day when the debates took place or later, but no later than 15 days since the closing of debates, with the possibility of postponing the pronouncement of the judgment only once. Although part of the court proceedings, the pronouncement of the judgment does not take place at a hearing, but at a public session. The accused may attend that session.[68] If the accused was not present at the trial itself but was present at the session at which the court pronounced judgment, according to Romanian law the proceedings are not considered to be *in absentia* proceedings, if he did not file an appeal, waived filing an appeal or withdrew the appeal.[69]

When an absent accused participates in the court proceedings via videoconference, s/he is considered to be present at those proceedings.[70]

4.4 Conclusion

The autonomous Union law meaning of the concept of a 'trial *in absentia*' is a trial at which the person concerned was not physically present. When comparing the various national law meanings of the concept of a 'trial *in absentia*' with the Union law meaning of that concept, a number of divergences appear.

67 RO, report, p. 9.
68 RO, report, p. 10.
69 RO, report, p. 10.
70 RO, report, p. 13.

Under Union law, all that is needed for a trial to be considered a trial *in absentia* is that the defendant was not physically present at that trial. Rather than defining the concept of a 'trial *in absentia*' in a *factual* manner, the national laws of the Member States give that concept a *technical* meaning. For example, some Member States *also* require that the defendant was either not summoned (properly) or summoned in a particular way, that s/he cannot justify his/her absence and/or that his/her (mandated) legal counsellor was also not present. In one Member State, the defendant must have a chosen legal counsellor for a waiver of the right to attend the hearing be effective. Another Member State no longer provides for trials *in absentia*, except for (petty) fiscal offences and petty offences; even though trials for other than those offences may be conducted *in the absence* of the accused, such trials are not considered trials *in absentia*, unless the requirements of the technical national concept of a 'trial in *absentia*' are met. As a result of these technical national definitions, the national law concepts are *more narrow* than the Union law concept of a 'trial *in absentia*'. The former comprise *less* situations than the latter. To give but one example: if an absent defendant is represented by his/her mandated legal counsellor, in the Netherlands the trial is not considered a trial *in absentia*.

Just to be clear, such divergences between the Union law meaning and a national law meaning do not necessarily mean that applying national law leads to results which are incompatible with Union law. To use the example again, representation by a mandated legal counsellor is one of the situations in which a trial *in absentia* may not lead to refusal of the EAW (Article 4a(1)(b) FD 2002/584/JHA) and in which a Member State may conduct a trial *in absentia* (Article 8(2)(b) Directive 2016/343/EU). However, divergences could cause misunderstandings in the application of Article 4a(1) FD 2002/584/JHA.

5 Trial Resulting in the Decision

5.1 Introduction

Together with the concept of 'appearance in person' – which was discussed in the previous chapter – the concept of a 'trial resulting in the decision' is the other key concept on which the application of Article 4a(1) FD 2002/584/JHA hinges. The concept of a 'trial resulting in the decision' determines the *scope* of Article 4a(1), *i.e.* it determines which proceedings and which decisions come within the ambit of the ground for refusal. After all, only when the person concerned did not appear in person at the 'trial resulting in the decision' may the executing judicial authority refuse to execute the EAW, unless one of the exceptions applies. Not surprisingly, the Court of Justice has held that this concept is an autonomous concept of Union law which must be interpreted uniformly (see also Section 3.5).[1]

As of yet, the Court of Justice has interpreted the concept of a 'trial resulting in the decision' in three judgments: *Tupikas*,[2] *Zdziaszek*[3] and *Ardic*.[4] In the first of these judgments, the Court of Justice held that the notion of a 'decision' in the concept of a 'trial resulting in the decision' refers to the "judicial decision which finally sentenced the person whose surrender is sought in connection with the execution of a European Arrest Warrant",[5] in other words to a final 'conviction'[6] or a 'final sentencing decision'.[7] A final conviction or a final sentencing decision comprises 'two distinct but related aspects': the finding of guilt and the handing down of a sentence.[8] This represents what one might call the ideal type of a 'trial resulting in the decision'.

In day-to-day practice, variants of that ideal type regularly present themselves. Some of those variants concern proceedings within one and the same instance. These variants,

1 ECJ, judgment of 10 August 2017, *Openbaar Ministerie v. Tadas Tupikas*, C-270/17 PPU, ECLI:EU:C:2017:628.

2 ECJ, judgment of 10 August 2017, *Openbaar Ministerie v. Tadas Tupikas*, C-270/17 PPU, ECLI:EU:C:2017:628.

3 ECJ, judgment of 10 August 2017, *Openbaar Ministerie v. Sławomir Andrzej Zdziaszek*, C-271/17 PPU, ECLI:EU:C:2017:629.

4 ECJ, judgment of 22 December 2017, *Samet Ardic*, C-571/17 PPU, ECLI:EU:C:2017:1026.

5 ECJ, judgment of 10 August 2017, *Openbaar Ministerie v. Tadas Tupikas*, C-270/17 PPU, ECLI:EU:C:2017:628, para. 74.

6 ECJ, judgment of 10 August 2017, *Openbaar Ministerie v. Tadas Tupikas*, C-270/17 PPU, ECLI:EU:C:2017:628, para. 75.

7 ECJ, judgment of 10 August 2017, *Openbaar Ministerie v. Tadas Tupikas*, C-270/17 PPU, ECLI:EU:C:2017:628, para. 76.

8 ECJ, judgment of 10 August 2017, *Openbaar Ministerie v. Sławomir Andrzej Zdziaszek*, C-271/17 PPU, ECLI:EU:C:2017:629, para. 77.

with regard to which the Court of Justice has not yet had the opportunity to clarify the concept of 'trial resulting in the decision', are the subject of Section 5.3. Other variants concern successive proceedings leading to successive decisions. In the context of such proceedings, *viz.* appeal proceedings, proceedings in which previously imposed penalties are merged into a new penalty and proceedings in which the suspension of the execution of a sentence is revoked, the Court of Justice has expounded how the concept of a 'trial resulting in the decision' is to be understood in the aforementioned *Tupikas, Zdziaszek* and *Ardic* judgments. Such proceedings are the subject of Section 5.4. Section 5.5 will deal with the related issue of EAWs which refer to multiple national judicial decisions.

However, before delving into the details of the concept of a 'trial resulting in the decision', we must first discuss an important distinction: the distinction between an *enforceable* decision (see Article 8(1)(c) FD 2002/584/JHA and section (b) of the EAW) and a *final* decision (see Article 4a(1) FD 2002/584/JHA and section (d) of the EAW).

5.2 Enforceable Decision versus Final Decision

In determining the meaning of the concept of a 'trial resulting in the decision', the Court of Justice drew a distinction which is most important for the practical application of Article 4a(1) FD 2002/584/JHA. Pursuant to Article 8(1)(c) FD 2002/584/JHA, the EAW must contain "evidence of an *enforceable* judgment, an arrest warrant or any other *enforceable* judicial decision having the same effect, coming within the scope of Articles 1 and 2",[9] which "evidence" the issuing judicial authority must proffer in section (b) of the EAW, entitled "Decision on which the warrant is based". In section (d) of the EAW, entitled "Indicate if the person appeared in person at the trial resulting in *the decision*",[10] the issuing judicial authority must tick the applicable box(es) concerning 'the decision' rendered *in absentia*. Now, according to the Court of Justice the 'decision' to which the concept of a 'trial resulting in the decision' refers – the decision of section (d) of the EAW –, is not necessarily the *enforceable* judicial decision on which the EAW is based – the enforceable judicial decision of section (b) of the EAW. The enforceability of a judicial decision is decisive in determining when an EAW may be issued.[11] Without an enforceable judicial decision no EAW can be issued. After all, following surrender, it is the enforceable domestic judicial decision which allows the competent authorities of the issuing Member State to enforce the custodial sentence or the detention order, not the EAW itself.[12] However,

9 Emphasis added.
10 Emphasis added.
11 ECJ, judgment of 10 August 2017, *Openbaar Ministerie v. Tadas Tupikas*, C-270/17 PPU, ECLI:EU:C:2017:628, para. 71.
12 Cf. ECJ, judgment of 6 December 2018, *IK*, C-551/18 PPU, ECLI:EU:C:2018:991, para 56.

according to the Court of Justice the notion of the *enforceability* of a decision is of lesser importance under Article 4a(1) FD 2002/584/JHA than the notion of the *finality* of a decision. From other provisions, the Court of Justice deduced that the 'trial resulting in the decision' is "the proceedings that led to the judicial decision which *finally* sentenced the person whose surrender is sought in connection with the execution of [an EAW]".[13] While in some cases, the *enforceable* judicial decision and the judicial decision which *finally* sentenced the person concerned *may coincide*, it is up to the national laws of the Member States to regulate whether the final decision actually is the enforceable decision.[14]

Depending on the national law of the issuing Member State, therefore, a final conviction may not be enforceable (yet). There may be any number of reasons for that state of affairs. The limitation period for enforcement may have expired (in which case the decision is no longer enforceable).[15] The national law of the issuing Member State may afford the convicted person a *terme de grâce* during which s/he may request a pardon. The execution of the final custodial sentence or detention order may be suspended, in which case the penalty is not enforceable as long as the suspension of the execution is not revoked.

It is perfectly understandable why the Court of Justice does not equate the judicial decision which finally sentenced the person concerned with the enforceable judicial decision. Automatically equating both decisions would make the scope of Article 4a(1) FD 2002/584/JHA dependent on the particularities of the national laws of the Member States with regard to the enforceability of judicial decisions. The ground for refusal would then be neither common nor clear and would, as a consequence, detract from the twin goals of enhancing the procedural rights of defendants and facilitating judicial cooperation. An example may illustrate this point. It may be that according to the national law of the issuing Member State the judgment of the court of first instance is the enforceable judicial decision when an appellate court upholds that judgment. But if the defendant was present at the first instance trial though not at the trial on appeal, designating the first instance judgment as the decision as referred to in Article 4a(1) FD 2002/584/JHA is problematic from the viewpoint of protecting the defendant's right of defence. In addition, if the only relevant decision were to be an enforceable decision, a Member State might no longer be able to guarantee a new trial or a retrial as one of the ways to prevent a refusal.

13 ECJ, judgment of 10 August 2017, *Openbaar Ministerie v. Tadas Tupikas*, C-270/17 PPU, ECLI:EU:C:2017:628, paras. 71-75.

14 ECJ, judgment of 10 August 2017, *Openbaar Ministerie v. Tadas Tupikas*, C-270/17 PPU, ECLI:EU:C:2017:628, para. 76.

15 Of course, in that situation issuing an EAW would not be possible at all.

5.3 Proceedings and Decisions within One Instance

5.3.1 Introduction

As we said before (see Section 5.1), in the day-to-day practice of executing judicial authorities a number of variants of the ideal type of the 'trial resulting in the decision' – *i.e.* the proceeding resulting in the 'final conviction' – present themselves. These variants concern proceedings *within one instance* in which:

1. an agreement between the defendant and the public prosecutor as to the penalty to be imposed was confirmed by a court (consensual proceedings);
2. a penalty was imposed on the defendant by a court without having held a trial and/or by an authority other than a court or a judge;
3. the defendant was not present at the trial, but was present at the hearing at which the judgment was pronounced;
4. the trial was spread out over two or more hearings and the defendant was present at one or more but not all of those hearings.

These variants raise the question whether the proceedings and the resulting decisions are covered by the concept of a 'trial resulting in the decision'.

5.3.2 Consensual Proceedings

A number of Member States involved in this project provide for consensual proceedings (guilty pleas and/or plea bargaining procedures).

In Belgium, when the defendant and the public prosecutor reach an agreement, a document mentioning date, hour and place of the court hearing is signed and a copy thereof is handed over to the defendant. The handing over of the document is considered as a summons. If both the defendant and his/her legal counsellor are absent at the hearing, the court will reject the agreement.[16]

In Poland, every agreement as to the sentence between the public prosecutor and the defendant must be accepted by the court in the form of a judgment sentencing the defendant. If the defendant appears at the session of the court, the judgment is rendered in his/her presence. If s/he fails to appear although duly summoned, the judgment is rendered *in absentia*.[17]

16 BE, report, p. 23.
17 PL, report, p. 58.

Romania distinguishes between a guilty plea and plea bargaining. A guilty plea can only be entered for offences for which the law requires a penalty of no more than 15 years of imprisonment and if the evidence sufficiently proves that such an offence was committed and that the defendant was its author. The plea agreement must be confirmed by the court by way of a judgment, following a public session and after hearing the public prosecutor, the defendant and his/her legal counsellor. The presence of the defendant at the hearing is *mandatory*. Therefore, it is unlikely that a judgment on a plea agreement will be rendered *in absentia*. If accepted by the court, the plea agreement results in a reduction of the custodial sentence with one-third. As regards plea bargaining: if the offence is not punishable by life imprisonment, the court will inform the defendant that, if s/he fully admits to having committed the offence, s/he may apply for a trial based only on the evidence submitted during the prosecution and on the documentary evidence submitted by the parties. A successful application reduces the limits of imprisonment with one-third. Having made such an application, the court shall hear the defendant and, after arguments by the public prosecutor and other parties, shall take a decision on the application.[18]

Are such consensual proceedings to be considered as a 'trial resulting in the decision' in the sense of Article 4(a(1) FD 2002/584/JHA? A common feature of all these kinds of proceedings is that, once the court confirms the agreement or accepts the plea agreement or plea bargain, it imposes a penalty on the defendant. A judicial decision imposing a penalty presupposes a finding of guilt by the court. If a court imposes a penalty following a guilty plea by the defendant, the court obviously accepts that guilty plea. In such circumstances, the finding of guilt may be said to be implicit. It is hard to see why a decision imposing a penalty on the defendant following consensual proceedings should not be considered a 'conviction' in the sense of the Court of Justice's case-law and, therefore, – provided that it is final – a decision in the sense of Article 4a(1).[19] Indeed, the *Dworzecki* judgment concerned a judgment of conviction rendered after *Dworzecki* had "pleaded guilty and accepted in advance the punishment suggested by the prosecutor".[20] However, it should be pointed out that, according to the ECtHR, "where the effect of plea bargaining is that a criminal charge against the accused is determined through an abridged form of

18 RO, report, p. 26.

19 Compare ECJ, judgment of 10 August 2017, *Openbaar Ministerie v. Tadas Tupikas*, C-270/17 PPU, ECLI:EU:C:2017:628, paras. 78 and 83; ECJ, judgment of 10 August 2017, *Openbaar Ministerie v. Sławomir Andrzej Zdziaszek*, C-271/17 PPU, ECLI:EU:C:2017:629, para. 77.

20 See the opinion of Advocate General Bobek of 11 May 2016, *Openbaar Ministerie v. Paweł Dworzecki*, C-108/16 PPU, ECLI:EU:C:2016:333, para. 62. Art. 335 of the Polish Code of Criminal Procedure was applied. See PL, report, p. 22 ("Issuing a conviction at the sitting of the court (Polish: *posiedzenie*)"). According to some German courts, such proceedings do not come within the ambit of Art. 4a(1). When no 'oral trial' ('mündliche Verhandlung') takes place, the German transposition of Art. 4a(1) is not applicable: *Oberlandesgericht Celle*, decision of 18 December 2012, 1 Ausl 56/12; *Kammergericht Berlin*, decision of 14 November 2017, (4) 151 AuslA 140/17 (200/17).

judicial examination, this amounts, in substance, to the waiver of a number of procedural rights". Therefore, a defendant who strikes a bargain with the prosecuting authority over the sentence and pleads no contest as regards the charge waives his right to have the criminal case against him examined on the merits.[21]

Those experts who have voiced an opinion on this subject agree that such final decisions come within the ambit of Article 4a(1).[22]

In the Belgian, Hungarian, Polish and Romanian cases which were examined in the course of this project, the *executing* judicial authorities were not confronted with EAWs concerning a penalty imposed by a judicial decision following consensual proceedings.[23]

The Dutch and the Irish *executing* judicial authority did encounter such cases. Both authorities have held that Article 4a(1) is applicable to such decisions.[24]

In none of the cases which were examined in the course of this project did the *issuing* judicial authorities experience any problems with consensual proceedings.[25] Of course, in Ireland no such situation could arise, because plea bargaining is not permitted under Irish law in any circumstances.[26]

5.3.3 *Penalties Imposed without a Trial or by a Non-Judicial Authority*

In some of the Member States involved in this project, it is not (entirely) excluded that (i) a court imposes a penalty without having held a trial and/or that (ii) an authority other than a court or a judge imposes a penalty.

In Belgium, *in the context of an EAW* the imposition of a penalty without having held a trial and/or by an authority other than a court or a judge is not possible.[27] As the issuing of an EAW for the enforcement of a penalty requires that a *custodial sentence* or a *detention order* of at least four months was imposed (Article 2(1) FD 2002/584/JHA), this answer clearly implies that under Belgian law a penalty or measure *involving deprivation of liberty* cannot be imposed without having held a trial and/or by an authority other than a court or a judge.

In Hungary, the court may adopt a 'concluding decision' against the defendant, with the omission of a trial, if the offence is punishable by not more than 3 years' imprisonment,

21 ECtHR, judgment of 29 April 2014, *Natsvlishvili and Tongonidze v. Georgia*, ECLI:CE:ECHR:2014:0429JUD000904305, § 91 and § 92.

22 BE, report, p. 23; HU, report, p. 19 (however, with the proviso that "it is possible to hold a trial instead"); NL, report, p. 64.

23 BE, report, p. 41 ("No information available"); HU, report, p. 33; PL, report, p. 79; RO, report, p. 40.

24 IE, report, p. 66; NL, report, pp. 101-102.

25 BE, report, p. 41; HU, report, p. 33; NL, report, p. 103; PL, report, p. 79; RO, report, p. 40.

26 IE, report, p. 67.

27 BE, report, p. 23.

the facts of the case are simple, the defendant is at large and the objective of punishment can be attained without holding a trial. Under Hungarian law, punishment can only be imposed by a court.[28]

In Ireland, the imposition of a penalty without having held a trial and/or the imposition of a penalty by an authority other than a court or a judge is not possible, except with regard to purely administrative financial penalties to which the EAW-system does not apply.[29]

In the Netherlands, the public prosecutor may issue a punishment order against the defendant with regard to misdemeanours and crimes not carrying a maximum penalty of more than 6 years imprisonment and impose a *non-custodial* penalty, such as the penalty of community service. It is not possible to impose an *alternative* custodial sentence if the person concerned does not comply with the non-custodial penalty. Punishment orders, therefore, can never be the – sole –[30] basis for issuing an EAW. If the defendant lodges an objection against the punishment order, a trial before the District Court will ensue. If s/he does not comply with the non-custodial penalty, the public prosecutor may indict him/her, in which case a trial before the District Court will also ensue.[31]

In Poland, the court may issue a penal order in the absence of the defendant at a court session. The defendant is not notified of the date of the session. Only a *non-custodial* penalty may be imposed. However, that penalty can later be converted into the penalty of imprisonment (and thus give rise to the issue of an EAW). The defendant may lodge an objection against the penal order. If an objection is lodged within the specific time limit, the penal order ceases to be valid and a trial under the normal rules will be held. Only a court may impose a penalty in Poland (not counting proceedings concerning petty offences in which a fine may be imposed by the police).[32]

In Romania, only a court can impose a penalty.[33]

Do judicial decisions imposing a penalty without having held a trial and decisions imposing a penalty by an authority other than a court or a judge fall within the ambit of Article 4a(1) FD 2002/584/JHA? Not holding a trial does not necessarily violate Article 6(1) ECHR. After all, the obligation to hold a trial is not absolute. In cases which do not carry any significant degree of stigma and which do not strictly belong to traditional criminal law, such as administrative penalties, Article 6(1) ECHR does not necessarily

28 HU, report, p. 19.

29 IE, report, p. 47.

30 Assuming that FD 2002/584/JHA does not prohibit so-called 'accessory surrender', an EAW could be issued for the purpose of the execution of a punishment order, if the EAW *also* pertains to an offence or a penalty which does comply with the requirements of Art. 2(1) FD 2002/584/JHA.

31 NL, report, p. 66.

32 PL, report, p. 58 in conjunction with p. 14 and pp. 22-23.

33 RO, report, p. 27.

apply with its full rigour as it does in regular criminal cases.[34] Although not holding a trial may be justified *only in rare cases*, "there may be proceedings in which an oral hearing may not be required, for example where there are no issues of credibility or contested facts which necessitate a hearing and the courts may fairly and reasonably decide the case on the basis of the parties' submissions and other written materials" and the domestic authorities may have regard to "the demands of efficiency and economy".[35]

In this respect it should be noted that Directive 2016/343/EU explicitly recognises proceedings in which no hearing is held. According to Article 8(5) Directive 2016/343/EU and recital (41) of the preamble, the provisions about the right to be present at the trial are not applicable to proceedings or certain stages thereof which are conducted *in writing, provided that these proceedings comply with the right to a fair trial*. The exceptions to the rule that the executing judicial authority may refuse to execute the EAW if the person concerned did not appear in person at the 'trial resulting in the decision' are intended to do just that: ensuring that his/her rights of defence, flowing from the general right to a fair trial, are fully respected. If a penalty was imposed by a court without having held a trial, this is all the more reason to (at least have the opportunity to) verify whether the rights of the defence were fully respected.

In any case, the judicial imposition of a penalty is a 'conviction' in the sense of the *Tupikas* and *Zdziaszek* judgments and, therefore, a 'decision' in the sense of Article 4a(1), provided that it is final.[36] The issuing judicial authority should mention in the EAW – either under point 4 of section (d) or in section (f) – when the 'decision' resulted from proceedings in which no hearing was held.

To the contrary, decisions imposing a penalty by a non-judicial authority can never form the – sole – basis for issuing an EAW. After all, the expression 'decision' in Article 4a(1) FD 2002/584/JHA refers to "the *judicial* decision which finally sentenced the person whose surrender is sought in connection with the execution of a European Arrest Warrant".[37] This decision need not necessarily be the 'enforceable judgment' or 'any other enforceable judicial decision having the same effect' as referred to in Article 8(1)(c) FD

34 ECtHR, judgment of 23 November 2006, *Jussila v. Finland* [GC], ECLI:CE:ECHR:2006:1123JUD007305301, § 43.

35 ECtHR, judgment of 23 November 2006, *Jussila v. Finland* [GC], ECLI:CE:ECHR:2006:1123JUD007305301, § 41. See for offences of a minor character ECtHR, decision of 17 May 2011, *Suhaldolc v. Slovenia*, ECLI:CE:ECHR:2011:0517DEC005765508 and ECtHR, decision of 17 May 2016, *Van Velzen v. the Netherlands*, ECLI:CE:ECHR:2016:0517DEC002149610.

36 With regard to the predecessor of Art. 4a(1), the *Oberlandesgericht* Köln was of a different opinion. It ruled that Art. 5(1) FD 2002/584/JHA did not apply to a Slovakian *Strafbefehl* (punishment order). According to the *Oberlandesgericht*, a *Strafbefehl* did not equate to a judgment *in absentia*, because in the proceedings resulting in the adoption of the *Strafbefehl* no hearings were held: *Oberlandesgericht* Köln, decision of 10 June 2005, Ausl 22/05-14/05.

37 ECJ, judgment of 10 August 2017, *Openbaar Ministerie v. Tadas Tupikas*, C-270/17 PPU, ECLI:EU:C:2017:628, para. 74 (emphasis added).

2002/584/JHA (see Section 5.2),[38] but it must be a *judicial* decision. It follows that a *non*-judicial decision imposing a penalty as such does not come within the ambit of Article 4a(1) FD 2002/584/JHA.

One may object that this line of reasoning would undermine the high-level protection of the person concerned which Article 4a(1) seeks to provide. On closer inspection, however, one must concede that this objection is groundless. Without the existence of an enforceable *judgment* or any other *judicial* decision having the same effect, no EAW for the enforcement of a penalty imposed by a *non*-judicial decision can even be issued (Article 8(1)(c) FD 2002/584/JHA).

In this regard it is relevant that – according to a well-settled line of case-law beginning with the *Öztürk*-judgment – Article 6 ECHR does not exclude an *administrative* authority from imposing a penalty, *on condition* that the person concerned may take this decision before a 'tribunal' that does offer the guarantees of Article 6 ECHR and has full jurisdiction.[39] It is only the final decision of such a tribunal that comes within the ambit of Article 4a(1) FD 2002/584/JHA.

As to the question whether Article 4a(1) is applicable to judicial decisions imposing a penalty without having held a trial, the Dutch expert is of the opinion that Article 4a(1) is indeed applicable, essentially for the reasons given earlier.[40] The Hungarian expert is of the opinion that Article 4a(1) is not applicable, because that provision supposes that at least one hearing is held.[41] As to the question whether Article 4a(1) is applicable to non-judicial decisions imposing a penalty, the Belgian, Dutch and Romanian experts point out that no EAW may be issued based solely on a decision of a non-judicial authority.[42] The other experts did not directly answer the first and/or second questions. Rather, they discussed whether such decisions were possible under *national* law.[43]

In the Belgian, Hungarian, Irish and Romanian cases which were examined in the course of this project, the *executing* judicial authorities were not confronted with EAWs concerning judicial decisions imposing a penalty without having held a trial or decisions imposing a penalty by a non-judicial authority.[44]

38 ECJ, judgment of 10 August 2017, *Openbaar Ministerie v. Tadas Tupikas*, C-270/17 PPU, ECLI:EU:C:2017:628, para. 76.

39 *See, e.g.*, ECtHR, judgment of 21 February 1984, *Öztürk v. Germany*, ECLI:CE:ECHR:1984:0221JUD000854479, § 56; ECtHR, judgment of 24 February 1994, *Bendenoun v. France*, ECLI:CE:ECHR:1994:0224JUD001254786, § 41; ECtHR, judgment of 23 July 2002, *Janosevic. v. Sweden*, ECLI:CE:ECHR:2002:0723JUD003461997, § 81.

40 NL, report, pp. 64-65.

41 HU, report, p. 19.

42 BE, report, p. 23; NL, report, p. 65; RO, report, p. 27.

43 IE, report, pp. 46-47; PL, report, p. 58.

44 BE, report, p. 41; HU, report, p. 33; IE, report, p. 66; RO, report, p. 40.

In the Netherlands, the *executing* judicial authority did come across final decisions taken either by a public prosecutor or by a court without having held a trial or during 'written proceedings'. A decision by an Italian public prosecutor concerned the merger of previously imposed sentences. Because in merging those sentence the public prosecutor lacked any margin of discretion, his decision was not considered to fall within Article 4a(1). A number of court decisions taken following 'written proceedings' also concerned the merger of previously imposed sentences. In these proceedings, the Hungarian and German courts, respectively, could dispose of a margin of discretion. Therefore, Article 4a(1) was held to be applicable. In one case, appeal proceedings in Latvia took place in written proceedings during which the defendant was not allowed to be present. Article 4a(1) was held to apply to those proceedings.[45]

In none of the cases which were examined in the course of this project did the *issuing* judicial authorities report any difficulties with judicial decisions imposing a penalty without having held a trial or decisions imposing a penalty by an authority other than a court or a judge.[46] As regards Ireland, no such situation could ever arise. Under the Irish Constitution, the administration of justice is reserved to judges appointed under, or in accordance with, the Constitution. Only a court can impose a penalty involving imprisonment or deprivation of liberty.[47]

5.3.4 *Absence at the Trial, Presence at the Pronouncement*

In the experience of the Dutch executing judicial authority, some issuing judicial authorities seem to interpret the expression 'the trial resulting in the decision' in points 1 and 2 of section (d) of the EAW as the 'hearing at which the judgment was pronounced'. Taken at face value, this might mean that those issuing judicial authorities are of the opinion that presence at the pronouncement of the judgment, in itself, is determinative for the applicability of Article 4a(1) FD 2002/584/JHA. From a Dutch perspective, this is puzzling. In Dutch criminal procedural law, the trial and the pronouncement of the judgment are distinct procedural steps. The trial ends when the president of the court closes the examination of the case. The judgment may be pronounced immediately after the examination of the merits of the case is closed, but usually the judgment is pronounced at a public hearing two weeks later.

Against this background, the question was raised whether the presence of the defendant at the pronouncement of the judgment is enough to preclude the applicability of that provision when s/he was absent at the trial.

45 NL, report, pp. 102-103.
46 BE, report, p. 41; HU, report, p. 33; NL, report, p. 103; PL, report, p. 79; RO, report, p. 40.
47 IE, report, p. 67.

If the requested person did not appear in person at the 'trial resulting in the decision', the executing judicial authority may refuse to execute the EAW, unless the rights of the defence were fully respected, *i.e.* unless the situations referred to in Article 4a(1)(a) to (d) FD 2002/584/JHA apply. It follows that underlying Article 4a(1) is a presumption that the rights of the defence were indeed respected when the requested person appeared in person at that trial (see Section 3.1). Put differently, according to the internal logic of Article 4a(1), presence in person at the trial obviates any check as to whether the rights of the defence were fully respected during that trial.

From the wording of Article 4a(1) – 'trial *resulting* in the decision' – and from the definition given by the Court of Justice to the concept of a 'trial resulting in the decision' – "the proceeding that *led* to the judicial decision which finally sentenced the person whose surrender is sought in connection with the execution of a European Arrest Warrant" –[48] it follows that the trial and the decision are distinct and that, therefore, the trial and the pronouncement of the decision are necessarily distinct, too.

Unless the trial and the pronouncement of the judgment took place at the same date and the defendant was also present at the trial, the mere presence of the defendant at the pronouncement of the judgment of conviction cannot support the conclusion that the rights of the defence were fully respected during the trial leading to that judgment. If one were to interpret Article 4a(1) in such a way that *mere* presence at the pronouncement of the judgment would suffice to preclude the applicability of that provision, that interpretation would blatantly run counter to one of its objectives: to enhance the procedural rights of persons subject to criminal proceedings (Article 1(1) FD 2009/299/JHA).

The experts agree that the presence of the defendant at the pronouncement of the judgment is *not* enough to preclude the applicability of that provision when s/he was absent at the trial.[49]

According to the Irish expert, Irish courts treat the concept of a 'trial resulting in the decision' as covering any substantive hearing culminating in a verdict on the issue of guilt (in cases where the accused has pleaded not guilty and has contested his/her criminal liability) and/or (if the accused has pleaded guilty) culminating in a decision/judgment on the imposition of a sentence.[50] The question whether mere presence at the pronouncement of the judgment is enough to preclude the applicability of Article 4a(1) has not arisen for consideration before the Irish courts.

According to the four Polish judges who were interviewed in the course of this project, the trial is not held *in absentia* if the defendant was present at least at one hearing. It should

48 ECJ, judgment of 10 August 2017, *Openbaar Ministerie v. Tadas Tupikas*, C-270/17 PPU, ECLI:EU:C:2017:628, para. 74.

49 BE, report, p. 24; HU, report, p. 20; IE, report, p. 67; NL, report, p. 67; PL, report, p. 60; RO, report, p. 27.

50 IE, report, p. 48.

be stressed that Polish judges rather connect the notion of a 'trial *in absentia*' in criminal proceedings with specific proceedings which may be conducted with reference to fiscal offences (*postępowanie w stosunku do nieobecnych*; see Section 4.3.6). Therefore, if the defendant was present at the hearing at which the judgment was pronounced, but failed to appear at previous hearings, the proceedings are not considered to be conducted *in absentia*. The presence of the defendant at some of the hearings, but his/her absence at the hearing at which the judgment was pronounced is also not classified as *in absentia*. Such an interpretation is supported by the wording of Article 540b of the CCP. However, a different approach seems to be taken by Polish judges when acting as *issuing* judicial authority. The analysis of EAWs issued by three Polish courts shows that in some cases presence at some of the hearings as to the merits of the case, but absence at the hearing at which the judgment was pronounced was designated as *in absentia*, whereas in other cases presence at some but not all hearings as to the merits of the case but absence at the hearings at which the judgment was pronounced was classified as 'personal presence'. The former cases seem to prevail. Although in the former cases it might appear to executing judicial authorities that the issuing judicial authority interpreted the concept of a 'trial resulting in the decision' as 'the hearing at which the judgment was pronounced' (see the Dutch experiences related earlier), what is decisive for the classification as *in absentia* proceedings is not non-appearance at the pronouncement of the judgment, but non-appearance at some of the hearings as to the merits of the case.[51] This view is supported by the fact that according to Polish law non-appearance of a defendant at the hearing at which a judgment is rendered does not preclude pronouncement of the judgment (Article 419 of the CCP), while non-appearance of a defendant at the hearing as to the merits of the case, if duly justified, shall preclude conducting the hearing (Article 117 §2 of the CCP).

As regards the experiences of the *executing* judicial authorities, in Belgium there is insufficient accurate information available to confirm or deny that Belgian executing judicial authorities were confronted with the issue at hand.[52]

In Romania, no difficulties were reported.[53]

Likewise in Ireland. However, it seems likely that the Irish executing judicial authority would not afford the words 'the trial resulting in the decision' such a narrow interpretation as 'the hearing at which the judgment was pronounced'. On the contrary, the likelihood is that the definition would be regarded as including all parts of the procedure, including the announcement of the decision or judgment as coming within the definition.[54]

51 PL, report, pp. 60 and 81.
52 BE, report, p. 41.
53 RO, report, p. 41.
54 IE, report, p. 67.

In the Netherlands, the executing judicial authority regularly encounters EAWs – especially EAWs issued by Polish issuing judicial authorities – in which the standard phrase 'the trial resulting in the decision' is rendered as 'the hearing at which the judgment was pronounced' or a similar wording. In such cases, the executing judicial authority will disregard that statement and will examine whether the person concerned appeared in person at 'the trial resulting in the decision' and, if so, whether any of the situations referred to in Article 4a(1)(a) to (d) applies.[55]

According to the Polish judges who were interviewed in the course of this project, it is decisive whether the requested person was aware of the trial. Most important is the requested person's participation in the hearings at which the merits of the case were examined, both at first instance and on appeal. Case file analysis shows that the executing judicial authority rather checks whether the requested person was aware of the proceedings. Because Article 607r § 3 CCP provides for an optional ground for refusal, this issue is not analysed in a very detailed manner, but it is taken into account when raised by the requested person.[56]

5.3.5 *Presence at Some But Not All Hearings*

Another issue emerging from the experiences of the Dutch executing judicial authority is the issue of divergent practices of issuing judicial authorities regarding trials consisting of several hearings where the defendant was present at some of those hearings and absent at others. Some issuing judicial authorities designate such situations as 'appearance in person', others as 'non-appearance in person'.

The situation that the defendant was present at some but not all of the hearings held within one and the same instance raises a number of questions: (1) if the trial resulting in an *in absentia* judgment of conviction consisted of several hearings and the defendant was present at one or more but not all of these hearings, has the condition that 'the person did not appear in person at the trial resulting in the decision' been met; (2) does it matter what transpired at the hearing(s) at which the defendant was present or is the mere presence of the defendant at one of the hearings enough to preclude the applicability of Article 4a(1) and (3) if it does matter what transpired at the hearing(s) at which the defendant was present, on the basis of which criteria does one establish whether the defendant was present 'at the trial resulting in the decision'?

To reiterate, Article 4a(1) FD 2002/584/JHA

55 NL, report, p. 103 in conjunction with pp. 97-98.
56 PL, report, p. 80.

> seeks to guarantee a *high* level of protection and to allow the executing judicial authority to surrender the person concerned despite that person's failure to attend the trial which led to his conviction, while *fully* respecting his rights of defence.[57]

Because Article 4a(1) FD 2002/584/JHA is only applicable on condition that the requested person did not appear in person at the trial which resulted in his/her conviction, it, therefore, necessarily follows that there is a *presumption* that the requested person's rights of defence were *fully* respected if s/he was *present* at the trial which resulted in his/her conviction (see Section 3.1).

Against this background, three possible interpretations present themselves: (1) to exclude the applicability of Article 4a(1), the defendant must have been present at *every* hearing; (2) to exclude the applicability of Article 4a(1), it suffices that s/he was present at *only one* of the hearings, regardless of what transpired at that hearing and (3) to exclude the applicability of Article 4a(1), the defendant must have been present at the hearing(s) at which the court dealt with the *merits of the case.*

The first interpretation has the advantage of practicability. It will be relatively easy for the judicial authorities to conclude whether Article 4a(1) is applicable or not. On the other hand, the first interpretation may be asking too much. Consider a hearing which was adjourned immediately after the opening of the hearing, because of the non-attendance of a witness. Is the fact that the defendant was not present at this hearing, while s/he was present at all of the other hearings, in itself, enough to conclude that his/her rights of defence were not fully respected? An affirmative answer to this question does not seem to recommend itself. Moreover, the first interpretation does not square with one of the objectives of Article 4a(1): to facilitate judicial cooperation in criminal matters (Article 1(1) FD 2009/299/JHA).

The second interpretation is also practicable. However, against the background of the presumption underlying Article 4a(1), the second interpretation may be asking too little. Consider again a hearing which was adjourned because of non-attendance of a witness. Is the presence of the defendant at this hearing, in itself, enough to conclude that his/her rights of defence were fully respected? It would seem not.

One could, of course, argue that, having once attended a hearing, it is the responsibility of the defendant to enquire after the date and place of the next hearing. Such a line of reasoning, however, conflates the question of the applicability of Article 4a(1) with the question whether – once applicable – there are circumstances which enable the executing judicial authority to ensure that the surrender of the person concerned does not entail a

57 ECJ, judgment of 10 August 2017, *Openbaar Ministerie v. Tadas Tupikas*, C-270/17 PPU, ECLI:EU:C:2017:628, para. 58 (emphasis added).

breach of his/her rights of defence. Furthermore, such a line of reasoning would significantly lower the high level of protection Article 4a(1) is designed to ensure and would, therefore, not be in line with another objective of Article 4a(1): to enhance the procedural rights of persons subject to criminal proceedings (Article 1(1) FD 2009/299/JHA).

A third possible interpretation is that to exclude the applicability of Article 4a(1), the defendant must have been present at the hearing(s) at which the court dealt with the merits of the case. A disadvantage of this interpretation is that it may not always be easy to distinguish between hearings at which the merits of the case were dealt with and other hearings.

This interpretation is in line with the presumption underlying Article 4a(1), identified earlier (see Section 3.1). If the defendant was present at the hearing(s) at which the court dealt with the merits of the case, one may safely assume that s/he had the opportunity to defend him/herself and that, therefore, the executing judicial authority can order his/her surrender in the knowledge that his/her rights of defence were *fully* respected. In comparison with the second interpretation, the third interpretation accords well with the aim of seeking to guarantee a *high* level of protection. It enhances the procedural rights of the person concerned and at, the same time, facilitates judicial cooperation in criminal matters.

The third interpretation is also in line with Article 6 ECHR. The ECtHR's case-law shows that it is indeed relevant what transpired at a hearing at which the defendant was not present: *e.g.* whether at that hearing all the evidence was examined in the absence of the defendant[58] or whether, by contrast, at that hearing no activity took place which required the presence of the defendant.[59]

---

58 See ECtHR, judgment of 22 May 2012, *Idalov v. Rusland*, ECLI:CE:ECHR:2012:0522JUD000582603, § 178: the applicant was removed from the courtroom for improper behaviour; *all the evidence*, including witnesses, was examined in his *absence*; because the court had not warned the applicant or considered a short adjournment in order to make the applicant aware of the potential consequences of his ongoing behaviour, the ECtHR was unable to conclude that, notwithstanding his disruptive behaviour, the applicant had unequivocally waived his right to be present at his trial. His removal from the courtroom meant that s/he was not in a position to exercise that right. Compare ECtHR, judgment of 25 November 2008, *Boyarchenko v. Ukraine*, ECLI:CE:ECHR:2012:0522JUD000582603, § 3: the applicant was charged with an infringement of custom regulations; the applicant and the Customs Office participated in the court hearing, in which the applicant was given an opportunity to advance any arguments in his defence and provide any piece of evidence in support of his submissions; the court sent the case file back to the Customs Office for technical reasons; at the next hearings, at which the applicant was not present, the Customs Office did not offer any *new arguments* in support of their position; the applicant did not suggest that the court had *examined* any *new evidence or arguments* or that he had any *new arguments or proofs to present*: the ECtHR held that in these circumstances, the decision to continue with the case in the absence of the applicant did not disclose any unfairness.

59 ECtHR, decision of 8 December 2009, *Previti v. Italy*, ECLI:CE:ECHR:2009:1208DEC004529106, § 196-198: 108 hearings were held at first instance, 33 hearings in appeal and 8 hearings in cassation; the applicant was absent at only one of the hearings of the first instance court; the ECtHR ruled that when a considerable number of hearings were held, it will only be in exceptional circumstances that the absence of the defendant at one of these hearings can compromise the fairness of the entire proceedings; such exceptional circum-

The opinions of the experts can be neatly categorised into one of the three aforementioned interpretations.

In Hungary, the trial is considered to be unitary if it consists of several hearings. If the defendant was present at one or more but not all of these hearings, the condition that the defendant 'did not appear in person at the trial resulting in the decision' is met.[60] This opinion corresponds to the first interpretation (the defendant must have been present at every hearing).

As stated before, the common view of the four Polish judges interviewed in the course of the project is that the trial is not held *in absentia* if the defendant was present at least at one hearing. Therefore, if the defendant was present at one or more but not all hearings, the condition that 'the person did not appear in person' was not met.[61] However, the analysis of a representative number of case files of EAWs issued by Polish judicial authorities seems to support a different conclusion: non-appearance of the accused at some but not all of the hearings as to the merits of the case was mainly classified as *in absentia*; non-appearance at the hearing at which the judgment was pronounced is not decisive for that classification (see Section 5.3.4).

According to the Romanian expert, the presence of the defendant at one of the hearings precludes the applicability of Article 4a(1).[62]

The Romanian expert's opinion and the opinion of the Polish judges who were interviewed correspond to the second interpretation (presence at least at one of the hearings suffices to preclude the applicability of Article 4a(1)).

In Belgium, as a matter of national law it does matter what transpired at the hearing(s) at which the defendant was present. The condition that the defendant 'did not appear in person at the trial resulting in the decision' would be met, if s/he were absent at the hearing(s) at which the merits of the case were discussed or the charges were brought against him/her. However, if his/her absence did in no way affect his/her rights of defence, *e.g.* if s/he was absent at a hearing which was merely adjourned or if his/her legal counsellor was present at that hearing, the condition would not be met and Article 4a(1) would be inapplicable.[63]

In Ireland, the situation has never arisen, as was to be expected. However, on a purely hypothetical basis it seems unlikely that mere presence on one occasion would automatically preclude the applicability of Article 4a(1), particularly if that occasion involved a purely

stances did not present themselves in this case: at the one hearing at which the applicant was absent no activity took place which required the presence of the applicant in person "telle que, par exemple, *la production de moyens de preuve*" (emphasis added).

60 HU, report, p. 20.

61 PL, report, p. 60.

62 RO, report, p. 28.

63 BE, report, pp. 24-25.

procedural hearing in the preliminary stages of the criminal procedure (*e.g.* involving an application to vary a bail condition, or the seeking of a witness summons).[64]

In the Netherlands, from the perspective of the executing judicial authority the mere presence of the defendant at one of the hearings is not enough to preclude the applicability of Article 4a(1). What matters is his/her presence at the hearing(s) at which the merits of the case were examined.[65]

The Belgian, Dutch and Irish experts' opinions correspond to the third interpretation (to preclude the applicability of Article 4a(1), the defendant must have been present at the hearing(s) at which the merits of the case were dealt with or at the hearing(s) which were not of a purely procedural nature). The case files of EAWs issued by Polish judicial authorities which were analysed in the course of the project seem to indicate that Polish issuing judicial authorities mainly adhere to this interpretation.

Turning to the experiences of the *executing* judicial authorities, in Belgium there have been many EAWs concerning trials which consisted of several hearings, but there is no specific information available to confirm that the EAW also mentioned that the defendant was not present at all of these hearings. Not a single decision to refuse surrender on such a basis was reported.[66]

In Hungary,[67] Poland[68] and Romania,[69] no difficulties have been reported. In Poland, according to the judges who were interviewed what matters is that the defendant was present at least at one of the hearings as to the merits of the case, because this means that s/he was aware of the trial. Such a perspective is supported by the wording of Article 607r § 3 of the Polish CCP. This provision uses the general word 'summoning to the proceedings' and suggests that what matters is awareness of the judicial proceedings. To reiterate, *issuing* Polish judicial authorities mainly seem to be of a different opinion. As issuing judicial authorities they rather adhere to the wording of section (d) of the EAW-form which clearly refers to the 'trial resulting in the decision'.

In Ireland, up until the *Zdziaszek* and *Ardic* judgments the executing judicial authority had consistently taken the position that if the requested person was present at any time during the trial resulting in the decision then s/he was not tried *in absentia*. The requested person who was voluntarily absent for another part of the remainder of the trial could be regarded as having had notice of the proceedings and/or having been aware of them and therefore as having waived his/her right to be present throughout. Consequently, if the

64 IE, report, pp. 48-49.

65 In this regard Dutch EAW law differs from Dutch criminal procedural law.

66 BE, report, p. 42.

67 HU, report, p. 34. The case referred to in the response did not concern a situation in which the defendant was present at some but not all of the hearings.

68 PL, report, p. 81.

69 RO, report, p. 41.

EAW in that situation mentioned that the person concerned appeared in person at the trial resulting in the decision then *prima facie* that was the end of the matter. In the light of both judgments, a somewhat more nuanced approach may be required, differentiating, where appropriate, between the trial of the issue of criminal liability and the trial of the issue as to the appropriate sentence to be imposed.[70]

In the Netherlands, the executing judicial authority regularly encounters situations in which the person concerned was present at some but not all of the hearings. After a period of wavering case-law, the executing judicial authority recently adopted a more strict approach to the issue. According to this new line of case-law, the person concerned cannot be deemed to have appeared in person at 'the trial resulting in the decision' if s/he was not present at the hearing(s) at which the court dealt with the merits of the case.[71]

As regards the experiences to the *issuing* judicial authorities, in Belgium, Hungary, Ireland, the Netherlands and Romania no difficulties were reported.[72]

In Poland, the issuing judicial authorities have encountered some problems. In 7 (out of 68 EAWs issued in the period 2016-2017), the Lublin Regional Court was asked to provide information about the participation of the defendant in particular hearings. In 4 (out of 52 EAWs issued in the period 2016-2017), the Warsaw Regional Court was asked to provide similar information. In none of these cases, the execution of the EAWs was refused on the grounds that the defendant was not present at some of the hearings.[73]

5.4 SUCCESSIVE PROCEEDINGS AND DECISIONS

5.4.1 *Introduction*

As we have seen earlier, the 'decision' in the expression 'trial resulting in the decision' is a judicial decision which finally sentences the requested person, *i.e.* a final conviction (see Section 5.1). Referring to the ECtHR's case-law on Article 5(1)(a) ECHR, the Court of Justice describes a conviction as encompassing "both a finding of guilt after it has been established in accordance with the law that there has been an offence, and the imposition of a penalty or other measure involving deprivation of liberty".[74] Whereas the previous section was dedicated to variants of the ideal type of a 'trial resulting in the decision' in the context of proceedings within one instance, this section will focus on variants of that

70 IE, report, pp. 67-68.
71 NL, report, p. 104.
72 BE, report, p. 42; HU, report, p. 35; IE, report, p. 68; NL, report, p. 105; RO, report, p. 41.
73 PL, report, p. 81.
74 ECJ, judgment of 10 August 2017, *Openbaar Ministerie v. Tadas Tupikas*, C-270/17 PPU, ECLI:EU:C:2017:628, para. 78.

ideal type in the context of *successive proceedings leading to successive decisions.* The Court of Justice already ruled on two variants of the ideal type of a 'trial resulting in the decision', *viz.* (1) appeal proceedings (Section 5.4.2) and (2) proceedings in which the nature or the *quantum* of a previously imposed penalty is modified (Section 5.4.3).

5.4.2 *Appeal Proceedings*

5.4.2.1 Case-Law

According to the well-settled case-law of the ECtHR, Article 6 ECHR does not compel the Contracting States to set up courts of appeal (or of cassation),[75] but when they do so the guarantees of Article 6 ECHR must be complied with.[76] Appeal proceedings (and cassation proceedings) are an 'extension' of the original trial process.[77] After all, the 'charge' against the defendant is not 'determined' as long as the judgment of conviction or acquittal has not become final.[78] Article 6 ECHR, therefore, applies to such proceedings,[79] but the manner in which Article 6 ECHR is to be applied to such proceedings depends, *inter alia*, on the special features of the proceedings involved.[80]

With respect to appeal proceedings, the *personal attendance* of the defendant "does not take on the same crucial significance for an appeal hearing as it does for a trial hearing".[81] Even if the appellate court has jurisdiction to review the case *both as to facts and as to law*, Article 6 ECHR does not always require a *right to appear in person*. Whether the defendant has a right to appear in person on appeal depends on, *inter alia*,

> the specific features of the proceedings in question and to the manner in which the applicant's interests were actually presented and protected before the appellate court, particularly in the light of the nature of the issues to be decided by it.[82]

No such right is required, *e.g.*, when the defendant did not raise any questions of law or fact which could not be adequately resolved on the basis of the case file, s/he was charged

75 Art. 2(1) of Protocol No 7 to the ECHR guarantees everyone convicted of a criminal offence by a tribunal the right of appeal. Protocol No 7 is ratified by all but three Member States (DE, NL, UK).

76 *See, e.g.*, ECtHR, judgment of 17 January 1970, *Delcourt v. Belgium*, ECLI:CE:ECHR:1970:0117JUD000268965, § 25.

77 ECtHR, judgment of 12 April 2007, *Mevlüt Kaya v. Turkey*, ECLI:CE:ECHR:2007:0412JUD000138302, § 19.

78 ECtHR, judgment of 17 January 1970, *Delcourt v. Belgium*, ECLI:CE:ECHR:1970:0117JUD000268965, § 25.

79 *See, e.g.*, ECtHR, decision of 7 September 1999, *Jodko v. Lithuania*, ECLI:CE:ECHR:1999:0907DEC003935098.

80 ECtHR, judgment of 17 January 1970, *Delcourt v. Belgium*, ECLI:CE:ECHR:1970:0117JUD000268965, § 26.

81 ECtHR, judgment of 18 October 2006, *Hermi v. Italy* [GC], ECLI:CE:ECHR:2006:1018JUD001811402, § 60.

82 ECtHR, judgment of 18 October 2006, *Hermi v. Italy* [GC], ECLI:CE:ECHR:2006:1018JUD001811402, § 62.

with a minor offence and the sentence could not be increased on appeal.[83] However, when an appellate court

> has to examine a case as to the facts and the law and make a *full* assessment of the *issue of guilt or innocence*, it cannot determine the issue without a direct assessment of the evidence given in person by the accused for the purpose of proving that he did not commit the act allegedly constituting a criminal offence.[84]

The difference between this situation and situations in which there is no right to appear in person, although the appellate court has jurisdiction to examine the case both as to the facts as to the law is that the defendant claims that s/he did not commit the offence, which then becomes the principal issue for determination by the appellate court.[85]

The ECtHR's ruling on appellate courts which have to make a full assessment of the issue of guilt or innocence is the basis for the Court of Justice's ruling in the *Tupikas* case:

> Moreover, the European Court of Human Rights has held on several occasions that, where appeal proceedings are provided for, they must comply with the requirements flowing from Article 6 of the ECHR, in particular where the remedy available against the decision given at first instance is a full appeal, the second-instance court having jurisdiction to re-examine the case, by assessing the merits of the accusations in fact and in law, and thus to determine the guilt or innocence of the person concerned on the basis of the evidence presented (...).[86]

After adding the argument that the defendant's presence at the first instance trial does not necessarily mean that Article 6 ECHR was complied with when the defendant was absent

83 ECtHR, judgment of 29 October 1991, *Fejde v. Sweden*, ECLI:CE:ECHR:1991:1029JUD001263187, § 33.

84 ECtHR, judgment of 18 October 2006, *Hermi v. Italy* [GC], ECLI:CE:ECHR:2006:1018JUD001811402, § 64 (emphasis added).

85 ECtHR, judgment of 26 May 1988, *Ekbatani v. Sweden*, ECLI:CE:ECHR:1988:0526JUD001056383, § 32; ECtHR, judgment of 27 June 2000, *Constantinescu v. Romania*, ECLI:CE:ECHR:2000:0627JUD002887195, § 55; ECtHR, judgment of 16 July 2019, *Styrmir Þór Bragason v. Iceland*, ECLI:CE:ECHR:2019:0716JUD003629214, § 64.

86 ECJ, judgment of 10 August 2017, *Openbaar Ministerie v. Tadas Tupikas*, C-270/17 PPU, ECLI:EU:C:2017:628, para. 79. However, it should be pointed out that, even in such circumstances and even if none of the exceptions of Art. 4a(1)(a)-(d) applies, a trial *in absentia* on appeal does not necessarily constitute a violation of Art. 6 ECHR: ECtHR, judgment of 17 December 2015, *Sobko v. Ukraine*, ECLI:CE:ECHR:2015:1217JUD001510210, § 73-83. In other words, this confirms that the former provision *does not fully codify the ECtHR's case-law* concerning the latter provision and that, consequently, the Framework Decision *provides for a higher level of protection* than the ECHR (see Sections 3.1 and 8.1).

on appeal, the Court of Justice formulates the interpretation of the concept of 'trial resulting in the decision' in the context of proceedings which have taken place at several instances and have given rise to successive decisions, at least one of which was given *in absentia*:

> the instance which led to the *last* of those decisions, provided that the court at issue made a *final ruling* on the *guilt of the person concerned* and *imposed a penalty on him*, such as a custodial sentence, following an *assessment, in fact and in law, of the incriminating and exculpatory evidence*, including, where appropriate, the taking account of the individual situation of the person concerned.[87]

The Court of Justice's criterion rules out proceedings in which *only questions of law* are dealt with, such as cassation proceedings. This is perfectly in accordance with the ECtHR's case-law. Although such proceedings are part of the determination of a criminal charge as referred to in Article 6(1) ECHR, they may comply with the requirements of Article 6(1) ECHR even where the defendant was not given an opportunity of being heard in person by the cassation court.[88]

The Court of Justice's criterion *limits* the scope of the concept or a 'trial resulting in the decision' in the context of proceedings in several instances and resulting in successive decisions to the *last* of those proceedings and the *last* of those decisions, provided that the decision consisted of a *final* ruling on guilt and an imposition of a penalty. Consequently, if the person concerned appeared in person at the trial at which the merits of the case were re-examined, Article 4a(1) does not apply, even though s/he did not appear in person at the first instance trial. However, if s/he did appear in person at the first instance trial, but did not appear in person at the trial concerning a re-examination of the merits of the case, Article 4a(1) does apply.

According to the Court of Justice, the *last* decision, holding a *final* ruling on guilt and an imposition of a penalty, is *decisive* for the defendant "since it directly affects his personal situation with regard to the finding of guilt and, where appropriate, the determination of the custodial sentence to be served". Therefore, it is at that stage of the proceedings that the defendant "must be able to fully exercise his rights of defence in order to assert his point of view in an effective manner and thereby to influence the final decision which could lead to the loss of his personal freedom". Moreover, focussing on the *last* decision

87 ECJ, judgment of 10 August 2017, *Openbaar Ministerie v. Tadas Tupikas*, C-270/17 PPU, ECLI:EU:C:2017:628, paras. 80-81 (emphasis added).

88 *See, e.g.*, ECtHR, judgment of 26 July 2002, *Meftah and Others v. France* [GC], ECLI:CE:ECHR:2002:0726JUD003291196, § 41.

holding a *final* ruling on guilt and an imposition of a penalty best ensures the objective pursued by FD 2009/299/JHA, which is to facilitate and accelerate judicial cooperation in criminal matters on the basis of the principle of mutual recognition. Including previous decisions would "inevitably prolong or even seriously impede" the surrender procedure. Finally, the Court of Justice points out that a reading of section (d) of the EAW-form confirms that the information to be provided by the issuing judicial authority *only* pertains to the *last* instance at which the merits of the case were examined.[89]

Excluding from the scope of Article 4a(1) all but the *last* decision, containing a *final* ruling on guilt and an imposition of a penalty, is in accordance with Article 6(1) ECHR. The ECtHR has repeatedly held that an appeal in which the defendant was entitled to participate and which opened up the possibility of a fresh determination of the merits of the charge redresses the violation which may have occurred by a conviction *in absentia*.[90]

The scope of appeal (and cassation) proceedings may vary from Member State to Member State. With the exception of Ireland, all Member States involved in the project provide for a legal recourse in which the merits of the case can be re-examined with regard to both the law and the facts.[91] Poland distinguishes between ordinary and extraordinary appeal measures. An ordinary appeal is directed against a first instance judgment which is not final and not legally binding and results in the examination of the merits of the case within the limits of the appeal (see below), both as to the facts of the case and as to the law applied by the first instance court. An extraordinary appeal (such as a cassation appeal) is directed at a final and legally binding judgment of an appellate court ending the proceedings.[92] In Ireland, the general right of appeal in indictable cases is confined to a review of the legality of the trial (issues relating to the admissibility of evidence, the fairness of the trial procedure, the adequacy and correctness of legal instructions given to the jury and issues of substantive criminal law relating to the definition of the offence charged and the application/interpretation of relevant statutory provisions or common law rules).[93] In some Member States involved in the project, when lodging an appeal the defendant may restrict the scope of that appeal,[94] *e.g.*, to questions of law only[95] or to a part of the judg-

89 ECJ, judgment of 10 August 2017, *Openbaar Ministerie v. Tadas Tupikas*, C-270/17 PPU, ECLI:EU:C:2017:628, paras. 87-89.

90 *See, e.g.*, ECtHR, judgment of 1 March 2006, *Sejdovic v. Italy* [GC], ECLI:CE:ECHR:2006:0301JUD00565810, § 126; ECtHR, judgment of 3 October 2016, *Baratta v. Italy*, ECLI:CE:ECHR:2015:1013JUD002826309, § 78; ECtHR, decision of 3 October 2017, *Giurgiu v. Romania*, ECLI:CE:ECHR:2017:1003DEC002623909, § 96.

91 BE, report, pp. 11-14; HU, report, p. 10; NL, report, p. 34; PL, p. 40; RO, report, pp. 15-18.

92 PL, report, pp. 36 and 40.

93 IE, report, p. 21.

94 HU, report, p. 10.

95 PL, report, p. 41. *See, e.g.*, ECtHR, judgment of 9 June 2009, *Sobolewski (no. 2) v. Poland*, ECLI:CE:ECHR:2009:0609JUD001984707, § 20 and § 41; ECtHR, judgment of 9 June 2009, *Strzałkowski v. Poland*, ECLI:CE:ECHR:2009:0609JUD003150902, § 9 and § 47.

ment.[96] In none of the Member States involved in the project, the cassation court – as a court of final instance – is – currently –[97] empowered to make a fresh determination of the merits of the case.[98]

Given that only a small group of Member States' national laws were analysed, that some Member States involved in the project allow for restricting the scope of an appeal and that in at least one Member State the cassation court at one time did have the power to make a fresh determination of the merits of the case, it seems that the mere fact that a decision is rendered by an appeal court or a cassation court may be insufficient to determine whether Article 4a(1) applies to that decision.

Apparently, the Court of Justice is of the opinion that section (d) of the EAW is clear with regard to its applicability in the context of appeal proceedings. However, the plain fact of the matter is that section (d) of the EAW merely refers to 'the decision'. The structure of section (d) does not force the issuing judicial authority to specify the decision(s) to which it deems that section applicable.

5.4.2.2 Application in Practice

5.4.2.2.1 Questions

In day-to-day practice, issuing judicial authorities:

- do not always mention that proceedings have taken place at several instances, restricting themselves to mentioning the first or second instance decision which was upheld in subsequent proceedings (in section (b) of the EAW-form);
- when mentioning that proceedings have taken place at several instances, do not always explain the nature of second or third instance proceedings and/or simply refer to the first instance decision in section (d).

This raises the question of what the executing judicial authority should do, if:

1. the EAW does not mention appeal proceedings, although it is apparent that such proceedings have taken place;
2. the EAW does mention appeal proceedings, but does not give any information on the nature and/or outcome of these proceedings;

96 BE, report, pp. 13 and 14. The same holds true for NL, although this was not addressed in the Dutch report.

97 Apparently, under previous legislation the Romanian High Court of Cassation and Justice was empowered to make a fresh determination of the merits of the charge, after having quashed the judgment *a quo*: *see*, e.g., ECtHR, judgment of 2 October 2018, *Bivolaru v. Romania (No 2)*, ECLI:CE:ECHR:2018:1002 JUD006658012, § 133.

98 BE, report, p. 15; HU, report, p. 12; IE, report, p. 23; NL, report, pp. 41-42 (after having quashed the judgment *a quo*, the Supreme Court may only deal with the case itself, if this can be done without having to re-examine the facts); PL, report, p. 45 (with one exception: if the Supreme Court holds that a conviction is manifestly unjust, it may acquit the defendant); RO, report, p. 18.

3. the EAW also mentions appeal proceedings, but does not make clear to which proceedings section (d) is applicable.

5.4.2.2.2 Opinions of the Experts

The prevailing opinion among the experts seems to be that the executing judicial authority should request supplementary information, if need be.

With regard to the first question, the Belgian expert is of the opinion that such a situation would not lead to refusal, but to a request for supplementary information, if need be. As to the second question, he is of the opinion that providing information about the existence and the outcome of successive proceedings is mandatory, especially if no legal recourse is available. Such information could be brief, but merely mentioning that the decision is final does not suffice. Concerning the third question, the Belgian expert puts forward that supplementary information would be requested, unless it could be assumed that section (d) only relates to the first instance decision.[99]

According to the Hungarian expert, with regard to the first question it is irrelevant what decisions were rendered at first instance, if subsequent proceedings were conducted *in absentia*. If the defendant appeared at the first instance proceeding, but not on appeal, section (d) must be filled in with regard to the latter proceedings. With regard to the second and first questions, the Hungarian expert points out that these situations do not constitute a reason for refusal, but could lead to a request for supplementary information.[100]

According to the Irish expert, taking into account the requested person's objections to surrender and applying the Court of Justice's case-law, the executing judicial authority must establish what stage of the proceedings relate to the 'trial resulting in the decision' and must satisfy itself whether section (d) actually relates to that trial. If need be, it must request supplementary information.[101]

The Dutch expert takes the view that the answer to all three questions should be that – unless information from other sources is available – supplementary information must be requested. In the circumstances indicated in the first question, the executing judicial authority does not have the necessary information to validly decide on the execution of the EAW. The same holds true for the second question: on the basis of the *Tupikas* judgment, the mere mention of proceedings in appeal is not enough to conclude that Article 4a(1) applies to the decision on appeal. In the circumstances of the third question, the executing judicial authority cannot verify whether the rights of the defence were fully respected with regard to the relevant decision.[102]

99 BE, report, pp. 33-34.
100 HU, report, pp. 26-27.
101 IE, report, pp. 54-56.
102 NL, report, pp. 84-85.

The Polish expert relates that some of the judges who were interviewed in the course of the project pointed out that they mainly take into consideration the first instance proceedings, since those proceedings usually concern the merits of the case. All judges underlined the importance of the statements (explanations) provided for by the requested person at the session of the executing judicial authority. If the requested person raises any objections as to the fairness of the proceedings conducted against him/her in the issuing Member State, the executing judicial authority will assess such objections and, if need be, will request supplementary information.[103]

The Romanian expert is of the opinion that all three situations are subject to a request for supplementary information.[104]

5.4.2.2.3 Experiences of Executing Judicial Authorities

In the experience of Belgian executing judicial authorities, in all cases in which section (d) did not state which decision mentioned in section (b) it referred to, section (d) applied to the first instance judgment of conviction mentioned in section (b)2 of the EAW. It is often mentioned that the first instance decision was upheld on appeal, sometimes accompanied by the mention that the legal counsellor of the defendant lodged the appeal and, occasionally, that cassation proceedings were unsuccessful. In such circumstances attention is sometimes drawn to the fact that it is the decision in first instance that becomes enforceable and that only this decision can be the object of the EAW. The information in section (d) then reflects on the first instance proceedings. As a result of the legal counsellor representing the defendant on appeal, apparently the issuing judicial authority considers the judgment on appeal not to be rendered *in absentia*.[105]

The Hungarian executing judicial authority has had a case in which problems concerning appeal proceedings arose. The EAW stated that the defendant was not present at the trial, but that s/he mandated a legal counsellor who was present at the trial. The supplementary information requested by the executing judicial authority made it clear that the issuing authority considered the second instance proceedings as 'the trial resulting in the decision'. It turned out that there were several hearings in the first instance proceedings at which the defendant and his/her legal counsellor were present. As s/he was aware of the second instance trial and as his/her legal counsellor was present at that trial, the court decided not to refuse the execution of the EAW.[106]

The Irish executing judicial authority was confronted with an EAW concerning a 'non-conclusive' conviction while appeal proceedings were pending; because the person con-

103 PL, report, pp. 68-69.
104 RO, report, pp. 34-35.
105 BE, report, pp. 44-545.
106 HU, report, p. 37 in conjunction with p. 34.

cerned would be regarded as a convicted person under Irish law, and because the issuing judicial authority would not guarantee a retrial, the Irish executing judicial authority refused to surrender the person concerned.[107]

In most cases, in the circumstances referred to in the three questions the Dutch executing judicial authority requested supplementary information, unless information from other sources, such as the statement of the requested person, allowed it to verify whether Article 4a(1) was applicable.[108]

In Poland, executing judicial authorities have reported a few problems with EAWs concerning successive proceedings.[109]

5.4.2.2.4 *Experiences of Issuing Judicial Authorities*

In Belgium, some EAWs issued by the public prosecutor at the sentence enforcement court (*strafuitvoeringsrechtbank*) referring to that court's judgment to revoke a conditional release led to requests for supplementary information related to the functioning and the competence of the sentence enforcement court. The problems were resolved by pointing out that the basis for the EAW was the judgment of conviction. The fact that the remainder of the sentence mentioned in the decision of the sentence enforcement court differed from the original sentence should not be interpreted as being the outcome of a review of the *quantum* of the sentence, as it was in fact the result of a deduction of time already served or the application of legal rules that leave no margin for discretion.[110]

In the case files which were examined, the Hungarian issuing judicial authorities did not experience any problems with EAW concerning successive proceedings.[111]

The same goes for the Romanian issuing authorities.[112]

The Dutch issuing judicial authority has issued EAWs concerning successive proceedings, but has not experienced any problems in this regard.[113]

In Poland, only in one of the case files which were analysed an issuing judicial authority was asked to provide information about the character of the appellate proceedings which resulted in upholding the first instance judgment and was, furthermore, asked to fill in section (d) of the EAW with respect to the judgment of the appellate court. The issuing judicial authority explained that the presence of the defendant at the appellate

107 IE, report, p. 90 in conjunction with pp. 63-65.
108 NL, report, pp. 114-115.
109 PL, report, p. 85 in combination with pp. 57 and 68-69.
110 BE, report, p. 45.
111 HU, report, p. 37.
112 RO, report, p. 43.
113 NL, report, p. 115.

hearing was not mandatory and that the EAW concerned the first instance judgment which was upheld by the appellate court.[114]

Ireland, of course, has never issued an EAW for a person tried *in absentia*.[115]

5.4.3 *Proceedings to Amend Previously Imposed Penalties*

5.4.3.1 Case-Law

In the *Zdziaszek* judgment, the Court of Justice clarified the concept of a 'trial resulting in the decision' in the context of appeal proceedings which resulted in a final 'conviction' such as at issue in the *Tupikas* judgment, followed by proceedings resulting in amending the *quantum* of the penalty previously imposed and finally determining the penalty.

Both proceedings come within the ambit of Article 4a(1): the former with regard to the final finding of guilt, the latter with regard to the final determination of the *quantum* of the penalty. A conviction has 'two distinct, but related aspects': the finding of guilt and the imposition of a sentence. The *final finding of guilt* in the appeal proceedings directly affects the situation of the person concerned, as it constitutes the legal basis for the custodial sentence which s/he must serve. The person concerned should be able to fully exercise his/her rights of defence before such a final decision is taken.[116]

With regard to the *final determination of the quantum of the penalty*, the Court of Justice distinguishes between a decision modifying the *quantum* of penalties previously imposed and a decision relating to the methods of execution of a sentence. This distinction is supported by the ECtHR's case-law: Article 6(1) ECHR does not apply to "questions concerning the methods for executing a sentence, in particular those relating to provisional release".[117] In the particular proceedings at issue, a cumulative sentence was handed down, consisting in commuting into a single sentence one or more sentences handed down previously. The result of such proceedings is necessarily more favourable for the person concerned, because the cumulative sentence may be less than the sum of the separate sentences.

114 PL, report, p. 85.

115 IE, report, p. 90.

116 ECJ, judgment of 10 August 2017, *Openbaar Ministerie v. Sławomir Andrzej Zdziaszek*, C-271/17 PPU, ECLI:EU:C:2017:629, paras. 76-82.

117 The Court of Justice refers to ECtHR, judgment of 3 April 2012, *Boulois v. Luxembourg* [GC], ECLI:CE:ECHR:2012:0403JUD003757504, § 87. See also ECtHR, judgment of 17 September 2009, *Enea v. Italy* [GC], ECLI:CE:ECHR:2009:0917JUD007491201, § 97; ECtHR, decision of 23 October 2012, *Ciok v. Poland*, ECLI:CE:ECHR:2012:1023DEC000049810, § 38. The European Commission of Human Rights had already held that a decision to revoke the suspension of a sentence and a decision to rescind a provisional release do not amount to a 'determination of a criminal charge' within the meaning of Art. 6 ECHR: ECHR, decision of 5 October 1967, *X. v. the Federal Republic of Germany*, ECLI:CE:ECHR:1967:1005DEC000242865; ECHR, decision of 6 December 1977, *X. v. Switzerland*, ECLI:CE:ECHR:1977:1206DEC000764876; ECHR, decision of 9 May 1994, *Sampson v. Cyprus*, ECLI:CE:ECHR:1994:0509DEC001977492.

Again, the Court of Justice refers to Strasbourg case-law: Article 6 ECHR does not only apply to the finding of guilt but also to the determination of the sentence;[118] therefore, the person concerned has a right to be present at the hearing "because of the significant consequences which it may have on the quantum of the sentence to be imposed".[119] Such significant consequences could arise where the proceedings for determining an overall sentence are

> not a purely formal and arithmetic exercise but entail a margin of discretion in the determination of the level of the sentence, in particular, by taking account of the situation or personality of the person concerned, or of mitigating or aggravating circumstances.[120]

In this respect, it does not matter whether the competent court has jurisdiction to increase the sentence previously imposed.[121] Nor is it relevant that the new sentence is hypothetically more favourable to the requested person: after all, the level of the sentence is not determined in advance. Because the proceedings at issue determine the *quantum* of the sentence which the person concerned will ultimately serve, s/he must be able to effectively exercise his/her rights in order to influence a favourable outcome. To sum up, proceedings giving rise to a cumulative sentence and leading to a new determination of the level of custodial sentences previously imposed fall within the ambit of Article 4a(1), if they entail a margin of discretion for the competent authority and give rise to a decision which finally determines the sentence.[122]

---

118 The Court of Justice refers to ECtHR, judgment of 28 November 2013, *Aleksandr Dementyev v. Russia*, ECLI:CE:ECHR:2013: 1128JUD004309505, § 23.

119 The Court of Justice refers to ECtHR, judgment of 21 September 1993, *Kremzow v. Austria*, ECLI:CE:ECHR: 1993:0921JUD001235086, § 67.

120 The Court of Justice refers to ECtHR, judgment of 15 July 1982, *Eckle v. Germany*, ECLI:CE:ECHR:1982: 0715JUD000813078, § 77 and ECtHR, judgment of 28 November 2013, *Aleksandr Dementyev v. Russia*, ECLI:CE:ECHR: 2013:1128JUD004309505, § 23 and 26.

121 The Court of Justice refers to ECtHR, judgment of 26 May 1988, *Ekbatani v. Sweden*, ECLI:CE:ECHR:1988: 0526JUD001056383, § 32 and ECtHR, judgment of 18 October 2006, *Hermi v. Italy* [GC], ECLI:CE:ECHR: 2006:1018JUD001811402, § 65.

122 ECJ, judgment of 10 August 2017, *Openbaar Ministerie v. Sławomir Andrzej Zdziaszek*, C-271/17 PPU, ECLI:EU:C:2017:629 paras. 85-92. It should be pointed out that, even in proceedings which do not involve a 'purely formal and arithmetic exercise' and in which the competent court consequently enjoys a margin of discretion, Art. 6 ECHR does not always require the presence of the defendant at the hearing: ECtHR, judgment of 28 November 2013, *Aleksandr Dementyev v. Russia*, ECLI:CE:ECHR:2013:1128JUD004309505, § 43-47. Given the limited scope for sentencing (a prison sentence ranging from 1 day to 2 months) and the fact that the original sentences were not imposed *in absentia*, the domestic court could dispense with a direct assessment of the evidence given by the applicant in person. This is yet another illustration of the fact that Art. 4a(1) FD 2002/584/JHA *does not fully codify the case-law of the ECtHR* on trials *in absentia* and, consequently, *provides for a higher level of protec*tion than Art. 6 ECHR (see Sections 3.1 and 8.1).

According to the Court of Justice, providing information on both the final finding of guilt and the final determination of the sentence does not increase the workload of the issuing judicial authority: the EAW-form already requires it to provide information not only on the offence(s) but also on the penalty imposed.[123] Of course, that is correct, but the wording and the structure of section (d) of the EAW-template are not very helpful in this regard, restricting itself to referring to 'the decision' (see also Section 5.4.2). Section (d) is not tailored to situations in which two judgments or judicial decisions come within the ambit of Article 4a(1) and may, by its very wording and structure, lead issuing and executing judicial authorities to believe that section can only apply to *one* decision.

In the *Ardic* judgment, concerning decisions to revoke the suspension of the execution of a previously imposed custodial sentence, the Court of Justice further refined its distinction between decisions modifying the *quantum* of the sentence and decisions relating to the methods of the execution of a sentence.

Again referring to Strasbourg case-law, the Court of Justice pointed out that, whereas a final conviction, including a final determination of the sentence, squarely falls within Article 6 ECHR, that provision does not apply to "questions relating to the detailed rules for the execution or application of such a custodial sentence".[124] However, decisions concerning the latter category only come within the ambit of Article 6 ECHR, where, "following a finding of guilt of the person concerned and having imposed a custodial sentence on him, a new judicial decision modifies either the nature or the quantum of sentence previously imposed".[125] The Court of Justice gave two examples of such a decision: (1) a prison sentence is replaced by an expulsion order[126] and (2) the duration of the detention previously imposed is increased.[127] Therefore, the concept of a 'decision' referred to in Article 4a(1) does not cover a

> decision relating to the execution or application of a custodial sentence previously imposed, except where the purpose or effect of that decision is to modify either the nature or quantum of that sentence and the authority which adopted it enjoyed some discretion in that regard.[128]

123 ECJ, judgment of 10 August 2017, *Openbaar Ministerie v. Sławomir Andrzej Zdziaszek*, C-271/17 PPU, ECLI:EU:C:2017:629 para. 95, referring to point 55 of the conclusion of Advocate General Bobek, ECLI:EU:C:2017:612.

124 The Court of Justice refers to, *inter alia*, ECtHR, judgment of 3 April 2012, *Boulois v. Luxembourg* [GC], ECLI:CE:ECHR:2012:0403JUD003757504, § 87.

125 ECJ, judgment of 22 December 2017, *Samet Ardic*, C-571/17 PPU, ECLI:EU:C:2017:1026, para. 76.

126 The Court of Justice refers to ECtHR, judgment of 15 December 2009, *Gurguchiani v. Spain*, ECLI:CE:ECHR:2009:1215JUD001601206, § 40, 47 and 48.

127 The Court of Justice refers to ECtHR, judgment of 9 October 2003, *Ezeh and Connors v. United Kingdom* [GC], ECLI:CE:ECHR:2003:1009JUD003966598.

128 ECJ, judgment of 10 August 2017, *Openbaar Ministerie v. Sławomir Andrzej Zdziaszek*, C-271/17 PPU, ECLI:EU:C:2017:629, paras. 75-77.

The decisions at issue in the *Ardic* case did not affect the nature or the *quantum* of the custodial sentences imposed by the final judgments of conviction. In the proceedings, the competent court only had to determine whether non-compliance with certain conditions attached to the suspension of the execution of those custodial sentences justified requiring the person concerned to serve, in part or in full, the custodial sentences originally imposed. In doing so, the competent court did not dispose of discretion with regard to the level or the nature of the original sentences, but only with regard to revoking the suspension or not. Therefore, the decisions at issue were not covered by Article 4a(1).[129]

When read together, the *Tupikas, Zdziaszek* and *Ardic* judgments seem to support the applicability of Article 4a(1) to a category of cases not specifically dealt with in those judgments: cases in which an *appeal* was directed *against the sentence only* and led to a *final* determination of the sentence by an authority which enjoyed a *margin of discretion* with regard to the level or the nature of the sentence. In such cases, it seems likely that Article 4a(1) applies to two decisions as well: the decision holding a final ruling on guilt and the final decision on appeal.

Although the Court of Justice's reasoning and the criterion it adopted are fairly clear, the Court of Justice muddied the waters, so to speak, by adding some remarks about the obligations of Member States. According to the Court of Justice, even though the decisions at issue are not covered by Article 4a(1), this does not absolve the Member States from their "obligation to respect the fundamental rights and fundamental legal principles enshrined in Article 6 TEU, including the right of defence of persons subject to criminal proceedings, nor of the obligation to ensure that those rights and principles are respected by their judicial authorities" with regard to such proceedings. In this respect, the Court of Justice also refers to the opinion of Advocate General M. Bobek, who points out that "all Member States are party to the ECHR and must effectively guarantee the respect of all the rights enshrined therein, irrespective of whether the proceedings in question relate to the execution of an EAW" and that, therefore, the obligation to respect the right to be heard is incumbent on the *issuing* Member State and "must be protected in connection with the implementation of domestic remedies and procedures".[130] Given the particular context of the *Ardic* case – involving decisions to revoke the suspension of the execution of a custodial sentence –, both the reference to Article 6 TUE and the reference to the ECHR are somewhat puzzling. As regards Article 6 TUE, the Court of Justice itself has repeatedly held that criminal procedures for the enforcement of a custodial sentence or a detention order lie *outside* the scope of FD 2002/584/JHA and Union law. Such procedures are, therefore,

129 ECJ, judgment of 10 August 2017, *Openbaar Ministerie v. Sławomir Andrzej Zdziaszek*, C-271/17 PPU, ECLI:EU:C:2017:629, paras. 78-82.

130 Opinion of 20 December 2017, *Samet Ardic*, C-571/17 PPU, ECLI:EU:C:2017:1013, paras. 76-77.

outside the scope of Article 6 TUE.[131] As regards the ECHR, the Court of Justice has also repeatedly held that, although such procedures lie outside the scope of FD 2002/584/JHA and Union law, Member States remain bound to observe the fundamental rights, laid down in, *inter alia*, the ECHR and their national law. But as the Court of Justice itself observed, Article 6 ECHR does not apply to a decision such as the one at issue in the *Ardic* case.

The Court of Justice further points out that the obligation to respect fundamental rights and fundamental legal principles *reinforces* the high level of trust that must exist between Member States and, as a result, the principle of mutual recognition, which is based on mutual trust between the Member States that their national legal systems are capable of providing protection of fundamental rights that is equivalent to and just as effective as the protection Union law provides. It concludes that in order to *foster* mutual trust, the issuing and executing judicial authorities "must make full use of the instruments provided for, in particular in Art. 8(1) and Art. 15 of [FD 2002/584/JHA]".

Perhaps the Court of Justice is only trying to say that one must trust that the issuing Member State complies with the obligation to respect fundamental rights and fundamental legal principles even with regard to decisions which are outside the scope of Article 4a(1); by demonstrating in the EAW – hence the reference to Article 8(1) – that this trust is justified also in this particular case – *e.g.* by mentioning that the person concerned can still exercise his/her right to be heard, as the German issuing judicial authority had done – the issuing judicial authority fosters mutual trust and, therefore, facilitates judicial cooperation on the basis of mutual recognition. For the rest, the obligation to respect the right to be heard in proceedings which do not come within the ambit of Article 4a(1) FD 2002/584/JHA is the *primary* responsibility of the issuing Member State. Therefore, it is up to the national law of that Member State to remedy a breach of that right. That, at least, seems to be the gist of Advocate General Bobek's opinion, to which the Court of Justice refers.

In any case, given the subsequent judgment in the *LM* case, it seems likely that a breach of the right to be heard in the issuing Member State could only lead to a refusal to execute the EAW, if such a breach could be qualified as a breach of the *essence* of the right to a fair trial.[132] Furthermore, it seems probable that the executing judicial authority could only examine the risk of such a breach after first having established that there is a real risk, on account of *systemic* or *generalised* deficiencies in the issuing Member State, of the essence of the fundamental right to a fair trial being compromised.[133]

131 ECJ, judgment of 30 May 2013, Jeremy *F. v. Premier ministre*, C-168/13 PPU, EU:C:2013:358, para. 48; ECJ, judgment of 25 July 2018, *Minister for Justice and Equality (Deficiencies in the system of justice)*, C-216/18 PPU, EU:C:2018:586, para. 57.

132 Cf. ECJ, judgment of 25 July 2018, *Minister for Justice and Equality (Deficiencies in the system of justice)*, C-216/18 PPU, EU:C:2018:586, para. 59.

133 Cf. ECJ, judgment of 25 July 2018, *Minister for Justice and Equality (Deficiencies in the system of justice)*, C-216/18 PPU, EU:C:2018:586, paras. 60, 61 and 68.

5.4.3.2 Application in Practice

5.4.3.2.1 Questions

The judgments in the *Zdziaszek* and *Ardic* cases raise a number of practical questions:

1. if the EAW refers to a later decision modifying the nature or the *quantum* of the penalty originally imposed, but contains no information on the basis of which the executing judicial authority can verify whether the conditions set out in *Zdziaszek* and *Ardic* judgments were met, what, if any, consequences should this have for the decision on the execution of the EAW;
2. if the EAW refers to a later decision which does not meet the conditions set out in those judgments, but contains no information on the basis of which the executing judicial authority can verify whether the fundamental rights of the person concerned were respected, what, if any, consequences should this have for the decision on the execution of the EAW;
3. if the EAW refers to a later decision which does not meet the conditions set out in those judgments, but does not provide information about the proceedings leading to that decision, and the executing judicial authority concludes that the fundamental rights of the person concerned were not respected, what, if any, consequences should this have for the decision on the execution of the EAW?

5.4.3.2.2 Opinions of the Experts

The answers of the experts hailing from Member States which have transposed Article 4a(1) as a *mandatory* ground for refusal more or less correspond. The Dutch, Hungarian and Irish experts advocate requesting supplementary information in reply to the first question.[134] The Hungarian and Irish experts give the same answer to the second question,[135] whereas the Dutch expert is of the opinion that – given the fundamental presumption that all Member States respect fundamental rights, which is capable of rebuttal only in exceptional circumstances – the executing judicial authority should rely on that presumption unless presented with evidence capable of rebutting it.[136] Both the Hungarian and the Irish experts are of the opinion that surrender should be refused in the circumstances of the third question,[137] whereas the Dutch expert is of the opinion that the *Ardic* judgment does not make it clear what the executing judicial authority should do when it concludes that the fundamental rights of the requested person were not respected and that the executing judicial authority probably should seek guidance from the Court of Justice.[138]

134 HU, report, p. 28; IE, report, p. 56; NL, report, p. 87.
135 HU, report, p. 28; IE, report, p. 56.
136 NL, report, p. 88.
137 HU, report, p. 29; IE, report, p. 56.
138 NL, report, p. 89.

With regard to the first question, the expert from Belgium points out that further information needs to be gathered in order to identify the Member States whose legal systems allow for a revision by a court of the *quantum* of the original penalty and allow their courts a certain discretion in that regard. Information about possible legal recourses against such decision is also necessary. This could prevent drawing conclusions based on insufficient or inadequate information. With respect to the second and third question, he is of the opinion that the *Ardic* judgment should not be read as allowing for an examination of respect for fundamental rights beyond the situations identified in *Aranyosi and Căldăraru*[139] (and subsequent judgments).[140]

The Polish expert relates the opinion of Polish judges who were interviewed that section (d) of the EAW should refer to the decision or the judgment which is to be executed after surrender and that, if information regarding such a decision is lacking, they would request supplementary information. In the circumstances of the third question, surrender should be refused, because Article 607p § 1 CCP provides that the execution of an EAW shall be denied if surrendering the person concerned would violate the human rights of the requested person.[141]

The Romanian expert describes a number of national proceedings which can result in amending the *quantum* of the original penalty but which in her opinion do not fall within the ambit of Article 4a(1).[142]

5.4.3.2.3 *Experiences of Executing Judicial Authorities*

In Belgium, no difficulties were reported, neither before nor after the *Zdziaszek* judgment. The *Ardic* judgment confirms earlier case-law of Belgian courts. No cases were reported in which the revocation decision changed the nature or the level of the originally imposed sentence.[143]

In Hungary, in the cases which were examined the executing judicial authority did not encounter any problems with regard to *Zdziaszek* and *Ardic* decisions.[144]

In Romania, likewise no problems were reported.[145]

139 ECJ, judgments of 5 April 2016, *Pál Aranyosi and Robert Căldăraru v. Generalstaatsanwaltschaft Bremen*, C-404/15 and C-659/15 PPU, EU:C:2016:198.
140 BE, report, pp. 35-37.
141 PL, report, pp. 71 and 72.
142 RO, report, pp. 36-37.
143 BE, report, pp. 45-46.
144 HU, report, p. 37.
145 RO, report, p. 43.

In Ireland, a decision to lift the suspension of a previously imposed sentence led to a preliminary reference to the Court of Justice,[146] which was withdrawn in the aftermath of the *Ardic* judgment.[147]

In the Netherlands, before the *Zdziaszek* judgment the executing judicial authority did not consider cumulative judgments as decisions coming within the ambit of Article 4a(1). Since that judgment, it is regularly confronted with EAWs concerning cumulative judgments such as at issue in the *Zdziaszek* judgment, but those EAWs rarely contain the necessary information about the original judgments of conviction. The Dutch executing judicial authority applies the *Zdziaszek* judgment by analogy to appeals which *only* concern the sentence imposed at first instance. Consequently, in such cases it will check whether both the first instance proceedings (with respect to the final finding of guilt) and the appeal proceedings (with respect to the final determination of the sentence) meet the requirements of Article 4a(1).[148] With regard to a Latvian decision to partially substitute a penalty of community service with a custodial sentence, after requesting supplementary information it turned out that the competent authority did not enjoy a margin of discretion concerning the level or the nature of that latter penalty. The same conclusion was drawn with regard to a Latvian decision to merge penalties into a new penalty. Before the judgment in the *Ardic* case, the Dutch executing judicial authority excluded decisions to revoke the suspension of the execution of a previously imposed penalty from the scope of Article 4a(1). Since that judgment, those decisions do not pose any problems, as they do not modify the nature or the *quantum* of that penalty.[149]

In Poland, in two out of the five cases in which an executing judicial authority refused to execute an EAW, the reason for refusal was that the proceedings in which the original non-custodial penalty was converted into the penalty of imprisonment were conducted *in absentia*. The person concerned was not informed about the decision. No promise of a retrial was provided by the issuing judicial authorities. In a third case, the EAW concerned a suspended penalty of imprisonment. The proceedings which resulted in the suspension being revoked were conducted *in absentia*. In all three cases supplementary information was requested from the issuing judicial authorities concerning these proceedings.[150]

---

146 In the *Lipinski* case, C-191/18 (*KN v. Minister for Justice and Equality*).

147 ECJ, order of 26 October 2018, *KN v. Minister for Justice and Equality*, C-191/18, ECLI:EU:C:2018:884.

148 The appeal proceedings in the *Tupikas* case turned out to be an appeal against a sentence: District Court of Amsterdam, judgment of 30 August 2017, ECLI:NL:RBAMS:2017:6273. Advocate General Bobek also seems to be of the opinion that an appeal does not necessarily has to deal with *both* a finding of guilt *and* an imposition of a sentence: opinion of 26 July 2017, *Openbaar Ministerie v. Tadas Tupikas*, C-270/17 PPU, ECLI:EU:C:2017:609, paras. 59 and 65 ("the question of guilt *or* the question of the penalty") (emphasis added).

149 NL, report, pp. 117-118.

150 PL, report, p. 85 in combination with p. 71.

5.4.3.2.4 *Experiences of Issuing Judicial Authorities*

In Belgium, so far the issuing judicial authorities have not reported any difficulties with decision such as those at issue in the *Zdziaszek* and *Ardic* judgments. Currently, national legislation does not provide for proceedings resulting in a cumulative judgment. The necessary legislation allowing for such proceedings has not entered into force and, in the light of upcoming legislation, that entry into force has become uncertain.[151]

In Hungary, Ireland and Romania no problems were reported.[152]

In the Netherlands, proceedings resulting in a cumulative judgment are not provided for. For the rest, the issuing judicial authority did not encounter any difficulties.[153]

In Poland, after the *Zdziaszek* judgment the issuing judicial authorities were confronted with requests for supplementary information with regard to cumulative judgments and requests to fill in section (d) with reference to cumulative judgments. One such request concerned the right to a retrial after surrender. Surrender was refused, after it was explained that Article 540b CCP provides for an optional ground for re-opening of the proceedings and does, therefore, not offer a right to a retrial. Other requests concerned the way the person concerned was summoned to the hearing which led to the cumulative judgment. At least two requests also concerned proceedings resulting in the execution of a suspended penalty.[154]

5.5 Multiple Decisions

Closely related to the issues discussed in the previous sections is the issue of EAWs which mention multiple decisions in section (b) of the EAW.

According to Article 8(1)(c) FD 2002/584/JHA, the EAW shall contain "evidence of an enforceable judgment, an arrest warrant or any other enforceable judicial decision having the same effect". Enforceability is decisive in determining the time from which an EAW may be issued.[155] Article 8(1)(c) corresponds to section (b) of the EAW-form ("Decision on which the warrant is based"). Point 1 of section (b) concerns enforceable domestic arrest warrants or other judicial decisions having the same effect and point 2 of section (b) concerns enforceable judgments.

Article 4a(1) FD 2002/584/JHA, on the other hand, refers to 'the decision'. This provision corresponds to section (d) of the EAW-form ("Indicate if the person appeared in person

151 BE, report, p. 46.

152 HU, report, p. 37; IE, report, p. 91; RO, report, p. 44.

153 NL, report, p. 119.

154 PL, report, p. 85.

155 ECJ, judgment of 10 August 2017, C-270/17 PPU, *Openbaar Ministerie v. Tadas Tupikas*, ECLI:EU:C:2017:628, para. 71.

at the trial resulting in the decision"). This 'decision' is the judicial decision which finally sentenced the person whose surrender is sought in connection with the execution of an EAW.[156]

The enforceable judgment or decision referred to in Article 8(1)(c) is not necessarily the decision which finally sentenced the requested person referred to in Article 4a(1), although these decisions may in some cases coincide, depending on the national procedural rules of the issuing Member State (see also Section 5.2).[157]

EAWs which mention multiple decisions in section (b)(2) of the EAW, but fail to mention to which of these decisions section (d) of the EAW-form applies, raise the question what, if any, consequences this should have for the decision on the execution of the EAW.

Most experts point to the possibility of requesting supplementary information (Article 15(2) FD 2002/584/JHA).[158] The Belgian expert adds that whether supplementary information will be requested depends, *inter alia*, on the (clarity of the) information included in the EAW and the discussions during the surrender proceedings.[159] The Polish expert relates that the Polish judges who were interviewed in the course of this project pointed out that the ground for refusal is an *optional* one. In accordance with the principle of mutual recognition and mutual trust, these judges will assume that the right to a fair trial was respected in the issuing Member State. However, in case of any doubts it is possible to ask for supplementary information on this issue. Additionally, during the surrender proceedings the court may ask the requested person whether s/he was aware of the proceedings referred to in section (b) of the EAW.[160]

As regards the experiences of *executing* judicial authorities, in Hungary and Romania the issue of multiple decisions did not present itself in the cases which were examined in the course of this project.[161]

In Belgium, the executing judicial authorities will presume that section (d) of the EAW relates to the first instance proceedings, if multiple decisions are mentioned in section (b) (*e.g.* first instance judgment, judgment on appeal, judgment in cassation). If the EAW mentions a decision in section (b)1 and a judgment in section (b)2, the executing judicial authority will consider the latter as the basis of the EAW. Should there be any discussion on this issue, the executing judicial authority will request supplementary information.[162]

---

156 ECJ, judgment of 10 August 2017, C-270/17 PPU, *Openbaar Ministerie v. Tadas Tupikas*, ECLI:EU:C:2017:628, para. 74.
157 ECJ, judgment of 10 August 2017, C-270/17 PPU, *Openbaar Ministerie v. Tadas Tupikas*, ECLI:EU:C:2017:628, paras. 71 and 76.
158 HU, report, p. 18; IE, report, p. 46; NL, report, p. 63; RO, report, p. 25.
159 BE, report, p. 22.
160 PL, report, p. 57.
161 HU, report, p. 33; RO, report, p. 40.
162 BE, report, p. 40.

In Ireland, the Netherlands and Poland, the issue of multiple decisions has arisen and has caused problems, in some cases eventually leading to a refusal to execute the EAW.

In Ireland, one of the problems concerned an EAW with regard to a 'non-conclusive' conviction while appeal proceedings were pending; because the person concerned would be regarded as a convicted person under Irish law, and because the issuing judicial authority would not guarantee a retrial, the Irish executing judicial authority refused to surrender the person concerned.[163]

In the Netherlands, problems were encountered with, *e.g.*, a Croatian EAW which mentioned the existence of a judgment and a decision in section (b) of the EAW, whereas point 3.4 of section (d) of the EAW referred to 'the decision'. The public prosecutor requested supplementary information and it turned out that point 3.4 applied to the judgment only. Another example concerns a Romanian EAW which mentioned two 'sentences'. From the answers to a request for supplementary information it emerged that the 'criminal sentence' mentioned in section (b)2 was a decision to revoke the conditional suspension of the execution of a custodial sentence, which was imposed by the other 'criminal sentence' mentioned elsewhere in the EAW. The 'criminal sentence' mentioned in section (d) was the decision to revoke the conditional suspension of execution.[164]

In Poland, the judges who were interviewed sometimes had to request supplementary information concerning cumulative judgments, *viz.* which judgment would be subjected to execution after surrender.[165] In a number of cases, surrender was refused because the successive proceedings in which a non-custodial sentence was converted into a penalty of imprisonment were conducted *in absentia.*[166]

As regards the experiences of *issuing* judicial authorities, in Hungary, Ireland and the Netherlands no cases were reported in which those authorities were confronted with problems arising from multiple decisions.[167] In the Netherlands, in case of multiple decisions the issuing judicial authority will clearly indicate this and will clearly distinguish between these decisions.[168] The issuing judicial authorities of the other Member States have reported problems with EAWs referring to multiple decisions.

In Belgium, in some cases in which the EAW was issued by the Belgian public prosecutor at the sentence enforcement court (*strafuitvoeringsrechtbank*), supplementary information was requested about the functioning and the jurisdiction of that court (see Section 5.4.2.2).[169]

---

163 IE, report, pp. 63-65.

164 NL, report, pp. 99 and 100.

165 PL, report, p. 77. Apparently, the Polish executing judicial authorities are of the opinion that section (d) of the EAW only concerns the judgment which is to be enforced in the issuing Member State after surrender (however, see Section 5.2).

166 PL, report, p. 77 in combination with p. 71.

167 HU, report, p. 33; IE, report, p. 65; NL, report, p. 101.

168 NL, report, p. 101.

169 BE, report, p. 40 in conjunction with p. 45.

In Romania, in some cases additional information was requested, including information on the Romanian legal system. In most cases, the decision of the foreign executing judicial authority was positive.[170]

In Poland, analysis of the EAWs issued by two issuing judicial authorities demonstrates difficulties regarding cumulative judgments. The EAWs issued by the Lublin Regional Court only referred to the cumulative judgment, resulting in a request for supplementary information concerning the judgments replaced by the cumulative judgment in three out of six cases. The other issuing judicial authority, the Warsaw Regional Court, referred to cumulative judgments in three different ways: (1) section (d) of one EAW only referred to the cumulative judgment; (2) section (d) of some EAWs referred to all judgments (the cumulative judgment *and* the judgments replaced by the former judgment) and (3) section (d) of some EAWs only referred to the cumulative judgment but provided additional explanations under point 4 with reference to the proceedings in which the replaced judgments were rendered. In three out of eight cases, the executing judicial authorities requested supplementary information. The requested information concerned the presence of the requested person in the proceedings resulting in the judgments which were replaced by the cumulative judgment and the reasons for the cumulative judgment (upon a motion of the person concerned or *ex officio*). The Polish judges who were interviewed added that in some cases the foreign executing judicial authority questioned the fairness of the proceedings in which the penalties were imposed which were later replaced by the cumulative judgment and refused the execution of the EAW with regard to these penalties, even though under Polish law the only penalty which may be executed is the cumulative penalty and not the previously imposed penalties which were merged into the cumulative penalty.[171] Further to this point, in some cases the foreign executing judicial authority wanted to know whether the information in section (d) of the EAW referred to the cumulative judgment or to the judgments which were replaced by the former judgment.[172]

5.6 Conclusion

What conclusions, if any, can be drawn from the preceding sections?

---

170 RO, report, p. 40.

171 PL, report, pp. 77-78. It may well be that according to Polish law the only penalty which may be executed is the cumulative penalty and not the previously imposed penalties which were merged into the cumulative penalty, but according to *Union* law the proceedings leading to the previously imposed penalties are also relevant under Art. 4a(1).

172 PL, report, p. 78.

Let us first look at the issues concerning *proceedings and decisions within one instance* (Section 5.3). The issue of consensual proceedings appears unproblematic. The executing judicial authorities of only two Member States have had any dealings with such proceedings. Both have ruled that Article 4a(1) is applicable to such proceedings. Those experts who have voiced an opinion on this subject agree. None of the issuing judicial authorities have reported any difficulties with this issue.

In practice, the second issue – imposition of a penalty without having held a trial or by a non-judicial authority – is equally unproblematic. Only the executing judicial authorities of two Member States have encountered EAWs concerning penalties imposed without having held a trial. They were of the opinion that Article 4a(1) applied, which is also the position of most experts who voiced an opinion on this issue. None of the issuing judicial authorities have reported any difficulties with this issue. A penalty imposed by an authority other than a court or a judge – *e.g.* by an administrative authority – cannot in itself lead to the issuing of an EAW, since each EAW must be based on a domestic *judicial* decision.

The third issue – presence at the pronouncement of the judgment only – *appears* to be somewhat more problematic. The experts agree that the mere presence of the person concerned at the pronouncement of the judgment is not enough to preclude the applicability of Article 4a(1). However, difficulties were reported by the Dutch executing judicial authority. Nevertheless, its assumption that Polish issuing judicial authorities – sometimes – interpret the words 'trial resulting in the decision' as 'the hearing at which the judgment was pronounced' was not confirmed by the analysis of Polish case files. It turns out that (non-)appearance at the hearing at which the judgment was pronounced is not actually decisive for classifying the proceedings as *in absentia* proceedings.

The fourth issue – presence at some but not all of the hearings – presents a real challenge. The impact of this issue on the day-to-day practice of judicial authorities seems to be relatively minor. Only the Dutch executing judicial authority and two Polish issuing judicial authorities have reported difficulties with this issue. However, given that the concept of a 'trial resulting in the decision' is an autonomous concept of Union law which must be uniformly interpreted, it is worrisome that – in the context of a trial consisting of several hearings – this concept is not interpreted uniformly by the experts nor by the executing and issuing judicial authorities. The respective positions fall into three different positions. To preclude the application of Article 4a(1): (1) the person concerned must have been present at every hearing, (2) it suffices that the person concerned was present at least at one hearing and (3) the person concerned must have been present at the hearing(s) at which the merits of the case were examined. In view of such divergence of opinion, until such time as the Court of Justice has clarified this issue, all that issuing judicial authorities can do to minimise potential problems is to describe in a clear, concise and factual way which hearings were held, whether the person concerned was present and what was done at those hearings.

Interestingly, with regard to the third and fourth issues some of the experts' opinions and the practice of some judicial authorities seem to correspond to the answer given in that part of the Questionnaire which is dedicated to *national criminal procedural law*. In other words, the interpretation of Union law concepts by those experts and judicial authorities seems to be governed by the meaning of national law concepts. The Belgian expert, *e.g.*, referred explicitly to national law concerning the issue of presence at some but not all of the hearings. In essence, his opinion on this issue corresponds to the answer given to question 5.[173] Of course, just because a national interpretation of a Union law concept corresponds to the meaning of a national law concept does not mean that this interpretation is incorrect. But equally, it does not mean that this interpretation is correct. Ultimately, the Court of Justice decides what the correct interpretation of an autonomous Union law concept is. Both issuing and executing judicial authorities should be aware of this and should be wary of assigning national law meanings to Union law concepts.

Let us now turn to *successive proceedings and decisions* (Section 5.4). Concerning appeal proceedings, both the executing and issuing judicial authorities of a number of Member States encountered difficulties with EAWs concerning appeal proceedings. All experts agree that these difficulties can be solved by requesting and providing supplementary information (if need be). It must be stressed that the EAW should contain information about the nature and outcome of successive proceedings. Again, providing a description in the EAW of each of the successive proceedings and decisions in a clear, concise and factual way could go a long way in preventing any misunderstandings, requests for supplementary information and, ultimately, refusals to execute the EAW. Unfortunately, section (d) of the EAW-form is not tailored to the description of more than one procedural instance and decision. Amending section (d) of the EAW-template in order to accommodate the description of successive proceedings and decisions should receive serious consideration.

The focus of some issuing and executing judicial authorities on *first* instance proceedings is disconcerting. This focus does not seem to be in accordance with the *Tupikas* judgment. According to that judgment, only the proceedings leading to the *last* decision are relevant under Article 4a(1), provided that the court made a final ruling on the guilt of the person concerned and imposed a sentence, following a review, in fact and in law, of the merits of the case. That last decision need not be the first instance judgment, but might well be the judgment on appeal. A possible cause for the focus on first instance proceedings might be that issuing and executing judicial authorities do not distinguish between the enforceable judgment and the final conviction (see Section 5.2). This supposition is confirmed by the opinion of Polish judges that section (d) of the EAW refers to the decision or the judgment

173 BE, report, pp. 9 and 24-25.

which is to be executed after surrender (see Section 5.4.3.2). Again, in the *Tupikas* judgment the Court of Justice held that the final decision might coincide with the enforceable decision or judgment, but that it is up to the national laws of the Member States to regulate whether the final decision actually is the enforceable decision or judgment. Union law determines which decision is the final decision and national law determines which decision is the enforceable decision. The 'decision or the judgment which is to be executed after surrender' is indeed the enforceable decision to which Article 8(1)(c) FD 2002/584/JHA and section (b) refer. However, which of the successive decisions to which Article 4a(1) and section (d) refer, will be determined by applying the *Tupikas* criterion. In offering practical instructions to issuing and executing judicial authorities, the distinction between enforceable decisions and final decisions should be stressed.

The issuing and executing judicial authorities of some Member States reported difficulties with EAWs concerning proceedings resulting in the modification of the nature or the level of a previously imposed penalty, in some cases even leading to a refusal to execute the EAW. Of course, these difficulties could be solved by requesting and providing clear, concise and factual information about those proceedings, but it is much better to provide such information in the EAW from the get-go. Another way to help facilitate judicial cooperation information is to gather and to spread information about the Member States who provide for such proceedings and under which conditions (*e.g.* do the competent authorities have a margin of discretion with regard to the nature or the level of the penalty; which legal recourse is open against the decision), as the Belgian expert pointed out. A simple way of doing this might be to disperse a questionnaire regarding such proceedings through Eurojust. As with appeal proceedings, the wording and structure of section (d) of the EAW-template are not really helpful in steering both issuing and executing judicial authority in the right direction – all the more reason for contemplating an amendment to section (d) of the EAW-template.

In the context of cumulative judgments, the focus of some issuing judicial authorities on the penalty which under national law is to be enforced after surrender is troubling. Again, a failure to distinguish between enforceable decisions and final decisions may lead to results contrary to the Court of Justice's case-law. The problem here is that, potentially, two sets of proceedings must comply with the requirements of Article 4a(1): not only the proceedings leading to the final determination of the sentence, but also the previous proceedings leading to the final decision on guilt. By focussing on the enforceable decision, one runs the risk of losing sight of the other decisions.

Lastly, let us look at the issue of multiple decisions. The issuing and executing judicial authorities of some Member States have reported difficulties with this issue, in some cases even resulting in a refusal to execute the EAW. As with the previous issues, difficulties can be resolved by providing clear, concise and factual information, but prevention is always better than cure: such information should already be contained in the EAW. Again, as with the previous issues, section (d) of the EAW provides insufficient guidance to issuing and executing judicial authorities.

Bringing all the different strands together, it is safe to conclude on the basis of this chapter that there is a great need:

1. for amending the wording and structure of section (d) of the EAW-form;
2. for improving – and keeping up to date – the knowledge of issuing and executing judicial authorities of the relevant case-law of the Court of Justice on Article 4a(1) (especially with respect to the distinction between enforceable decisions and final decisions) and
3. for ensuring that issuing judicial authorities describe the proceedings which led to the decisions to which Article 4a(1) is applicable in a clear, concise and factual way.

6 Summons; Mandated Legal Counsellor; Right to a Retrial: Decision Already Served

6.1 Introduction

All questions of *in absentia*, summoning, representation by legal counsel and legal recourses must be understood in the context in which they are placed by Framework Decision 2009/299 and that is that they give an answer to the question *whether* the executing judicial authority that has received an EAW *may* refuse the execution of the EAW in the situation that the accused did not appear in person at the trial (Article 4a(1)). This means that Framework Decision 2009/299 confirms the message of the mother-FD 2002/584 that in principle an executing Member State must comply with the EAW issued by the issuing Member State. In a cooperation system between the Member States of the European Union based on mutual recognition, refusals are the exception to the rule of surrender. The general rule stemming from Article 1(2) of the framework decision is the requirement for Member States to execute the EAW "on the basis of the principle of mutual recognition and in accordance with the provisions of this Framework Decision".

Advocate General Bobek stated *the logic of Article 4a(1)* as follows:

> Article 4a(1) introduced the possibility of refusing to execute an EAW where the person concerned did not appear in person at the trial which resulted in the decision. That possibility of not executing an EAW must be based on an examination by the executing judicial authority of the circumstances of each specific case. The possibility of non-execution ceases when the executing judicial authority establishes that a particular case is covered by one of the situations listed in Article 4a(1)(a) to (d) of the Framework Decision. In such a scenario, a refusal to execute the EAW is excluded and the requirement to surrender the person concerned becomes the rule once again.[1]

1 Opinion of Advocate General Bobek of 26 July 2017, *Openbaar Ministerie v. Tadas Tupikas*, C-270/17 PPU, ECLI:EU:C:2017:628, paras. 72-74. See also ECJ, judgment of 24 May 2016, *Openbaar Ministerie v. Paweł Dworzecki*, C-108/16 PPU, ECLI:EU:C:2016:346, paras. 34 and 35.

As the Court has stated several times, this means that grounds for refusals must be interpreted restrictively. Framework Decision 2009/299 sets the normative standard for the assessment of whether the situation at hand is such an exceptional situation that the executing Member State must make use of its competence to refuse. In that sense the framework decision harmonises this ground for refusal to a certain extent, but not completely. As we will see, not every element of the notions encompassed in Framework Decision 2009/299 has led to a completely common understanding, as some elements are ambiguous or lead to confusion in practice as to their meaning. As a consequence, Member States give their own interpretations, which may lead to frictions and misunderstandings.

Advocate General Bobek used strong words when describing the meaning of Article 1 FD:

> It should be recalled that, according to Article 1 of Framework Decision 2009/299, the *prohibition* on convictions in absentia pursues the objective of safeguarding the effectiveness of the rights of defence of the person concerned.[2]

However, the Court has not ruled out trials in the absence of the accused completely, but merely stated that the right to be present is not absolute.[3] In other words, there may be exceptions to the rule that the accused is present.

6.2 Summons

6.2.1 *Introduction*

The summons is the document by which the accused is informed that a criminal proceeding will be conducted against him/her.

The first remarkable thing is that the Framework Decision does not *define* what a summons is. Although the framework decision does not say so, implicitly it presumes that it concerns a document in writing.

However, in Article 4a(1)(a)(i) and in recital (9) of the preamble, the framework decision stipulates what *information* should be in the document. The summons should inform the accused:

2 Opinion of Advocate General Bobek of 26 July 2017, *Openbaar Ministerie v. Tadas Tupikas*, C-270/17 PPU, ECLI:EU:C:2016:333, para. 58 (emphasis added).

3 ECJ, judgment of 24 May 2016, *Openbaar Ministerie v. Paweł Dworzecki*, C-108/16 PPU, ECLI:EU:C:2016:346, para. 42.

- of the scheduled date and place of the trial;[4] and
- that a decision may be handed down if s/he does not appear.[5]

The framework decision does not stipulate anything in relation to whether the accused can read and can understand the language in which the document is written. Apparently the system is built on the presumption that written documents are the best method to convey the message about the upcoming trial. The shape or *form* in which the summons may take place is by and large traditional and is in writing. Romania also provides for e-mail, SMS or telephone.[6]

The underlying presumption of using a written form is that every human being is able to read and write and that no accused is illiterate. This will not be so in all cases. In addition, the framework decision does not state anything on whether the accused, who may be able to read as such, also understands the legal or formal language used. Concerning the language used, Article 3 of Directive 2010/64 on Interpretation and Translation stipulates that an indictment must be translated. Although there is no case-law on this yet, it seems reasonable to understand the notion of an 'indictment' as to encompass not only information on the charge, but also information on when and where the trial against the accused will be held.

The framework decision does not hide what the *purpose* of summoning an accused is. It is all about enabling the presence of the accused (preamble, recitals (1), (7) and (8)) as a means to facilitate him/her using the rights of the defence, not to deal with other specific rights. Or in the words of Advocate General Bobek,

> The purpose of Article 4a is not to incorporate all the procedural guarantees of Article 6 of the ECHR (or, by analogy, the potentially more extensive guarantees of Articles 47 and 48 of the Charter) as factors capable of justifying the refusal to execute an EAW. Article 4a exclusively covers the guarantees relating to the right to appear in person at the trial.[7]

While it is absolutely clear that the drafters of the framework decision regard a trial in the presence of the accused as the preferred situation, an accused should not be allowed to hold up the trial by deliberately refraining from being present at the trial. In other words,

4 General awareness of a proceeding is not enough, see Opinion of Advocate General Bobek of 11 May 2016, *Openbaar Ministerie v. Paweł Dworzecki*, C-108/16 PPU, ECLI:EU:C:2016:346, para. 74. The EU offers a higher level of protection than under the ECHR.

5 The FD does not oblige to inform the accused that s/he may have him/herself represented.

6 RO, report, p. 6; PL, report, pp. 9-10: Poland allows for communications other than in writing in urgent cases; HU, report, p. 5.

7 Opinion of Advocate General Bobek of 20 December 2017, *Samet Ardic*, C-571/17 PPU, ECLI:EU:C:2016:346, para. 58.

the ideal trial is a trial in the presence of the accused. When the accused choses to stay away from it, it will not prevent that justice is done. The accused has not been given the actual power to obstruct. Member States are free to provide for trials *in absentia*, but are not under an obligation to do so. If they do provide for *in absentia* trials, they are subject to the rules stipulated in the framework decision.[8] This also carries the notion that it is a choice, not an obligation, for the accused to be there. This purpose of summoning, to inform the accused about the choice that s/he must make, is further strengthened by other notions in the framework decision, such as that it is "unequivocally established that he was aware of the scheduled trial". The implicit presumption is that awareness must lead to action on behalf of the accused if s/he does not want the trial to continue with him/her being there. The elements stated earlier about the information that should be contained in the summons leads to the conclusion that the decision of the accused should be an informed decision. In other words, after having been provided with all the relevant information (including information about the potential consequences of a waiver), the accused may waive his/her right to be present. The waiver, as such, does not need to be explicit.

The contextual purpose of providing the accused with the possibility to defend him/herself with all necessary means is further safeguarded by inclusion of a *temporal element* with regard to providing him/her with the relevant information. This is expressed in the framework decision by the wording: 'in due time'. The function of providing the accused with information about the upcoming trial has two main functions (recital (7) of the preamble). The first is its relation to the right to have adequate time to prepare the defence. A fair trial is only possible, when the accused had sufficient time to prepare. Member States have objectified this by stipulating a specific number of days that must elapse between handing over the summons to the accused and the trial. The second function more prominently relates to the right to be present. Because s/he has been informed with sufficient time ahead of the trial, s/he can make a thorough decision on whether s/he wishes to be there or not. Alternatively, whether s/he wishes defence counsel to represent him/her or not. The wording of recital (7) of the preamble seems to imply that the temporal notion is relevant for all alternative ways of informing the accused. Article 4a(1)(a) seems to limit this to the situation of 4a(1)(a) only.

What exactly is 'in due time' as mentioned in Article 4a(1)(a)? According to recital (7) of the preamble, 'in due time' means "sufficiently in time to allow [the person concerned] to participate in the trial and to effectively exercise his or her right of defence". The Polish report explicitly mentions that the Polish legislator did not transpose into national law the

8 Formally the FD of course does not oblige Member States to change anything, as the FD only deals with the question whether under the circumstances given, a Member State may refuse an EAW. In practice, and also in line with Directive 2016/343, adopted later, FD 2009/299 has an *indirect* harmonizing effect, as Member States must live up to the requirements of the Directive as interpreted by the Court anyway. See also Sections 3.5 and 4.1.

notion of 'in due time' as mentioned in Article 4a(1)(a).[9] Other Member States have transposed this notion and have interpreted it in much the same way as recital (7), *viz.* as the reasonable time the accused would need to prepare for and be present at the trial.[10]

However, with regard to *national criminal procedural law* most Member States have formalised the notion of 'due time' in a very specific way and have set a number of days.[11] On top of the formal criterion, the Belgian report introduces a more substantive element and relates it to the Directive that harmonises the Member States' legislation on the right to be present. It states

> See consideration 36 of Directive 2016/343: 'in due time' means leave sufficient time 'to enable him or her to become aware of the trial'. The definition of 'in due time' should however refer to more than just becoming aware of the trial.

Becoming aware of the trial should be interpreted in a broad sense, *i.e.* including disposing of sufficient time. In light of that interpretation, Member States that prescribe a fixed number of days should be aware that a fixed number of days may not in all circumstances comply with the 'due time' requirement. Therefore, depending on the circumstances, what is acceptable as *due time* may be longer in some cases than the number of days provided for in the national legislation. It is very likely that the time frame in which a summons must be delivered to the accused before trial was determined on the basis of the presumption that the accused would be within the country. In our day and age, and in view of increased free movement of EU-nationals throughout the EU, many accused find themselves outside the country. That requires more time to do the same: contact a lawyer and discuss what to do and travel to the Member State in which the trial will be conducted.[12]

---

9 PL, report, p. 62. See also Sections 2.2.2 and 3.6.

10 RO, report, p. 29; HU, report, p. 21; BE, report, p. 26.

11 HU, report, p. 21 has formalised that to at least eight days; BE, report, p. 26 and NL, report, p. 13 to 10 days; PL, report, p. 62.

12 In support of this conclusion, one could refer to Art. 7(3) of the European Convention on Mutual Assistance in Criminal Matters (ECMACM). According to this provision, a Party may declare that when it is requested by another Party to serve a foreign 'writ' on its territory – such as a summons –, that 'writ' should reach it at a given time before the date set for appearance. The purpose of this provision is to "enable the requested Party to transmit the writ in good time to the accused so that he may prepare his defence and travel to the place where he is due to appear" (*Explanatory Report to the European Convention on Mutual Assistance in Criminal Matters*, p. 8). However, the relevance of such declarations and such time frames is to a large extent superseded by Art. 5 of the Convention, established by the Council in accordance with Art. 34 of the Treaty on European Union, on Mutual Assistance in Criminal Matters between the Member States of the European Union (*OJ* 2000 C-197, p. 3). In principle, this provision allows for sending of procedural documents *directly by post, i.e.* without any intervention of the authorities of the Member State in whose territory the addressee resides. Art. 7(3) ECMACM is only applicable to situations in which the intervention of that Member State is requested in serving the procedural document to the addressee. The EU convention has been ratified by all but three Member States (France, Greece and Luxembourg).

Section (d) of the EAW-form does not contain an – explicit – reference to the concept of 'in due time'. However, point 3.1a of section (d) (summons in person) requires that the date at which the summons was served is filled in and point 3.1b of section (d) (actual official notification) requires an explanation 'how the relevant condition was met' (point 4 of section (d)). Both requirements present an opportunity for the issuing judicial authority to demonstrate that and for the executing judicial authority to check whether the person concerned was summoned or notified 'in due time'.

The framework decision is silent on the *consequences of the summons* except for the explicit reference that the summons should carry the information that a decision may be handed down without him/her being present. This must be regarded as a permission from the Union legislator for the national criminal justice system to allow for proceedings to be held without the accused being present. This is the only explicit consequence the framework decision refers to. An implicit one is that receiving the summons obliges the accused to take action if s/he does not want the case to continue without him/her. The inclusion of the words 'in due time' has an impact on the accused as well. If s/he receives the summons in compliance with the temporal rules, s/he subsequently must also act within the time limits set by the national system.

Compliance with the national procedures on summoning the accused is a precondition for the opening of the trial. Meaning that if the formal rules on summoning have been applied, the trial can start or continue without the accused being there (with some exceptions).[13] With the exception of Ireland, a failure of the accused to appear is not an impediment to start the trial. It is on this point that the major difference exists between Ireland and the other five project Member States. Under Irish law, the commencement of a trial is conditional on the presence of the accused. The trial cannot commence if the accused is not present. For the other five, commencement is conditional on his/her presence or on the compliance with the national formalities on summoning him/her. By allowing for the latter, these Member States have definitively fewer incentives to realise the presence of the accused. To realise the presence of the accused may be rather difficult, whereas it will be very easy to comply with at least one of the wide variety of formal procedures that allow the trial to start without the accused being present.

6.2.2 *Various Forms of Summoning*

6.2.2.1 **Summons in Person**

It is absolutely clear that the Union legislator considers the *summons in person* as the preferred transmission of the summons (Article 4a(1)(a)(i)/point 3.1a of section (d) of the

13 For some of these exceptions see PL, report, pp. 19-21.

EAW-form).[14] However, here also, the framework decision does not define what a summons in person is. Looking at the alternatives to a summons in person, which we will discuss below, these are subject to a qualitative standard and that is that the alternative to a summons in person must be able to meet the high standard of "unequivocally establishing that the accused was aware of the scheduled trial". From this, it may be deduced that, by definition, the summons in person itself complies with that standard. The Court has determined that it constitutes an autonomous concept of EU law and must be interpreted uniformly throughout the European Union.[15] Its meaning cannot be left to the discretion of the Member States. The Framework Decision does not stipulate anything on the evidence capable of proving the *in person* character. While they agree on the fact that 'in person' is the best way of summoning, Member States already differ on the question of what it exactly means. The Belgium report states for instance:

> Handing over a summons/document to a member of the family living under the same roof as the defendant or an employee or servant present at the time of service is not a personal service.[16]

This may not be the same for all other Member States. In Ireland, summonses are not commonly used in indictable cases. Typically, the person is charged in a police station on a charge sheet, rather than by being summonsed, and then is either brought immediately before a court, or is remanded on police bail to appear before a court on a specific date of which he/she is informed in person in the police station. However, if a summons is used in such cases actual personal service is required.[17]

---

14 Opinion of Advocate General Bobek of 11 May 2016, *Openbaar Ministerie v. Paweł Dworzecki*, C-108/16 PPU, ECLI:EU:C:2016:333, paras. 56 and 57: "the person concerned must have been summoned in person and have thus been informed of the scheduled date and place of the trial. As is apparent from the wording of Article 4a(1) of the Framework Decision, the subject of the summons in person is without question the person concerned. Thus, the fact that the determination of the procedural methods of the summons is a matter for the Member States does not suffice for the concept of 'summons in person' to be interpreted as resting on a fiction, namely that notification to a person other than the person concerned might be deemed to be a summons in person."

15 ECJ, judgment of 24 May 2016, *Openbaar Ministerie v. Paweł Dworzecki*, C-108/16 PPU, ECLI:EU:C:2016:346, para. 32. In the case of Sliczynski, the Irish Supreme Court in considering how the Irish EAW Act had transposed Art. 5(1) of FD 2002/584/JHA concluded that the word 'notified' in that article did not bear an autonomous meaning in EU law, and therefore that it had to interpret the transposing provision in accordance with the rules of statutory interpretation applicable to Irish statutes. However, the interpretation the Supreme Court arrived at accorded exactly with that subsequently afforded by the Court in *Dworzecki:* IE, report, p. 9.

16 BE, report, p. 6.

17 However, summonses are commonly used in summary cases and service by delivery of the document to the accused's usual or last known place of abode, or place of business within the state, either by hand delivery or by pre-paid registered post or other means of recorded delivery is permitted by statute and will in general suffice: IE report, pp. 4-6. In the event that delivery is disputed then proof of personal service in

The importance of the summons cannot be underestimated: respect for the rights of the accused and, in case of non-appearance, respect for the formal rules of summoning mean that the trial can go on and a verdict can be reached. There is a presumption that an accused has voluntarily waived his/her right to be present, once the formal rules of summoning have been followed.[18] However, there is not a single Member State (except for Poland) that explicitly raises that question, nor is there a single Member State (except for Poland) that informs the accused that if s/he does not appear, the proceedings may be continued in his/her absence and may result in an enforceable decision against him/her.[19]

The rules on summonses and especially their non-personal alternatives are constructed in such a way that a non-responsive accused cannot stop the process from going on. That as such is fine and could be kept. However, it is over the top, once you allow for the continuation of cases in which it is absolutely clear that the accused cannot possibly have had any knowledge of the trial. The systems do not require a positive indication that the accused is aware of the trial, as they have formalised the requirements and do not look into the material facts. This may be different when it comes to positive indications as to the fact that the accused does not wish to be tried in his/her presence. In addition to formalisations, the law of the Netherlands also recognises an informal direct indication from the accused: "a circumstance has otherwise occurred from which it follows that the defendant apparently does not wish to be tried in his presence" (Art. 590(3) CPC). This clearly indicates that the intentions of the legislator were very much efficiency-driven (nothing can stop a Dutch criminal trial) and not principle-oriented.

What to do if the whereabouts of the accused cannot be established? In Poland, Article 22 of the CCP stipulates that if the whereabouts of the accused cannot be established, the criminal proceedings shall be suspended.[20]

6.2.2.2 Summons by Other Means

This second best option of transmitting the summons to the accused also has not been defined (Art. 4a(1)(a)(i)/point 3.1b of section (d) of the EAW-form/recital (7) of the

---

the *Sliczynski* and *Dworzecki* sense, *i.e.*, that the accused received actual notification, would be required: IE, report, p. 9.

18 There is an interesting exception to this general presumption under Dutch law when it comes to the right to lodge an appeal. The defendant must lodge an appeal within 14 days after a circumstance has occurred from which it follows that the judgment is known to the defendant (Art. 408(2) CPC). This is a material criterion that prevails over the formal presumed knowledge of the accused.

19 In Poland the accused is informed about the content of Art. 376 and 377 of the CCP (containing the conditions for conducting the hearing in his absence even if his presence is mandatory). The obligation to inform the accused stems from Art. 353 § 4 of the CCP. Both provisions (Art. 376 and 377 of the CCP) state that the court may conduct the hearing without the presence of the accused. Thus, the accused is informed of this eventuality.

20 PL, report, p. 18.

preamble). As with the notion of a 'summons in person', the Court has ruled that the notion of a 'summons by other means' constitutes an autonomous concept of EU law, which must be interpreted uniformly throughout the European Union. The meaning of that concept cannot be left to the discretion of the Member States.[21]

The Union legislator has stipulated two standards with which the *summons by other means* must comply. The first relates to the result that it must achieve. The result is that it must be "unequivocally established that the accused was aware of the scheduled trial", or in the words of Advocate General Bobek: "an unambiguous factual result is required".[22] In this regard, Article 4a(1) seems more stringent than Article 6 ECHR. If the summons was delivered at the address given by the defendant to a family member of the defendant and if the defendant has never stated that he is no longer in contact with that family member, according to the ECtHR it is not unreasonable to *infer* that the defendant was aware of the proceedings against him.[23]

How a Member State can realise the standard of unequivocally established awareness has not been stipulated other than by the instruction on the informative elements that must also be adopted in the summons. Similarly as the summons in person, the summons by other means must inform the accused:

- of the scheduled date and place of the trial; and
- that a decision may be handed down if s/he does not appear.

Like the summons in person, the summons by other means is subject to the temporal requirement that it must be served in due time. The Framework Decision does not stipulate what evidence may prove that the accused received the summons *by other means*. One may read from the wording "unequivocally established that the accused was aware of the scheduled trial", that undisputable evidence must be provided. It is apparent that applying the formalities prescribed under national law may not lead to an understanding of an

21 ECJ, judgment of 24 May 2016, *Openbaar Ministerie v. Paweł Dworzecki*, C-108/16 PPU, ECLI:EU:C:2016:346, para. 32.

22 Opinion of Advocate General Bobek of 11 May 2016, *Openbaar Ministerie v. Paweł Dworzecki*, C-108/16 PPU, ECLI:EU:C:2016:333, para. 61.

23 See ECtHR, decision of 6 March 2018, *Nicolae Popa v. Romania*, ECLI:CE:ECHR:2018:0306DEC005524212, § 73; ECtHR, judgment of 2 February 2017, *Ait Abbou v. France*, ECLI:CE:ECHR:2017:0202JUD004492113, § 63-65. It should be stressed that Art. 6(1) ECHR does not confer on the defendant the right to obtain a *specific* form of service of court documents. However, in the interests of the administration of justice, that provision does require that the defendant should be notified of a court hearing in such a way as to not only have knowledge of the date, time and place of the hearing, but also to have enough time to prepare his or her case and to attend the court hearing: ECtHR, judgment of 28 November 2018, *Vyacheslav Korchagin v. Russia*, ECLI:CE:ECHR:2018:0828JUD001230716, § 65.

implied waiver.[24] To the contrary, when it was not possible to summon the accused in person, "an enhanced level of diligence is required of the national courts."[25]

How does the summons by other means take place in practice? Member States hold quite different views on what to do when they are unable to deliver the summons directly to the addressee.[26] When delivering the summons in person is unsuccessful, Member States may choose to opt for alternatives: indirect or substitute service.[27] Member States accept under a wide variety of conditions that other persons receive the summons on behalf of the accused. For instance:

- other persons living at the formal address[28]
- an address indicated by the accused[29]
- an employer's address[30]
- a police station or other state authority[31]
- the address of the chosen legal counsellor[32]
- leaving a notice at the door[33]
- leaving a notice at the door where to collect the summons[34]
- public announcement (including on a website)[35]
- report about the impossibility to deliver[36]

24 Although the Framework Decision does not use the word waiver, it is not ruled out. However, a waiver must be made explicit if the summons was not in person and cannot be deduced from the mere observance of the national rules on summoning the accused. Opinion of Advocate General Bobek of 11 May 2016, *Openbaar Ministerie v. Paweł Dworzecki*, C-108/16 PPU, ECLI:EU:C:2016:333, para. 68.

25 Opinion of Advocate General Bobek of 11 May 2016, *Openbaar Ministerie v. Paweł Dworzecki*, C-108/16 PPU, ECLI:EU:C:2016:333, para. 70.

26 In addition, Belgium and the Netherlands differ between two kinds of notifications: *kennisgevingen* and *betekeningen*. The latter requires to be handed over by a government official, the former does not.

27 PL, report, pp. 6-9.

28 RO, report, p. 7; PL, report, pp. 6-7; the accused is obliged to inform the court of a change of address; if s/he fails to do so, the presumption is that s/he received the summons at his/her old address; HU, report, p. 6; NL, report, p. 10.

29 RO, report, p. 6; PL, report, p. 7; HU, report, p. 5; NL, report, p. 14.

30 RO, report, p. 6; PL, report, pp. 8-9.

31 PL, report, p. 8.

32 RO, report, p. 6; PL, report, p. 10.

33 RO, report, p. 6; PL, report, p. 8; NL, report, p. 10.

34 PL, report, p. 8. Poland has become stricter since 2015: "It should be underlined once again that currently a summons concerning the first date of the hearing shall be served directly on a defendant. In the case of substitute service, a summons is deemed to have been served properly only if it is collected from the postal office by the defendant in person or not collected at all (such correspondence is deemed to have been served properly – Article 133 §2 of the CCP). With reference to the subsequent dates of the hearing (not the first one) all ways of service of a summons, as presented in part I of this chapter, may be applied.": PL, report, p. 17.

35 HU, report, p. 5.

36 RO, report, p. 7; HU, report, p. 6.

Under Polish legislation, not collecting a summons after a notice was put in the letterbox or presented in another visible way twice is regarded as a waiver of the right to be present (Article 133 § 2 of the CCP).[37] This is an interpretation based on absence of direct information from the accused. Article 136 § 1 of the CCP provides that a document is deemed to have been served if the addressee refuses to accept correspondence.[38] Pursuant to Article 139 § 1 of the CCP if the accused changes his/her place of residence without informing the court of the new address or does not reside at the address indicated by him/her, any correspondence sent to the original address is deemed to have been served. From 1 July 2015 the change of the place of residence caused by deprivation of liberty (*e.g.* detention on remand) is considered as voluntary. Thus, the accused is henceforth obliged to inform the court about such change of residence. The Polish report mentions that indirect service via an adult member of the household does not give certainty about the receipt by the accused.[39] The adult member may fail to deliver it to him/her. It is reported that information from the accused that s/he will not be present is extremely rare.[40]

Below the report for the Netherlands is quoted as it explains very well the ambiguities that may arise from different understandings of what a summons in person is or whether it is a summons by other means:

> Delivery of the summons or of the written notice to appear to the defendant *in person* undoubtedly constitutes a 'personal summons' in the sense of Art. 4a(1)(a)(i) FD 2002/584/JHA, because in such cases it is 'ensured that the person concerned has himself received the summons and, accordingly, has been informed of the date and place of his trial'. Delivery of the summons or of the written notice to appear to a person *authorised by the defendant* does not constitute a 'personal summons' in the sense of Art. 4a(1)(a)(i) FD 2002/584/JHA. It is not excluded that such a delivery of the summons constitutes service 'by other means' as a result of which the defendant has 'actually received official information of the scheduled date and place of that trial in such a manner that it is unequivocally established that he or she is aware of the scheduled trial' in the sense of Art. 4a(1)(a)(i) FD 2002/584/JHA, but in order to qualify as such a service it must be *unequivocally established* that the person authorised by the defendant *actually* passed the summons on to the person concerned and when s/he did so. The record of delivery as referred to in Art. 589 CPC will not indicate if and when this condition was met (see the answer to question 2a)

37 PL, report, p. 12. In practice, however, the notice is left in the letterbox.
38 PL, report, p. 48.
39 PL, report, p. 12.
40 PL, report, pp. 16-17.

> under J). One could argue that, if a defendant expressly authorises a third person in writing to collect a summons for him/her, it is not an unreasonable inference that this third party will pass the summons on to the defendant. However, it is questionable whether a reasonable inference is sufficient to unequivocally establish that the defendant actually received the summons. At any rate, a reasonable inference does not answer the question *when* the defendant actually received the summons. The answer to that question is relevant for determining whether the defendant was informed in due time of the date and the place of the trial (Art. 4a(1)(a)(ii) FD 2002/584/JHA). In conclusion, delivery of the summons to a person authorised in writing by the defendant does not *in and of itself* equate to service 'by other means' as referred to in Art. 4a(1)(a)(i) FD 2002/584/JHA. However, the case file may contain evidence that the person authorised by the defendant did indeed pass the summons on to the defendant and when s/he did so, *e.g.*, if the defendant requests in writing an adjournment of the hearing, stating that s/he has received the summons but is unable to attend the hearing.
> All other methods of delivery of the summons or of the written notice to appear do not constitute a 'personal summons' as referred to in Art. 4a(1)(a)(i) FD 2002/584/JHA, neither do they constitute, in and of itself, service 'by other means'. Again, the case file may contain evidence that the defendant actually received the summons or the written notice to appear and when s/he did so.[41]

This raises the question of how to bring *Dworzecki* in line with *Covaci*. The latter judgment allows, albeit in the context of the service of a penalty order, that a Member State may make

> it mandatory for an accused person not residing in that Member State to appoint a person authorised to accept service of a penalty order concerning him/her, provided that that accused person does in fact have the benefit of the whole of the prescribed period for lodging an objection against that order.[42]

It seems fair to assume that this period must be long enough for counsel and accused to contact each other and to discuss how to proceed. The interpretation that the period for lodging an objection only starts running when the accused *actually* received the penalty order not only seems reasonable, but would also align *Covaci* with *Dworzecki*.

41 NL, report, pp. 18-19, footnotes omitted.
42 ECJ, judgment of 15 October 2015, *Criminal proceedings against Gavril Covaci*, C-216/14, ECLI:EU:C:2015:586, para. 68.

6.2.3 *The Place Where the Summons Must Be Served*

6.2.3.1 Introduction

The Framework Decision does not make any distinction as to the place where the accused resides. It does not apply different standards depending on whether the accused was within the country or abroad, whether s/he was in detention or at freedom. That as such is logical in view of the fact that the rights of the defence and the right to a fair trial exist independent of these kind of factors. All accused, whether detained or not, whether abroad or not, are entitled to the same defence rights and the right to a fair trial.

6.2.3.2 Summons Abroad

The Framework Decision does not mention the possibility that the accused could find him/herself abroad already at the moment that the trial is about to start and that s/he must be summoned. As a consequence of the absence of any specific rule in the Framework Decision, the regular national rules on summons to be effected abroad apply. Before dealing with that, it is worth mentioning that the absence of any rules in the Framework Decision on summoning abroad in the context of EAWs for absent accused must be considered to be remarkable. Especially the fact that the accused is abroad before the actual start of the trial is a circumstance that at a later stage may very well contribute to a decision handed down in his/her absence. One might have expected the Framework Decision to deal with the specific situation of summoning an accused elsewhere in the EU. We will return to this issue when mentioning the recommendations.[43] There is another reason why it is rather strange that Member States distinguish between summonses within and outside the country, because the right at stake (the right to be present) does not distinguish between accused who are in the country and accused who are abroad nor between accused who are

43 It is recommended that the FD be amended as to provide for an obligation to assist each other in cases that the accused is abroad. Member States should then be obliged, on request of the state in which the trial will start, to personally hand over the summons to an accused residing on their territory. This will have a preventive effect and reduce the number of problematic cases. Art. 10 of the ECMACM provides for a specific invitation for witnesses, which might be remodeled to apply for accused:

"1. If the requesting Party considers the personal appearance of a witness or expert before its judicial authorities especially necessary, it shall so mention in its request for service of the summons and the requested Party shall invite the witness or expert to appear.
The requested Party shall inform the requesting Party of the reply of the witness or expert.

2. In the case provided for under para. 1 of this article the request or the summons shall indicate the approximate allowances payable and the travelling and subsistence expenses refundable.

3. If a specific request is made, the requested Party may grant the witness or expert an advance. The amount of the advance shall be endorsed on the summons and shall be refunded by the requesting Party."

detained and accused who are at liberty.[44] From an EU point of view, one may even question whether Member States are not obliged to treat all residences within the EU as equal to national residences, otherwise this could amount to discrimination.

While Member States of course cannot send their officials to an accused residing abroad, there is no positive evidence that they have attempted to bring such an accused in the same position as an accused living in their own state, in respect of informing him/her of the upcoming trial and making use of his/her rights of defence. To the contrary, Member States apply presumptions from which they deduce a waiver. For instance under Polish law, the accused residing abroad is obliged to inform the authorities of an address in Poland to which all correspondence will be sent. If s/he fails to do so, the correspondence sent to the last known address in Poland or – if such an address is not available – the correspondence attached to the case file will be deemed to be served properly.[45] Romania forces the accused residing abroad to arrange an address in Romania for further communication.[46] Such presumptions enhance the chances that an accused will not hear in a timely fashion that a case has been started against him/her.

All Member States provide for the transmission of the summons in compliance with the rules applicable to international cooperation in criminal matters with the specific Member State. The national reports state very little on the various requirements, but it is clear that the rules applicable on summoning abroad differ from Member State to Member State, depending on the specific bilateral relationship. Article 52 of the Convention implementing the Schengen Agreement (CISA)[47] allows Member States to send procedural documents directly by post. In this manner, the CISA opens an avenue of formal summoning without any knowledge about whether:

- the letter reached the address indicated;
- the address was (still) correct;
- the accused has received it;
- the accused is still alive;
- the accused has read and understood the summons.

44 The ECtHR held in the case of Hokkeling that the detention of the accused abroad does not rob him of his right to be present at the trial, see ECtHR, judgment of 14 February 2017, *Hokkeling v. the Netherlands*, ECLI:CE:ECHR:2017:0214JUD003074912.

45 PL, report, pp. 12-13.

46 RO, report, p. 6.

47 In essence, Art. 5 of the Convention, established by the Council in accordance with Art. 34 of the Treaty on European Union, on Mutual Assistance in criminal matters between the Member States of the European Union does the same thing. Not all Member States have ratified this convention.

6.2.4 *Evidence of Service*

Some Member States, but not all, provide for the requirement that evidence of the service of the summons shall be produced. This may be provided by a written report by the state official serving the document.[48] It may also be a return receipt signed by the accused or any other person to whom it may be delivered.[49] Most Member States report that a statement by the requested person or a document or record signed by the requested person suffices as proof that s/he received the summons in person.[50] Some Member States report that the statement of a third party in itself is not enough, when the requested person disputes that statement.[51] However, apparently there is the experience in Belgium, that in some cases the executing judicial authority questions the statement of a third party.

In this context, the Irish report mentions that

> it happens relatively frequently that a requested person will seek to dispute the fact of what has been certified at 3.1a, or 3.1b (...), as the case may be; and it is a respondent's legal entitlement to raise such an issue. The Irish High Court, as executing judicial authority approaches such disputes on the basis that, having regard to the principle of mutual recognition, it must accept without question that which is certified by the issuing judicial authority unless the respondent has adduced cogent evidence to the contrary, sufficient to put the executing judicial authority on enquiry. The court will refuse to embark on any such enquiry on the basis of a requested person's mere assertion that what is certified is incorrect. To trigger an enquiry the assertion must be backed up by evidence, and the evidence must reach a threshold level of cogency such that it raises a real concern in the mind of the executing judicial authority about the possibility of there having been some genuine error or mistake. In that regard, the requested person is said to bear an evidential burden.[52]

The Irish position seems to be in line with the Court's case-law: when ensuring that the conditions of Article 4a(1)(a) are met, 'it may also rely on other evidence', *i.e.* evidence other than the evidence indicated in the EAW, "including circumstances of which it became aware when hearing the person concerned".[53]

---

48 RO, report, pp. 29-30.

49 HU, report, p. 22.

50 BE, report, pp. 26-27; HU, report, p. 22; IE, report, p. 50; NL, report, p. 73; PL, report, p. 63.

51 HU; IE; NL.

52 IE, report, p. 69.

53 ECJ, judgment of 24 May 2016, *Openbaar Ministerie v. Paweł Dworzecki*, C-108/16 PPU, ECLI:EU:C:2016:346, para. 49.

The Irish example relates to a dilemma for the executing Member State: to what extent does the obligation deriving from mutual recognition that the issuing Member State should be believed that what it states is correct, prevail over respect for the human rights of the accused/requested person? As this does not concern an absolute human right, there does not seem to be a reason not to give priority to mutual trust and recognition.

6.2.5 *Remedies for Non-compliance*

Most Member States apply the rule that non-compliance with the procedure for summoning can be remedied by the appearance of the accused[54] at the trial or by representation by a chosen[55] or *ex officio* defence counsel.[56] This must be regarded as in line with the case-law of the Court. From the fact that the Court in *Tupikas* regards the last trial as *the trial resulting in the decision* for the purposes of Article 4a(1)(a)(i) in a situation in which the accused was not present at the first instance, but was present at the second instance, it can be deduced that a potential problem with the summons in first instance may be remedied by the appearance of the accused in the second instance.[57] This leads to the important conclusion that Member States providing for criminal proceedings in which the merits of the case may be assessed in two instances have two chances to summon the accused in an appropriate manner. The Court stated it as follows:

> where the issuing Member State has provided for a criminal procedure involving several degrees of jurisdiction which may thus give rise to successive judicial decisions, at least one of which has been handed down in absentia, the concept of 'trial resulting in the decision', within the meaning of Art. 4a(1) of the Framework Decision, must be interpreted as relating only to the instance at the end of which the decision is handed down which finally rules on the guilt of the person concerned and imposes a penalty on him, such as a custodial sentence, following a re-examination, in fact and in law, of the merits of the case.[58]

---

54 RO, report, p. 7.
55 RO, report, p. 7.
56 RO, report, p. 7.
57 ECJ, judgment of 10 August 2017, *Openbaar Ministerie v. Tadas Tupikas*, C-270/17 PPU, ECLI:EU:C:2017:628, paras. 81 and 85.
58 ECJ, judgment of 10 August 2017, *Openbaar Ministerie v. Tadas Tupikas*, C-270/17 PPU, ECLI:EU:C:2017:628, para. 98.

One may debate whether the Court would allow a trial without a summons in a case that the accused was obliged to stay within the country and left in breach of that obligation. This idea emerges from the case of *Ardic*, in which it held:

> it is precisely the fact that the person concerned left the German territory, in breach of an express condition of the grant of suspension, which made it impossible for the competent German authorities to notify him personally of the information relating to the introduction of proceedings seeking revocation of the suspension previously granted and, consequently, the adoption in his absence of the revocation decisions at issue in the main proceedings.[59]

However, in the case of *Hokkeling*, the accused left the Netherlands while his criminal proceedings were still pending before the Court of Appeal. Subsequently, he was arrested in Norway on suspicion of a new offence and was unable to be present in the Netherlands. The Dutch Court of Appeal proceeded with the trial in spite of repeated requests to adjourn the hearing in order for Hokkeling to be present, as there was no legal possibility to transfer him (temporarily) to the Netherlands to be present at the trial. The ECtHR found a violation of the right to be present as Hokkeling did not intend to waive his right to be present and his absence when the merits of the case were decided in the last instance could not be compensated by his presence at the first instance and the active defence of his counsel at the second.[60] It is of note, that, at present, there is no EU legislation providing for the (temporary) transfer of a defendant who is detained abroad to another Member State in order to participate in the trial[61] nor is there a legal basis in EU law for participating in the trial from abroad via video link technology (see also Section 4.2.4).

6.2.6 *Overall Notions Applicable to All Varieties of Summonses*

There are two all-encompassing notions to be distinguished that apply to all varieties of summonses. It is national law that governs the rules on summoning. This becomes clear from the wording of Article 4a(1) "in accordance with further procedural requirements

---

59 ECJ, judgment of 22 December 2017, *Samet Ardic*, C-571/17 PPU, ECLI:EU:C:2017:1026, para. 84. The Court's reasoning is in line with the Strasbourg Court's case-law. *See, e.g.*, ECtHR, decision of 4 December 2018, *Năstase v. Republic of Moldova*, ECLI:CE:ECHR:2018:1204DEC007444411.

60 ECtHR, judgment of 14 February 2017, *Hokkeling v. the Netherlands*, ECLI:CE:ECHR:2017:0214 JUD003074912.

61 Art. 9 of the Convention established by the Council in accordance with Art. 34 of the Treaty on European Union, on Mutual Assistance in Criminal Matters between the Member States of the European Union (*OJ* 2000, L 194, p. 3) only provides for temporary transfer of a person held in custody for the purpose of *investigation.*

defined in the national law of the issuing Member State." The second is that "when considering whether the way in which the information is provided is sufficient to ensure the person's awareness of the trial, particular attention could, where appropriate, also be paid to the diligence exercised by the person concerned in order to receive information addressed to him or her" (recital (8) of the preamble).[62] The first notion once again strengthens the message that the Framework Decision does not harmonise the rules on summoning. It remains fully within the competence of the Member States to regulate those rules. The second notion is that the law may provide for certain obligations for the accused to enable the authorities to get into touch with him/her. In other words, an accused who has carefully informed the authorities about his/her places of residence is entitled to different treatment than the accused who used every trick in the book to disappear from the radar.

6.2.7 *The Practice of the Project Member States*

Some Member States make a distinction between first and subsequent summonses. Whereas the first summons is safeguarded with the highest standards available in the national legal system, this is different in some Member States for subsequent summonses and notifications once the trial has started. However, it is not explicitly provided for that the first summons must have reached the accused before allowing for different standards to summon him/her once the trial has started. This is not the case in Ireland where the same rules apply to service of all documents in the course of proceedings. In indictable matters, actual personal service of subsequent documents will usually be effected lest there be any issue as to the adequacy of service. At any rate, it must be capable of being established that the accused received actual notification.[63] In Belgium, in principle there is no difference between the first and subsequent summonses. Only if the court decides that 'notification' of the subsequent hearing suffices – Belgian law distinguishes between summonses and notifications –, will the defendant be notified of the date of the next hearing. A notification can only be issued if the defendant or his legal counsellor was present at the hearing at which the trial was adjourned.

All Member States strive for realising the first summons to be served 'in person', meaning that the individual who is the addressee receives the summons him/herself, either at home or in prison. However, they also consider various other ways than the delivery in the hands of the accused as a delivery *in person*.[64] Member States tend to be far less strict

62 See also ECJ, judgment of 24 May 2016, *Openbaar Ministerie v. Paweł Dworzecki*, C-108/16 PPU, ECLI:EU:C:2016:346, para. 51.

63 IE, report, pp. 3-6 and 19.

64 See especially Poland: PL, report, p. 12. In Poland, only 'substitute service' (leaving a notification in the closest postal office twice for 7 days) is treated as having equal consequences as personal service.

when there is evidence that the defendant at least has knowledge about a trial. Under Romanian law, *e.g.*, the accused will not be summoned to the next hearing when he was present in person or represented by a chosen legal counsellor, unless the accused specifically asks the court to formally issue a summons (*e.g.* in order to be used as a justification with regard to his/her employer). Again in Romania, if the accused has applied – orally or in writing – for the proceedings to take place in his/her absence, the accused will not be summoned to the next hearing. All project Member States provide that the summons for an accused for a next hearing can be delivered orally.[65] The date of the next hearing is announced in court and is recorded in the official record of the hearing. In the Netherlands, if the defendant is not present or if the court adjourns *sine die*, the defendant will be summoned to the next hearing. The latter is also the case in Belgium.

Not respecting the formalities of the rules on the summons is not problematic when it appears by other means that the accused did have knowledge.

6.2.8 Consequences of State Practice for Filling in the Form

National laws of some Member State operate with *formal* understanding of summonses in person or with *legal presumptions* (BE, HU, NL, PL, RO). Such formal understandings/legal presumptions raise the question whether the summons is served in such a way that it is unequivocally established that the defendant actually received it. These formal understandings of summonses raise serious doubts as to whether they are in compliance with the Court of Justice's case-law (in particular, since the *Dworzecki* case) and cause problems with executing EAWs.

National rules on service of summonses seem to shape the way issuing judicial authorities interpret Article 4a(1) and section (d) of the EAW-form. Because in some Member States service of the summons on an adult member of the household of the defendant who undertakes to hand over the summons to the defendant constitutes a valid way of summoning a defendant, issuing judicial authorities of these Member States tick point 3.1b of section (d) of the EAW-form, indicating that s/he was served *by other means.*[66]

It is apparent that Member States' authorities occasionally mix the factual description of what actually happened with a legal-qualitative approach of summoning when filling in the form. In other words, they tick the box of 'summoned in person' when what factually happened could *under their national legal system* be qualified as a summons in person. However, this may not be in line with the interpretation the Court has given to the provi-

65 *See, e.g.*, RO, report, p. 6; HU, report, p. 5.

66 *See, e.g., Minister for Justice and Equality v. Iacobuta* [2019] IEHC 250 (20 March 2019), para. 112, with regard to service on relatives of the person concerned and to public service (notification on the door of the Town Council building).

sions of the Framework Decision. This practice raises the urgent question of how to interpret the terminology used in the Framework Decision and the EAW-form. Are the terms used in the context of the Framework Decision and the Form to be regarded as of an autonomous European nature or can they be further interpreted in a national manner? From *Dworzecki* it follows that the notion of a 'summons in person' and the notion of a 'summons by other means' are of an autonomous European character and cannot be replaced by anything else (see also Section 3.5).

6.3 Mandated Legal Counsellor

6.3.1 *Introduction*

As a second best option to the summons in person or the summons by other means, the Framework Decision provides for the possibility that the accused was not present him/herself, but represented by a mandated legal counsellor at the trial. Most Member States (BE, HU, NL, PL, RO) allow for defence/representation of an absent defendant by a legal counsellor; Ireland only does so exceptionally.[67]

Representation by a mandated legal counsellor should not lead to a refusal of the EAW. The triggering precondition is that the accused, "being aware of the scheduled trial" (Article 4a(1)(b)/recital (10) of the preamble/point 3.2 of section (d) of the EAW-form) has given a mandate to a legal counsellor, either appointed by him/herself or assigned to him/her by the state.

6.3.2 *Awareness of the Scheduled Trial*

Article 4a(1)(b) FD 2002/584/JHA concerns situations in which the defendant "must be deemed to have waived, voluntarily and unambiguously, his right to be present at his trial",[68] which requires that the defendant had sufficient awareness of the proceedings and the charges against him (see also Section 8.2). The case-law of the ECtHR confirms that in cases in which the defendant had no knowledge of the proceedings against him/her and was defended in his/her absence by a legal counsellor who was not appointed by him/herself, there can be no voluntary waiver of the right to be present at the trial.[69]

67 IE, report, pp. 15-17. In general a trial will not proceed in the absence of the accused.

68 ECJ, judgment of 25 February 2013, *Stefano Melloni v. Ministerio Fiscal*, C-399/11, ECLI:EU:C:2013:107, para. 52.

69 *See, e.g.*, ECtHR, judgment of 1 March 2006, *Sejdovic v. Italy* [GC], ECLI:CE:ECHR:2006:0301JUD005658100, § 101. See also ECtHR, judgment of 21 July 2009, *Seliwiak v. Poland*, ECLI:CE:ECHR:2009:0721JUD

The Framework Decision does not define *awareness* of the scheduled trial. The standard of awareness to be applicable here seems to be more general than required when the summons is served in person. In the latter situation, the accused must have specific knowledge of the date and place of the trial. In the former, general awareness is enough,[70] in the sense that the accused is more or less aware that a trial might be pending or coming up against him/her, but s/he does not know the exact dates and location of the hearings. The other possible explanation is that specific awareness is required; knowledge of the concrete date, time and place of the hearing.[71]

In some Member States,[72] there is a legal presumption that an absent defendant who is defended/represented by a legal counsellor is aware of the proceedings/scheduled trial.[73] In one Member State (IE) the defendant will always have knowledge of the proceedings; in another Member State (PL), the defendant will always be informed about the appointment of an *ex officio* legal counsellor, but such an appointment does not release the authorities from their obligation to summon the defendant to the trial; in yet another Member State (HU) there is no need to inform the defendant of the proceedings/scheduled trial. One Member State requires actual knowledge of the date/place of the trial (RO), for others awareness or a reasonable expectation of an impending trial suffices (HU, NL, PL; IE: *Sliczynski* (awareness of the actual date of the trial))[74] or *Fiszer* (awareness of anticipated/intended trial).[75] Belgium requires that the defendant be informed of the date and the place of the hearing.

000381804, § 63: the applicant was not aware of the appointment of a new *ex officio* legal counsellor; the ECtHR held: "The Court further observes that in the present case the applicant was ultimately not represented before the appellate court by the lawyer who had represented him before the trial court, but by a new one. In the absence of any communication between the new legal-aid lawyer and the applicant, who was deprived of the possibility of instructing the lawyer, the mere fact that the lawyer prepared the appeal and attended the hearing was not sufficient, in the Court's view, to ensure that the proceedings complied with the requirements of fairness". Compare ECtHR, judgment of 31 October 2013, *Janyr v. Czech Republic*, ECLI:CE:ECHR:2013:1031JUD004293708, § 71: "La Cour relève en outre que le requérant n'est à aucun moment resté sans représentant devant les juridictions tchèques, qu'il a été au courant de la désignation de Me F. [son avocat d'office] et de ses coordonnées (voir, *a contrario*, *Seliwiak c. Pologne*, no 3818/04, § 60, 21 juillet 2009) et qu'il n'a pas refusé ses services (voir *a contrario*, *Sakhnovski c. Russie* [GC], no 21272/03, § 91, 2 novembre 2010). (...)".

70 HU, report, p. 23.

71 RO, report, p. 31.

72 BE, report, pp. 9-10; NL, report, p. 24. RO has specifically mentioned that this is the case only with regard to a *chosen* legal counsel. It may be expected that this is similar for other Member States.

73 Compare ECtHR, judgment of 10 May 2011, *Shkalla v. Albania*, ECLI:CE:ECHR:2011:0510JUD002686605, § 72: "The fact that the applicant was defended on appeal by a counsel appointed by his father does not mean that he had prior effective knowledge of the proceedings against him. The domestic courts did not examine this question at all and the Government did not submit any proof to the contrary".

74 *Minister for Justice Equality and Law Reform v. Sliczynski* [2008] IESC 73 (19 December 2008).

75 *Minister for Justice & Equality v. Fiszer* [2015] IEHC 664 (27 October 2015).

The Framework Decision does not indicate at which moment the accused must have become aware of the scheduled trial.

Belgian law interestingly presumes an awareness of the convicted person, once an *ex officio* legal counsellor lodges an appeal; the understanding is that the defendant knows about the hearing.[76] Under Hungarian law there is no need to inform the defendant of the proceedings/scheduled trial, if s/he has waived the right to be present.[77] The examples of awareness in this section seem to amount to a formal deduction based on the rules on how to formally summon the accused and do not necessarily mean that the accused actually is aware of the scheduled trial.

The Framework Decision is ambiguous on what the starting point of the acceptance of the mandate of legal counsellor is. On the one hand, it is obvious that awareness is the key to mandating a legal counsellor. On the other hand, the Framework Decision also explicitly provides for assigning the accused *ex officio* counsel. The latter may be appointed without the accused being aware of the fact that a trial is about to start.

6.3.3 *Function of the Mandated Legal Counsellor*

The *function* of the mandated legal counsellor is to represent the absent defendant. Article 4a(1)(b) introduces a qualitative condition: "and was indeed defended". Some Member States have introduced specific rules. For instance Hungary has stipulated that the presence of defence counsel in *in absentia* proceedings is obligatory.[78] Under Polish law, counsel may not replace the accused when the presence of the accused has been declared mandatory.[79]

6.3.4 *Mandate*

Pursuant to recital (10) of the preamble to FD 2009/299/JHA, it is understood that the person concerned "should deliberately have chosen to be represented by a legal counsellor instead of appearing in person at the trial". Next to a cognitive element ('being aware of the scheduled trial'), Article 4a(1)(b) therefore also requires a volitional element: the accused must have chosen to be represented in his absence.

Furthermore, Article 4a(1)(b) requires that the person concerned had given a 'mandate' to the legal counsellor. What is *the meaning* of a mandate? The Framework Decision does not define the concept of a 'mandate'. According to the traditional canons of interpretation,

76 BE, report, p. 28.
77 HU, report, p. 8.
78 HU, report, p. 8.
79 PL, report, p. 30.

that concept is an autonomous concept of Union law.[80] This interpretation is supported by recital (10) of the preamble to FD 2009/299/JHA, which *only* refers to the "appointment of the legal counsellor and related issues" as matters belonging to *national* law. The legislative history of Article 4a(1) shows that this reference does not concern the meaning of the notion of a 'mandate' itself.[81]

It is of note that recital (10) of the preamble to FD 2009/299/JHA speaks of a person who was defended at the trial by a legal counsellor to whom he or she had given a mandate to do so and then adds the words "ensuring that legal assistance is practical and effective", thus indicating a causal connection between defence by a mandated legal counsellor on the one hand and the practicality and effectiveness of that defence on the other.[82] Put negatively, without a mandate given by the defendant, it is not ensured that legal assistance by the legal counsellor is practical and effective.

The expression 'had given a mandate to a legal counsellor' presupposes at least some form of contact between the accused and his/her legal counsellor about acting on behalf of the accused. This interpretation is confirmed by the legislative history of Article 4a(1)(b). Some Member States advocated deleting the reference to a 'mandate', but the reference was retained, precisely because otherwise a person could be considered to have been defended by a legal counsellor, even though s/he had not deliberately decided to be defended by a legal counsellor and had not had any contact with the legal counsellor. Moreover, it was felt that deleting the reference would mean that the requirements of Article 6 ECHR would no longer be met.[83] The case-law of the ECtHR demonstrates that the absence of awareness of the appointment of an *ex officio* legal counsellor and of any contact with the legal counsellor is indeed problematic under Article 6 ECHR (see Section 6.3.2).

Hungary, Poland and Romania distinguish between *ex officio* and *chosen lawyers*. For the chosen legal counsellor there is the obligation to present a power of attorney, signed by the client.[84] The *ex officio* legal counsellor will be appointed by the court. This means that the court knows that s/he has been given a mandate. Hungary does not require a mandate for the *ex officio* legal counsellor or any contact with the accused; it is sufficient for the defendant to be aware of the appointment and the contact details of the legal counsellor. The court informs the defendant and the *ex officio* legal counsellor about each

80 Art. 4a(1)(b) of FD 2002/584/JHA does not refer to the law of the Member States for the purpose of determining the meaning and the scope of the notion of a 'mandate'. Cf. ECJ, judgment of 24 May 2016, *Openbaar Ministerie v. Paweł Dworzecki*, C-108/16 PPU, ECLI:EU:C:2016:346, paras. 28-30; ECJ, judgment of 10 August 2017, *Openbaar Ministerie v. Tadas Tupikas*, ECLI:EU:C:2017:628, paras. 65-67.

81 Council document 8074/08, 8 April 2008, p. 7.

82 Compare the French language version: "(...) a été défendue au procès par un conseil juridique, auquel elle a donné mandat à cet effet, **afin que l'assistance juridique soit concrète et effective**. (...)".

83 Council document 8074/08, 8 April 2008, pp. 5-7.

84 HU, report, p. 23.

other's contact details in the order appointing the *ex officio* legal counsellor.[85] In Romania, it is the duty of the *ex officio* legal counsellor to try to contact the defendant and to report his or her efforts to the court. In cases in which the *ex officio* legal counsellor could not establish contact with his/her client, s/he cannot be considered to have been given a mandate by his/her client. In case of an *ex officio* legal counsellor, the hearing may only be continued in his/her presence. If a defendant in Poland requests an *ex officio* legal counsellor and if the court appoints one, the court will inform both the defendant (of the name and address of the *ex officio* legal counsellor) and the *ex officio* legal counsellor (of the name and address of the defendant). The same procedure applies in cases of mandatory defence.[86] In all six project Member States, defendants cannot have a chosen and an *ex officio* legal counsellor at the same time.

Concerning the expression 'given a mandate', some Member States (BE, IE, NL) require awareness of appointment, contact with the legal counsellor and/or consent with representation; some Member States only require awareness (HU, PL), while another Member State has no requirement at all (RO). In Poland, an *ex officio* legal counsellor either is appointed at the request of the defendant or is appointed by the court in case of mandatory defence, in which case both the defendant and the *ex officio* legal counsellor are informed of the appointment and each other's names and addresses. The mandate lasts until the case is finally adjudicated. Romania distinguishes between chosen legal counsellors and *ex officio* legal counsellors. Chosen counsel must present a copy of his/her mandate. If the *ex officio* legal counsellor is in contact with the defendant, s/he may become the defendant's chosen legal counsellor.

The Framework Decision is silent on how the mandate is *formalised*. Under the principle of procedural autonomy, this is left to national law to determine. National systems differ as to whether a mandate requires a formal agreement between the accused and his/her counsel and whether counsel must be able to prove that s/he received a mandate from his/her client, or whether a mandate is presumed when counsel states that s/he is mandated by his/her client.

In the Netherlands and in Belgium defence counsel has to state that s/he has been mandated by the accused.[87] If counsel does so, no further evidence is required. In most other Member States, a written mandate is required. In Poland, the defendant or his chosen legal counsellor must provide the court with a written declaration signed by the defendant, confirming that the legal counsellor was appointed by him/her. However, it is also possible to give a mandate orally during the hearing. In such a case, the act of giving a mandate is recorded in the minutes of the hearing.

85 HU, report, p. 23.
86 PL, report, p. 30.
87 NL, report, p. 25; BE, report, pp. 9-10.

There seems to be a tendency among executing judicial authorities to take their national standards as the standard of measurement when assessing what happened in the issuing Member State.[88] In some Member States the legal counsellor's mandate cannot be examined by the courts (BE, NL). For example, a Member State under which legal system defence counsel must submit a written form that proves that the accused mandated him/her will be inclined to ask the issuing Member State for that form when executing an EAW concerning *in absentia* proceedings in which a mandated legal counsellor represented the accused. For a Member State that applies an entirely different system, namely that if the defence counsellor states that s/he has a mandate, no proof is necessary, this is asking for the impossible. In such a Member State it is probably the Code of Conduct of the Bar that safeguards that counsel will only declare to have a mandate if that corresponds to the truth on pain of elimination from the Bar or other sanctions relating to a breach of trust.

In the opposite situation, an issuing Member State with an explicit proof of mandate requirement will not be requested to provide supplementary information on the mandate from an executing Member State practising the implicit system, even in the case that there was no written proof of such mandate. It demonstrates that Member States assess questions of compliance with formalities from the angle of their own legal system. Although this is entirely understandable, it is conceptually wrong. The only formalities that must be respected at the moment of the mandate are those that are applicable in that specific Member State. At that moment, it is impossible to anticipate any potential later debate in the context of EAW-proceedings. Should one require that the formalities of the (later known) executing Member State are respected, one is asking for the impossible. It would require Member States to take into consideration all the formalities of all EU Member States, as in theory, all Member States could at an unknown point in time be asked to execute an EAW.

Under the principle of procedural autonomy, it is, again, national law that determines what *the scope* of the mandate is. On the one extreme, there are the Member States that allow for a general instruction to do everything that is in the interest of the accused. On the other extreme, there may be Member States requiring an explicit instruction for each individual procedural step. Some Member States (IE, NL)[89] require that the legal counsellor is instructed by the defendant; some Member States do not.[90]

In Poland, a chosen legal counsellor shall do what is requested by the defendant; the agreement between the legal counsellor and the defendant indicates the scope of the mandate. An *ex officio* legal counsellor may appeal or take any other procedural decision

88 It is for instance reported that as an executing Member State, Germany requires an explicit declaration of power of attorney from the Netherlands, which under the latter's legislation does not exist.

89 IE, report, pp. 16 and 17.

90 HU, report, p. 8; PL, report, p. 31.

in favour of a defendant, whether or not the defendant consents.[91] The defendant may withdraw the appeal or the request for a retrial lodged by the legal counsellor, except in cases of mandatory defence. However, the mandated *ex officio* legal counsellor must have the explicit consent of his/her client for *waiving* an appeal.[92] In other words: under Polish law, a mandate in case of an *ex officio* legal counsellor means that counsel is entitled to any step that otherwise the defendant could take him/herself, with the exception of acquiescing in the judgment.

Only the Belgian report deals with the potential dispute of an *ex officio* lawyer and the requested person, when the latter is confronted with an EAW.[93]

National rules also differ as to *the end* of the mandate. Under Irish law defence counsel is not allowed to withdraw without the permission of the court, even in cases of loss or withdrawal of confidence. This is the same for Romania and Poland for *ex officio* lawyers.

6.4 Right to a Retrial: Decision Already Served

6.4.1 *Introduction*

Article 4a(1)(c) Framework Decision does not explicitly state in which situations it applies. From the logic of the article, one can deduce that it concerns situations in which neither the conditions with respect to the summons (Article 4a(1)(a)), nor the conditions with respect to representation by a mandated legal counsellor (Article 4a(1)(b)), were met. In these situations, both the issuing Member State and the accused get another chance for a trial in his/her presence.

6.4.2 *Service of the Decision*

The Framework Decision requires that the convicted person was served with the decision. It does not mention the formalities that are applicable, from which it may be deduced that in accordance with the principle of procedural autonomy it is national law that determines how such a service takes place. Most Member States apply the rules on service of the summons before the start of the trial also when a judgment must be served.[94]

91 PL, report, p. 31.
92 PL, report, pp. 31-32.
93 BE, report, p. 43.
94 BE; HU; NL; PL; RO.

'After being served with the decision' means for some Member States[95] service *in person*[96] or at least service in such a way that the requested person is *actually aware* of the judgment and of the possible recourses.

The question what the concept 'After being served with the decision' means has led to a debate on the question whether this relates to an autonomous concept of EU law. The Belgian report is clear on this. The concept 'After being served with the decision' does not have an autonomous nature, because the Framework Decision refers to national law. On the other hand the report for the Netherlands refers to the *Dworzecki* case to make the case for an autonomous nature of the concept. In that case, the Court held that 'summoning in person' is an autonomous concept of EU law. As a consequence, the Netherlands' report draws the conclusion that then also 'serving the judgment' must be.

These two points of view might not be so distinct as they seem at first sight. There is a difference between the wording of Article 4a (1)(a) ('summoned in person') and Article 4a (1)(c) ('served with the decision'). From this one can deduce that service under (c) not necessarily is the same as summoned in person, but may be broader.[97] 'Served with the decision' must be regarded as an autonomous concept aiming at the result. That enables the Member States to apply any procedure provided for under national law that realises this result. In other words, there are two distinct autonomous concepts: the first being 'summoned in person', which leaves very little discretion to the Member States and 'being served with the decision', which allows for more differences in how to serve the decision on the accused. The latter might also allow for a service of the judgment on counsel for the accused,[98] as long as that service does comply with the qualitative requirements of *informing* the accused about the retrial or appeal rights. Although the Member States have more discretion as to serving the judgment, these qualitative requirements presume that the judgment and the information about the retrial or appeal *actually* reached the accused (see also Section 6.4.4).[99]

95 BE; HU; IE; NL; PL, report, p. 15.

96 BE: as defined by national law.

97 German case-law reaches the opposite conclusion: because Art. 4a(1)(d) refers to situations in which the person concerned "was not *personally* served with the decision", Art. 4a(1)(c) must be interpreted as also requiring personal service ("eine persönliche Zustellung"): *Kammergericht Berlin*, decision of 10 October 2018, (4) 151 AuslA 162/18 (176/18). Affixing a notice on the notice board of the court (a so-called öffentliche Zustellung) or a legal presumption ("Zustellungsfiktion") does not suffice: *Kammergericht Berlin*, decision of 15 March 2019, (4) 151 AuslA 167/18 (178/18).

98 HU, report, p. 9 allows for service of the judgment on counsel when the accused waived the right to be present.

99 According to the ECtHR, the object of expressly informing the defendant of the right to a retrial or an appeal is to enable him to exercise that right in accordance with the law of issuing Member State: ECtHR, judgment of 1 March 2011, *Faniel v. Belgium*, ECLI:CE:ECHR:2011:0301JUD001189208, § 30. When serving a judgment of conviction on the defendant, particularly when at the moment of service he is detained or not represented by a legal counsellor, he must be informed in an reliable and official manner of the possible recourses against that judgment and the time frame within which to exercise those recourses: ECtHR,

If a national legal system works with legal presumptions for summonses, it will most likely do so as well for serving the judgment. That does not seem to be in compliance with the demands of the Framework Decision. As with serving the summons, the service of the decision has an *informative function*. It enables the accused to make informed decisions on how to proceed. However, compliance with the requirement of being served with the decision on the side of the authorities triggers consequences for the accused. If s/he wishes to have a retrial or to appeal, s/he must take swift action. Not doing so, after being served, could result in the loss of the right to a retrial and to an appeal and could, therefore, entail that his/her absence at the trial cannot be a ground for refusing the execution of the EAW (see Section 6.4.4).

A particular situation exists in Poland. The legislation does not provide for a service in person when the judgment is delivered without the accused being present: in principle the first instance judgment is not served on the accused except upon his/her motion.[100] It does not apply the same rules as to the summons for the first hearing. Service of the judgment may be done by any manner.[101] If s/he requests so within seven days, Polish law provides that the judgment shall be served upon the accused.[102]

6.4.3 *Right to a Retrial or an Appeal*

The Framework Decision does not state what a retrial or an appeal is, but does express what it must embody at least: the accused has the right to participate in the trial, the merits of the case must be assessed, fresh evidence may be introduced, the case must be re-examined and last but not least, it may lead to the original decision being reversed. Of course, according to the principle of procedural autonomy it is national law that determines what the procedure looks like; however, it must allow for the possibility of another outcome than the conviction that is the object of the EAW.

The meaning of the concept of the 'right to retrial or an appeal' – which also figures in Article 4a(1)(d) – will be discussed at length in Chapter 7.

---

judgment of 1 March 2011, *Faniel v. Belgium*, ECLI:CE:ECHR:2011:0301JUD001189208, § 30. *Apropos* the time frame see ECtHR, judgment of 29 June 2010, *Hakimi v. Belgium*, ECLI:CE:ECHR:2010:0629JUD000066508, § 36. The object of expressly informing the defendant of his rights could be achieved by providing him with a document which indicates the formalities and the time frame to be respected when exercising the right to a retrial or an appeal in such a way that it does not require the interpretation of the applicable legislation or the advice of a legal counsellor: ECtHR, judgment of 24 May 2007, *Da Luz Domingues Ferreira v. Belgium*, ECLI:CE:ECHR:2007:0524JUD005004999, § 58.

100 See three exceptions mentioned PL, report, pp. 19 and 32-33.

101 PL, report, pp. 24 and 33-35, with the exception of a penal order, which must be sent to the defendant personally.

102 PL, report, pp. 32-33.

6.4.4 Non-exercise of the Right to a Retrial or an Appeal

Being served with the decision and having the right to a retrial or an appeal is not enough to trigger the exception of Article 4a(1)(c). There are two alternative additional conditions. These conditions concern situations in which the requested person has the right to a retrial or an appeal but does not exercise that right:
- s/he expressly states that s/he does not contest the decision;
- s/he does not request a retrial or an appeal within the applicable time frame.

The meaning of these two conditions must be read together. The first is abundantly clear: only an express statement, not a presumed answer, qualifies. The Framework Decision does not state how this statement should take place. In light of the importance of the right to be present, any shape in which such an express statement is performed will count: whether in writing or orally, as long as it is clear that s/he does not contest the decision.[103] In view of the fact that the service of the decision is the first moment at which the convicted person learns of the fact that proceedings were conducted against him/her, the same high standard of awareness and evidence should apply as concerning the summons preceding the trial. This is also underlined by the wording of the fourth option of Article 4a(1)(d) Framework Decision, that deals with the situation that the convicted person "was not personally served with the decision".

That is the same for the second situation in which the convicted person does not do anything. This is the only difference with the first situation, in which the convicted person acts. However, both situations require exactly the same degree of clarity as to the service of the decision and awareness of what is going on. The standard for the service of the decision is equal to the standard for the summons that initiates the proceedings except for one element. The latter requires that the accused will be informed of the fact that a decision may be handed down if s/he does not appear. The Framework Decision does not require this information to be given to the convicted individual: if you do not apply for a retrial or an appeal, the decision will become final.

6.5 Conclusions

It seems to be that one of the problems is that Article 4a(1) and the EAW-form use terminology that may be interpreted in a qualitative manner, whereas it might be better to understand it as a factual description of what happened in reality. In other words, the explanation for the problems emerging is that issuing Member States seem to consider the

103 We hesitate on whether there must be proof of informed consent.

Framework Decision/EAW-form as giving them leeway to interpret boxes and categories under their own terms, whereas a European autonomous way is meant.[104] With the exception of Ireland, Member States seem to be much stricter when executing than when issuing EAWs. They tend to interpret the Framework Decision's notion of personally informed in line with the case-law of the Court in a material sense when executing other Member States' EAWs and demonstrate an entirely different attitude when issuing EAWs.

Concerning the summons it is interesting to see that Member States appear to have lost track of the original reason of summoning the accused: to realise the presence of the accused at the trial. That goal no longer seems to be the main effort for five of the six project Member States. It looks as if they have compromised the ideal situation of the presence of the accused at the hearing for a set of formalities that make sure that nothing can stop the trial from being held. In other words: the presence of the accused no longer seems the main purpose of the summons, it is the trial that must continue. Compliance with the formalities constitutes a rationalisation and pays lip service to the formal goal of achieving the presence of the accused. However, the driving force is the continuation of the trial under almost all circumstances. In this context, it may help to raise a rhetorical question. What is it that can stop the continuation of criminal proceedings on the continent? Is it the absence of the accused? No, that is not problematic, but what is problematic is disrespect for formalities. The formalities around the summons have become a goal of its own.

Residence or detention abroad is a factor which may contribute to a trial in the absence of the accused. In this respect, the focus on compliance with formalities and the absence of EU instruments providing for participation in the trial by accused who reside or are detained abroad either via video link technology or by temporary transfer only heighten the chances that the trial is conducted in their absence.

Member States consider themselves to be in line with the case-law of the Court. However, with the exception of Ireland, it is doubtful whether this is the case. Especially on the first option, the summons in person/summons by other means, Member States do apply formalities that are not in compliance with the case-law of the Court. Illustrative is the way in which the project Member States summon accused who reside abroad. The applicable rules do not require any evidence that the summons actually reached the accused in time. The consequence ought to be that point 3.1 of section (d) of the EAW-form cannot be ticked and that another option must be used to prevent the executing Member State from refusing.

104 Opinion of Advocate General Bobek of 11 May 2016, *Openbaar Ministerie v. Paweł Dworzecki*, C-108/16 PPU, ECLI:EU:C:2016:333, para. 30: "It must be emphasised that the role of independent review carried out by the executing authority is limited to verifying the legal classification (points 3.1b, 3.2 or 3.3 of the form) of the facts as presented by the issuing authority (point 4 of the form)."

As to the second option, defence by a mandated legal counsellor, the autonomous concept of 'being aware of the scheduled trial' requires that the accused must be aware that a trial is anticipated or intended, but not that s/he has knowledge of the specific date and place of that trial. National rules show a wide range of positions: one project Member State operates with a legal presumption of awareness, another uses a reasonable expectation of an impending trial, whereas yet a third requires awareness of the actual date and place of the trial. As for the autonomous concept of a 'mandate', we do not know yet, whether for an absent accused, represented by counsel, general, specific or no instructions at all are required to comply with the minimum standards of EU human rights, although that concept presupposes that the accused was aware of the appointment of the legal counsellor, that s/he wanted to be represented by the legal counsellor and that s/he at least had some form of contact with the legal counsellor about acting on the accused's behalf. Obviously, the requirement of a 'mandate' given by the person concerned can be particularly problematic when the legal counsellor is appointed by the State *ex officio*. With regard to the formalisation, the scope and the end of the 'mandate', national rules diverge. These divergences can hinder judicial cooperation.

With regard to the third option, the judgment was already served on the accused who had a right to a retrial or an appeal but did not exercise it (in a timely fashion), there are differences of opinion as to what the autonomous concept of Union law 'being served with the decision' means. This concept aims at the result that the person concerned is informed of the judgment. Since Article 4a(1)(c) also requires that the person concerned was informed about the right to a retrial or an appeal, this provision requires that the judgment and the information about the right to a retrial or an appeal must have actually reached the person concerned. Furthermore, the additional alternative conditions, non-contest/non-exercise, require the same standard of awareness.

7 Right to a Retrial: Decision Served after Surrender

7.1 Introduction

7.1.1 *Fourth Exception*

The fourth exception to the rule that the executing judicial authority may refuse to execute the EAW in case of non-appearance of the person concerned at the trial resulting in the decision concerns situations in which

> the executing judicial authority is required to execute the [EAW], even though the person concerned is entitled to a retrial, because the arrest warrant indicates (...) that [the person concerned] will be expressly informed of his right to a retrial.[1]

The fourth exception, which is laid down in Article 4a(1)(d) FD 2002/584/JHA, seems to be very important for the day-to-day practice of issuing and executing judicial authorities. In the majority of EAWs concerning judgments *in absentia* dealt with by one of the Polish executing judicial authorities, the issuing judicial authorities had ticked the box of point 3.4 of section (d) of the EAW. As a result, in the majority of cases points 2 and 3 were not examined at all.[2] Also in the experience of Belgian executing judicial authorities, point 3.4 is often ticked.[3] A statistical analysis of EAWs handled by the Dutch executing judicial authority in 2017 shows that in 50 of 121 *in absentia* EAWs point 3.4 was ticked, whereas that authority ruled that in 70 of those 121 cases the assurances of Article 4a(1)(d) were needed because none of the other exceptions applied (see also Section 1.1).[4] The importance of the fourth exception justifies dedicating a separate chapter to it.

The exception relates to cases in which the authorities have been unable to contact the person concerned "in particular because he or she sought to evade justice" (recital (12) of the preamble). Despite that, the right to be present is considered so important that the EU

1 ECJ, judgment of 26 February 2013, *Stefano Melloni v. Ministerio Fiscal*, C-399/11, ECLI:EU:C:2013:103, para. 52.

2 PL, report, p. 80.

3 Together with point 3.1b: BE, report, p. 26.

4 NL, report, p. 149.

legislator yet gave him/her another chance to be present at his/her trial. This exception differs from the third exception both as to the moment when the decision is served, namely after the surrender has been effected, and as to its form, namely personal service.

For the exception to be applicable, the person concerned must not have been *personally* served with the 'decision', *i.e.* with the final conviction. Situations in which the person concerned already was served with the 'decision' are the subject of another exception (Article 4a(1)(c) FD 2002/584/JHA; see Section 6.4). In light of the *Dworzecki* judgment, it seems likely that the concept of 'personal service' must be interpreted as actually handing over the 'decision' to the surrendered person.[5]

7.1.2 Assurances

In essence, Article 4a(1)(d) FD 2002/584/JHA requires a number of *assurances* by the issuing judicial authority,[6] *viz.*: (1) the assurance that the person concerned will be personally served with the decision "without delay after surrender", (2) the assurance that the person concerned, when served with the decision, "will be expressly informed of his or her right to a retrial, or an appeal" which retrial or appeal must conform to the characteristics mentioned in Article 4a(1)(d)(i) FD 2002/584/JHA and (3) the assurance that the person concerned will also be informed of the time frame within which s/he has to request such a retrial or appeal, which time frame must be mentioned in the EAW.

Point 3.4 of section (d) of the EAW-template corresponds to Article 4a(1)(d) FD 2002/584/JHA. If that provision is applicable, all the issuing judicial authority has to do is to tick the box of point 3.4 and fill in the applicable time frame. It is not mandatory to provide "information about how the relevant condition has been met": point 4 of section (d) does not apply when point 3.4 is ticked.

7.1.3 Serving the Decision and Informing the Person Concerned

Article 4a(1)(d) FD and point 3.4 of section (d) of the EAW-form state that the person concerned must be personally served (see Section 7.1.1) with the decision "without delay after surrender" and that s/he must be 'expressly' informed both of his/her right to a retrial or an appeal and of the time frame within which to request the retrial or the appeal. The issue of informing the person concerned about the applicable time frame will be dealt with separately (see Section 7.2.3).

---

5 Cf. ECJ, judgment of 24 May 2016, *Openbaar Ministerie v. Paweł Dworzecki*, C-108/16 PPU, ECLI:EU:C:2016:346, para. 45.

6 See recitals (6) and (12) of the preamble to FD 2009/299/JHA and ECJ, judgment of 10 August 2017, *Openbaar Ministerie v. Sławomir Andrzej Zdziaszek*, C-271/17 PPU, ECLI:EU:C:2017:629, para. 104.

Both serving the decision and informing the person concerned of his/her rights will take place 'after the surrender' and, therefore, on the territory of the issuing Member State. Since the surrendered person will necessarily be in the custody of the issuing Member State – on the basis either of a national arrest warrant or of an enforceable judgment –[7] this should not be an undue burden on that Member State. This also means that service of the decision will be performed in a manner provided for under its legislation, in accordance with the principle of procedural autonomy (see Section 6.4.2).

EU Member States have varying practices of informing defendants of their rights, as deriving from Article 4a(1)(d)(i and ii) FD 2002/584/JHA.

In Belgium, at the moment of being served with a (copy of) the judgment, the person concerned receives a specific document containing the relevant information regarding the possible recourses. This document is in the same language as the *in absentia* judgment. Similarly, in the Netherlands, when serving the defendant with a notification of the judgment in accordance with Article 366 NL-CPC, a leaflet is attached to the notification of the judgment, explaining whether the defendant may appeal the judgment and, if so, within which time frame and in which manner. While this is not a national legal requirement, it is common practice.

In Hungary, the court will inform the defendant during the first hearing of this right. If the court rendered a judgment following proceedings *in absentia*, the written judgment will contain the information about the right to a retrial or an appeal and the applicable time frame. In the view of Romanian authorities, the defendant is informed about his/her rights to legal recourses via the executing judicial authority (when they ask for the *in absentia* judgment). If that is not done, the information is provided immediately after the defendant's surrender.

In Poland, different courts issuing EAWs seem to deal with the matter differently. As the right to a retrial under Article 540b of the PL-CCP usually is not indicated in the EAW as an effective measure available for surrendered persons after surrender to Poland, judges are rarely confronted with such cases.

7.1.4 *Characteristics of a Retrial or an Appeal*

The characteristics of the retrial or the appeal must be (1) that the person concerned has the right to participate in the retrial or the appeal, (2) that the retrial or the appeal allows the merits of the case, including fresh evidence, to be re-examined and (3) that the retrial or the appeal may lead to the original decision being reversed. One cannot fail to notice the similarities between those characteristics and the remedy which according to the case-

7 Cf. ECJ, judgment of 6 December 2018, *IK*, C-551/18 PPU, ECLI:EU:C:2018:991, para. 56.

law of the ECtHR should be available to someone who was convicted *in absentia* and who did not waive his/her right to appear and to defend him/herself: a fresh determination of the merits of the charge, in respect of both law and fact, by a court which has heard him/her.[8] Clearly, the rationale of Article 4a(1)(d) is the same as the rationale of such a fresh determination: a retrial or an appeal with the characteristics enumerated in that provision can remedy a breach of the rights of the defence that occurred during first instance *in absentia* proceedings.[9]

Compared to its predecessor – Article 5(1) FD 2002/584/JHA – a number of differences stand out. Firstly, whereas Article 4a(1)(d) refers to a *right* to a retrial, or an appeal, Article 5(1) only spoke of the *opportunity* to *apply* for a retrial. Secondly, whereas Article 4a(1)(d) describes the main characteristics of such a retrial or an appeal, Article 5(1) did not. Thirdly, whereas Article 4a(1)(d)(i) prescribes a specific assurance concerning the right to a retrial or an appeal, Article 5(1) left the adequacy of the assurance entirely up to the discretion of the executing judicial authority. These differences may be explained, partly by the wish to establish a *common* and *clear* ground for refusal[10] and partly by the aim of ensuring a *high* level of protection and of allowing the executing judicial authority to surrender the person concerned notwithstanding his/her failure to attend the trial which led to his/her conviction, while *fully* respecting the rights of the defence.[11]

Since the wording of Article 4a(1)(d) does not refer to the law of the issuing Member State for the purpose of its meaning and scope, it follows that such concepts as 'the right to a retrial, or an appeal' and the characteristics of the retrial or the appeal enumerated in that provision are *autonomous* concepts of Union law which must be interpreted *uniformly*.[12] This conclusion – which however is not shared by all experts (see Section 3.5) – fits well both with the desire of establishing common and clear grounds for refusal and with the objective of ensuring a high level of protection.

As discussed at length in Sections 3.5 and 4.2.1, Article 4a(1) only harmonises the ground for refusal, not the national rules concerning trials *in absentia*. This means that, as far as the right to a retrial or an appeal after surrender is concerned, Article 4a(1) does not oblige Member States to provide for the right to a retrial or an appeal with the charac-

8 *See, e.g.*, ECtHR, judgment of 1 March 2006, *Sejdovic v. Italy* [GC], ECLI:CE:ECHR:2006:0301JUD005658100, § 82.

9 Cf. ECJ, judgment of 11 August 2017, *Openbaar Ministerie v. Tadas Tupikas*, C-270/17 PPU, ECLI:EU:C:2017:628, para. 82. *See also, e.g.*, ECtHR, judgment of 1 March 2006, *Sejdovic v. Italy* [GC], ECLI:CE:ECHR:2006:0301JUD00565810, § 126; ECtHR, judgment of 3 October 2016, *Baratta v. Italy*, ECLI:CE:ECHR:2015:1013JUD002826309, § 78; ECtHR, decision of 3 October 2017, *Giurgiu v. Romania*, ECLI:CE:ECHR:2017:1003DEC002623909, § 96.

10 Recitals (3) and (4) of the preamble to FD 2009/299/JHA.

11 Recital (4) of the preamble to FD 2009/299/JHA; ECJ, judgment of 10 August 2017, *Openbaar Ministerie v. Tadas Tupikas*, C-270/17 PPU, ECLI:EU:C:2017:628, para. 58.

12 Cf. ECJ, judgment of 11 August 2017, *Openbaar Ministerie v. Tadas Tupikas*, C-270/17 PPU, ECLI:EU:C:2017:628, paras. 65-67.

teristics enumerated in Article 4a(1)(d)(i). If, however, the law of the issuing Member States provides for a retrial or an appeal in some form, that legal recourse must – at least – present those characteristics in order for Article 4a(1)(d) to apply. If one or more of these characteristics are missing, then Article 4a(1)(d) is not applicable and the issuing judicial authority should not tick the box of point 3.4 of section (d) of the EAW. Of course, in such circumstances the issuing judicial authority could still describe the legal recourse open to the surrendered person under point 4 of section (d) of the EAW, in the hope that the executing judicial authority would be guided by the *Dworzecki* and *Tupikas* judgments and draw the conclusion that, even though none of the exceptions applies, surrendering the person concerned would not entail a breach of his/her rights of defence.[13]

The wording of Article 4a(1)(d) makes it abundantly clear that a legal recourse in which *only* points of law are re-examined does not qualify as a retrial or an appeal as referred to in that provision. A re-examination of points of law only is quite obviously not a re-examination of 'the merits of the case, including fresh evidence'.[14]

The phrase "which *allows* the merits of the case, including fresh evidence, to be re-examined" might suggest that it is sufficient that the competent court in the issuing Member State has discretion as to the re-examination of fresh evidence.[15] Recital (12) of the preamble to FD 2009/299/JHA, however, points to another possible interpretation: "Such a retrial, or appeal, is aimed at guaranteeing the rights of the defence and is characterised by the following elements: (…), the merits of the case *are* re-examined (…)."[16] When read against the background of the case-law of the ECtHR, perhaps the more likely interpretation of the word 'allows' is that it is open and indeed up to the defendant to ask the appellate court to admit new evidence. In the words of the ECtHR:

> (…) in cases where an accused has been convicted *in absentia* at first instance, it is for the appellate court to provide a forum for the fresh factual and legal determination of the merits of the criminal charge. *It is then for the accused to avail themselves of the remedies for their defence that are provided for by domestic law.*

13 Cf. ECJ, judgment of 24 May 2017, *Openbaar Ministerie v. Paweł Dworzecki*, C-108/16 PPU, ECLI:EU:C:2016:346, paras. 50-52; ECJ, judgment of 11 August 2017, *Openbaar Ministerie v. Tadas Tupikas*, C-270/17 PPU, ECLI:EU:C:2017:628, paras. 96-97.

14 In the same vein: *Minister for Justice and Equality v. Jefisovas* [2019] IEHC 248 (08 April 2019), paras. 63-68.

15 Emphasis added. Compare the French version "qui *permet* de réexaminer l'affaire sur le fond, en tenant compte des nouveaux éléments de preuve" (emphasis added).

16 Emphasis added.

In such cases, Article 6 ECHR does not require the appellate court to act *ex proprio motu.*[17] Based on, *inter alia*, recital (12), the German Constitutional Court (*Bundesverfassungsgericht*) held that Article 4a(1)(d)(i) *entitles* the surrendered person to a (re-)examination of any exculpatory evidence s/he puts forward and that this interpretation is an *acte clair.*[18] This ruling evidently presupposes that the defendant actually asks the appellate court to consider such evidence.

7.1.5 *Providing a Copy of the Judgment before Surrender*

It is interesting to see that, even though the person concerned will only be formally served with the judgment after the issuing Member State has obtained his/her surrender, s/he may already receive a copy of the decision in the executing Member State. Article 4a(2) FD 2002/584/JHA stipulates that the requested person may request to be provided with such a copy, if Article 4a(1)(d) applies and the requested person has not previously received any official information about the existence of the criminal proceedings against him/her. Upon such a request, the issuing judicial authority must 'immediately' provide him/her with a copy via the executing judicial authority. The Framework Decision does not state that the executing judicial authorities must inform him/her of this right. It also does not state what the consequences are in case a request is not complied with. However, it does state that the request shall not delay the surrender procedure and the decision on the execution of the EAW and that providing the judgment cannot be regarded as a formal service. Providing a copy of the judgment does not activate any time limits for requesting a retrial

---

17 ECtHR, judgment of 30 October 2018, *Gestur Jónsson and Ragnar Halldór Hall v. Iceland*, ECLI:CE:ECHR:2018:1030JUD006827314, § 69 (emphasis added). The case was referred to the Grand Chamber. See also ECtHR, decision of 3 October 2017, *Giurgiu v. Romania*, ECLI:CE:ECHR:2017:1003DEC002623909, § 96: "In this connection, the Court reiterates that – given that the defendant was allowed to appeal against the conviction in absentia and was entitled to attend the hearing in the court of appeal, thus opening up the **possibility** of a fresh factual and legal determination of the criminal charge – the proceedings as a whole may be said to have been fair (*see,* mutatis mutandis, *Jones v. the United Kingdom* (dec.), no. 30900/02, 9 September 2003)" (emphasis added).

18 *Bundesverfassungsgericht*, judgment of 15 December 2015, 2 BvR 2735/14, paras. 88-104 and 125, accessible at www.bundesverfassungsgericht.de. The case concerned an Italian EAW. At issue was Art. 603(4) of the Italian Code of Criminal Procedure, which provided that the court of appeal would only allow fresh evidence to be presented if the defendant *showed* that he was unable to appear at the first instance trial on account of *force majeure*, that he did not have any knowledge of the first instance summons through no fault of his own or that he did not voluntarily seek to avoid knowledge of the first instance proceedings. This problem seems to have been solved by the Italian judiciary. In 2016, the Italian *Corte di cassazione* held that a person who was convicted *in absentia* and who, because he was unaware of the proceedings, was given a new time frame for lodging an appeal has the right to an *integral* re-examination on appeal. Because of the need to interpret the national provisions in accordance with Art. 6 ECHR, the limitations contained in Art. 603(4) CCP do not apply to him/her. See *Corte di cassazione*, judgment of 30 November 2016, Num. 51041, accessible at www.cortedicassazione.it.

or an appeal, but is for information purposes only. In addition to the duty to mention the applicable time frame in the EAW (see Section 7.2.3), this is another safeguard for the person concerned, which is intended to ensure that s/he will not find him/herself with only a very short time in which to request the retrial or the appeal.

Guaranteeing the right of the accused to 'immediately' receive a copy of the judgment before surrender does not seem to be a problem in the project Member States. All project Member States have legal provisions and/or practices in place that guarantee the right of the requested person to receive a copy of the judgment before surrender. Usually, the executing judicial authority[19] will contact the issuing judicial authority, request a copy of the judgment and hand it over to the accused (or to his/her legal counsellor if the person sought can no longer be reached (Belgium)) as soon as possible.[20]

In Romania, upon the demand of the requested person, the judge shall postpone the case only once, for at least 5 days, and request the issuing judicial authority to deliver, in copy and in a language which the requested person understands, the decision rendered *in absentia*. However, failure by the issuing judicial authority to deliver the decision rendered *in absentia* shall neither have an effect on surrender procedure nor on the surrender of the requested person.[21]

7.1.6 *Relationship with Article 5(3) FD 2002/584/JHA*

If the person concerned has the right to a retrial, or an appeal, as referred to in Article 4a(1)(d), his/her situation "is comparable to that of a person who is the subject of [an EAW] for the purposes of prosecution". Provided that the person concerned is a national or a resident of the executing Member State, the executing judicial may also apply Article 5(3) of FD 2002/584/JHA and subject the execution of the EAW to the condition "that the person, after being heard, is returned to the executing Member State in order to serve there the custodial sentence or detention order passed against him in the issuing Member State".[22]

In this way, both the important goal of reintegrating into society and the rights of defence are given their due weight. If applying Article 4a(1)(d) and Article 5(3) *cumulatively* were not possible, the national or resident concerned would be constrained to waive the right to a retrial or an appeal "in order to ensure that his sentence may, pursuant to Article 4(6) of Framework Decision 2002/584, be executed in the Member State where he is [a

19 In Romania, the public prosecutor will contact the issuing authority: RO, report, p. 22.

20 BE, report, p. 19; HU, report, p. 15; NL, report, p. 59; PL, report, p. 54. In Poland, the submission of the request does not stop the execution of the EAW. It has happened in cases where the accused has consented to the surrender that s/he was surrendered before a copy of a judgment could be served on him/her.

21 RO, report, p. 22.

22 Cf. ECJ, judgment of 21 October 2010, *I.B.*, C-306/09, ECLI:EU:C:2009:626, para. 57. This judgment concerns Art. 5(1) FD 2002/584/JHA.

national or a] resident within the meaning of the relevant provisions of that framework decision".[23]

7.2 Issues Concerning Interpretation and Application

7.2.1 *Introduction*

The interpretation and application of Article 4a(1)(d) raise a number of issues. First of all, what does the expression 'the right to retrial, or an appeal' mean? If that right is dependent on any other condition than that the requested person was not personally served with the decision and that the retrial or the appeal is lodged within the applicable time frame and in the manner prescribed by national law, does that right qualify as the 'right' referred to in Article 4a(1)(d)?

Second, if the issuing judicial authority ticked the box of point 3.4 of section (d) of the EAW-form but deleted words which form an integral part of the standard text of point 3.4, what, if any, consequence should this have for the decision on the execution of the EAW?

Third, if the issuing judicial authority did not mention in point 3.4. of section (d) of the EAW-form the applicable time frame for requesting a retrial or an appeal, what, if any, consequences should this have for the decision on the execution of the EAW?

Fourth, if the issuing judicial authority ticked the box of point 3.4 of section (d) of the EAW-form – and thus assured that the person concerned had the right to a retrial or an appeal – but provided information *proprio motu* which seems to contradict that assurance, what, if any, consequences should this have for the decision on the execution of the EAW?

7.2.2 *Right to a Retrial or an Appeal*

What does the concept of a 'right to a retrial, or an appeal' mean? One thing is perfectly clear.

From the wording of Article 4a(1)(d) it follows that the retrial or the appeal will not take place *automatically* upon surrender. Because Article 4a(1)(d)(ii) refers to the time frame "within which [the person concerned] *has to request* such a retrial or appeal",[24] it is evident that, after surrender, it is up to the surrendered person to take the necessary steps to give effect to his/her right to a retrial or an appeal. The wording of Article 4a(3) supports

23 ECJ, judgment of 21 October 2010, *I.B.*, C-306/09, ECLI:EU:C:2009:626, paras. 58-59.

24 Emphasis added.

this reading. According to this provision, once the surrendered person "*has requested* a retrial or appeal" the detention of that person awaiting such retrial or appeal shall be reviewed on a regular basis or upon request until these proceedings are finalised.[25]

In determining the meaning of the concept of a 'right to a retrial, or an appeal', it is important to recall that Article 4a(1) FD 2002/584/JHA seeks to guarantee a *high* level of protection in order to allow the executing judicial authority to surrender the person concerned while *fully* observing his/her rights of defence.[26] Furthermore, Article 4a(1)(d)(ii) FD 2002/584/JHA explicitly refers to "*his* or *her* right to a retrial, or an appeal",[27] thus indicating that what is meant is the legal recourse that is open *in this particular case* to *this requested person*, not possible recourses which might be open *in general*. The retrial or appeal is "aimed at *guaranteeing* the rights of the defence" (recital (11) of the preamble to FD 2009/299/JHA).[28] Moreover, when ticking point 3.4 of section (d) of the EAW, the issuing judicial authority *guarantees* that the defendant has a *right* to a retrial or an appeal (recital (12) of the preamble to FD 2009/299/JHA). According to the Court of Justice, Article 4a(1)(c) and (d) sets out situations where the person concerned is *entitled* to retrial.[29] Once the surrendered person has requested a retrial or an appeal, the retrial or appeal 'shall begin' within due time after the surrender (Article 4a(3) FD 2002/584/JHA). Against this background, one might be forgiven for thinking that, once the surrendered person has put in the request, the court in the issuing Member State *must* grant him/her a retrial or an appeal.

However, it does not seem too bold a supposition that the legal systems of the Member States normally subject a legal recourse *to conditions for admissibility, e.g.* conditions with respect to the manner in which and to the time frame within which to lodge that legal recourse. Consequently, the competent court will normally check whether a request for a retrial or an appeal is admissible. In this sense, too, a retrial or an appeal is not automatic. It is hardly conceivable, then, that such an admissibility check would, in itself, preclude the applicability of Article 4a(1)(d). Indeed, that provision itself *explicitly* refers to one condition for admissibility: the "time frame within which [the person concerned] has to request" a retrial or an appeal. *Implicitly*, by referring to a request, that provision could be understood to refer to formalities concerning the manner in which to request a retrial or an appeal. Subjecting the right to a retrial or an appeal to such conditions for admissibility,

25 Emphasis added.
26 ECJ, judgment of 10 August 2017, *Openbaar Ministerie v. Tadas Tupikas*, C-270/17 PPU, ECLI:EU:C:2017:628, para. 58.
27 Emphasis added.
28 Emphasis added.
29 ECJ, judgment of 26 February 2013, *Stefano Melloni v. Ministerio Fiscal*, C-399/11, ECLI:EU:C:2013:107, para. 52; ECJ, judgment of 10 August 2017, *Openbaar Ministerie v. Tadas Tupikas*, C-270/17 PPU, ECLI:EU:C:2017:628, para. 57.

in itself, does not violate Article 6 ECHR. The ECtHR has repeatedly held that the right of access to a court is not absolute, but may be subject to implied limitations "notably as regards the requirements for an appeal to be admissible". Nevertheless, the limitations must not "restrict the access left to the individual in such a way or to such an extent that the very essence of the right is impaired", must "pursue a legitimate aim" and must be reasonably proportionate to that aim.[30]

Similarly, there may come a point where a condition for admissibility is such that it can no longer be said that the convicted person's *right* to a retrial or an appeal is *effectively guaranteed*. This may be the case when a person who was convicted *in absentia* has to *prove* that s/he was not seeking to evade justice or that his/her absence was due to *force majeure*. Such a condition was held by the ECtHR to be in contravention of Article 6 ECHR.[31] Therefore, such a condition would fail to meet the requirements of Article 4a(1)(d). On the other hand, that same court ruled that it is open "to the national authorities to assess whether the person concerned showed good cause for his absence or whether there was anything in the case file to warrant finding that he had been absent for reasons beyond his control".[32] Such a discretion does not seem compatible with the explicit wording of Article 4a(1)(d); if the national authorities could deny a retrial or an appeal on the basis of such an assessment, the person concerned cannot be considered to have the right to a retrial or an appeal.[33] In this regard, the requirements of Article 4a(1)(d) seem to be more strict than the requirements of Article 6 ECHR.[34]

There is no unanimity among the experts on the issue of the meaning of the concept of a 'right to a retrial'. Two strands of thought clearly emerge. According to one strand of thought, the 'right to a retrial' is nothing more than the *possibility* to ask for a retrial. Consequently, admissibility conditions are not problematic at all. According to the other strand of thought, only some admissibility conditions are acceptable. This strand of thought implies that the 'right to a retrial' is more than just a possibility to ask for a retrial.

30 *See, e.g.*, ECtHR, judgment of 25 July 2002, *Papon v. France*, ECLI:CE:ECHR:2002:0725JUD005421000, § 90.

31 *See, e.g.*, ECtHR, judgment of 12 February 1985, *Colozza v. Italy*, ECLI:CE:ECHR:1985:0212JUD000902480, § 30.

32 See ECtHR, judgment of 1 March 2006, *Sejdovic v. Italy* [GC], ECLI:CE:ECHR:2006:0301JUD005658100, § 88, with reference to ECtHR, judgment of 14 June 2001, *Medenica v. Switzerland*, ECLI:CE:ECHR:2001:0614 JUD002049192, § 57.

33 Compare *Oberlandesgericht Hamm*, decision of 29 October 2015, 2 Ausl. 105/15; *Kammergericht Berlin*, decision of 15 March 2019, (4) 151 AuslA 167/18 (178/18); *Brandenburgisches Oberlandesgericht*, decision of 8 July 2019, 2 AR 6/29. These German courts apply the criterion that a retrial or an appeal may only be dependent on the will of the defendant ("dass die Erneuerung der Hauptverhandlung (...) allein vom Willen des Verfolgten abhängt"). See also *Minister for Justice and Equality v. Iacobuta* [2019] IEHC 250 (20 March 2019), with regard to a guarantee which seemed to guarantee a retrial only to the extent that the requested person demonstrated that national legal rules as to service were violated; the Irish High Court found it doubtful whether the requirements of point 3.4 had been met.

34 The same interpretation applies to Art. 4a(1)(c).

The Belgian expert points out that, in his opinion, given recital (14) of the preamble of FD 2009/299/JHA, Article 4a(1)(d) does *not* introduce an autonomous concept of legal recourses that must be interpreted uniformly in all Member States. According to him, from the wording of Article 4a(1)(d) and of Article 9 of Directive 2016/343/EU and from para. 52 of the *Dworzecki* judgment,[35] it follows that the right to a retrial means *the possibility to request a retrial.* In other words: the right to a retrial requires having access to a legal recourse after surrender that *could* lead to a retrial. Consequently, the executing judicial authorities do not have to assess if the legal recourse would be successful or effective. This line of reasoning is not contradicted by recitals (11) and (12) of the preamble to FD 2009/299/JHA: these recitals do not imply that a request for a retrial must always lead to a retrial.[36]

The Dutch, Hungarian and Irish experts are all of the opinion that the right to a retrial or an appeal cannot be made dependent on any other condition than that the requested person was not personally served with the decision and that the retrial or the appeal is lodged within the applicable time frame and in the manner prescribed by national law.[37]

The Polish expert relates the view of one of the interviewed Polish judges that no other conditions should apply than those which usually apply to a motion for a retrial (*viz.* the formal conditions that the motion should be lodged within the applicable time frame and should be prepared and submitted by a legal counsellor).[38] In essence, this view is in accordance with the opinion of the Dutch, Hungarian and Irish experts. The Polish judges stressed that during the surrender proceedings they inform the requested person of his/her right to a retrial after surrender if the EAW refers to this right. In case of serious doubts as to the conditions for a retrial, the court may ask for supplementary information.[39]

With respect to experiences of the *executing* judicial authorities, only the Dutch executing judicial authority reported difficulties with EAWs in which point 3.4 of section of the EAW was ticked. The Dutch executing judicial authority will accept no other conditions than those relating to the manner in which to exercise the right to a retrial or an appeal and to the time frame within which to exercise that right. If the defendant is required to show that s/he was absent through no fault of his/her own and/or that s/he had no

35 ECJ, judgment of 24 May 2016, *Openbaar Ministerie v. Paweł Dworzecki*, C-108/16 PPU, ECLI:EU:C:2016:346. It does not follow from para. 52 of that judgment that the 'right to a request a retrial' to which the Polish Government referred before the Court of Justice is the equivalent of the 'right to a retrial' as mentioned in Art. 4a(1)(d)(i). There is no reference to Art. 4a(1)(d) in the judgment at all. Indeed, the judgment does not even reproduce the text of that provision (see para. 6). Moreover, the issuing judicial authority had not ticked the box of point 3.4 of the EAW against Dworzecki, as one of the authors of this report – who was closely involved in the proceedings in the *Dworzecki* case – can confirm.

36 BE, report, p. 32.

37 HU, report, p. 25; IE, report, p. 53 ('It could be strongly argued that they cannot [make a retrial dependent on other conditions]'; NL, report, p. 82.

38 PL, report, p. 67.

39 PL, report, p. 67.

knowledge of the date and place of the trial or of the judgment, the assurance does not comply with Article 4a(1)(d). Equally, if the court in the issuing Member State is required to determine whether the person concerned had knowledge of the proceedings or of the judgment and voluntarily waived his/her right to appear at the trial, the assurance is deemed inadequate.[40]

Polish assurances which refer to Article 540b of the Polish CCP are regularly deemed insufficient by the Dutch executing judicial authority, either because the person concerned must show that s/he was not aware of the proceedings or of the judgment or because that provision is not applicable when the summons was served in a particular way. Incidentally, this is in line with the opinion of some Polish judges who were interviewed in the course of this project. Even if all the conditions of Article 540b are met, a re-opening of the proceedings is *optional*, not mandatory. That is why these judges do not consider Article 540b a basis for a retrial under Article 4a(1)(d)[41] and why Article 540b is usually not indicated in the EAW as an effective legal recourse available to the surrendered person.[42]

Italian assurances which refer to Article 175 of the Italian CCP, as in force until 2005, are not considered valid guarantees by the Dutch executing judicial authority, because this provision requires the person concerned to prove that s/he had no effective knowledge of the judgment and that s/he had not deliberately refused to take cognisance of the procedural steps. Its judgment in the *Sejdovic* case, the ECtHR ruled that this provision "did not guarantee with sufficient certainty that the applicant would have the opportunity of appearing at a new trial to present his defence".[43] Article 175, as in force between 2005 and 2014 shifted the burden of proof to the Italian 'judicial authorities'. If the issuing Italian judicial authority declares that there are no indications that the person concerned had effective knowledge of the proceedings or that s/he had refused to appear or to appeal the judgment, an assurance based on that version of Article 175 CCP is accepted.

When a *Dutch national* or *resident* is convicted *in absentia*, some particular problems may present itself. Under the Dutch transposition of Article 4(6) FD 2002/584/JHA, it is not allowed to surrender a Dutch national or resident for the purpose of enforcement of a final custodial sentence or detention order.[44] In Belgian cases, the Dutch criminal record sometimes mentions that the Belgian conviction *in absentia* is final, whereas in the EAW

40 NL, report, p. 112.

41 PL, report, pp. 39 and 48.

42 PL, report, p. 53.

43 ECtHR, judgment of 1 March 2006, *Sejdovic v. Italy* [GC], ECLI:CE:ECHR:2006:0301JUD005658100, § 104.

44 In more than one respect, this Dutch provision is not in accordance with Art. 4(6). See ECJ, judgment of 21 June 2017, *Daniel Adam Popławski*, C-579/15, ECLI:EU:C:2017:503.

point 3.4 is ticked, thus prompting the Dutch executing judicial authority to ask the issuing judicial authority to confirm that the conviction is not in fact final.[45]

The Belgian, Hungarian, Irish, Polish and Romanian executing judicial authorities reported no difficulties with EAWs in which point 3.4 of section (d) was ticked.[46]

With respect to experiences of *issuing* judicial authorities, Irish judicial authorities, of course, have never issued an EAW seeking the surrender of a person tried *in absentia*.[47] As the Dutch issuing judicial authority only deals with cases in which the judgment is *final*, it has never ticked point 3.4 of section (d) of the EAW.[48] No difficulties were reported by the Hungarian issuing judicial authorities.

However, Belgian *issuing* judicial authorities have encountered many requests by executing judicial authorities, wishing to know whether a retrial would be held automatically and whether it would be a full retrial.[49] Romanian issuing judicial authorities reported that the executing judicial authorities of some Member States repeatedly called for additional safeguards (*i.e.* that the requested person would be expressly informed when serving the judgment that s/he had the right to an effective remedy or a re-examination of the case). After providing such guarantees, the requested persons were surrendered.[50]

Polish issuing judicial authorities only exceptionally tick point 3.4 of section (d) of the EAW. Sometimes, executing judicial authorities want to know whether the requested person would be granted a retrial, mainly with reference to EAWs issued for the enforcement of an *in absentia* judgment rendered in so-called 'simplified proceedings'.[51] In a number of EAWs issued by the Lublin Regional Court, point 3.4 of section (d) of the EAW was ticked with regard to *in absentia* judgments rendered after 'simplified proceedings'. Probably, the issuing judicial authority had in mind the possibility of requesting the reinstatement of the time limit for lodging an objection against the judgment. Two EAWs issued by the Regional Court in Zamość referred to the same recourse. One of these EAWs

45 NL, report, p. 126. The information in Dutch criminal records about a conviction of a Dutch national *in another Member State* is provided by that Member State, in accordance with Framework Decision 2009/315/JHA.

46 BE, report, p. 44; HU, report, p. 36; IE, report, p. 89; PL, report, p. 84; RO, report, p. 42.

47 IE, report, p. 90.

48 NL, report, p. 113.

49 BE, report, p. 44.

50 RO, report, pp. 42-43.

51 PL, report, p. 84. Before 1 July 2015, the presence of the defendant at the hearing was mandatory. However, Polish criminal procedural law provided for so-called 'simplified proceedings' which applied on condition that the preparatory proceedings were held in the form of an inquiry and which concerned less severe cases. In simplified proceedings, the court could conduct *in absentia* proceedings and pronounce a judgment *in absentia*, when the accused and his/her defence counsel were absent. Due to the transitional regime, proceedings initiated before 1 July 2015 could still be conducted under the old rules and an *in absentia* judgment could be rendered. See PL, report, p. 15.

concerned a judgment issued in the 'penal order procedure'.[52] A German executing judicial authority refused to execute this EAW.[53]

7.2.3 Time Frame

From the wording of Article 4a(1)(d)(ii) it clearly follows that the time frame within which the surrendered person has to request the retrial or the appeal after surrender must be mentioned in the EAW ("the time frame (...) as mentioned in the relevant [EAW]"). Point 3.4 of section (d) of the EAW clearly indicates that the applicable time frame must be mentioned and where it must be mentioned ("the person will be informed of the time frame within which he or she has to request a retrial or appeal, which will be .... days"). Apparently, the Union legislator wanted to make sure that the person concerned is aware of and alert to the applicable time frame for requesting a retrial or an appeal *even before his/her eventual surrender* in order to afford him/her an *effective* right to obtaining a retrial or an appeal. Given the obstacles facing a detainee – especially a foreign detainee – in instructing a legal counsellor and/or in requesting a retrial or appeal him/herself, this seems to be a sensible precaution.[54] Advance notice of (the right to a retrial and of) the applicable time frame affords the person concerned the opportunity to prepare for lodging the request as soon as possible after surrender.

In this context it is also relevant to refer to the right of the requested person to appoint a legal counsellor in the issuing Member State conferred by Article 10(5) and (6) of Directive 2013/48 on the Right of Access to a Lawyer. Exercising this right will enable the requested person to make the appropriate assessment of how to apply the rights of the defence, especially to make use of a right to a new trial within the time limits provided under national law.

In view of the potential need for interpretation and translation of the judgment and the information about the right to a retrial or an appeal and the potential need for consultation with counsel, a national time limit that in the given circumstances is so short as to make that right practically inexistent should be extended. The standard imposed by the Court in *Covaci* is that the "accused person does in fact have the benefit of the whole of

---

52 In a judgment rendered following a penal order procedure, no penalty of imprisonment may be imposed. It is only possible to impose a fine up to 200 daily units or a penalty of limitation of liberty: PL, report, p. 23. It necessarily follows that the penalty originally imposed was subsequently converted into a custodial sentence. See PL, report, p. 58.

53 PL, report, p. 84.

54 Cf. ECtHR, judgment of 1 March 2006, *Sejdovic v. Italy* [GC], ECLI:CE:ECHR:2006:0301JUD005658100, § 54.

the prescribed period for lodging an objection against that order."[55] As a result of the *Sleutjes* case, it means that both the judgment and the information about the time frame for requesting a new trial must be available in a language the surrendered person understands when the time limit starts to run.[56]

The answers given by the experts concerning the potential consequences of not mentioning the applicable time frame show a wide range of viewpoints. According to the Belgian expert, not mentioning the time frame should have no consequences at all. He raises the issue why the EAW should mention the applicable time frame at all, because the information about the applicable legal recourse and the applicable time frame should only be provided *after* surrender.[57]

The Hungarian expert points out that not mentioning the applicable time frame is not a ground for refusal but adds that the executing judicial authority may request supplementary information.[58]

The Polish judges who were interviewed in the course of the project stress that the ground for refusal is only optional. The executing judicial authority can try to clarify this issue during the surrender proceedings by asking the requested person whether s/he is aware of the time frame for requesting a retrial or an appeal. In case of doubt, it may request supplementary information.[59]

According to the Dutch expert, the conditions of Article 4a(1)(d) are not met if the EAW does not mention the applicable time frame. Therefore, the executing judicial authority should enquire after the applicable time frame.[60] The opinion of the Dutch expert implies that, if the issuing judicial authority does not provide the applicable time frame as requested and if none of the other exceptions to the rule that the execution of the EAW may be refused applies, the executing judicial may – and according to Dutch legislation: must – refuse to execute the EAW.

The opinion of the Irish expert is more or less the same. Point 3.4 amounts to an assurance from one judicial authority to another, which on the basis of the principle of mutual recognition is intended to be taken at face value. Precision is therefore essential and the time frame needs to be specified. If the omission is due to mere oversight, additional

55 ECJ, judgment of 15 October 2015, *Criminal proceedings against Gavril Covaci*, C-216/14, ECLI:EU:C:2015:586, para. 68.
56 ECJ, judgment of 12 October 2017, *Criminal proceedings against Frank Sleutjes*, C-278/16, ECLI:EU:C:2017:757.
57 BE, report, p. 32.
58 HU, report, p. 25.
59 PL, report, p. 67.
60 NL, report, p. 82.

information could be requested to remedy the defect.[61] If, however, the omission appears to have been deliberate, or if the issuing judicial authority refuses to provide the applicable time frame when requested to do so, then arguably the defect would be fatal to any possibility of surrender based on the assurance of point 3.4. It does not seem to be the kind of problem that amplifying the supplementary information provided at point 4 could overcome.[62]

With respect to experiences of the *executing* judicial authorities, only the Dutch executing judicial authority reported any cases in which the EAW did not mention the applicable time frame. The issuing judicial authority was requested to provide the time frame. If the executing judicial authority has *ex officio* knowledge that the law of the issuing Member State does not provide for a time frame for requesting the retrial or the appeal, it will refrain from requesting supplementary information.[63]

With respect to experiences of *issuing* judicial authorities, no difficulties were reported by any of the Member States involved in the project.

7.2.4 *Modification of Assurances*

For Article 4a(1)(d) to apply, the EAW must state the assurances referred to in that provision. In this respect, section (d) of the EAW-form is user-friendly. Point 3.4 of section (d) repeats word for word the assurances mentioned in Article 4a(1)(d). If the issuing judicial authority is of the opinion that Article 4(1)(d) applies to the situation at hand, all it has to do is to tick the box of point 3.4.[64] If, on the other hand, it takes the view that point 3.4 is not (fully) applicable and, therefore, that it cannot give the assurances, it should refrain from ticking that box. There is no need for the issuing judicial authority to *add* anything to the standard text (except for the applicable time frame, see Section 7.2.3) and it should not *delete* anything from that text, because point 3.4 reflects the conditions of Article 4a(1)(d). As regards the *substance* of the assurances, nothing more is needed and nothing less is acceptable.

According to the Romanian expert, deletion of passages which form an integral part of the standard text of point 3.4 is not considered as a ground for refusal.[65] The Hungarian expert concurs, but adds that the executing judicial authority may request supplementary

---

61 In *Minister for Justice and Equality v. Tache* [2019] IEHC 68 (11 February 2019) the EAW did not mention the applicable time frame. The Irish Central Authority requested supplementary information. In reply, the issuing judicial authority provided the requested information.

62 IE, report, p. 53.

63 NL, report, p. 113, footnote 266.

64 And to mention the applicable time frame (see Section 7.2.3).

65 RO, report, p. 34.

information.[66] The Polish judges stress the optional nature of the ground for refusal and point out that in case of doubt the executing judicial authority could request supplementary information.[67] According to the Belgian expert, deletion of passages which form an integral part of the standard text of point 3.4 raises the presumption that the issuing judicial authority is not able to comply with the requirements set out in the standard text of the EAW-form. However, before refusing to surrender, the executing judicial authority should request supplementary information in order to confirm or to rebut that presumption.[68] According to the Irish expert, a certain Irish precedent would seem to suggest that surrender would have to be refused. However, in the light of the *Dworzecki* and *Tupikas* judgments it could be argued that if the issuing judicial authority offered an explanation for the deletion and if that explanation allayed any concerns that the requested person's right of defence would not be respected, surrender is possible. If, on the other hand, no explanation is proffered, the executing judicial authority should probably seek confirmation that the assurances were in fact being offered in the prescribed form or an explanation for the deletion and alternative assurances with respect to how the defendant's rights of defence could and would be respected.[69] The Dutch expert points out that, if an integral part of the standard text of point 3.4 is deleted, it necessarily follows that the corresponding part of the conditions of Article 4a(1)(d) is not met.[70]

With respect to experiences of the *executing* judicial authorities, only the Dutch executing judicial authority reported difficulties with EAWs in which passages were deleted which form an integral part of the standard text of point 3.4. In one such case, *e.g.*, point 3.4. was ticked, but the entire text after the words "the person was not served the decision personally, but the decision will be served him/her personally without delay after his/her handing over" was deleted. In another case, the issuing judicial authority used the *old* version of section (d) of the EAW,[71] stated that it was still possible to oppose the *in absentia* judgment and referred to the applicable provisions of the CCP. When requested to clarify this statement, the issuing judicial authority limited its response to reproducing the text of one of those provisions. The executing judicial authority decided to request supplementary information yet again. From the response of the issuing judicial authority it did not follow that the surrendered person would have the right to participate in the

66 HU, report, p. 26.
67 PL, report, p. 67.
68 BE, report, p. 32.
69 IE, report, p. 54.
70 NL, report, p. 82. In the same vein: *Minister for Justice and Equality v. Iacobuta* [2019] IEHC 250 (20 March 2019), para. 113.
71 The EAW was issued on 5 September 2017 (!).

new proceedings nor that the new proceedings allowed the merits of the case, including fresh evidence, to be re-examined and could lead to the original decision being reversed.[72]

With respect to experiences of *issuing* judicial authorities, no difficulties were reported by any of the Member States involved in the project.

7.2.5 Contradictory Information

Point 4 of section (d) of the EAW is not applicable, when point 3.4 is ticked. In ticking point 3.4, the issuing judicial is under no obligation to provide information *proprio motu* about how the conditions of Article 4a(1)(d) are met.

However, if the issuing judicial authority decides to provide information under point 4, this information should not contradict the assurances of point 3.4. Otherwise, the assurances given under point 3.4 could be called into question.

As to the consequences of contradictory information, the majority of the experts refer to the possibility of requesting supplementary information.[73] The Hungarian expert adds that contradictory information does not constitute a ground for refusal. The Irish expert, however, does not exclude the possibility of refusal, if the ostensibly contradictory information is, in itself, clear and unambiguous. According to the Polish expert, the executing judicial authority could try to clarify this issue at the EAW-hearing. The Romanian expert points out that Romanian executing judicial authorities have not been confronted with the issue of contradictory information.[74]

None of the issuing and executing judicial authorities of the Member States involved in this project have reported cases in which point 3.4 was contradicted by the information given under point 4.

7.3 Interrelationship of the Four Exceptions

Now that all four exceptions to the rule that the executing judicial authority may refuse to execute the EAW if the person concerned did not appear in person at the trial resulting in the decision have been discussed, it is time to examine their interrelationship.

72 NL, report, p. 113. This is probably the case referred to in BE, report, p. 52 ("Some questions are without purpose e.g. when section 3.4 of box D was ticked, asking if the defendant has the right to be present at the retrial while this is a condition that has to be met before ticking that section"). If only the issuing judicial authority had used the *current* version of section (d) –, there probably would have been no need to request supplementary information in the first place. In the end, the issuing judicial authority did what it should have done from the beginning and stated that the standard text of point 3.4 was applicable. The person concerned was surrendered to Belgium.

73 BE, report, p. 33; HU, report, p. 26; IE, report, p. 54; NL, report, p. 83; PL, report, p. 67.

74 RO, report, p. 34.

As to the four situations in which a final decision that was reached without the accused being present at the trial resulting in that decision cannot lead to a refusal of the EAW, it is clear that Article 4a(1) gives preference to the accused being summoned in such a way that s/he was actually aware of the date and the place of the trial. If no such summoning took place, s/he may be represented by his/her mandated legal counsellor. Both situations may not lead to the refusal of the EAW. These two situations of an absent accused do not lead to a new trial, but instead respect the outcome of the *in absentia* trial. A Member State may not make surrender conditional on a new trial being conducted in those circumstances. The Court stated in *Melloni*:

> This literal interpretation of Article 4a(1) of Framework Decision 2002/584 is confirmed by an analysis of the purpose of the provision. The object of Framework Decision 2009/299 is, firstly, to repeal Article 5(1) of Framework Decision 2002/584, which, subject to certain conditions, allowed for the execution of a European arrest warrant issued for the purposes of executing a sentence rendered in absentia to be made conditional on there being a guarantee of a retrial of the case in the presence of the person concerned in the issuing Member State and, secondly, to replace that provision by Article 4a. That provision henceforth restricts the opportunities for refusing to execute such a warrant by setting out, as indicated in recital 6 of Framework Decision 2009/299, 'conditions under which the recognition and execution of a decision rendered following a trial at which the person concerned did not appear in person should not be refused'.[75]

This is slightly different in the other two situations. Both the third exception – service of the judgment after completion of the trial – and the fourth exception – service of the judgment after the EAW has led to a surrender – may lead to a retrial (or an appeal). However, a retrial will not necessarily follow, as the convicted may decide not to apply for it. The system of the Framework Decision was designed to evade final refusals. A finding that the preferred respect for formalities (summons or representation) did not take place can be remedied either by the service after the judgment or by the service after the surrender and by guaranteeing the right to a retrial. In other words, as long as the issuing Member States give the guarantee that a retrial may take place upon request of the person concerned, the EAW-proceedings cannot end with a refusal. Ultimately, refusals are only possible in those situations in which the issuing Member State does not give a sufficient guarantee.

75 ECJ, judgment of 26 February 2013, *Stefano Melloni v. Ministerio Fiscal*, C-399/11, ECLI:EU:C:2013:107, para. 41.

The logic of the system of the EAW is that if one of the situations of a (the absent accused was summoned in person) or b (the absent accused was represented by counsel) applies or if the issuing Member State guarantees a new trial, there is no reason to refuse the EAW and the requested person must be surrendered.

7.4 Conclusions

The exception referred to in Article 4a(1)(a)(d) is an important exception in the day-to-day practice of issuing and executing judicial authorities.

Given the importance of this exception, it gives cause for concern that the experts are not unanimous on the *nature* of a key concept of that exception, 'the right to as retrial, or an appeal'. The majority of the experts consider this concept to be an autonomous concept of Union law, whereas one expert is of the opinion that it is not. Whether the concept is or is not an autonomous concept of Union law has far-reaching consequences for the interpretation and application of the exception. In the former case, a Union wide standard is applicable. In the latter case, there are as many standards as there are Member States. Equally worrisome is the fact the experts are not unanimous on the meaning of the concept of a 'right to a retrial', especially in the context of admissibility conditions. The majority of the experts take the view that the 'right to a retrial' is something more than the possibility to ask for a retrial and that, consequently, only some admissibility conditions are allowed, whereas one expert is of the opinion that the right to a retrial is nothing more than the possibility to ask for a retrial and that, therefore, the executing judicial should not assess whether requesting a retrial would be effective.

Only the Dutch executing judicial authority has encountered any difficulties in this regard. However, the experiences of issuing judicial authorities show that the executing judicial authorities from non-project Member States are critical of the assurances given under point 3.4 also.

Until such time as the Court of Justice decides on the nature and the meaning of the concept of a 'right to a retrial', one can only hope to prevent any problems by describing in the EAW in a factual way which conditions the surrendered person has to meet in order to obtain a retrial or an appeal.

The issue of the consequences not mentioning the time frame in the EAW elicited a wide range of opinions from the experts, ranging from questioning the requirement of mentioning the applicable time frame to refusal of surrender. Again, this is worrisome, given that both Article 4a(1)(d) and section (d) clearly require mentioning the applicable time frame. Moreover, it is hard to see how the requirement of mentioning the applicable time frame could inconvenience the issuing judicial authority.

Again, only the Dutch executing judicial authority reported any problems in this regard. None of the other executing judicial authorities and none of the issuing judicial authorities encountered any problems.

The experts differed widely on the issue of modifying the standard text of the assurances also. Their opinions ranged between the two extremes of 'not a ground for refusal' and 'could lead to refusal', the middle ground being taken up by 'requesting supplementary information'.

Yet again, only the Dutch executing judicial authority reported any problems with this issue. None of the other executing judicial authorities and none of the issuing judicial authorities encountered any difficulties.

Both the issue of the applicable time frame and the issue of modifying the standard text demonstrate the need to issue clear and practical instructions to issuing judicial authorities on ticking point 3.4 of section (d) of the EAW. Even if points 3.1-3.3 are not applicable, the issuing judicial authority is not under any obligation to tick point 3.4. An issuing judicial authority should only tick that point, if it is *fully* applicable, without adding to (except for the applicable time frame) and deleting from the standard text. The wording of point 3 of section (d) of the EAW-template is somewhat misleading in this regard ("3. If you have ticked the box under point 2, please confirm the existence of one of the following") and there is some evidence that it actually creates the misguided impression that the issuing judicial authority must tick one of the boxes of point 3, even if that particular point is not fully applicable to the situation at hand.[76] Therefore, consideration should be given to clarifying the wording of point 3 of section (d) of the EAW-form.

On the issue of contradictory information, most experts referred to the possibility of requesting supplementary information, while one expert excluded refusal of surrender whereas others did not.

This issue seems to be of theoretical importance only, because none of the issuing and executing judicial authorities encountered any problems.

It is striking that only the Dutch executing judicial authority reported any problems with regard to the first three issues. The fact that the Netherlands transposed Article 4a(1) as a *mandatory* ground for refusal cannot (fully) explain this state of affairs. Hungary and Ireland also transposed that provision as a mandatory ground for refusal, yet their executing judicial authorities reported no difficulties. The fact that the Netherlands vested the power to execute EAWs in *one specialised* court offers no (full) explanation either. Hungary and Ireland also appointed central executing judicial authorities. A possible (additional) explanation may be that the Dutch executing judicial authority deals with much more

76 NL, report, pp. 56-57 and 125.

EAWs than the executing judicial authorities in Hungary and Ireland. A larger volume of cases logically entails a larger volume of potentially problematic cases.[77]

77 In the period 2004-2015, Ireland received a total of 402 EAWs: *Report on the operation of the European Arrest Warrant Act 2003 (as amended) for the year 2016 made to the Houses of the Oireachtas by the Central Authority in the person of the Minister for Justice and Equality pursuant to section 6(6) of the European Arrest Warrant Act 2003*, p. 6. In 2015 alone, the Netherlands received 901 EAWs. There is no data on the EAWs received by Hungary: HU, report, p. 41.

8 Margin of Discretion

8.1 Introduction

In the previous chapters we focussed, firstly, on the situations in which Article 4a(1) is applicable, *i.e.* situations in which the person concerned did not appear in person at the trial resulting in the decision (Chapters 4 and 5). Subsequently, we discussed the situations in which, notwithstanding the absence of the person concerned at the trial resulting in the decision, the executing judicial authority may not refuse to execute the EAW, *viz.* the person concerned was summoned in person, was defended by a mandated legal counsellor, was served with the decision in person but did not make use of the right to a retrial or will be served with the decision and will be informed of that right (Chapters 6 and 7).

It cannot be excluded, in a particular case, that none of those four exceptions applies and that, therefore, the executing judicial authority has the power to refuse the execution of the EAW. But even so, in such a case the executing judicial authority possesses a *margin of discretion* to refrain from exercising that power.

After all, the Court of Justice has held that even after the executing judicial authority has found that the cases referred to in Article 4a(1)(a) to (d) FD 2002/584/JHA do not cover the situation of the requested person, it may take into account "other circumstances that enable it to ensure that the surrender of the person concerned does not entail a breach of his rights of defence".[1] This is so, because Article 4a(1) provides for an *optional* ground for refusal.[2]

In the context of the assessment whether the surrender does not entail a breach of the requested person's rights of defence the executing judicial authority may "have regard to the conduct of the person concerned", in particular "to any manifest lack of diligence on the part of the person concerned, notably where it transpires that he sought to avoid service of the information addressed to him".[3]

The four exceptions (see Chapters 6 and 7) do not represent the only situations in which the surrender does not entail a breach of the requested person's rights of defence.

1 ECJ, judgment of 24 May 2016, *Openbaar Ministerie v. Paweł Dworzecki*, C-108/16 PPU, ECLI:EU:C:2016:346, para. 50; ECJ, judgment of 10 August 2017, *Openbaar Ministerie v. Tadas Tupikas*, C-270/17 PPU, ECLI:EU:C:2017:628, para. 96; ECJ, judgment of 10 August 2017, C-271/17 PPU, *Openbaar Ministerie v. Sławomir Andrzej Zdziaszek*, ECLI:EU:C:2017:629, para. 107.

2 ECJ, judgment of 24 May 2016, *Openbaar Ministerie v. Paweł Dworzecki*, C-108/16 PPU, ECLI:EU:C:2016:346, para. 50.

3 ECJ, judgment of 24 May 2016, *Openbaar Ministerie v. Paweł Dworzecki*, C-108/16 PPU, ECLI:EU:C:2016:346, para. 51.

Although the situations covered in Article 4a(1)(a) to (d) FD 2002/584/JHA relate to situations in which – according to the relevant case-law of the ECtHR – *in absentia* proceedings do not infringe Article 6(1) ECHR, these situations do not *fully* codify that case-law. In other words, even though none of the situations in Article 4a(1)(a) to (d) FD 2002/584/JHA applies, this does not necessarily mean that surrender for the purpose of the enforcement of an *in absentia* conviction would breach the rights of defence of the person concerned (see also Section 3.1).

In leaving the executing judicial authority a margin of discretion, FD 2002/584/JHA

> does not prevent the executing judicial authority from ensuring that the rights of the person concerned are upheld by taking due consideration of all the circumstances characterising the case before it, including the information which it may itself obtain, provided that compliance with the deadlines laid down in Article 17 of that Framework Decision is not called into question.[4]

The national laws of the Member States which transposed Article 4a(1) as a *mandatory* ground for refusal do not allow taking into account "circumstances that enable it to ensure that the surrender of the person concerned does not entail a breach of his rights of defence".[5] The national laws of the Member States which transposed Article 4a(1) as an *optional* ground for refusal do (see also Section 3.3).[6]

This chapter will deal with two issues concerning the margin of discretion: which circumstances are sufficient to enable the executing judicial authority to ensure that the surrender of the requested person does not entail a breach of his/her rights of defence (Section 8.2) and whether the executing judicial authority may refrain from refusing to execute the EAW even if it finds that the surrender does entail a breach of the requested person's rights of defence (Section 8.3). Finally, this chapter will devote some attention to the consequences of an eventual refusal to execute an EAW (Section 8.4).

---

4 ECJ, judgment of 10 August 2017, *Openbaar Ministerie v. Tadas Tupikas*, C-270/17 PPU, ECLI:EU:C:2017:628, para. 97; ECJ, judgment of 10 August 2017, *Openbaar Ministerie v. Sławomir Andrzej Zdziaszek*, C-271/17 PPU, ECLI:EU:C:2017:629, para. 108.

5 HU, report, p. 29; IE, report, p. 57 (however, the relevant case was decided before the *Dworzecki, Tupikas* and *Zdziaszek* judgments); NL, report, p. 90.

6 BE, report, p. 37; PL, report, p. 72. According to RO, report, p. 38, there is no specific provision in Romanian law allowing for taking into account such circumstances.

8.2 Other Circumstances Justifying Surrender[7]

Because of the highly casuistic nature of the case-law of the ECtHR, it is impossible to list exhaustively circumstances other than those enumerated in Article 4a(1) (a) (d) which would justify the conclusion that the surrender of the requested person would not entail a breach of his/her rights of defence.

What follows is an indication of circumstances derived from the ECtHR's case-law which might act as building blocks to support such a conclusion.

Such circumstances will most likely occur only in cases in which, although the defendant was not summoned in person or otherwise officially informed about the date and the place of the trial, *s/he had sufficient knowledge of the charges against him/her and the proceedings*[8] and

- either unequivocally waived his/her right to attend the trial; or
- displayed a lack of diligence in taking proper measures to receive official notifications about the date and the place of the trial.

The ECtHR distinguishes between an express waiver and a tacit waiver of the right to be present.[9] It is a prerequisite for a valid waiver - either express or tacit - that the person concerned was sufficiently aware of the proceedings and the charges against him.[10] After all, waiving a right presupposes that the person concerned knows of the existence of that right and, therefore, of the proceedings within which to exercise that right.[11]

Against this background, the *mere* fact that the defendant was informed during the *police-investigations* that:

---

7 This paragraph is based on NL, report, pp. 90-95.

8 See ECtHR, judgment of 1 March 2006, *Sejdovic v. Italy* [GC], ECLI:CE:ECHR:2006:0301JUD005658100, § 101.

9 ECtHR, judgment of 1 March 2006, *Sejdovic v. Italy* [GC], ECLI:CE:ECHR:2006:0301JUD00565810, § 86. On this distinction see also ECtHR, judgment of 12 June 2018, *M.T.B. v. Turkey*, ECLI:CE:ECHR:2018:0612 JUD004708106, § 49-50.

10 ECtHR, judgment of 1 March 2006, *Sejdovic v. Italy* [GC], ECLI:CE:ECHR:2006:0301JUD00565810, § 101. *See also*, e.g., ECtHR, judgment of 23 May 2006, *Kounov v. Bulgaria*, ECLI:CE:ECHR:2006:0523JUD 002437902, § 50; ECtHR, decision of 12 December 2006, *Battisti v. France*, ECLI:CE:ECHR:2006:1212DEC 002879605; ECtHR, decision of 16 January 2010, *Sulejmani v. Albania*, ECLI:CE:ECHR:2012:0619DE C001611410; ECtHR, judgment of 12 June 2018, *M.T.B. v. Turkey*, ECLI:CE:ECHR:2018: 0612JUD004708106, § 49. In this respect, the decision in *Sulejmani v. Albania* is particularly relevant: the applicant had signed a copy of a power of attorney in which he referred to the charges against him and by which he acknowledged the start of the proceedings against him and appointed lawyers B. and J. to represent him. The ECtHR held that "(b)y choosing to leave the country, the applicant must be considered to have intentionally and unequivocally waived his rights under Article 6 of the Convention and could reasonably have foreseen the consequences of his conduct".

11 *See, e.g.*, ECtHR, judgment of 4 March 2014, *Dilipak and Karakaya v. Turkey*, ECLI:CE:ECHR:2014: 0304JUD000794205, § 87.

- *in the event of a prosecution* s/he would be summoned at the address given by him/her and
- he was obliged by national law to notify the proper authorities of any change in residence,

in and of itself would probably not suffice.[12] What is lacking here is, to begin with, sufficient knowledge of the charges against him/her.[13] However, if the defendant is aware of the

12 The Romanian expert is of the opinion that these circumstances might suffice, since at least the second circumstance is covered by Romanian legislation: RO, report, p. 38. The Hungarian expert disagrees; these circumstances do not suffice, because the defendant has the right to be aware of a hearing and the authorities must do everything to find out his/her residence: HU, report, p. 29. The Polish expert refers to the common opinion of Polish judges that a defendant who was provided with the written instruction as to his/her rights and duties at the pre-trial stage of the proceedings should collect correspondence sent to him/her by judicial authorities. Failure to collect correspondence properly sent to the address indicated by the accused shall be treated as a waiver of the right to participate actively in the criminal proceedings: PL, report, p. 73. The Irish expert points out that evidence of conduct on the part of the requested person tending to suggest a waiver of the right to be present in person would be potentially relevant to supporting a conclusion that the requested person's rights would not be disrespected by a surrender: IE, report, p. 57.

13 See ECtHR, judgment of 23 May 2006, *Kounov v. Bulgaria*, ECLI:CE:ECHR:2006:0523JUD002437902, § 48-50: "48. La Cour a envisagé que dans certaines hypothèses, même en l'absence d'une notification à personne, il ne pouvait être exclu que certains faits avérés puissent démontrer sans équivoque qu'un individu est au courant des poursuites, connaît la nature et la cause des accusations contre lui et n'a pas l'intention de prendre part au procès ou entend se soustraire à la justice (…). 49. Toutefois, la Cour estime que tel n'est pas le cas du requérant en l'espèce. Ainsi, même en admettant la thèse du Gouvernement dans le sens que l'intéressé se serait enfui du commissariat, la Cour considère qu'en l'absence de notification au requérant des charges retenues contre lui, rien dans les éléments produits devant elle ne permet d'établir qu'il a été au courant de l'ouverture des poursuites, de son renvoi en jugement ou de la date de son procès. En effet, les tentatives des autorités de faire exécuter le mandat d'arrêt se sont révélées infructueuses et aucun des actes de la procédure n'a été notifié à l'intéressé, mais à l'avocat commis d'office. *Ayant été interrogé sur les faits par les policiers*, le requérant pouvait seulement supposer que des poursuites allaient être engagées *mais ne pouvait en aucun cas avoir une connaissance précise des charges qui allaient être retenues*. 50. Au vu de ces observations, la Cour *n'estime pas établi* en l'occurrence que le requérant *avait une connaissance suffisante des poursuites et des accusations à son encontre* pour être en mesure de décider de se soustraire à la justice ou de renoncer, de manière non équivoque, à son droit de comparaître en justice et de se défendre (…)" (emphasis added). See also ECtHR, judgment of 24 April 2012, *Haralampiev v. Bulgaria*, ECLI:CE:ECHR:2012:0424JUD002964803, § 38-44: the applicant was interrogated by the police in the presence of a legal counsellor; he, therefore, had "une connaissance suffisante des poursuites et des accusations à son encontre pour savoir que le dossier serait probablement renvoyé devant le parquet et que lui-même serait par la suite cité à comparaître et traduit devant les juridictions". The ECtHR nevertheless examined whether the applicant "avait eu **une connaissance exacte des accusations portées contre lui**" and stated that one could not conclude that the applicant "a tenté à se soustraire à la justice ou qu'il a manifesté de manière non équivoque son refus de comparaître devant les tribunaux" (emphasis added). Compare ECtHR, decision of 26 March 2019, *Vybornova v. Russia*, ECLI:CE:ECHR:2019:0326DEC003483911, § 30. The police had questioned the applicant as a suspect before she left for the Czech Republic. She applied for asylum in the Czech Republic, stating that she was being prosecuted in Russia on charges related to the YUKOS scandal and that she feared an unfair trial. Her request for asylum was allowed. Russian requests for extradition were rejected. The ECtHR concluded: "(…) it is evident to the Court that the applicant decided to stay away from Russia and to refrain from direct involvement in the criminal proceedings against her long before the trial. **In such circumstances she may be regarded as having been sufficiently aware**

proceedings and the charges, a failure to comply with the duty of notifying a change of address can be considered as a lack of diligence on the part of the defendant (see also below) and can lead to a refusal to grant the defendant a retrial or an appeal.[14]

The fact that the defendant made a deal with the public prosecutor as to the penalty *to be imposed by the court* necessarily implies that the defendant had sufficient knowledge of the charges against him/her, but it does not, in and of itself, imply a waiver of the right to be present at the trial.[15]

It does, however, follow from the deal that the defendant could have reasonably expected to be summoned at the address s/he had provided.[16] In such circumstances, it is up to the defendant to take appropriate measures to ensure receipt of his/her mail.[17] A lack of dili-

---

of the prosecution and the charges against her and as having deliberately chosen not to attend the hearings at the first-instance and appeal courts". Compare ECtHR, decision of 2 September 2004, *Kimmel v. Italy*, ECLI:CE:ECHR:2004:0902DEC003282302: the applicant, who was interrogated by the investigating judge, **was aware of the proceedings against her**, but upon release chose to have every judicial notification delivered at the address of her legal counsellor. "Aux yeux de la Cour, **la requérante aurait dû savoir qu'à la suite de son élection de domicile, aucun acte ne lui aurait été personnellement communiqué**, et qu'il lui appartenait de prendre contact avec [son avocat] pour obtenir toute information relative au déroulement des instances. Ayant omis d'agir dans ce sens, la requérante pouvait raisonnablement s'attendre à être jugée par contumace, étant représentée à l'audience par son conseil. La Cour conclut partant que l'intéressée a renoncé de manière non équivoque à son droit de comparaître et de se défendre personnellement" (emphasis added).

14 For the interplay between the duty to inform the authorities of any change of address imposed on the defendant by national law, his awareness of the proceedings and of the charge and the minimum level of diligence required of him *see, e.g.*, ECHR, judgment of 24 October 2013, *Ioannis Papageorgiou v. Greece*, ECLI:CE:ECHR:2013:1024JUD004584709, § 42, 44 and 45.

15 A-G Bobek, opinion of 11 May 2016, *Openbaar Ministerie v. Paweł Dworzecki*, C-108/16 PPU, ECLI:EU:C:2016:333, para. 68. *See*, however, ECtHR, judgment of 29 April 2014, *Natsvlishvili and Togonidze v. Georgia*, ECLI:CE:ECHR:2014:0429JUD000904305, § 92: "The Court thus observes that by striking a bargain with the prosecuting authority over the sentence and pleading no contest as regards the charges, the first applicant waived his right to have the criminal case against him examined on the merits".

16 ECtHR, judgment of 26 January 2017, *Lena Atanasova v. Bulgaria*, ECLI:CE:ECHR:2017:0126JUD005200907, § 48 and § 53.

17 *See, e.g.*, ECtHR, judgment of 16 December 1992, *Hennings v. Germany*, ECLI:CE:ECHR:1992:1216 JUD001212986, § 26 ("The Court (…) considers that the applicant could reasonably have been expected to obtain a key to his letter-box in order to have ready access to any mail addressed to him, particularly since he must have foreseen that proceedings would be brought against him as a result of his failure to reply to the letter of 9 August 1984 from the public prosecutor's office (…). The authorities cannot be held responsible for barring his access to a court because he failed to take the necessary steps to ensure receipt of his mail and was thereby unable to comply with the requisite time-limits laid down under German law"); ECtHR, decision of 15 September 2005, *Maass v. Germany*, ECLI:CE:ECHR:2005:0915DEC007159801 ("The authorities cannot, however, be held responsible for barring an applicant's access to court because he or she failed to take the necessary steps to ensure receipt of his or her mail and was thereby unable to comply with the requisite time-limits laid down in domestic law (…). The Court notes that, after having been questioned by the police, the applicant knew that criminal proceedings were pending against her. Even assuming that the applicant in fact had not received any of the letters sent to her by the German authorities, she could therefore reasonably be expected to take the necessary steps to secure receipt of her mail, especially as she had stated that several other letters had also not reached her or her neighbours"); ECtHR, judgment of 8 October 2015, *Aždajić v. Slovenia*, ECLI:CE:ECHR:2015:1008JUD007187212, § 56 ("(…) the Court

gence in this regard may lead to the conclusion that the *in absentia* proceedings did not breach Article 6 ECHR. Indeed, the preamble of FD 2002/584/JHA itself explicitly refers to this line of case-law:

> (…) In accordance with the case law of the European Court of Human Rights, when considering whether the way in which the information is provided is sufficient to ensure the person's awareness of the trial, particular attention could, where appropriate, also be paid to the diligence exercised by the person concerned in order to receive information addressed to him or her.[18,19]

Of course, if the defendant is lawfully deprived of his/her freedom, one can hardly reproach him/her for having failed to take the necessary steps to ensure receipt of his/her mail at his/her regular address. On the contrary, in such circumstances the defendant may reasonably expect the authorities to be aware of this fact and to be able to ascertain his/her whereabouts.[20] After all, it is the responsibility of the State "to make available to the courts effective access to information about persons deprived of their liberty at the time of the trial" and it is for the courts "to ensure, by making the necessary administrative arrangements, that the court correspondence [is] served" on a defendant who at the time of the trial is in custody.[21] If the authorities are aware that the defendant is incarcerated *abroad* and if there are no indications that s/he intends to waive his/her right to appear at the trial and to defend him/herself, they should consider measures to enable the defendant to make use of that right.[22] In the absence of legal instruments enabling the transfer of the defendant, an adjournment of the trial may be the only solution.

If a defendant who was sufficiently aware of the proceedings against him/her was absent at the hearing while his/her legal counsellor was present, s/he could have asked his/her

agrees with the Government that the applicant might have expected that an action could be lodged against her. Therefore, in view of the fact that she planned to be absent from her home for two months, it would not be unreasonable to expect from her that she would take some measures to ensure the receipt of her mail in order to be able to comply with the requisite time-limits laid down in the domestic law, in case of institution of proceedings against her").

18 Recital (8), *in fine*.

19 The Belgian expert refers to such circumstances as: refusing to open the door in order to avoid being served with the summons in person, refusing to empty the mailbox, refusing to collect a registered letter at the post office: BE, report, p. 38.

20 ECHR, report of 16 October 1996, *Menckeberg v. the Netherlands*, ECLI:CE:ECHR:1996:1016REP002551494, § 50.

21 ECtHR, judgment of 21 July 2009, *Seliwiak v. Poland*, ECLI:CE:ECHR:2009:0721JUD000381804, § 60.

22 ECtHR, judgment of 28 August 1991, *F.C.B. v. Italy*, ECLI:CE:ECHR:1991:0828JUD001215186, § 33; ECtHR, judgment of 14 February 2017, *Hokkeling v. the Netherlands*, ECLI:CE:ECHR:2017:0214JUD003074912, § 61.

legal counsellor about the progress of the proceedings. Failing to do so is relevant in reaching the conclusion that the defendant waived his/her right to be present.[23]

If the defendant was aware of the date of the first hearing, it is up to him/her to contact his/her legal counsellor – or the registrar of the court – and to enquire after any subsequent hearings.[24]

A defendant who was present at the first instance trial and who lodges an appeal against the first instance judgment can reasonably expect to be summoned to appear at the hearing

---

23 See ECtHR, decision of 2 September 2004, *Kimmel v. Italy*, ECLI:CE:ECHR:2004:0902DEC003282302 ("Aux yeux de la Cour, la requérante aurait dû savoir qu'à la suite de son élection de domicile, aucun acte ne lui aurait été personnellement communiqué, et **qu'il lui appartenait de prendre contact avec Me F. [son avocat d'office] pour obtenir toute information relative au déroulement des instances**"); ECtHR, decision of 14 September 2006, *Booker v. Italy*, ECLI:CE:ECHR:2006:0914DEC001264806 ("La Cour en conclut que le requérant était au courant de la date de l'audience (...). Cependant, il décida de son plein gré de ne pas y participer. **Le requérant a également omis de prendre contact avec son conseil, présent à l'audience incriminée, pour se renseigner quant au déroulement de la procédure et à la date de l'audience suivante, fixée par le juge en présence des représentants des parties**"); ECtHR, decision of 23 November 2006, *Zaratin v. Italy*, ECLI:CE:ECHR:2006:1123DEC003310406 ("(...) la Cour note que dans chacune des procédures en cause le requérant était au courant des poursuites entamées à son encontre. (...) A la lumière de ce qui précède, la Cour considère que **le requérant aurait pu, à l'occurrence par l'intermédiaire des avocats de son choix, se renseigner quant aux dates des audiences, auxquelles ces derniers ont participé**. Il avait donc une possibilité effective d'être présent aux débats; il a cependant de son plein gré choisi de ne pas s'en prévaloir"); ECtHR, decision of 22 May 2007, *Böheim v. Italy*, ECLI:CE:ECHR:2007:0522DEC003566605 ("La Cour en conclut que le requérant était au courant des accusations portées contre lui et des conséquences qui auraient pu découler de son inertie. Cependant, il a décidé de son plein gré de ne pas élire domicile en Italie, de ne pas nommer un avocat de son choix et **de ne contacter ni les autorités ni l'avocat d'office**, pour se renseigner quant au déroulement de la procédure et aux dates des audiences"); ECtHR, decision of 28 September 2010, *Tedeschi v. Italy*, ECLI:CE:ECHR:2010:0928DEC002568506: "Force est de constater qu'à aucun moment, le requérant ne rectifia l'élection de domicile auprès du cabinet de [son avocat]. Au contraire, il réitéra expressément ladite élection de domicile lors de l'appel introduit le 4 février 2001. Aux yeux de la Cour, le requérant aurait dû savoir qu'à la suite de son élection de domicile, et faute de rectification de sa part, aucun acte ne lui serait personnellement communiqué, **et qu'il lui appartenait de prendre contact avec [son avocat] pour obtenir toute information relative au déroulement des instances** (...)" (emphasis added).

24 ECtHR, decision of 20 October 2015, *Di Silvio v. Italy*, ECLI:CE:ECHR:2015:1020DEC005663513, § 33-34: "La Cour estime aussi établi que le requérant avait connaissance de la date initialement fixée pour les débats d'appel, à savoir le 21 janvier 2011. En effet, il a produit un certificat médical dans le but d'obtenir le renvoi de cette audience (...). (...) Dans ces circonstances, la Cour considère **qu'il appartenait au requérant de prendre contact avec le conseil de son choix pour savoir si le renvoi sollicité avait été octroyé et, dans l'affirmative, quelle date avait été fixée pour les débats d'appel** (...). **L'intéressé aurait pu également s'adresser au greffe de la cour d'appel pour se renseigner quant au déroulement de son procès**" (emphasis added). Of course, if the defendant was aware of the date and the place of the trial and was defended at that trial by a legal counsellor appointed by him, there is no problem under Art. 6 ECHR: ECJ, judgment of 17 April 2018, *Pirozzi v. Belgium*, ECLI:CE:ECHR:2018:0417JUD002105511, § 70. See also ECtHR, decision of 28 November 2006, *Holowiński v. Poland*, ECLI:CE:ECHR:2006:1128DEC003671104: the applicant was present at the first three hearings, knew about the date of the final hearing but failed to inform the domestic court about his absence in due time and in writing, and to justify it. The domestic court relied on information that the applicant was being sought for the purpose of serving a prison sentence imposed in another criminal case, but had gone into hiding. In the circumstances, the ECtHR concluded that the applicant had waived the right to appear at the hearing in an unequivocal manner.

on appeal at the address s/he gave to the authorities.[25] Again, in such circumstances, it is up to the defendant to take appropriate measures to ensure receipt of his/her mail and, again, a lack of diligence in this regard may lead to the conclusion that the *in absentia* proceedings did not breach Article 6 ECHR.

This case must be distinguished from cases in which the public prosecutor lodges an appeal against the first instance judgment and the defendant does not have sufficient knowledge of the proceedings on appeal. The mere fact that the defendant was present at the trial at first instance which resulted in his/her acquittal and that s/he, therefore, could reasonably expect the public prosecutor to lodge an appeal does not justify, in and of itself, the conclusion that s/he waived his/her right to be present on appeal.[26]

If the defendant, who had sufficient knowledge of the proceedings against him/her and who was assisted by a legal counsellor changed his/her address without notifying the proper

25 ECtHR, decision of 23 February 1999, *De Groot v. the Netherlands*, ECLI:CE:ECHR:1999:0223DEC003496697. See also ECtHR, judgment of 24 May 2007, *Da Luz Domingues Ferreira v. Belgium*, ECLI:CE:ECHR:2007:0524JUD005004999, § 50: "La Cour relève avec le Gouvernement que **le requérant a interjeté lui-même appel** du jugement du tribunal correctionnel d'Arlon en février 1994 et qu'**il savait donc depuis cette date qu'il serait cité à comparaître en appel**. (…)".

26 *See, e.g.*, ECtHR, judgment of 25 March 2008, *Gaga v. Romania*, ECLI:CE:ECHR:2008:0325JUD000156202: the first instance court acquitted the applicant in his absence of murder. The public prosecutor appealed against that judgment. The second instance court rejected the appeal in the presence of the applicant. The public prosecutor appealed against that judgment. The applicant was summoned for the third instance hearing at the address of his former wife, who earlier had notified the second instance court that the applicant had not resided there since 1995 and had explicitly asked the court to stop sending summonses of her former husband to her address. The third instance court convicted the applicant to a custodial sentence *in absentia*. The ECtHR rejected the argument of Romania that the applicant could have been informed of the date of the third instance hearing by other means (*via* his former wife). According to the ECtHR such vague and informal knowledge does not suffice to conclude that the applicant waived his right to be present at the third instance hearing. What is noteworthy here is that – although one could argue that the applicant, having been acquitted twice, should reckon with another appeal by the public prosecutor and should, therefore, take the necessary steps to receive the summons for the third instance hearing –, there is not the slightest indication that the ECtHR found the applicant's responsibility for the receipt of his mail or the fact that he could have reckoned with an appeal by the public prosecutor relevant to this case. Of course, the Romanian authorities gave notification of the third instance hearing at an address of which they were aware it was no longer the applicant's address. It could be that the ECtHR felt that this error on the part of the Romanian authorities was decisive or at least weighed far heavier than any responsibility on the part of the applicant. See also ECtHR, judgment 22 May 2018, *Muca v. Albania*, ECLI:CE:ECHR:2018:0522JUD005745611, § 34-37: the applicant was present at the first instance trial, was assisted by his chosen legal counsellor, was acquitted and went abroad. The defendant was not informed of the appeal lodged by the public prosecutor, but his legal counsellor was. The defendant's chosen legal counsellor continued to represent him on appeal and the defendant was convicted *in absentia*. However, the ECtHR held that it could not be inferred that the legal counsellor was acting on the defendant's express instructions. Furthermore, in later retrial proceedings the same legal counsellor represented the defendant, having been appointed by the court. The ECtHR concluded that the applicant did not have sufficient knowledge of the appeal proceedings and found a violation of Art. 6 ECHR. Again, there is no inkling that the ECtHR found relevant that the applicant should have reckoned with an appeal lodged by the public prosecutor or that he should have remained in contact with his legal counsellor. What seems to be decisive in this case is that the applicant was not aware of the proceedings on appeal.

authorities of his/her new address, even though a restriction was imposed on him/her not to leave his/her residence without the authorisation of the public prosecutor's office, s/he by his/her own actions brought about a situation that made him/her unavailable to be informed of and to participate in the trial. In such circumstances the *in absentia* proceedings do not breach Article 6 ECHR.[27,28]

A judgment commuting into a single sentence one or more sentences previously imposed on the person concerned comes within the ambit of Article 4a(1), where the proceedings resulting in that judgment

> are not a purely formal and arithmetic exercise but entail a margin of discretion in the determination of the level of the sentence, in particular, by taking account of the situation or personality of the person concerned, or of mitigating or aggravating circumstances.[29]

This is so, because compliance with the requirement of a fair trial

---

27 ECtHR, judgment of 28 February 2008, *Demebukov v. Bulgaria*, ECLI:CE:ECHR:2008:0228JUD006802001, § 57. The Belgian expert also referred to this judgment: BE, report, p. 38. See also ECtHR, decision of 20 May 2003, *Riekwel v. the Netherlands*, ECLI:CE:ECHR:2003:0520DEC007420801: the applicant might reasonably have been expected, either through his representative or in person, to ensure that his change of address was communicated to the registrar of the Supreme Court; ECtHR, decision of 28 September 2010, *Tedeschi v. Italy*, ECLI:CE:ECHR:2010:0928DEC002568506: "Force est de constater qu'à aucun moment, le requérant ne rectifia l'élection de domicile auprès du cabinet de [son avocat]. Au contraire, il réitéra expressément ladite élection de domicile lors de l'appel introduit le 4 février 2001. Aux yeux de la Cour, le requérant aurait dû savoir qu'à la suite de son élection de domicile, et **faute de rectification de sa part**, aucun acte ne lui serait personnellement communiqué, et qu'il lui appartenait de prendre contact avec [son avocat] pour obtenir toute information relative au déroulement des instances (...)"; ECtHR, judgment of 26 January 2017, *Lena Atanasova v. Bulgaria*, ECLI:CE:ECHR:2017:0126JUD005200907, § 52: "En conclusion, compte tenu des circonstances spécifiques de l'espèce, la Cour estime que la situation dénoncée par la requérante ne s'analyse pas en une restriction injustifiée de son droit de participer à l'audience de son affaire pénale. La requérante avait été dûment informée de l'existence d'une procédure pénale à son encontre et des charges retenues contre elle. Elle avait reconnu les faits, s'était déclarée prête à négocier les termes de sa condamnation et pouvait donc raisonnablement s'attendre à être citée à comparaître devant les tribunaux. **Elle a pourtant quitté l'adresse qu'elle avait préalablement communiquée aux autorités sans leur signaler le changement de son domicile.** Son allégation selon laquelle elle aurait donné aux autorités l'adresse de son compagnon est restée complètement non étayée. Les autorités ont entrepris les démarches raisonnablement nécessaires afin d'assurer sa comparution devant le tribunal de district pendant son procès: elles ont d'abord cherché à la convoquer à l'adresse qu'elle leur avaient laissée et qu'elle avait quittée sans les prévenir; elles ont ensuite cherché à établir les autres adresses connues de la requérante et à la convoquer à celles-ci; elles ont cherché à la localiser dans les établissements pénitentiaires; elles se sont assurées qu'elle n'avait pas quitté le territoire du pays. A la lumière de toutes ces circonstances, la Cour considère que la requérante a sciemment et valablement renoncé, de manière implicite, à son droit de comparaître en personne devant les tribunaux dans le cadre de la procédure pénale menée à son encontre. (...)" (emphasis added).

28 See also ECtHR, decision of 4 December 2018, *Năstase v. the Republic of Moldova*, ECLI:CE:ECHR:2018:1204 DEC007444411, with regard to the obligation not to leave his village.

29 ECJ, judgment of 10 August 2017, *Openbaar Ministerie v. Sławomir Andrzej Zdziaszek*, C-271/17 PPU, ECLI:EU:C:2017:629, para. 88.

> entails the right of the person concerned to be present at the hearing [resulting in the determination of a sentence] because of the significant consequences which it may have on the quantum of the sentence to be imposed (…).[30]

However, even though the competent court has a margin of discretion, when the *scope for sentencing* is *limited* and when the *original sentences* were *not imposed in absentia*, the competent court can determine the new sentence on the basis of the case file and written submissions.[31]

8.3 Limits to the Margin of Discretion

Under Article 4(6) FD 2002/584/JHA, the executing judicial authority must have a margin of discretion 'as to whether or not it is appropriate to refuse to execute the [EAW]', but it may only exercise the option to refuse the EAW if it finds that "there is a legitimate interest which would justify the sentence imposed in the issuing Member State being enforced in the executing Member State" in light of the objective pursued by that provision.[32] In other words, the margin of discretion is not limitless. Only a legitimate interest justifies exercising the option to refuse the EAW.

Under Article 4a(1) it is less clear whether there are any limits to the margin of discretion. The Court of Justice seems to be attempting to guide the executing judicial authority towards exercising its margin of discretion in accordance with the objective of that provision: the executing judicial authority *may* take 'other circumstances' into account in order to allow surrender *provided that* the rights of defence are respected. The difference with Article 4(6) FD 2002/584/JHA is that the Court of Justice, as yet, has not ruled that the executing judicial authority *must* have a margin of discretion under Article 4a(1) (see Section 3.3) nor that it *must* exercise that discretion in a particular way.

It is true that the Court of Justice has already held that an executing judicial authority "*cannot tolerate* a breach of fundamental rights", in the context of EAW-proceedings in which, after having requested supplementary information once, "it still has not obtained the necessary assurances as regards the rights of defence of the person concerned during the relevant proceedings". Although the words "cannot tolerate a breach of fundamental

30 ECJ, judgment of 10 August 2017, *Openbaar Ministerie v. Sławomir Andrzej Zdziaszek*, C-271/17 PPU, ECLI:EU:C:2017:629, para. 87.

31 ECtHR, judgment of 28 November 2013, *Aleksandr Dementyev v. Russia*, ECLI:CE:ECHR:2013:1128JUD004309505, § 45-47. The domestic court had to commute a sentence of six months' community work into a prison sentence, **ranging from 1 day to 2 months**.

32 ECJ, judgment of 13 December 2018, *Ministère public v. Marin-Simion Sut*, C-514/17, ECLI:EU:C:2018:1016, paras. 33 and 36-37.

rights" seem to indicate an obligation to refuse to execute the EAW in such circumstances, the Court of Justice nonetheless concluded that the executing judicial authority *may* refuse to execute the EAW.[33]

As a result, it is yet undecided whether the executing judicial authority may refrain from refusing to execute the EAW if it finds that the surrender of the requested person entails a breach of his/her rights of defence. However, it can be strongly argued that this question should be answered in the negative.

According to the case-law of the ECtHR, extraditing someone would be contrary to Article 6 ECHR in circumstances where the person concerned had suffered or risked suffering a 'flagrant denial of justice' in the requesting country. A 'flagrant denial of justice' requires a "nullification, or destruction of the very essence" of the right to a fair trial.[34] Such a 'flagrant denial of justice' would occur

> where a person convicted *in absentia* is unable subsequently to obtain from a court which has heard him a fresh determination of the merits of the charge, in respect of both law and fact, where it has not been unequivocally established that he has waived his right to appear and to defend himself.[35]

This case-law also applies to situations in which the requesting State is a Member State of the European Union.[36]

Article 47(2) Charter corresponds to Article 6(1) ECHR.[37] Article 52(3) Charter declares that Charter-rights which correspond to ECHR-rights have the same meaning and scope as the latter rights. As the Court of Justice recently held, this provision

---

33 ECJ, judgment of 10 August 2017, *Openbaar Ministerie v. Sławomir Andrzej Zdziaszek*, C-271/17 PPU, ECLI:EU:C:2017:629, paras. 104-105 (emphasis added).

34 ECtHR, judgment of 17 January 2012, *Othman (Abu Qatada) v. United Kingdom*, ECLI:CE:ECHR:2012:0117JUD000813909, § 260. According to Advocate General Sharpston this criterion is too strict: opinion of 18 October 2012, *Ciprian Vasile Radu*, C-396/11, ECLI:EU:C:2012:648, paras. 82-83.

35 *See, e.g.*, ECtHR, decision of 16 October 2011, *Einhorn v. France*, ECLI:CE:ECHR:2001:1016DEC007155501, § 33.

36 *See, e.g.*, ECtHR, decision of 4 October 2007, *Cenaj v. Albania and Greece*, ECLI:CE:ECHR:2007:1004DEC001204906; ECtHR, decision of 1 February 2011, *Mann v. Portugal and the United Kingdom*, ECLI:CE:ECHR:2011:0201DEC000036010; ECtHR, judgment of 17 April 2018, *Pirozzi v. Belgium*, ECLI:CE:ECHR:2018:0417JUD002105511, § 71. We shall not discuss the rebuttable presumption of equivalent protection which applies under the ECHR when authorities of a Member State implement legal obligations arising from that Member State's membership of the EU, as this is outside the scope of the project. *See, e.g.*, ECtHR, judgment of 23 May 2016, *Avotiņš v. Latvia* [GC], ECLI:CE:ECHR:2016:0523JUD001750207.

37 ECJ, judgment of 25 July 2018, *Minister for Justice and Equality (Deficiencies in the system of justice)*, C-216/18 PPU, ECLI:EU:C:2018:586, para. 33.

> seeks to ensure the necessary consistency between the rights contained in it and the corresponding rights guaranteed by the ECHR, without thereby adversely affecting the autonomy of EU law and that of the Court of Justice of the European Union.[38]

Therefore, the level of protection of Article 47(2) Charter must not be 'in conflict' with that guaranteed by Article 6 ECHR, as interpreted by the ECtHR.[39] In other words, Article 47(2) Charter must not be interpreted in such a way that it affords *less* protection than Article 6(1) ECHR. It follows that *at least* in situations in which executing the EAW would expose the person concerned to a 'flagrant denial of justice' – as defined by the case-law of the ECtHR –, Article 47(2) Charter would impose an obligation on the executing judicial authority to refuse to execute the EAW.[40]

Although Advocate General Tanchev advised the Court of Justice to adopt the criterion of a 'flagrant denial of justice' in the context of a potential violation of the right to a fair trial in the issuing Member State,[41] that court gave expression to the autonomy of Union law and introduced its own criterion for determining whether the executing judicial authority should refrain from giving effect to the EAW: the criterion of a 'breach of the essence of the right to a fair trial'.[42]

As an *in absentia* conviction of someone who has not voluntarily waived his/her right to be present and who does not have the right to a retrial or an appeal constitutes a 'flagrant denial of justice', it seems likely that such a conviction would also constitute a 'breach of the essence of the right to a fair trial', as guaranteed by Article 47 Charter, and would, therefore, act as a bar to surrender.

---

38 ECJ, judgment of 12 February 2019, *TC*, C-492/18 PPU, ECLI:EU:C:2019:108, para. 57.

39 Cf. ECJ, judgment of 20 March 2018, *Criminal proceedings against Luca Menci*, C-524/15, ECLI:EU:C:2018:197, para. 62.

40 Of course, as follows from the second sentence of Art. 52(3) Charter, Union law may provide for *more* protection than Art. 6(1) ECHR affords.

41 Opinion of 28 June 2018, *Minister for Justice and Equality (Deficiencies in the system of justice)*, C-216/18 PPU, ECLI:EU:C:2018:517, paras. 72-85.

42 ECJ, judgment of 25 July 2018, *Minister for Justice and Equality (Deficiencies in the system of justice)*, C-216/18 PPU, ECLI:EU:C:2018:586, para. 78. It does not necessarily follow that the Court of Justice's own criterion is less strict – *i.e.* affords more protection – than the criterion of a 'flagrant denial of justice'. Given the Strasbourg court's description of what a 'flagrant denial of justice' is – a "nullification, or destruction of the very essence" of the right to a fair trial – it rather seems that the Court of Justice's criterion is, at the least, close to that of the Strasbourg court. British and Irish courts are even of the opinion that the Court of Justice in substance did not adopt a different criterion than the Strasbourg court: *Lis & Ors v. Regional Court in Warsaw, Poland & Ors* [2018] EWHC 2848 (Admin) (31 October 2018); *The Minister for Justice and Equality v. Celmer No.5* [2018] IEHC 639 (19 November 2018).

8.4 Consequences of a Refusal

A refusal to execute an EAW on the basis of Article 4a(1) of FD 2002/584/JHA means that the requested person will not undergo the sentence in the *issuing* Member State. As all Member States have now transposed FD 2008/909/JHA on the mutual recognition of custodial sentences,[43] transferring the execution of the custodial sentence to the *executing* Member State might seem an alternative to surrender. However, if the execution of the EAW was refused on the basis of Article 4a(1), transferring the execution of the sentence to the executing Member State is not really an option. FD 2008/909/JHA provides for a regime concerning *in absentia* judgments which closely resembles that of Article 4a(1) (Article 9(1)(i) of FD 2008/909/JHA). If the requirements of Article 4a(1) are not met, neither are the requirements of Article 9(1)(i). Applying Article 4a(1) to refuse the execution of an EAW, therefore, creates a risk of impunity of the requested person.

However, a decision to refuse the execution of an EAW on the basis of Article 4a(1) is not necessarily the end of the matter.

Any refusal to execute an EAW must be accompanied by the reasons for the refusal (Article 17(6) FD 2002/584/JHA). The duty to provide the reasons for a refusal allows the issuing judicial authority to assess whether it can remedy the defect(s) established by the executing judicial authority in a new EAW with regard to the same person, the same offence(s) and the same judgment. If, *e.g.*, surrender was refused, because the EAW did not contain any evidence that the requested person actually received the summons which was served on a third party, the issuing judicial authority could remedy this defect by mentioning this evidence in a new EAW.

In this regard, it should be stressed that a decision to refuse to execute an EAW does not have any *ne bis in idem* effect. Such a decision is not an 'acquittal' or a 'conviction' as referred to in Article 50 Charter. The European Commission is of the opinion that there is no duty to withdraw an EAW, when the executing judicial authority refused to execute it. After all, the executing judicial authority of *another* Member State 'may still be able to execute it'.[44] In the context of a refusal on the basis of Article 4a(1), ideally the executing judicial authorities of all Member States will apply the national laws transposing that provision in the same way. However, Article 4a(1) does allow the Member States some latitude,

43 Council Framework Decision 2008/909/JHA of 27 November 2008 on the application of the principle of mutual recognition to judgments in criminal matters imposing custodial sentences or measures involving deprivation of liberty for the purpose of their enforcement in the European Union, *OJ* 2008 L 327, p. 27, as amended by FD 2009/299/JHA. See the Table of Implementation on the website of the European Judicial Network (https://www.ejn-crimjust.europa.eu/ejn/libdocumentproperties/EN/739), last accessed on 6 August 2019. In Bulgaria, the legislation adopted to transpose FD 2008/909/JHA will enter into force on 1 January 2020.

44 *Handbook on how to issue and execute a European Arrest Warrant, OJ* 2017 C-335, p. 41.

e.g., with regard to the discretion of the executing judicial authority. As a consequence, the same set of circumstances which resulted in a refusal in Member State A could result in a surrender in Member State B. It follows, *a fortiori*, that it is open to the issuing judicial authority to withdraw the EAW and, at a later date, issue a new EAW concerning the same person, the same offence(s) and the same judgment, in particular if a previously established 'defect' is remedied.

It does not matter whether such a new EAW is sent to another Member State or to the Member State in which the execution of the previous EAW was refused. A previous refusal by an executing judicial authority does not relieve an executing judicial authority of the *same* Member State of its duty to take a decision on the execution of a new EAW with regard to the same person and the same offence(s).[45]

If the 'defect' which led to the previous refusal cannot be repaired, transferring the proceedings from the issuing Member State to the executing Member State may be the only means to avoid impunity.[46] The European Convention on the Transfer of Proceedings in Criminal Matters (ECTPCM) regulates such a transfer. Article 8(1)(h) and (2) ECTPCM enables the Contracting State in which the person concerned has already been finally sentenced to request another Contracting State to undertake criminal proceedings, if the requesting State is not able to enforce the sentence itself even by having recourse to extradition and if the requested State refuses to enforce that sentence. The aim is to prevent the person concerned "from evading punishment for an act committed by him, because the requesting State is unable to enforce a sentence passed in its territory, or to have it enforced by another State".[47] However, not all Member States have ratified this Convention.[48] At present, there is no Union instrument enabling the transfer of proceedings in such circumstances.

8.5 CONCLUSIONS

The four exceptions to the rule that the executing judicial authority may refuse to execute the EAW because the person concerned did not appear in person at the trial resulting in the decision do not fully codify the case-law of the ECtHR concerning *in absentia* proceed-

45 ECJ, judgment of 25 July 2018, *AY*, C-268/17, ECLI:EU:C:2018:602, paras. 32-36.

46 Art. 50 of the Charter in combination with Art. 54 CISA would not be an obstacle to proceedings in the executing Member State against the same person for the same offence(s), because the penalty imposed in the issuing Member State would not have been enforced, would not actually be in the process of being enforced and would still be enforceable. Cf. ECJ, judgment of 27 May 2014, *Zoran Spasic*, C-129/14 PPU, ECLI:EU:C:2014:586.

47 *Explanatory report*, p. 19 (accessible at https://www.coe.int/en/web/conventions/search-on-treaties/-/conventions/treaty/073).

48 The convention was ratified by fourteen Member States.

ings. Therefore, even if none of these four exceptions applies, surrendering the person concerned would not necessarily breach the rights of defence of the person concerned.

Because of its optional nature, Article 4a(1) confers on the executing judicial authority a margin of discretion with regard to the decision on the execution of the EAW in cases in which none of the four exceptions applies. When national law has left that margin of discretion untouched, the executing judicial authority may decide to refrain from refusing to execute the EAW if it finds that surrender would not entail a breach of the rights of defence of the person concerned.

The case-law of the ECtHR on *in absentia* proceedings constitutes a treasure trove of circumstances which would allow for just such a conclusion.

If, however, the executing judicial authority were to reach the conclusion that surrendering the person concerned would entail a 'flagrant denial of justice' – in which case it would probably also entail a 'breach of the essence of the right to a fair trial' –, it seems likely that Article 47(2) of the Charter would require a refusal to execute the EAW.

A refusal to execute the EAW on the basis of Article 4a(1) creates a risk of impunity of the requested person. However, such a refusal is not necessarily the end of the matter. Once it has identified why the execution of the EAW was refused, the issuing judicial authority may decide to issue a new EAW with regard to the same person, the same offence(s) and the same judgment(s), in which it addresses the 'defect' which caused the refusal.

If the 'defect' cannot be repaired, transferring the proceedings to the executing Member State could avoid impunity. However, at present there is no Union instrument on the transfer of proceedings and not all Member States are bound by the Council of Europe Convention on the transfer of proceedings.

9 Conclusions and Recommendations

9.1 Introduction

In Chapters 4-8, the different component parts of Article 4a(1) were analysed and discussed one by one. The conclusions which were drawn in those chapters are summarised in Section 9.2.

In Section 9.3, the recommendations following from all the preceding chapters are presented and the reasons for those recommendations are set out.

The recommendations will be discussed in the following order: recommendations at micro-level (recommendations to issuing and/or executing judicial authorities: Section 9.3.1), recommendations at meso-level (recommendations to the Member States, Section 9.3.2) and recommendations at macro-level (recommendations to the European Union, Section 9.3.3).

9.2 Summary of Conclusions

Chapter 4 concerns the meaning of the expression 'trial *in absentia*'. The conclusions may be summarised as follows:

- in Union law the autonomous expression 'trial *in absentia*' denotes a trial at which the person concerned was not *physically* present;
- in contrast with the *factual* nature of the autonomous Union law meaning of the concept of a 'trial *in absentia*', the legal orders of the project Member States employ national law meanings of a *technical* nature;
- when comparing the Union law meaning of the concept of a 'trial *in absentia*' with the various national law meanings, divergences appear, but these divergences do not necessarily imply that applying national law leads to results which are incompatible with Union law.

Apart from the expression 'trial *in absentia*', the other concept upon which the operation of Article 4a(1) hinges is the concept of a 'trial resulting in the decision'. Chapter 5 is devoted to that autonomous concept of Union law in the context of proceedings within one instance, successive proceedings and multiple decisions. The conclusions may be summarised as follows:

- the *final* 'decision' referred to in Article 4a(1) is not necessarily the same as the *enforceable* 'decision' referred to in Article 8(1)(c) on which the EAW is based, although in some cases these decisions may coincide depending on the national laws of the Member States. The exclusive focus of some issuing and executing judicial authorities on the first instance decision and on the decision modifying the original penalties because according to national law these decisions *will be enforced after surrender* is not in accordance with the *Tupikas*[1] and *Zdziaszek*[2] judgments. This suggests that it is necessary to improve and to keep up to date judicial authorities' knowledge of the Court of Justice's case-law;

- the interpretation and application at national level of autonomous *Union* law concepts seems to be governed by notions of *national* criminal procedural law, which may cause misunderstandings in EAW-proceedings;
- problems relating to the autonomous concept of a 'trial resulting in the decision' could be minimised by describing the relevant proceedings in section (d) of the EAW in a clear, concise and, above all, *factual* way, rather than using national legal terminology;
- given the Court of Justice's case-law on successive proceedings and on subsequent decisions amending the nature or the level of the original penalty, the structure and the wording of section (d) of the EAW-form no longer accurately reflect the requirements of Article 4a(1), provide insufficient guidance to issuing and executing judicial authorities and may, therefore, cause misunderstandings.

Having discussed two pivotal concepts of Article 4a(1) in Chapters 4 and 5, Chapter 6 focusses on three of the four exceptions to the rule that the executing judicial authority may refuse to execute the EAW if the person concerned did not appear in person at the trial resulting in the decision: the person concerned was summoned in person or was otherwise actually officially informed of the date and the place of the trial (Article 4a(1)(a)), the person concerned was aware of the scheduled trial and was defended by his/her mandated legal counsellor (Article 4a(1)(b)) and the decision was served on the person concerned, but s/he did not exercise his/her right to a retrial or an appeal (Article 4a(1)(c)). The conclusions of this chapter may be summarised as follows:

- Article 4a(1) and section (d) of the EAW-form use *autonomous* concepts of Union law. When issuing EAWs, Member States seem to interpret those concepts as if they were concepts of *national* law, whereas when executing EAWs they tend to interpret those concepts in accordance with the case-law of the Court of Justice;

1 ECJ, judgment of 10 August 2017, *Openbaar Ministerie v. Tadas Tupikas*, C-270/17 PPU, ECLI:EU:C:2017:628.

2 ECJ, judgment of 10 August 2017, *Openbaar Ministerie v. Sławomir Andrzej Zdziaszek*, C-271/17 PPU, ECLI:EU:C:2017:629.

- with regard to summoning the accused, Member States seem to strive for complying with the formalities of summoning instead of providing the accused with an effective opportunity of exercising the right to be present at the trial;
- residence or detention abroad is a factor which may contribute to a trial in the absence of the accused. The focus on compliance with formalities and the absence of EU legislation on participating in the trial from abroad by a temporary transfer or by video link technology only heighten the chances of non-appearance at the trial;
- although Member States consider themselves to be in line with the case-law of the Court of Justice, it is doubtful whether this is the case (with the exception of Ireland), because they employ legal presumptions and formal understandings which are not in compliance with that case-law. Again, cases of residence or detention abroad are illustrative: the applicable national and Union rules on mutual assistance in criminal matters do not require any evidence that the summons actually reached the accused in time;
- with regard to defence by a mandated legal counsellor, first of all, the autonomous concept of 'being aware of the scheduled trial' requires that the accused must be aware that a trial is anticipated or intended, but not that s/he has knowledge of the specific date and place of that trial. However, Member States' positions on this point vary from a legal presumption via a reasonable expectation of an impending trial to awareness of the actual date and place of the trial. Second, although it is not yet clear whether the autonomous concept of a 'mandate' requires specific or no instructions at all, this concept does presuppose awareness of the appointment of the legal counsellor, consent with representation by the legal counsellor and at least some form of contact with the legal counsellor about acting on the accused's behalf. These requirements are particularly problematic with regard to *ex officio* legal counsellors. Concerning the concept of a 'mandate', Member States' rules differ on the formalisation, the scope and the end of the mandate. These divergences can hinder judicial cooperation;
- with regard to situations in which the judgment was served on the person concerned and s/he had a right to a retrial or an appeal, but did not exercise it, although there are differences of opinion as to the meaning of the autonomous expression of 'being served with the decision', it is clear that the judgment must be served and the information about the right to a retrial or an appeal must be provided in such a way that the judgment and the information actually reached the person concerned;

The fourth exception is the subject of Chapter 7: the decision has not been served on the person concerned, but will be served on him/her in person after surrender and s/he will be expressly informed of his/her right to a retrial or an appeal and of the applicable time limit for requesting that legal recourse (Article 4a(1)(d)). The conclusions of this chapter may be summarised as follows:

- in practice, the fourth exception is a most important exception;
- according to the regular canons of interpretation of Union law, the concept of a 'right to a retrial, or an appeal' is an *autonomous* concept of Union law;
- that concept refers to more than a mere possibility of a retrial or an appeal. Admissibility requirements going beyond the manner in which and the time limit within which the person concerned must lodge the request for a retrial or an appeal do not seem to be in accordance with Article 4a(1);
- the wording of point 3.1-3.4 of section (d) of the EAW does not make it sufficiently clear that an issuing judicial authority should only tick the box of a particular point, if that point is fully applicable. In other words, the issuing judicial authority should not tick the box of, *e.g.*, point 3.4 and, at the same time, delete any part of the standard text of that point;
- equally, the wording of section (d) does not make it sufficiently clear that the issuing judicial authority should always mention the applicable time frame for requesting a retrial or an appeal when ticking the box of point 3.4.

If none of the four exceptions applies, the executing judicial authority has a margin of discretion with regard to the decision whether or not to execute the EAW. After all, Article 4a(1) contains an *optional* ground for refusal. If, in transposing Article 4a(1), the national legislator has left that margin of discretion intact, the executing judicial authority may decide to refrain from refusing to execute the EAW when it has established that surrendering the person concerned would not entail a breach of his/her rights of defence. Chapter 8 discusses the margin of discretion. The conclusions of this chapter may be summarised as follows:

- the four exceptions of Article 4a(1)(a)-(d) *do not represent* the *only* situations in which surrendering the requested person does not entail a breach of his/her rights of defence. In other words, this provision *does not fully codify* the ECtHR's case-law concerning *in absentia* proceedings;
- that case-law provides the building blocks upon which the executing judicial authority may base its conclusion that surrendering the requested person would not entail a breach of the rights of defence, even if none of the four exceptions applies. Such a conclusion may most likely be reached in situations in which the requested person had sufficient knowledge of the charges and of the proceedings and either unequivocally waived the right to be present at the trial or displayed a lack of diligence in taking proper steps to receive official notifications about the (outcome of the) trial;
- the margin of discretion conferred on the executing judicial authority does not seem to be limitless. There is a strong argument to be made that the executing judicial authority must refuse to execute the EAW at least in circumstances in which surrendering the person concerned would expose him/her to a 'flagrant denial of justice', in

which case surrendering the person concerned would probably also constitute a 'breach of the essence of the right to a fair trial';

- a refusal to execute the EAW on the basis of Article 4a(1) can lead to *de facto* impunity, but such a refusal is not necessarily the end of the matter. The executing judicial authority must give reasons for a refusal, allowing the issuing judicial authority to identify the 'defect' which caused the refusal. It is open to the issuing judicial authority to issue a new EAW with regard to the same person, the same offence(s) and the same judgment in which the 'defect' which led to the previous refusal is repaired. If the 'defect' cannot be repaired, transferring the proceedings to the executing Member State may be the only means to avoid impunity. However, at present there is no legal instrument which is binding on all Member States and which provides for such a transfer.

9.3 Recommendations

9.3.1 *Judicial Authorities*

9.3.1.1 Issuing Judicial Authorities

Issuing judicial authorities are recommended to:

1) always fill in section (d) of the EAW-form;

The issuing judicial authority should always fill in section (d) of the EAW, even if it is of the opinion that Article 4a(1) is not applicable. Leaving section (d) open can trigger a request for supplementary information and, therefore, can cause – unnecessary – delays (see Section 2.4.2.1).

2) use the correct EAW-form/use the prescribed standard text of section (d);

Although the use of the EAW-form as amended by FD 2009/299/JHA is mandatory, it seems that issuing judicial authorities of some Member States continue to use the old EAW-form (see Section 2.3.3).

Section (d) of the amended EAW-form is tailored to the requirements of Article 4a(1), whereas section (d) of the old EAW-form is not. In using the amended EAW-form, it is ensured that the prescribed standard text of section (d) is used. Using the old form can trigger a request for supplementary information and, therefore, can cause – unnecessary – delays.

3) use the consolidated language versions of section (d) and not to prepare ad hoc *translations*;
Although consolidated versions of the EAW-form are available in each of the official languages of the Member States, issuing judicial authorities of some Member States translate the *entire* EAW (*i.e.* the information added by the issuing judicial authority *and the standard texts*) into the official or designated language of the executing Member State, instead of using the version of the EAW-form in that language and translating only the information which the issuing judicial authority added to the EAW-form (Section 2.3.4). This course of action can give rise to discrepancies with regard to the standard text of section (d). Such discrepancies, in turn, can lead to a request for supplementary information and, therefore, can cause – unnecessary – delays.

Please note that the FD 2002/584/JHA and the EAW-form are available in all official languages of the Union (with the exception of Irish). They are published at exactly the same pages in the Official Journal of the European Union in all languages of the Union at the time of adoption of the Framework Decisions (with the exception of Irish): *OJ* 2002, L 190, pp. 1-18, amended as of 28 March 2009 by FD 2009/299/JHA, *OJ* 2009, L 81, pp. 24-36. For those Member States which became Members of the Union after the adoption of FD 2002/584/JHA and/or FD 2009/299/JHA, there are 'Special Editions' of the Official Journal, containing the text of both Framework Decisions and the EAW-form in the official languages of those Member States.

4) provide information in a clear, correct, comprehensive and factual manner and avoid legal qualifications on the basis of their own national law when providing information;
Providing information – either in the EAW or on the basis of Article 15(2) or (3) of FD 2002/584/JHA – in a clear, correct, comprehensive and factual way may avoid misunderstandings. Misunderstanding can give rise to requests for supplementary information, delays and even to decisions to (refuse to) execute the EAW which in hindsight are incorrect (incorrect in the sense that had the information been correct, clear, consistent, comprehensive and factual, the executing judicial authority would have taken another decision) (see Section 2.4.2.3).

Using legal terms derived from the law of the issuing Member State should be avoided as it can cause misunderstandings, because these terms can have a different meaning according to the legal system of the executing Member State (see, *e.g.*, Sections 4.3 and 6.2.8). For instance, the non-appearance of the person concerned, how the summons was effected, whether the accused was present at the hearing (and at which hearing(s)), whether counsel represented the accused or how the judgment was served should be described purely factually.

5) explain why Article 4a(1) is not applicable to a particular decision, if that is the opinion of the issuing judicial authority;
Explaining why in the opinion of the issuing judicial authority Article 4a(1) is not applicable to a particular decision enables the executing judicial authority to check whether it agrees with the conclusion drawn by its counterpart and, if not, to request supplementary information. If the issuing authority does not explain why Article 4a (1) is not applicable, it is most likely that information requests will be made.

6) ensure that the cause of a refusal is addressed in a subsequent EAW so as to repair it and prevent that a subsequent EAW to the same or another Member State will be refused again on the same grounds;
If, *e.g.*, the execution of the EAW was refused because the issuing judicial authority did not mention any evidence on which it based its conclusion that the person concerned actually received the summons, such evidence (if available) should be mentioned in any new EAW against the same person, for the same offence(s) and with respect to the same judgment. Mentioning the evidence may prevent another refusal (see Section 8.4).

9.3.1.2 Executing Judicial Authorities

Executing judicial authorities are recommended to:

7) request supplementary information only when needed on specific issues applicable in the case at hand;
According to the Court of Justice, asking for supplementary information should be the *ultima ratio*: the executing judicial authority should apply Article 15(2) of FD 2002/584/JHA "only as a last resort in exceptional cases in which the executing judicial authority considers that it does not have the official evidence necessary to adopt a decision on surrender as a matter of urgency".[3]

Because (frequent) requests for supplementary information have a negative impact on mutual trust (see Section 2.4.2.2) and can lead to delays (see Section 2.4.3), executing judicial authorities should use their power to request supplementary information prudently. In practice, however, executing judicial authorities do not always limit themselves to requesting relevant information, but instead ask for general information about the legal system of the issuing Member State (see Sections 2.4.2.1 and 2.4.2.3). In other words: general questions about the structure of the criminal process and the right to be present should not be sent out without reason.

3 ECJ, judgment of 23 January 2018, *Dawid Piotrowski*, C-367/16, ECLI:EU:C:2018:27, para. 61.

8) refrain from sending standard questionnaires;
One Member State systematically uses a standard questionnaire with general questions in each EAW case (see Sections 2.4.2.1 and 2.4.2.3).

Because a request for supplementary information should be the *ultima ratio* (see earlier), Article 15(2) cannot be used, 'as a matter of course', to request 'general information'.[4]

9) formulate their requests for supplementary information in an abundantly clear manner;
The potential impact on mutual trust (see Section 2.4.2.2), the need to comply with time limits (see Section 2.4.3) and the *ultima ratio* character of a request for supplementary information (see Section 2.4.2.1) dictate that the executing judicial authority should make abundantly clear which information it needs.

The executing judicial authority should not ask open-ended questions, but rather formulate questions which allow for a clear, correct, comprehensive and factual answer by the issuing judicial authority (see Section 9.3.1.1, recommendation 4)). To facilitate such answers, the executing judicial authority should identify specific parts of section (d) of the EAW which in its view are unclear, insufficient, contradictory or obviously incorrect, and indicate what kind of information is needed (see Section 2.4.2.3).

The executing judicial authority should not leave its counterpart guessing as to the reason why a certain piece of information is needed. Explaining the reason behind the request for supplementary information with reference to relevant case-law of the Court of Justice helps the issuing judicial authority in providing that information and may also provide it with an opportunity to clear up any misunderstandings in the initial assessment of the executing judicial authority (see Section 2.4.2.3).

10) apply the autonomous categories of Article 4a(1) on the basis of factual descriptions and not according to national legal classifications;
Insofar as Article 4a(1) contains autonomous concepts of Union law, these concepts should be interpreted uniformly throughout the Union. The meaning of such concepts cannot be determined by national law (see Section 3.5).

Moreover, using national legal terminology may cause misunderstandings, because that terminology may not have the same meaning in other Member States (see, *e.g.*, Section 4.3 (trial *in absentia*), Section 5.4 (successive proceedings and decisions), Section 6.2.8 (summons) and Section 6.3.4 (mandated legal counsellor)).

4 ECJ, judgment of 25 July 2018, C-220/18, *Generalstaatsanwaltschaft (Conditions of detention in Hungary)*, ECLI:EU:C:2018:589, para. 80.

11) consider, before deciding on an EAW, whether the issue at stake is a matter that needs to be clarified by the Court of Justice;
Given that Article 4a(1) of FD 2002/584/JHA contains autonomous concepts of Union law (see Section 3.5), many of which the Court of Justice has not yet elucidated, that the execution of an EAW can have human rights implications and that a refusal to execute the EAW should be the exception rather than the rule and creates a risk of impunity (see Section 9.3.1.3, recommendations 15) and 16)), the executing judicial authority should consider whether it is necessary to verify its interpretation of (the national transposition of) Article 4a(1) with the Court of Justice.

See for further assistance provided by the Court itself: *Recommendations to national courts and tribunals in relation to the initiation of preliminary ruling proceedings, OJ* 2018, C-257, p. 1.

12) clearly explain the reasons for their decision, when refusing to execute an EAW on the basis of Article 4a(1);
According to Article 17(6) of FD 2002/584/JHA, the executing judicial authority must give its reasons for any refusal to execute an EAW.

The reasons for a refusal allow the issuing judicial authority to assess whether it can remedy the defect established by the executing judicial authority. If so, the issuing judicial authority may consider issuing a new EAW against the same person, for the same offence(s) and with respect to the same judgment, in which the defect is repaired (see Section 9.3.1.1, recommendation 6)).

The executing judicial authority should also ensure that the reasons for refusing to execute an EAW on the basis of Article 4a(1) are accurately communicated to the issuing judicial authority, especially when its Member State has designated a Central Authority for the transmission of official correspondence relating to EAWs (see Article 7(2) of FD 2002/584/JHA).

9.3.1.3 Both Issuing and Executing Judicial Authorities

Both issuing and executing judicial authorities are recommended to:

13) use a common language when communicating with each other (e.g. *English);*
Insofar as the applicable legal regime permits[5] and taking into account the rights of the person concerned,[6] the requirement to observe the time limits of Article 17 of FD 2002/584/JHA strongly suggests that the issuing and the executing judicial authorities

5 See Art. 8(2) of FD 2002/584/JHA concerning translation of the EAW.
6 See Art. 3(6) of Directive 2010/64/EU on the right to interpretation and translation in criminal proceedings, concerning translation of the EAW.

communicate with one another in a language which they both understand, thus obviating as far as possible the need for any translation.

14) recognise that the issues addressed in Article 4a(1) FD relate to autonomous concepts of Union law and that attaching a national legal meaning to them may give rise to misunderstandings;

When issuing an EAW or deciding on the execution of an EAW, national law notions sometimes seem to dictate the interpretation and application of the legislation adopted to transpose Article 4a(1) (see, *e.g.*, Sections 5.4, 6.2.8 and 6.3.4).

However, Article 4a(1) of FD 2002/584/JHA contains autonomous concepts of Union law, which must be interpreted uniformly throughout the European Union, "irrespective of classifications in the Member States". Assigning a national law meaning to an autonomous concept of Union law not only negates the autonomous character of such concepts, but can also cause misunderstandings. After all, the national law meaning of one Member State does not necessarily correspond to the national law meaning of other Member States (see, *e.g.*, Section 4.3) – and even less to the autonomous meaning of the respective concept under European Union law.

15) be mindful of the fact that, in principle, a refusal should be prevented;

In accordance with the principle of mutual recognition, executing the EAW is the general rule, whereas refusing to execute the EAW is the exception (see Sections 6.1 and 7.3). Both issuing and executing judicial authorities should bear this in mind. Moreover, the principle of sincere cooperation requires of the issuing and executing judicial authorities that they try in earnest to avoid, as far as possible, a refusal on the basis of Article 4a(1).

16) be mindful of the fact that a refusal to execute the EAW can result in de facto *impunity;*

This recommendation is closely connected to the previous recommendation. A refusal to execute an EAW for the purpose of enforcing a sentence imposed after a trial at which the person concerned did not appear in person will mean that the person concerned is not surrendered to the issuing Member State and, therefore, will not undergo his/her sentence in that Member State.

If the requirements of Article 4a(1)(a) to (d) of FD 2002/584/JHA are not met, equally the requirements for taking over the execution of the sentence are not met (Article 9(1)(i) of FD 2008/909/JHA). In such circumstances, the competent authority of the executing Member State may refuse to recognise and enforce the sentence imposed in the issuing Member State.

A refusal to execute the EAW on the basis of Article 4a(1), therefore, creates a risk of impunity (see Section 8.4).

However, this risk is offset by the fact that the requested person's rights of defence were not fully observed (after all, the requirements of Article 4a(1) were not met). Therefore, this recommendation should not be read as advising executing judicial authorities to surrender the requested person in cases in which the requirements of Article 4a(1)(a) to (d) were not met and they could not establish that surrendering the requested person would not entail a breach of his/her rights of defence (see Section 8.3). Rather, issuing and executing judicial authorities should cooperate to establish, where possible, that the requirements of Article 4a(1) were met or that surrendering the requested person would not entail a breach of his/her rights of defence.

9.3.2 *Member States*

9.3.2.1 All Member States

All Member States are recommended:

17) to recognise that the issues addressed in Article 4a(1) FD relate to autonomous concepts of Union law and that attaching a national legal meaning to them may give rise to misunderstandings;
The explanation for recommendation 14) applies *mutatis mutandis* to *all* authorities of the Member States, including the legislator.

18) to change the mandatory ground for refusal into an optional one (if applicable);
Three of the project Member States transposed Article 4a(1) of FD 2002/584/JHA as an optional ground for refusal, the other three as a mandatory ground for refusal (see Section 3.3).

Member States which transposed Article 4a(1) of FD 2002/584/JHA as a mandatory ground for refusal deny their executing judicial authorities the possibility of refraining from refusing to execute the EAW when these authorities are satisfied that executing the EAW would not entail a breach of the rights of defence of the requested person, even though none of the situations covered by Article 4a(1)(a) to (d) applies (see Sections 3.3 and 8.2).

19) to amend their legislation on summoning an accused in all proceedings so as to meet the requirements of the Dworzecki *judgment;*
Making national criminal procedural legislation 'Dworzecki-proof' will enhance the chances of execution of EAWs for the purpose of enforcing sentences imposed following a trial at which the person concerned did not appear in person, although Article 4a(1)(a) of FD

2002/584/JHA, as interpreted by the Court of Justice in its *Dworzecki* judgment,[7] in and of itself does not require any changes in the legislation concerning summoning an accused (see Section 4.2.1).

20) do the utmost to ensure that the accused has an effective opportunity to exercise the right to be present at the trial;
In five of the project Member States, the national rules on summonses and especially the non-personal alternatives for summoning seem to be constructed in such a way that non-participation by the accused cannot stop the proceedings from carrying on. These rules do not require a positive indication that the accused is aware of the date and the place of the trial, because they formalise the requirements and do not take account of the material facts. Continuing the proceedings, not ensuring that the accused can effectively exercise his/her right be present, seems to be the ultimate goal of these rules (see Section 6.2.2.1).

21) to pay specific attention to the fact that a summons abroad should meet the same high standards as a domestic summons, but that the factual and legal circumstances are quite different;
The circumstance that the accused resides (or is detained) abroad at the time of the trial can easily result in non-participation in the trial.

Neither FD 2009/299/JHA nor Directive 2016/343/EU contains any rules on Member States assisting each other in serving the summons when the accused resides (or is detained) in another Member State.

Member States distinguish between summonses within and outside their respective territories. Although the rules applicable on summoning abroad differ from Member State to Member State, all Member States seem to employ formal understandings or legal presumptions which increase the risk that an accused will not hear in a timely fashion that a case has been started against him/her. Article 52 Convention implementing the Schengen agreement allows Member States to send procedural documents directly by post. As a result, it is not established whether the summons *actually* reached the accused (see Section 6.2.3).

22) to explore the possibilities for a virtual presence of the accused;
This recommendation is closely connected to the previous recommendation.

In four of the six project Member States it is possible for the accused to be present at the trial via videoconference (see Section 4.3).

7 ECJ, judgment of 24 May 2016, *Openbaar Ministerie v. Paweł Dworzecki*, C-108/16 PPU, ECLI:EU:C:2016:346.

Especially when the accused resides (or is detained) abroad, videoconferencing is a useful tool to prevent that circumstance alone from resulting in non-participation in the trial.

23) not to substitute delivery of the summons to the legal counsellor of the accused for summons in person;
Delivery of the summons to the legal counsellor (instead of delivering the summons to the accused in person) operates on the formal understanding or the legal presumption that the accused is thus aware of the date and the place of the trial.

Such formal understandings and legal presumptions raise the question whether the summons is served in such a way that it is unequivocally established that the accused *actually* received it, raise serious doubts as to whether they are in compliance with the *Dworzecki* judgment and cause problems with executing EAWs (see Section 6.2.8).

24) to make abundantly clear what the ambit of a legal counsellor's mandate is under the national legal system;
For the purposes of Article 4a(1)(b) of FD 2002/584/JHA, the legal counsellor - a legal counsellor either appointed by the accused ('chosen legal counsellor') or by the Member State ('*ex officio* legal counsellor') - must have been given a 'mandate' by the accused. Although the FD does not define the concept of a 'mandate', it is clear that a mandate at least requires that the accused was aware of the appointment of the legal counsellor, that s/he wanted to be represented by the legal counsellor and that s/he at least had some form of contact with the legal counsellor about acting on the accused's behalf (see Section 6.3.4).

National rules diverge with regard to the formalisation, the scope and the end of the mandate (see Section 6.3.4). This divergence might hinder judicial cooperation on the basis of the EAW.

25) to provide for a legal basis for a transfer of proceedings when the execution of an EAW is refused on the basis of Article 4a(1);
All Member States transposed FD 2008/909/JHA on the mutual recognition of custodial sentences.[8] This Framework Decision provides a legal basis for recognising and enforcing a custodial sentence imposed on a national or on a non-national resident of the executing Member State (see Article 4(1)(c) in combination with Article 4(7)(a) of FD 2008/909/JHA).

8 Council Framework Decision 2008/909/JHA of 27 November 2008 on the application of the principle of mutual recognition to judgments in criminal matters imposing custodial sentences or measures involving deprivation of liberty for the purpose of their enforcement in the European Union, *OJ* 2008 L 327, p. 27, as amended by FD 2009/299/JHA.

Recognising and enforcing a custodial sentence on the basis of FD 2008/909/JHA can be an alternative for surrendering a requested person for the purpose of enforcing that custodial sentence (cf. Article 4(6) of FD 2002/584/JHA). However, if the custodial sentence was imposed by an *in absentia* judgment, both alternatives are subject to essentially the same legal regime (compare Article 4a(1) FD 2002/584/JHA with Article 9(1)(i) FD 2008/909/JHA). If the requirements of Article 4a(1) are not met, neither are the requirements of Article 9(1)(i). Therefore, even if the regime of FD 2008/909/JHA is applicable *ratione personae*, recognising and enforcing a custodial sentence is not a viable instrument to avoid the impunity that may result from a refusal to execute the EAW on the basis of Article 4a(1) FD 2002/584/JHA.

In order to prevent impunity, Member States should therefore provide for a legal basis for transferring the proceedings from the issuing Member State to the executing Member State in such circumstances. Article 8(1)(h) and (2) of the European Convention on the Transfer of Proceedings in Criminal Matters – which Convention is not ratified by all Member States – may serve as a template. These provisions enable the Contracting State in which the person concerned has already been finally sentenced to request another Contracting State to undertake criminal proceedings, if the requesting State is not able to enforce the sentence itself even by having recourse to extradition and if the requested State refuses to enforce that sentence (see Section 8.4).

26) to organise the attribution of the competence to issue EAWs and the competence to execute EAWs in such a way that it is prevented that judicial authorities only have occasion to issue or to execute an EAW on an incidental basis;
This recommendation aims at improving both quality and speed of the surrender process.

Attributing the competence to issue and to execute EAWs to a large number of different judicial authorities within one Member State can have an adverse effect on the quality of the EAWs and on the cost-effectiveness of EAW-proceedings. Some of those judicial authorities may have only limited experience with EAWs and, therefore, only limited incentive to follow the relevant case-law and to keep their knowledge up to date. Furthermore, if a judicial authority only issues an EAW or decides on the execution of an EAW once in a very long while, each time it has to reacquaint itself with the relevant rules and the relevant case-law.

In that sense, this recommendation also is closely related to recommendation 27 (see below).

27) to set up training programmes for issuing and executing judicial authorities with a view to regularly updating them on the case-law of the Court of Justice and the ECtHR;
With the increasing number of judgments issued by the Court of Justice on the EAW and other relevant forms of mutual recognition and the ever-expanding case-law of the ECtHR,

it is of the utmost importance that Member States provide training for their issuing and executing authorities. With the high number of relevant decisions authorities must be backed by permanent training programmes.

28) to register data on issuing and executing EAWs;
Some project Member States do not register data on the execution of EAWs or do not distinguish between prosecution-EAWs and execution-EAWs, let alone EAWs concerning *in absentia* judgments (see Section 1.3).

9.3.2.2 Project Member States

Ireland is recommended to:

29) review its case management procedures in execution cases;

30) take steps to expedite its execution court procedures so as to ensure greater compliance with the 60-day and 90-day time limits and in any case to reduce the time taken to process surrender requests;
Although under Irish law surrender proceedings are seen as having a *sui generis* character, in practice these proceedings have taken on the characteristics of *adversarial* proceedings.

This development and the practice of requesting comprehensive supplementary information[9] result in frequent non-compliance with the time limits of Article 17 of FD 2002/584/JHA (see Section 2.4.3).

9.3.3 *European Union*

The European Union is recommended to:

31) adopt legislation on the international judicial assistance to be delivered to summoning accused who reside (or is detained) abroad;
This recommendation is closely connected to the recommendation to Member States to pay specific attention to the fact that a summons abroad should meet the same high standards as a domestic summons. The reasons underpinning this recommendation are set out earlier (see Section 9.3.2.1, recommendation 21)).

The legislation envisaged in this recommendation should provide for an obligation for Member States to hand over the summons to an accused residing (or being detained) in their territory in person, if another Member State so requests, and to produce an official

9 On account of Irish judges' lack of familiarity with most Member States' (civil law) legal systems.

record of serving the summons. Article 10 of the European Convention on Mutual Assistance in Criminal Matters could act as a template (see Section 6.2.3.2).

32) adopt legislation on the presence of the accused who resides (or is detained) abroad at the trial via videoconference;
As with the previous recommendation, this recommendation aims at preventing non-participation in the trial, merely because the accused resides (or is detained) abroad. The reasons for the present recommendation are set out earlier (see Section 9.3.2.1, recommendation 22)).

At present, Union law provides for questioning the accused who resides (or is detained) in another Member State via videoconference, which is not the same as affording him the opportunity to be present at the trial via videoconference (see Section 4.2.4).

33) adopt legislation on the temporary transfer of the accused who is detained abroad in order to be present at the trial;
If the accused is detained in another Member State and has not waived his/her right to be present at the trial, in the absence of instruments providing for participation in the trial via video link technology or regulating a temporary transfer in order to stand trial, adjournment of the trial would be the only means to ensure that the accused's right to be present at the trial is respected.[10] Depending on the duration of the accused's detention, such an adjournment could cause problems with regard to prescription, the availability of evidence and, more generally, the need for swift criminal justice.

At present, Union law only provides for a temporary transfer for the purpose of *investigation* (see Section 6.2.5).

34) adopt legislation to amend and clarify the wording and structure of the relevant parts of the EAW-form;
In light of the case-law of the Court of Justice on Article 4a(1) of FD 2002/584/JHA, the wording and structure of section (d) of the EAW-form no longer accurately reflect the requirements of that provision as interpreted by the Court of Justice.

Some examples. The 'decision' referred to in section (d) (and in Article 4a(1)) is not necessarily the 'decision' referred to in section (b) (and in Article 8(1)(c)) (see Sections 5.2 and 5.4.2.1). Furthermore, the wording of section (d) suggests that it is applicable only to one decision. However, in some cases Article 4a(1) applies to two decisions (see Section 5.4.3.1).

A concrete proposal for amendment of the EAW-form is annexed to this report.

10 See ECtHR, judgment of 14 February 2017, *Hokkeling v. the Netherlands*, ECLI:CE:ECHR:2017:0214 JUD003074912.

35) adopt legislation on the transfer of proceedings when the execution of an EAW is refused on the basis of Article 4a(1);
See the explanation of recommendation 25) (Section 9.3.2.1). Unilateral legislative action by the Member States may not be enough to prevent impunity.

36) publish all declarations concerning translation of the EAW in the Official Journal;
Some project Member States deposited a declaration with the General Secretariat concerning translation of the EAW (Article 8(2) of FD 2002/584/JHA). However, contrary to Article 34(2) of FD 2002/584/JHA, these declarations were not published in the Official Journal, which raises the question whether they are legally binding (see Section 2.3.4).

37) further develop and maintain the Manual and the Guide set up by this project;
The Manual and the Guide set up by this project are just a first step in facilitating Member States' authorities to improve both quality and speed of the surrender process. Case-law and legal and factual circumstances will change in the future. Maintenance of both tools is required.

38) develop and implement the proposal for e-learning delivered by this project and set up a digital interactive version of the Manual;
Developing and implementing the proposal for e-learning and setting up a digital interactive version of the Manual will further facilitate judicial authorities to improve both speed and quality of the surrender process (see recommendation 37)).

39) specifically investigate the causes of exceeding time limits and see whether legal remedies against EAW decisions are one of the explanations;
In two of the six project Member States, the time limits of Article 17 of FD 2002/584/JHA are frequently exceeded (see Section 2.4.3).

40) adopt legislation on automatically providing the requested person in the executing Member State with the full judgment and its translation in a language s/he understands, if that judgment has not yet been served on the requested person in person (see Article 4a(1)(d) of FD 2002/584/JHA);
Currently, the requested person may ask for a copy of the judgment (Article 4a(2) of FD 2002/584/JHA). Once a requested person is surrendered to the issuing Member State, s/he is confronted with many practical obstacles when deciding whether or not to apply for a retrial or an appeal: (*e.g.*) s/he is in custody in the issuing Member State; s/he may not understand the language of the issuing Member State (see Section 7.1.5).

Given the importance of the right to a retrial or an appeal (see Section 7.1.1) and given those obstacles, Article 4(2) of FD 2002/584/JHA should be amended in such a way that the person concerned is automatically provided with a copy of the judgment in a language s/he understands in the executing Member State, in order to protect his/her rights and give him/her adequate time for (refraining from) requesting a retrial or an appeal.

Of course, automatically providing a copy of the judgment in the executing Member State should not activate the time limits for requesting a retrial or an appeal (cf. the present Article 4a(2)).

Table of European Cases

European Commission of Human Rights

ECHR, decision of 5 October 1967, *X. v. the Federal Republic of Germany*, ECLI:CE:ECHR:1967:1005DEC000242865

ECHR, decision of 6 December 1977, *X. v. Switzerland*, ECLI:CE:ECHR:1977:1206DEC000764876

ECHR, decision of 9 May 1994, *Sampson v. Cyprus*, ECLI:CE:ECHR:1994:0509DEC001977492

ECHR, report of 16 October 1996, *Menckeberg v. the Netherlands*, ECLI:CE:ECHR:1996:1016REP002551494

European Court of Human Rights

ECtHR, judgment of 17 January 1970, *Delcourt v. Belgium*, ECLI:CE:ECHR:1970:0117JUD000268965

ECtHR, judgment of 15 July 1982, *Eckle v. Germany*, ECLI:CE:ECHR:1982:0715JUD000813078

ECtHR, judgment of 21 February 1984, *Öztürk v. Germany*, ECLI:CE:ECHR:1984:0221JUD000854479

ECtHR, judgment of 12 February 1985, *Colozza v. Italy*, ECLI:CE:ECHR:1985:0212JUD000902480

ECtHR, judgment of 26 May 1988, *Ekbatani v. Sweden*, ECLI:CE:ECHR:1988:0526JUD001056383

ECtHR, judgment of 28 August 1991, *F.C.B. v. Italy*, ECLI:CE:ECHR:1991:0828JUD001215186

ECtHR, judgment of 29 October 1991, *Fejde v. Sweden*, ECLI:CE:ECHR:1991:1029JUD001263187

ECtHR, judgment of 16 December 1992, *Hennings v. Germany*, ECLI:CE:ECHR:1992:1216JUD001212986

ECtHR, judgment of 21 September 1993, *Kremzow v. Austria*, ECLI:CE:ECHR:1993:0921JUD001235086

ECtHR, judgment of 24 February 1994, *Bendenoun v. France*, ECLI:CE:ECHR:1994:0224JUD001254786

ECtHR, decision of 23 February 1999, *De Groot v. the Netherlands*, ECLI:CE:ECHR:1999:0223DEC003496697

ECtHR, decision of 7 September 1999, *Jodko v. Lithuania*, ECLI:CE:ECHR:1999:0907DEC003935098

ECtHR, judgment of 27 June 2000, *Constantinescu v. Romania*, ECLI:CE:ECHR:2000:0627JUD002887195

ECtHR, judgment of 14 June 2001, *Medenica v. Switzerland*, ECLI:CE:ECHR:2001:0614JUD002049192

ECtHR, judgment of 23 July 2002, *Janosevic. v. Sweden*, ECLI:CE:ECHR:2002:0723JUD003461997

ECtHR, judgment of 25 July 2002, *Papon v. France*, ECLI:CE:ECHR:2002:0725JUD005421000

ECtHR, judgment of 26 July 2002, *Meftah and Others v. France* [GC], ECLI:CE:ECHR:2002:0726JUD003291196

ECtHR, decision of 20 May 2003, *Riekwel v. the Netherlands*, ECLI:CE:ECHR:2003:0520DEC007420801

ECtHR, judgment of 9 October 2003, *Ezeh and Connors v. United Kingdom* [GC], ECLI:CE:ECHR:2003:1009JUD003966598

ECtHR, decision of 2 September 2004, *Kimmel v. Italy*, ECLI:CE:ECHR:2004:0902DEC003282302

ECtHR, decision of 15 September 2005, *Maass v. Germany*, ECLI:CE:ECHR:2005:0915DEC007159801

ECtHR, judgment of 1 March 2006, *Sejdovic v. Italy* [GC], ECLI:CE:ECHR:2006:0301JUD005658100

ECtHR, judgment of 23 May 2006, *Kounov v. Bulgaria*, ECLI:CE:ECHR:2006:0523JUD002437902

ECtHR, decision of 14 September 2006, *Booker v. Italy*, ECLI:CE:ECHR:2006:0914DEC001264806

ECtHR, judgment of 5 October 2006, *Marcello Viola v. Italy*, ECLI:CE:ECHR:2006:1005JUD004510604

ECtHR, judgment of 18 October 2006, *Hermi v. Italy* [GC], ECLI:CE:ECHR:2006:1018JUD001811402

ECtHR, decision of 9 November 2006, *Golubev v. Russia*, ECLI:CE:ECHR:2006:1109DEC002626002

ECtHR, decision of 23 November 2006, *Zaratin v. Italy*, ECLI:CE:ECHR:2006:1123DEC003310406

ECtHR, judgment of 23 November 2006, *Jussila v. Finland* [GC], ECLI:CE:ECHR:2006:1123JUD007305301

ECtHR, decision of 28 November 2006, *Holowiński v. Poland*, ECLI:CE:ECHR:2006:1128DEC003671104

ECtHR, decision of 12 December 2006, *Battisti v. France*, ECLI:CE:ECHR:2006:1212DEC002879605

ECtHR, judgment of 12 April 2007, *Mevlüt Kaya v. Turkey*, ECLI:CE:ECHR:2007:0412JUD000138302

ECtHR, decision of 22 May 2007, *Böheim v. Italy*, ECLI:CE:ECHR:2007:0522DEC003566605

ECtHR, judgment of 24 May 2007, *Da Luz Domingues Ferreira v. Belgium*, ECLI:CE:ECHR:2007:0524JUD005004999

ECtHR, decision of 4 October 2007, *Cenaj v. Albania and Greece*, ECLI:CE:ECHR:2007:1004DEC001204906

ECtHR, judgment of 28 February 2008, *Demebukov v. Bulgaria*, ECLI:CE:ECHR:2008:0228JUD006802001

ECtHR, judgment of 25 March 2008, *Gaga v. Romania*, ECLI:CE:ECHR:2008:0325JUD000156202

ECtHR, judgment of 25 November 2008, *Boyarchenko v. Ukraine*, ECLI:CE:ECHR:2012:0522JUD000582603

ECtHR, judgment of 9 June 2009, *Sobolewski (no. 2) v. Poland*, ECLI:CE:ECHR:2009:0609JUD001984707

ECtHR, judgment of 9 June 2009, *Strzałkowski v. Poland*, ECLI:CE:ECHR:2009:0609JUD003150902

ECtHR, judgment of 21 July 2009, *Seliwiak v. Poland*, ECLI:CE:ECHR:2009:0721JUD000381804

ECtHR, judgment of 17 September 2009, *Enea v. Italy* [GC], ECLI:CE:ECHR:2009:0917JUD007491201

ECtHR, decision of 8 December 2009, *Previti v. Italy*, ECLI:CE:ECHR:2009:1208DEC004529106

ECtHR, judgment of 15 December 2009, *Gurguchiani v. Spain*, ECLI:CE:ECHR:2009:1215JUD001601206

ECtHR, decision of 16 January 2010, *Sulejmani v. Albania*, ECLI:CE:ECHR:2012:0619DEC001611410

ECtHR, judgment of 29 June 2010, *Hakimi v. Belgium*, ECLI:CE:ECHR: 2010:0629JUD000066508

ECtHR, decision of 28 September 2010, *Tedeschi v. Italy*, ECLI:CE:ECHR: 2010:0928DEC002568506:

ECtHR, decision of 1 February 2011, *Mann v. Portugal and the United Kingdom*, ECLI:CE:ECHR:2011:0201DEC000036010

ECtHR, judgment of 1 March 2011, *Faniel v. Belgium*, ECLI:CE:ECHR: 2011:0301JUD001189208

ECtHR, judgment of 10 May 2011, *Shkalla v. Albania*, ECLI:CE:ECHR: 2011:0510JUD002686605

ECtHR, decision of 17 May 2011, *Suhaldolc v. Slovenia*, ECLI:CE:ECHR: 2011:0517DEC005765508

ECtHR, decision of 16 October 2011, *Einhorn v. France*, ECLI:CE:ECHR: 2001:1016DEC007155501

ECtHR, judgment of 17 January 2012, *Othman (Abu Qatada) v. United Kingdom*, ECLI:CE:ECHR: 2012:0117JUD000813909

ECtHR, judgment of 3 April 2012, *Boulois v. Luxembourg* [GC], ECLI:CE:ECHR: 2012:0403JUD003757504

ECtHR, judgment of 24 April 2012, *Haralampiev v. Bulgaria*, ECLI:CE:ECHR: 2012:0424JUD002964803

ECtHR, judgment of 22 May 2012, *Idalov v. Rusland*, ECLI:CE:ECHR: 2012:0522JUD000582603

ECtHR, decision of 23 October 2012, *Ciok v. Poland*, ECLI:CE:ECHR: 2012:1023DEC000049810

ECtHR, judgment of 24 October 2013, *Ioannis Papageorgiou v. Greece*, ECLI:CE:ECHR: 2013:1024JUD004584709

ECtHR, judgment of 31 October 2013, *Janyr v. Czech Republic*, ECLI:CE:ECHR:2013:1031JUD004293708

ECtHR, judgment of 28 November 2013, *Aleksandr Dementyev v. Russia*, ECLI:CE:ECHR:2013:1128JUD004309505

ECtHR, judgment of 4 March 2014, *Dilipak and Karakaya v. Turkey*, ECLI:CE:ECHR:2014:0304JUD000794205

ECtHR, judgment of 29 April 2014, *Natsvlishvili and Tongonidze v. Georgia*, ECLI:CE:ECHR:2014:0429JUD000904305

ECtHR, judgment of 8 October 2015, *Aždajić v. Slovenia*, ECLI:CE:ECHR:2015:1008JUD007187212

ECtHR, decision of 20 October 2015, *Di Silvio v. Italy*, ECLI:CE:ECHR:2015:1020DEC005663513

ECtHR, judgment of 17 December 2015, *Sobko v. Ukraine*, ECLI:CE:ECHR:2015:1217JUD001510210

ECtHR, judgment of 16 February 2016, *Yevdokimov e.a. v. Russia*, ECLI:CE:ECHR:2016:0216JUD002723605

ECtHR, decision of 17 May 2016, *Van Velzen v. the Netherlands*, ECLI:CE:ECHR:2016:0517DEC002149610

ECtHR, judgment of 23 May 2016, *Avotiņš v. Latvia* [GC], ECLI:CE:ECHR:2016:0523JUD001750207

ECtHR, judgment of 3 October 2016, *Baratta v. Italy*, ECLI:CE:ECHR:2015:1013JUD002826309

ECtHR, judgment of 26 January 2017, *Lena Atanasova v. Bulgaria*, ECLI:CE:ECHR:2017:0126JUD005200907

ECtHR, judgment of 2 February 2017, *Ait Abbou v. France*, ECLI:CE:ECHR:2017:0202JUD004492113

ECtHR, judgment of 14 February 2017, *Hokkeling v. the Netherlands*, ECLI:CE:ECHR:2017:0214JUD003074912

ECtHR, decision of 3 October 2017, *Giurgiu v. Romania*, ECLI:CE:ECHR:2017:1003DEC002623909

ECtHR, decision of 6 March 2018, *Nicolae Popa v. Romania*, ECLI:CE:ECHR:2018:0306DEC005524212

ECtHR, judgment of 17 April 2018, *Pirozzi v. Belgium*, ECLI:CE:ECHR:2018:0417JUD002105511

ECtHR, judgment 22 May 2018, *Muca v. Albania*, ECLI:CE:ECHR:2018:0522JUD005745611

ECtHR, judgment of 12 June 2018, *M.T.B. v. Turkey*, ECLI:CE:ECHR:2018:0612JUD004708106

ECtHR, judgment of 2 October 2018, *Bivolaru v. Romania (No. 2)*, ECLI:CE:ECHR:2018:1002JUD006658012

ECtHR, judgment of 30 October 2018, *Gestur Jónsson and Ragnar Halldór Hall v. Iceland*, ECLI:CE:ECHR: 2018:1030JUD006827314

ECtHR, judgment of 28 November 2018, *Vyacheslav Korchagin v. Russia*, ECLI:CE:ECHR:2018:0828JUD001230716

ECtHR, decision of 4 December 2018, *Năstase v. Republic of Moldova*, ECLI:CE:ECHR:2018:1204DEC007444411

ECtHR, decision of 26 March 2019, *Vybornova v. Russia*, ECLI:CE:ECHR:2019:0326DEC003483911

ECtHR, judgment of 16 July 2019, *Styrmir Þór Bragason v. Iceland*, ECLI:CE:ECHR:2019:0716JUD003629214

COURT OF JUSTICE OF THE EUROPEAN UNION

ECJ, judgment of 24 October 1996, *Aannemersbedrijf P.K. Kraaijeveld BV e.a. v. Gedeputeerde Staten van Zuid-Holland*, C-72, 95, ECLI:EU:C:1996:404

ECJ, judgment of 3 May 2007, *Advocaten voor de Wereld VZW v. Leden van de Ministerraad*, C-303/05, ECLI:EU:C:2007:261

ECJ, judgment of 17 July 2008, *Proceedings concerning the execution of a European arrest warrant issued against Szymon Kozłowski*, C-66/08, ECLI:EU:C:2008:437

ECJ, judgment of 6 October 2009, *Dominic Wolzenburg*, C-123/08, ECLI:EU:C:2009:616

ECJ, judgment of 16 November 2010, *Gaetano Mantello*, C-261/09, ECLI:EU:C:2010:683

ECJ, judgment of 21 October 2010, *I.B.*, C-306/09, ECLI:EU:C:2009:626

ECJ, judgment of 5 September 2012, *João Pedro Lopes Da Silva Jorge*, C-42/11, ECLI:EU:C:2012:517

ECJ, judgment of 26 February 2013, *Stefano Melloni v. Ministerio Fiscal*, C-399/11, ECLI:EU:C:2013:107

ECJ, judgment of 30 May 2013, *Jeremy F. v. Premier ministre*, C-168/13 PPU, ECLI:EU:C:2013:358

ECJ, judgment of 27 May 2014, *Zoran Spasic*, C-129/14 PPU, ECLI:EU:C:2014:586

ECJ, judgment of 16 July 2015, *Minister for Justice and Equality v. Francis Lanigan*, C-237/15 PPU, ECLI:EU:C:2015:474

ECJ, judgment of 15 October 2015, *Criminal proceedings against Gavril Covaci*, C-216/14, ECLI:EU:C:2015:586

ECJ, judgment of 5 April 2016, *Pál Aranyosi and Robert Căldăraru v. Generalstaatsanwaltschaft Bremen*, C-404/15 and C-659/15 PPU, ECLI:EU:C:2016:198

ECJ, judgment of 24 May 2016, *Openbaar Ministerie v. Paweł Dworzecki*, C-108/16 PPU, ECLI:EU:C:2016:346

ECJ, judgment of 7 July 2016, *Ivo Muladi v. Krajský úřad Moravskoslezského kraj*, C-447/15, ECLI:EU:C:2016:533

ECJ, judgment of 28 July 2016, *JZ v. Prokuratura Rejonowa Łódź – Śródmieście*, C-294/16 PPU, ECLI:EU:C:2016:610

ECJ, judgment of 10 November 2016, *Openbaar Ministerie v. Krzysztof Marek Poltorak*, C-452/16 PPU, ECLI:EU:C:2016:858

ECJ, judgment of 10 November 2016, *Openbaar Ministerie v. Ruslanas Kovalkovas*, C-477/16 PPU, ECLI:EU:C:2016:861

ECJ, judgment of 15 March 2017, *Lucio Cesare Aquino v. Belgische Staat*, C-3/16, ECLI:EU:C:2017:209

ECJ, judgment of 29 June 2017, *Daniel Adam Popławski*, C-579/15, ECLI:EU:C:2017:503

ECJ, judgment of 10 August 2017, *Openbaar Ministerie v. Tadas Tupikas*, C-270/17 PPU, ECLI:EU:C:2017:628

ECJ, judgment of 10 August 2017, *Openbaar Ministerie v. Sławomir Andrzej Zdziaszek*, C-271/17 PPU, ECLI:EU:C:2017:629

ECJ, judgment of 12 October 2017, *Criminal proceedings against Frank Sleutjes*, C-278/16, ECLI:EU:C:2017:757

ECJ, judgment of 5 December 2017, *Criminal proceedings against M.A.S. and M.B.*, C-42/17, ECLI:EU:C:2017:936

ECJ, judgment of 22 December 2017, *Samet Ardic*, C-571/17 PPU, ECLI:EU:C:2017:1026

ECJ, judgment of 23 January 2018, *Dawid Piotrowski*, C-367/16, ECLI:EU:C:2018:27

ECJ, judgment of 20 March 2018, *Criminal proceedings against Luca Menci*, C-524/15, ECLI:EU:C:2018:197

ECJ, judgment of 25 July 2018, *Minister for Justice and Equality (Deficiencies in the system of justice)*, C-216/18 PPU, ECLI:EU:C:2018:586

ECJ, judgment of 25 July 2018, *Generalstaatsanwaltschaft (Conditions of detention in Hungary)*, C-220/18 PPU, ECLI:EU:C:2018:589

ECJ, judgment of 25 July 2018, *AY*, C-268/17, ECLI:EU:C:2018:602

ECJ, judgment of 17 October 2018, *UD*, C-393/18, ECLI:EU:C:2018:835

ECJ, order of 26 October 2018, *KN v. Minister for Justice and Equality*, C-191/18, ECLI:EU:C:2018:884

ECJ, judgment of 6 December 2018, *IK*, C-551/18 PPU, ECLI:EU:C:2018:991

ECJ, judgment of 13 December 2018, *Ministère public v. Marin-Simion Sut*, C-514/17, ECLI:EU:C:2018:1016

ECJ, judgment of 12 February 2019, *TC*, C-492/18 PPU, ECLI:EU:C:2019:108

ECJ, judgment of 27 May 2019, *Minister for Justice and Equality v. OG and PI*, C-508/18 and C-82/19 PPU, ECLI:EU:C:2019:456

ECJ, judgment of 27 May 2019, *Minister for Justice and Equality v. PF*, C-509/18, ECLI:EU:C:2019:457

Part II
Proposal to Amend the EAW-Form

1 Amendment of Section (d) of the EAW-Form (proposed changes in bold)

(d) Personal presence at the trial resulting in the decision or the judgment

A Final Conviction

Part A concerns the <u>last</u> decision or judgment in which a court or a judge made a <u>final</u> ruling on the guilt of the person concerned and imposed a penalty on him, following an assessment, in fact and in law, of the inculpatory and exculpatory evidence, including, where appropriate, the taking account of the individual situation of the person concerned.

Indicate if the person appeared in person at the trial resulting in **that** decision **or that judgment**:

A.1. [ ] Yes, the person appeared in person at the trial resulting in **that** decision **or that judgment.**

A.2. [ ] No, the person did not appear in person at the trial resulting in **that** decision **or that judgment.**

A.3. If you have ticked the box under point A.1, please state the number of hearings, the date(s) of the hearing(s) and, in case of multiple hearings, the hearing(s) at which the person concerned was present and the extent to which the merits of the case were dealt with at that/those hearing(s):

....

....

A.4. If you have ticked the box under point A.2, please confirm the existence of one of the following **(should a particular point be only <u>partially</u> applicable, please do not delete the non-applicable part of that point, but rather refrain from ticking the corresponding box; if none of the points A.4.1a, A.4.1b, A.4.2, A.4.3 or A.4.4 is fully applicable, please do not tick any of the corresponding boxes, but rather explain under point A.5 why in your opinion surrender would nonetheless not entail a breach of the rights of defence of the requested person)**:

[ ] **A.4.1a.** the person was summoned in person on ... (day/month/year) and thereby informed of the scheduled date and place of the trial which resulted in the decision and

was informed that a decision may be handed down if he or she does not appear for the trial;

OR

[ ] **A.**4.1b. the person was not summoned in person but by other means actually received official information of the scheduled date and place of the trial which resulted in the decision, in such a manner that it was unequivocally established that he or she was aware of the scheduled trial, and was informed that a decision may be handed down if he or she does not appear for the trial;

OR

[ ] **A.**4.2. being aware of the scheduled trial, the person had given a mandate to a legal counsellor, who was either appointed by the person concerned or by the State, to defend him or her at the trial, and was indeed defended by that counsellor at the trial;

OR

[ ] **A.**4.3. the person was served with the decision on ... (day/month/year) and was expressly informed about the right to a retrial or appeal, in which he or she has the right to participate and which allows the merits of the case, including fresh evidence, to be reexamined, and which may lead to the original decision being reversed, and

[ ] the person expressly stated that he or she does not contest this decision,

OR

[ ] the person did not request a retrial or appeal within the applicable time frame;

OR

[ ] **A.**4.4. the person was not personally served with the decision, but

- the person will be personally served with this decision without delay after the surrender, and
- when served with the decision, the person will be expressly informed of his or her right to a retrial or appeal, in which he or she has the right to participate and which allows the merits of the case, including fresh evidence, to be re-examined, and which may lead to the original decision being reversed, and
- the person will be informed of the time frame within which he or she has to request a retrial or appeal, which will be ... days **(please fill in the period within which the request must be made)**.

[ ] **A.**5. If you have ticked the box under points **A.**4.1b, **A.**4.2 or **A.**4.3 above, please provide information about how the relevant condition has been met. **In particular, please state with regard to point A.4.1.b: how and when the person concerned actually received the information about the date and the place of the trial; with regard to point A.4.2: whether the legal counsellor was appointed by the person concerned or by the State and, in the latter case, how the person concerned was made aware of that appointment and whether he/she had any contact with the legal counsellor; with regard to point**

A.4.3: how and when the person concerned actually received the judgment and the information about the right to a retrial or an appeal:

....

....

B FINAL DETERMINATION OF THE SENTENCE

Part B concerns proceedings subsequent to the final conviction (part A) in which the level or the nature of the original penalty was modified by an authority which enjoyed a margin of discretion as to that level or that nature and which led to a decision or judgment finally determining the sentence. If such proceedings have taken place, not only must you fill in part A but also part B.

Indicate if the person appeared in person at the trial resulting in that decision or that judgment:

B.1. [ ] Yes, the person appeared in person at the trial resulting in that decision or that judgment.

B.2. [ ] No, the person did not appear in person at the trial resulting in that decision or that judgment.

B.3. If you have ticked the box under point B.1, please state the number of hearings, the date(s) of the hearing(s) and, in case of multiple hearings, the hearing(s) at which the person was present and the extent to which the merits of the case were dealt with at that/those hearing(s):

....

....

B.4. If you have ticked the box under point B.2, please confirm the existence of one of the following (should a particular point be only partially applicable, please do not delete the non-applicable part of that point, but rather refrain from ticking the corresponding box; if none of the points B.4.1a, B.4.1b, B.4.2, B.4.3 or B.4.4 is fully applicable, please do not tick any of the corresponding boxes, but rather explain under point B.5 why in your opinion surrender would nonetheless not entail a breach of the rights of defence of the requested person):

[ ] B.4.1a. the person was summoned in person on ... (day/month/year) and thereby informed of

the scheduled date and place of the trial which resulted in the decision and was informed that a decision may be handed down if he or she does not appear for the trial;

OR

[ ] B.4.1b. the person was not summoned in person but by other means actually received official information of the scheduled date and place of the trial which resulted in the decision, in such a manner that it was unequivocally established that he or she was aware of the scheduled trial, and was informed that a decision may be handed down if he or she does not appear for the trial;

OR

[ ] B.4.2. being aware of the scheduled trial, the person had given a mandate to a legal counsellor, who was either appointed by the person concerned or by the State, to defend him or her at the trial, and was indeed defended by that counsellor at the trial;

OR

[ ] B.4.3. the person was served with the decision on ... (day/month/year) and was expressly informed about the right to a retrial or appeal, in which he or she has the right to participate and which allows the merits of the case, including fresh evidence, to be reexamined, and which may lead to the original decision being reversed, and

[ ] the person expressly stated that he or she does not contest this decision,

OR

[ ] the person did not request a retrial or appeal within the applicable time frame;

OR

[ ] B.4.4. the person was not personally served with the decision, but

- **the person will be personally served with this decision without delay after the surrender, and**
- **when served with the decision, the person will be expressly informed of his or her right to a retrial or appeal, in which he or she has the right to participate and which allows the merits of the case, including fresh evidence, to be re-examined, and which may lead to the original decision being reversed, and**
- **the person will be informed of the time frame within which he or she has to request a retrial or appeal, which will be ... days (please fill in the period within which the request must be made).**

B.5. If you have ticked the box under points B.4.1b, B.4.2 or B.4.3 above, please provide information about how the relevant condition has been met. In particular, please state with regard to point B.4.1.b: how and when the person concerned actually received the information about the date and the place of the trial; with regard to point B.4.2: whether the legal counsellor was appointed by the person concerned or by the State and, in the latter case, how the person concerned was made aware of that appointment and whether he/she had any contact with the legal counsellor; with regard to point B.4.3: how and when the person concerned actually received the judgment and the information about the right to a retrial or an appeal:

....

....

2 Amendment of Section (c) (Proposed Changes in Bold)

(c) Indications on the length of the sentence:

1. Maximum length of the custodial sentence or detention order which may be imposed for the offence(s):

....

....

2. Length of the custodial sentence or detention order imposed:

....

....

If that sentence or that detention order results from a decision modifying the level or the nature of a sentence or sentences previously imposed (see section (d)(B)), please mention the authority which issued the decision and the date of the decision:

....

....

Remaining sentence to be served:

....

....

Part III
Case-Law Guide

1 Introduction

The aim of the Guide is to provide practitioners with easy access to the case-law of the European Court of Human Rights (hereafter: ECtHR) and the Court of Justice of the European Union (hereafter: Court of Justice) concerning *in absentia* trials and the interpretation of Article 4a(1) of FD 2002/584/JHA. The latter provision was drafted with due respect of the requirements of Article 6 of the ECHR and the relevant case-law of the ECtHR. Thus, it reflects the main requirements of a fair trial conducted *in absentia* and determines the structure of the Guide.

Conceived as a tool for issuing and executing authorities, the Guide offers summaries of important judgments and decisions of both European Courts regarding the main concepts used in Article 4a(1) of FD 2002/584/JHA which at the same time form the conditions for fairness of *in absentia* criminal proceedings: the requirements concerning summoning of a defendant; his/her representation by a lawyer; serving a judgment on a defendant and the right to retrial. While the Manual is elaborated in order to assist judicial authorities in filling in and assessing section (d) of the EAW-form, the Guide provides practitioners who want to know more of the background of the Manual with compendious information about the proper interpretation of Article 4a(1) of FD 2002/584/JHA and European standards of protection of the right to a fair trial.

2 Scope of Application of the ECHR to Proceedings Concerning the Execution of EAWs – General Remarks

2.1 Applicability to Proceedings Concerning the Execution of EAWs

According to well-established case-law of the ECtHR, Article 6 of the ECHR does not apply to proceedings concerning extradition, neither under its civil 'limb' nor under its criminal 'limb': the decision to extradite someone is not a determination of his or her civil rights nor is it a determination of a criminal charge.[1]

That case-law does not distinguish between extradition and the execution of an EAW: the EAW replaces extradition between the Member States of the European Union and has the same objectives as extradition (delivering a person who is suspected or convicted of an offence to another state). Execution of an EAW, therefore, does not enter the field of application of Article 6 of the ECHR either.

The decision *Monedero Angora v. Spain* is leading. A French judicial authority had issued an EAW against Monedero Angora, a Spanish national, for the purpose of executing a custodial sentence. His complaint that in deciding on the execution of the EAW the Spanish courts had violated his right to a fair trial before an independent and impartial court within a reasonable time was declared inadmissible *ratione materiae*, because the procedure did not concern the determination of a criminal charge.[2]

2.2 General European Standard for *In Absentia* Trials

Even though Article 6 of the ECHR is not directly applicable, the case-law of the ECtHR under that provision is relevant for the application of Article 4a(1) of FD 2002/584/JHA.

Because Article 4a(1) "strengthens the procedural rights of persons subject to criminal proceedings, guaranteeing them a high level of protection by ensuring full observance of

1 *See, e.g.*, ECtHR, judgment of 4 February 2005, *Mamatkulov and Askarov v. Turkey* [GC], ECLI:CE:ECHR:2005:0204JUD004682799, § 82.

2 ECtHR, decision of 7 October 2008, *Monedero Angora v. Spain*, ECLI:CE:ECHR:2008:1007DEC004113805. See also ECtHR, decision of 24 March 2015, *Martuzevičius v. the United Kingdom*, ECLI:CE:ECHR:2015:0324DEC001356613; ECtHR, decision of 25 June 2019, *West v. Hungary*, ECLI:CE:ECHR:2019:0625DEC000538012, § 65.

their rights of defence, flowing from the right to a fair trial, enshrined in Article 6 of the ECHR", it must be "interpreted and applied in accordance with the requirements of Article 6 of the ECHR and the relevant case-law of the European Court of Human Rights".[3]

3 ECJ, judgment of 22 December 2017, *Samet Ardic*, C-571/17 PPU, ECLI:EU:C:2017:1026, paras. 73-74.

3 Scope of Application of the EU Charter of Fundamental Rights to Proceedings Concerning Execution of EAWs

Currently, two Union law instruments set general standards for *in absentia* trials: Directive 2016/343/EU and FD 2009/299/JHA. The former instrument harmonises national rules on conducting criminal trials in the absence of the accused.[1] Not all Member States are bound by this Directive.[2] The latter instrument only harmonises the ground for refusal to execute an EAW which is issued for the purpose of enforcing a decision rendered following a trial at which the person concerned did not appear in person.

The EU Charter of Fundamental rights is applicable as regards the Member States (and, therefore, their judicial authorities) "only when they are implementing Union law" (Article 51(1) of the Charter).

When the authorities of the Member States apply the provisions of national law adopted to transpose FD 2002/584/JHA, FD 2009/299/JHA or Directive 2016/343/EU,[3] they are implementing Union law. In doing so, they are bound by the Charter, in particular by Article 47 (the right to an effective judicial remedy and the right to a fair trial) and Article 48(2) (the rights of the defence) of the Charter.[4]

Article 4a(1) of FD 2002/584/JHA is compatible with Article 47 and Article 48(2) of the Charter.[5] Directive 2016/343/EU is intended to enhance the right to a fair trial in criminal proceedings as enshrined in Article 47 and Article 48 of the Charter.[6]

1 Directive 2016/343/EU of the European Parliament and of the Council of 9 March 2016 on the strengthening of certain aspects of the presumption of innocence and of the right to be present at the trial in criminal proceedings, *OJ* 2016, L 65, p. 1.

2 Denmark, Ireland and the United Kingdom are not bound by Directive 2016/343/EU.

3 Cf. ECJ, judgment of 5 April 2016, *Pál Aranyosi and Robert Căldăraru v. Generalstaats- anwaltschaft Bremen*, C-404/125 and C-659/15 PPU, ECLI:EU:C:2016:198, para. 84.

4 *See,* as regards the right to a fair trial, ECJ, judgment of 25 July 2018, *Minister for Justice and Equality (Deficiencies in the system of justice)*, C-216/18 PPU, ECLI:EU:C:2018:586:586.

5 ECJ, judgment of 26 February 2013, *Stefano Melloni v. Ministerio Fiscal*, C-399/11, ECLI:EU:C:2013:107, para. 54.

6 Recital (9) of the preamble in connection with recital (1) thereof.

4 Fair *In Absentia* Criminal Proceedings under the ECHR and under EU Law

4.1 Stages of Judicial Examination of the Case Relevant for the Assessment Whether the Proceedings Were Conducted *In Absentia*

4.1.1 *Under the Case-Law of the ECtHR*

Determination of the charge

Article 6(1) of the ECHR guarantees everyone the right to a fair trial "(i)n the determination (...) of any criminal charge against him". The concept of a 'determination of a criminal charge' covers the whole proceedings in question (including appeal proceedings) from the moment of the charge to the final decision on the determination of the charge. In case of a conviction, there is no final determination of the charge as long as the sentence (the penalty imposed) is not definitively fixed.[1]

Appellate and cassation proceedings

Article 6 of the ECHR does not oblige the Parties to the ECHR to provide for *appellate and cassation proceedings*. Nonetheless, if they do so, those proceedings will also be covered by Article 6 of the ECHR. The ECtHR has held so many times, *e.g.*, in *Kudła v. Poland*:

> 122. The Court reiterates that Article 6 § 1 does not compel the States to set up courts of appeal or of cassation. Nevertheless, a State which does institute such courts is required to ensure that persons amenable to the law shall enjoy before them the fundamental guarantees contained in Article 6 (see, among other authorities, the *Delcourt v. Belgium* judgment of 17 January 1970, Series A no. 11 pp. 13-15, § 25, and the *Brualla Gómez de la Torre v. Spain* judgment of 19 December 1997, Reports 1997-VIII, p. 2956, § 37).
> While the manner in which Article 6 is to be applied in relation to courts of appeal or of cassation depends on the special features of the proceedings in question, there can be no doubt that appellate or cassation proceedings come

1 ECtHR, judgment of 15 July 1982, *Eckle v. Germany*, ECLI:CE:ECHR:1982:0715JUD000813078, § 77.

> within the scope of Article 6 (see, mutatis mutandis, the *Twalib v. Greece* judgment of 9 June 1998, Reports 1998-IV, pp. 1427-28, § 46). (...)[2]

Full jurisdiction on appeal

If on *appeal*, the appellate court has to examine a case *as to the facts and the law* and make a *full* assessment of the issue of guilt or innocence of the defendant, it *must in principle hear* the defendant, as the ECtHR held, *e.g.*, in *Seliwiak v. Poland*[3] and *Hokkeling v. the Netherlands*:

> 58. The Court has also held that although proceedings that take place in the accused's absence are not of themselves incompatible with Article 6 of the Convention, a denial of justice nevertheless undoubtedly occurs where a person convicted in absentia is unable subsequently to obtain from a court which has heard him a fresh determination of the merits of the charge, in respect of both law and fact, where it has not been established that he has waived his right to appear and to defend himself or that he intended to escape trial (see Sejdovic, cited above, § 82, with further references). In particular, where an appellate court has to examine a case as to the facts and the law and make a full assessment of the issue of guilt or innocence, it cannot determine the issue without a direct assessment of the evidence given in person by the accused for the purpose of proving that he did not commit the act allegedly constituting a criminal offence (see *Hermi v. Italy* [GC], no. 18114/02, § 64, ECHR 2006-XII; see also, as a more recent authority, *Zahirović v. Croatia*, no. 58590/11, § 56, 25 April 2013). Still less can it do so where the appellate court is called upon to examine whether the applicant's sentence should be increased (Zahirović, § 57).[4]

Jurisdiction limited to questions of law

However, proceedings involving *questions of law only* – such as *cassation proceedings* – may comply with the requirements of Article 6 ECHR even where the defendant was not given an opportunity of being heard in person by the cassation court. Thus, in *Meftah and Others v. France*, the ECtHR held:

> 41. (...) The Court has held on a number of occasions that, provided that there has been a public hearing at first instance, the absence of public hearings at

2 ECtHR, judgment of 26 October 2000, *Kudła v. Poland* [GC], ECLI:CE:ECHR:2000:1026JUD003021096, § 122.

3 ECtHR, judgment of 21 July 2009, *Seliwiak v. Poland*, ECLI:CE:ECHR:2009:0721JUD000381804, § 56.

4 ECtHR, judgment of 14 February 2017, *Hokkeling v. the Netherlands*, ECLI:CE:ECHR:2017:0214 JUD003074912, § 58.

second or third instance may be justified by the special features of the proceedings at issue. Thus, proceedings for leave to appeal or proceedings involving only questions of law, as opposed to questions of fact, may comply with the requirements of Article 6 even where the appellant was not given an opportunity of being heard in person by the appeal or cassation court (see the following judgments: *Sutter v. Switzerland*, 22 February 1984, Series A no. 74, p. 13, § 30; *Monnell and Morris v. the United Kingdom*, 2 March 1987, Series A no. 115, p. 22, § 58; *Ekbatani v. Sweden*, 26 May 1988, Series A no. 134, p. 14, § 31; *Kamasinski v. Austria*, 19 December 1989, Series A no. 168, pp. 44-45, § 106; and *Bulut v. Austria*, 22 February 1996, Reports 1996-II, p. 358, § 41).

42. The special features of the procedure before the Criminal Division of the Court of Cassation must therefore be taken into account in determining whether the applicants' right to a fair trial was infringed (see Kamasinski, cited above, pp. 44-45, § 106). Under French law, the Court of Cassation carries out supervision which is limited to compliance with the law, including jurisdictional and procedural rules, to the exclusion of any examination of the facts in the strict sense, such examination being within the sole province of the courts below. Save for exceptions, the procedure before the Court of Cassation is essentially written, that rule applying also when a party is represented by a member of the Conseil d'Etat and Court of Cassation Bar. Members of the Conseil d'Etat and Court of Cassation Bar do not enjoy an absolute right to make oral observations: any member wishing to do so at the hearing must first contact the President of the Criminal Division in order to inform him or her of the points of law which they intend to raise and to determine by agreement the arrangements under which they will be allowed to do so (see paragraph 31 above).

43. In the present case, the Court notes that the appeals to the Court of Cassation were lodged after the applicants' arguments had been examined by both the trial courts and the courts of appeal, which had had full jurisdiction and, in compliance with the rules laid down by Article 6, had held hearings at which the applicants or their lawyer had appeared and presented their case.

44. As regards the right for appellants in the Court of Cassation to make oral representations at the hearing, it should be noted that any legal argument at a hearing before the Criminal Division of the Court of Cassation will be particularly technical and concern only points of law (see paragraph 24 above), as no further submissions may be made on the facts beyond the court of appeal stage, unless the case is remitted by the Court of Cassation. Thus, in the Court's view,

> it would be unduly formalistic to interpret the procedural requirements as meaning that the applicants should have been permitted to make oral representations at the hearing before the Court of Cassation. It is clear that, in addition to entailing a risk of negative repercussions in terms of increased litigation, such an approach would not assist in resolving issues that are essentially in written form and technical, and largely inaccessible to someone without legal training (see *Pham Hoang v. France*, judgment of 25 September 1992, Series A no 243, p. 23, § 40).[5]

Cumulative sentence

Proceedings in which two or more final sentences are merged into a new sentence (a so-called ***cumulative*** or *aggregate sentence*) fall within the scope of Article 6 ECHR if the determination of the new sentence is not merely an arithmetical exercise, but leaves some *discretion* to the competent authority as to *the level of the new sentence*, as the ECtHR held, *e.g.*, in *Aleksandr Dementyev v. Russia*:

> 23. The Court reiterates that, in criminal matters, Article 6 § 1 of the Convention covers the whole of the proceedings in question, including appeal proceedings and the determination of sentence (see, among other authorities, *Eckle v. Germany*, 15 July 1982, § 76-77, Series A no. 51, and *T v. the United Kingdom* [GC], no. 24724/94, § 108, 16 December 1999).
>
> 24. Turning to the circumstances of the present case, the Court observes that, after two guilty verdicts had been rendered and taken effect in respect of the applicant, it still remained necessary for the domestic judicial authorities to fix the aggregate sentence combining those previously imposed on the applicant in the course of two sets of criminal proceedings against him.
>
> 25. The Court cannot accept the Government's argument that the determination of the aggregate sentence was a mere "formality" and an "arithmetical" exercise (see, by contrast, Nurmagomedov, cited above, § 48, where the domestic court was solely called upon to match the constituent elements of a crime as established in the original conviction with the definitions of offences contained in the new Criminal Code and to replace the old references with the new). When determining the aggregate sentence in respect of the applicant, the domestic judicial authorities were to take into account his character, as well as the miti-

5 ECtHR, judgment of 26 July 2002, *Meftah and Others v. France* [GC], ECLI:CE:ECHR:2002:0726 JUD003291196, § 41-44.

> gating and aggravating circumstances of the crimes committed. It was for the court to decide whether the terms of both sentences were to be added up in full or in part (see paragraph 14).
>
> 26. Accordingly, the Court considers that the applicant's case should be distinguished from the case of Nurmagomedov. In the Court's view, it bears a close resemblance to the case of Eckle where the Court held, in the context of determining the length of the criminal proceedings, that there is no "determination ... of any criminal charge", within the meaning of Article 6 of the Convention, as long as the sentence is not definitively fixed (see Eckle, cited earlier, § 77). In the Court's view, the applicant was not in a position to calculate the aggregate term of the sentences on his own. While the conversion of the term of community work into the prison term was indeed an arithmetical exercise, the judicial authorities still had discretion to decide whether the converted sentence would be added in full or in part, regard being had to the particular circumstances of the case. Accordingly, the Court concludes that the applicant's complaint concerning the hearing for determination of his aggregate criminal sentence is compatible ratione materiae with the provisions of the Convention. It falls within Article 6 of the Convention under its criminal head.[6]

However, the applicability of Article 6 of the ECHR to such proceedings does not necessarily mean that the person concerned is always entitled to be heard in person. In *Aleksandr Dementyev v. Russia*, the ECtHR held as follows:

> 43. The Court observes that under Russian law, defendants have the right to attend hearings concerning aggregate sentences. They may also appoint a lawyer to represent them before the sentencing court (see paragraph 16).
>
> 44. This does not necessarily imply, however, that the presence of the applicant at the sentencing hearing is required by Article 6 § 1 of the Convention, as the requirements of that provision are autonomous in relation to those of national legislation.
>
> 45. In the instant case, the Court deems it appropriate to proceed on the basis of the following facts. The Regional Court had jurisdiction to rule solely on the conversion of the applicant's sentence to six months' community work into a

6 ECtHR, judgment of 28 November 2013, *Aleksandr Dementyev v. Russia*, ECLI:CE:ECHR:2013:1128JUD004309505, § 23-26.

> prison sentence according to an arithmetical formula established by law, whereby three days of community work should be replaced by one day of a prison sentence (see paragraph 15). The recalculated and converted sentence was then to be added in full or in part to the thirteen years' imprisonment the applicant was to serve following his other conviction. While it is true that the Regional Court, in carrying out the sentencing exercise, was to take into account, inter alia, the applicant's character and the mitigating and aggravating circumstances of each of the crimes committed, its task was purely to decide what period – ranging from one day to two months – was to be served by the applicant following his conviction for battery.
>
> 46. Given the limited scope of the issue to be dealt with by the Regional Court and the fact that the applicant was present and represented during both trials and was able to appeal against his convictions, the Court considers that the Regional Court, could – as a matter of fair trial – have properly examined the issue on the basis of the case-file and the parties' written submissions without a direct assessment of the evidence given by the applicant in person.[7]

Substitution of a sentence

Given that there is no 'determination of a criminal charge' as long as the sentence is not definitively fixed, Article 6 of the ECHR also applies to proceedings in which *a final penalty is substituted for another penalty*. Thus, the ECtHR held in *Gurguchiani v. Spain*:

> 47. La Cour a déjà conclu, au paragraphe 40 ci-dessus, que le remplacement de la peine infligée au requérant par une expulsion et une interdiction de territoire pour une durée de dix ans constituait une peine au sens de l'article 7 de la Convention. Elle rappelle par ailleurs qu'en cas de condamnation il n'a pas été « décidé » du « bien-fondé d'une accusation en matière pénale, au sens de l'article 6 § 1 de la Convention, aussi longtemps que la peine ne se trouve pas déterminée définitivement » (Eckle, précité, § 77).
>
> 48. Ces éléments suffisent à la Cour pour conclure à l'applicabilité de l'article 6 § 1 à la présente espèce.[8]

---

7 ECtHR, judgment of 28 November 2013, *Aleksandr Dementyev v. Russia*, ECLI:CE:ECHR:2013:1128 JUD004309505, § 43-46.

8 ECtHR, judgment of 15 December 2009, *Gurguchiani v. Spain*, ECLI:CE:ECHR:2009:1215JUD001601206. Unofficial translation in English:
47. The Court already concluded (para. 40 above) that the substitution of the penalty imposed on the applicant by the measure of expulsion and a ban to enter the territory for a duration of ten years constituted

Execution of a sentence

However, one should sharply distinguish proceedings concerning the *determination of a sentence* from proceedings concerning the *execution of a sentence.* Article 6 of the ECHR does not apply to the latter category of proceedings, *e.g.* proceedings concerning a request for provisional release,[9] proceedings concerning a request for temporary prison leave,[10] proceedings concerning the application of amnesty legislation to a final conviction,[11] proceedings concerning placement in a secure prison[12] and proceedings concerning the transfer of the enforcement of a foreign sentence.[13] Such proceedings do not constitute a 'determination of a criminal charge'.

Equally, proceedings concerning the *revocation of a suspended sentence* and proceedings concerning the *revocation of provisional release* do not amount to a 'determination of a criminal charge'. Thus, in *X. v. the Federal Republic of Germany*, the European Commission of Human Rights held as follows:

> Whereas the Applicant complains, more particularly, that the proceedings under which the Regional Court of Lüneburg revoked the suspension on … June 1964, were not brought against him within a reasonable time;
> Whereas the Commission observes in this respect that the Applicant in these proceedings did not have the status of a person charged with a criminal offence but that of a person convicted by a sentence which had become final although its execution had been suspended; whereas a court, when revoking the suspension of a sentence is not determining a civil right or obligation within the meaning of Article 6 (Art. 6) of the Convention, nor a criminal charge brought against the person in question;
> Whereas the provisions of Article 6 (Art. 6) therefore do not apply to such proceedings; whereas the Commission refers in this respect to its decisions in Applications Nos 864/60 – *X v. Austria* – Collection of Decisions 9, page 17

a penalty in the sense of Article 7 of the Convention. It recalls that in case of a conviction there is no determination of a criminal charge in the sense of Article 6 § of the Convention, as long as the penalty is not definitively fixed (Eckle, cited above, § 77).

48. These elements suffice for the Court to conclude that Article 6 § is applicable to the case at hand.

9 ECtHR, judgment of 25 November 2014, *Vasilescu v. Belgium*, ECLI:CE:ECHR:2014:1125JUD006468212, § 121.

10 ECtHR, judgment of 3 April 2012, *Boulouis v. Luxembourg* [GC], ECLI:CE:ECHR:2012:0403JUD003757504, § 87.

11 ECtHR, decision of 13 May 2003, *Montcornet de Caumont v. France*, ECLI:CE:ECHR:2003:0513DEC005929000.

12 ECtHR, judgment of 17 September 2009, *Enea v. Italy* [GC], ECLI:CE:ECHR:2009:0917JUD007491201, § 97

13 *See, e.g.*, ECtHR, decision of 23 October 2012, *Ciok v. Poland*, ECLI:CE:ECHR:2012:1023DEC000049810, § 38.

> and 1336/62 – *S v. Austria*; whereas it follows that this part of the application must also be rejected as incompatible with the Convention.[14]

However, imposing *additional* days of custody on account of (disciplinary) offences committed during the execution of a sentence and thus *extending* the *duration of the sentence* does constitute a 'determination of a criminal charge', as the ECtHR held in *Ezeh and Connors v. the United Kingdom.*[15]

4.1.2 *Under the Case-Law of the Court of Justice Concerning Article 4a(1) of FD 2002/584/JHA*

Trial resulting in the decision: final conviction

According to the Court of Justice, the decision which Article 4a(1) refers to is the 'judicial decision which finally sentenced the person whose surrender is sought in connection with the execution of a European Arrest Warrant',[16] in other words the final 'conviction'[17] or the 'final sentencing decision'.[18] Such a final conviction or a final sentencing decision comprises 'two distinct but related aspects': the finding of guilt and the handing down of a sentence.[19]

Trial resulting in the decision: appellate proceedings

Referring to the case-law of the ECtHR, in the *Tupikas* judgment the Court of Justice defined the concept of a 'trial resulting in the decision' in the context of successive proceedings leading to successive decisions (first instance – appeal) as "the instance which led to the *last* of those decisions, provided that the court at issue made a *final ruling* on the *guilt of the person concerned and imposed a penalty on him*, such as a custodial sentence, following

14 ECHR, decision of 5 October 1967, *X. v. the Federal Republic of Germany*, ECLI:CE:ECHR:1967:1005DEC000242865. See also ECHR, decision of 6 December 1977, *X. v. Switzerland*, ECLI:CE:ECHR:1977:1206DEC000764876; ECHR, decision of 9 May 1994, *Sampson v. Cyprus*, ECLI:CE:ECHR:1994:0509DEC001977492.

15 ECtHR, judgment of 9 October 2003, *Ezeh and Connors v. the United Kingdom* [GC], ECLI:CE:ECHR:2003:1009 JUD003966598, § 120-130.

16 ECJ, judgment of 10 August 2017, *Openbaar Ministerie v. Tadas Tupikas*, C-270/17 PPU, ECLI:EU:C:2017:628, para. 74.

17 ECJ, judgment of 10 August 2017, *Openbaar Ministerie v. Tadas Tupikas*, C-270/17 PPU, ECLI:EU:C:2017:628, para. 75.

18 ECJ, judgment of 10 August 2017, *Openbaar Ministerie v. Tadas Tupikas*, C-270/17 PPU, ECLI:EU:C:2017:628, para. 76.

19 ECJ, judgment of 10 August 2017, *Openbaar Ministerie v. Sławomir Andrzej Zdziaszek*, C-271/17 PPU, ECLI:EU:C:2017:629, para. 77.

an *assessment, in fact and in law, of the incriminating and exculpatory evidence*, including, where appropriate, the taking account of the individual situation of the person concerned":

> 78. As is clear from the case-law of the European Court of Human Rights, the term 'conviction' within the meaning of the ECHR refers to both a finding of guilt after it has been established in accordance with the law that there has been an offence, and the imposition of a penalty or other measure involving deprivation of liberty (see, to that effect, ECtHR, 21 October 2013, *Del Río Prada v. Spain*, CE:ECHR:2013:1021JUD004275009, § 123, and the case-law cited).
>
> 79. Moreover, the European Court of Human Rights has held on several occasions that, where appeal proceedings are provided for, they must comply with the requirements flowing from Article 6 of the ECHR, in particular where the remedy available against the decision given at first instance is a full appeal, the second-instance court having jurisdiction to re-examine the case, by assessing the merits of the accusations in fact and in law, and thus to determine the guilt or innocence of the person concerned on the basis of the evidence presented (see, to that effect, judgments of the ECtHR of 26 May 1988, *Ekbatani v. Sweden*, CE:ECHR:1988:0526JUD001056383, § 24 and 32; 26 October 2000, *Kudła v. Poland*, CE:ECHR:1988:0526JUD001056383, § 122; 18 October 2006, *Hermi v. Italy*, CE:ECHR:2006:1018JUD001811402, § 64 and 65; 25 April 2013, *Zahirović v. Croatia*, CE:ECHR:2013:0425JUD005859011, § 56; and of 14 February 2017, *Hokkeling v. Netherlands*, CE:ECHR:2017:0214JUD 003074912, § 56 and 58).
>
> 80. It is also clear from that case-law of the European Court of Human Rights that where two instances are provided for, the fact that the person concerned was actually able to exercise his rights of defence at first instance does not automatically lead to the conclusion that he necessarily enjoyed the guarantees laid down in Article 6 of the ECHR if the appeal proceedings took place in his absence (see, to that effect, judgment of 14 February 2017, *Hokkeling v. Netherlands*, CE:ECHR:2017:0214JUD 003074912, § 57, 58 and 61).
>
> 81. Consequently, in the event that proceedings have taken place at several instances which have given rise to successive decisions, at least one of which was given in absentia, it is appropriate to understand by 'trial resulting in the decision', within the meaning of Article 4a(1) of Framework Decision 2002/584, the instance which led to the last of those decisions, provided that the court at issue made a final ruling on the guilt of the person concerned and imposed a

penalty on him, such as a custodial sentence, following an assessment, in fact and in law, of the incriminating and exculpatory evidence, including, where appropriate, the taking account of the individual situation of the person concerned.

82. That interpretation is fully in line with the requirements of respect for the rights of the defence which Article 4a of Framework Decision 2002/584 precisely seeks to uphold, as is apparent from paragraphs 58 and 59 of the present judgment.

83. It is the judicial decision finally disposing of the case on the merits, in the sense that there are no further avenues of ordinary appeal available, which is decisive for the person concerned, since it directly affects his personal situation with regard to the finding of guilt and, where appropriate, the determination of the custodial sentence to be served.

84. Accordingly, it is at that procedural stage that the person concerned must be able to fully exercise his rights of defence in order to assert his point of view in an effective manner and thereby to influence the final decision which could lead to the loss of his personal freedom. The outcome of that procedure is irrelevant in that context.

85. In those circumstances, even assuming that the rights of the defence have not been fully respected at first instance, such a breach may validly be remedied in the course of the second-instance proceedings, provided that the latter proceedings provide all the guarantees with respect to the requirements of a fair trial.

86. In other words, when the person concerned appeared before the judge responsible for a fresh assessment of the merits of the case, but not at first instance, the provisions of Article 4a of Framework Decision 2002/584 do not apply. Conversely, the executing judicial authority must carry out the checks provided for in that article when the person concerned was present at first instance, but not in the proceedings concerned with a fresh assessment of the merits of the case.[20]

20 ECJ, judgment of 10 August 2017, *Openbaar Ministerie v. Tadas Tupikas*, C-270/17 PPU, ECLI:EU:C:2017:628, paras. 78-86.

Trial resulting in the decision: cassation proceedings

The Court of Justice's criterion, enounced in para. 81 of the *Tupikas* judgment (and cited earlier), makes it clear that proceedings concerning *questions of law only*, such as *cassation proceedings*, do not come within the ambit of Article 4a(1) of FD 2002/584/JHA.

Trial resulting in the decision: cumulative sentence

Referring to the case-law of the ECtHR, in the *Zdziaszek* judgment the Court of Justice distinguishes between a *decision modifying the quantum of penalties previously imposed* and a *decision relating to the methods of execution of a sentence*. As to the first category, it follows from the case-law of the ECtHR that Article 6 of the ECHR does apply not only to the finding of guilt but *also to the determination of the sentence*. Therefore, the person concerned has a right to be present at the hearing "because of the significant consequences which it may have on the quantum of the sentence to be imposed". Such significant consequences could arise where the proceedings for determining an overall sentence are "*not a purely formal and arithmetic exercise* but entail a *margin of discretion in the determination of the level of the sentence*, in particular, by taking account of the situation or personality of the person concerned, or of mitigating or aggravating circumstances":

> 83. Secondly, it is necessary to determine whether a decision at a later stage of the proceedings amending one or more of the custodial sentences previously imposed, such as the cumulative sentence at issue in the case in the main proceedings, is covered by Article 4a(1) of the Framework Decision.
>
> 84. As is apparent from the case file before the Court, first, such a decision, although taken after one or more decisions sentencing the person concerned to one or more penalties, does not affect the finding of guilt set out in the previous decisions, that conviction therefore being final.
>
> 85. Next, such a decision modifies the quantum of the penalty or penalties imposed. It is therefore necessary to make a distinction between measures of that type and those relating to the methods of execution of a custodial sentence. It is moreover apparent from the case-law of the European Court of Human Rights that Article 6(1) of the ECHR does not apply to questions concerning the methods for executing a sentence, in particular those relating to provisional release (see, to that effect, ECtHR, 3 April 2012, *Boulois v. Luxembourg*, CE:ECHR:2012:0403JUD003757504, § 87).
>
> 86. Finally, proceedings leading to a decision, such as the judgment handing down a cumulative sentence at issue in the main proceedings, consisting in

commuting into a single sentence one or more sentences handed down previously in respect of the person concerned, necessarily results in a more favorable result for that person. Thus, for example, a lighter penalty may be imposed following the entry into force of new legislation which penalises the relevant offence less severely. In addition, following several convictions, each of which involves the imposition of a sentence, the sentences may be combined to obtain a cumulative sentence which is less than the sum of the various sentences resulting from previous separate decisions.

87. In that regard, it is apparent from the case-law of the European Court of Human Rights that the guarantees laid down in Article 6 of the ECHR apply not only to the finding of guilt, but also to the determination of the sentence (see, to that effect, ECtHR, 28 November 2013, *Dementyev v. Russia*, CE:ECHR:2013:1128JUD004309505, § 23). Thus, compliance with the requirement of a fair trial entails the right of the person concerned to be present at the hearing because of the significant consequences which it may have on the quantum of the sentence to be imposed (see, to that effect, ECtHR, 21 September 1993, *Kremzov v. Austria*, CE:ECHR:1993:0921JUD001235086, § 67).

88. This is the case with respect to specific proceedings for the determination of an overall sentence where those proceedings are not a purely formal and arithmetic exercise but entail a margin of discretion in the determination of the level of the sentence, in particular, by taking account of the situation or personality of the person concerned, or of mitigating or aggravating circumstances (see ECtHR, 15 July 1982, *Eckle v. Germany*, CE:ECHR:1983:0621 JUD000813078, § 77, and 28 November 2013, *Dementyev v. Russia*, CE:ECHR: 2013:1128JUD004309505, § 25 and 26).

89. Furthermore, it is irrelevant in that regard whether the court concerned has jurisdiction to increase the sentence previously imposed (see, to that effect, ECtHR, 26 May 1988, *Ekbatani v. Sweden*, CE:ECHR:1988:0526JUD001056383, § 32, and 18 October 2006, *Hermi v. Italy*, CE:ECHR:2006:1018JUD001811402, § 65).

90. It follows that proceedings giving rise to a judgment handing down a cumulative sentence, such as that at issue in the main proceedings, leading to a new determination of the level of custodial sentences imposed previously, must be regarded as relevant for the application of Article 4a(1) of Framework

Decision 2002/584, where they entail a margin of discretion for the competent authority within the meaning of paragraph 88 of the present judgment and give rise to a decision which finally determines the sentence.

91. Given that such proceedings determine the quantum of the sentence which the convicted person will ultimately serve, that person must be able to effectively exercise his rights of defence in order to influence favourably the decision to be taken in that regard.

92. The fact that the new sentence is hypothetically more favourable to the person concerned is irrelevant since the level of the sentence is not determined in advance but depends on the assessment of the facts of the case by the competent authority and it is precisely the duration of the sentence to be served which is finally handed down which is of decisive importance for the person concerned.

93. In the light of the grounds set out above, it must be held that, in a case such as that at issue in the main proceedings, where, following appeal proceedings in which the merits of the case were re-examined, a decision finally determined the guilt of the person concerned and also imposed a custodial sentence on him, the level of which was however amended by a subsequent decision taken by the competent authority after it had exercised its discretion in that matter and which finally determined the sentence, both decisions must be taken into account for the purposes of the application of Article 4a(1) of Framework Decision 2002/584.[21]

Trial resulting in the decision: decision to revoke the suspension of the execution of a sentence

Again referring to the Strasbourg case-law, in the *Ardic* judgment the Court of Justice reiterates that, whereas a final conviction, including a final determination of the sentence, squarely falls within Article 6 of the ECHR, that provision does not apply to "questions relating to the detailed rules for the execution or application of such a custodial sentence". However, decisions concerning the latter category do come within the ambit of Article 6 of the ECHR, where, "following a finding of guilt of the person concerned and having imposed a custodial sentence on him, *a new judicial decision modifies either the nature or*

21 ECJ, judgment of 10 August 2017, *Openbaar Ministerie v. Sławomir Andrzej Zdziaszek*, C-271/17 PPU, ECLI:EU:C:2017:629, paras. 83-93.

the quantum of sentence previously imposed",[22] *e.g.* (1) when *a prison sentence is replaced by an expulsion order* or (2) when *the duration of the detention previously imposed is increased*. Therefore, the concept of a 'decision' referred to in Article 4a(1) does not cover a "decision relating to the execution or application of a custodial sentence previously imposed, *except where the purpose or effect of that decision is to modify either the nature or quantum of that sentence and the authority which adopted it enjoyed some discretion in that regard*".[23]

The decisions at issue in the *Ardic* judgment *did not affect the nature or the quantum of the custodial sentences imposed by the final judgments of conviction*. In the proceedings, the competent court only had to determine whether non-compliance with certain conditions attached to the suspension of the execution of those custodial sentences justified requiring the person concerned to serve, in part or in full, the custodial sentences originally imposed. In doing so, *the competent court did not dispose of discretion with regard to the level or the nature of the original sentences*, but only with regard to revoking the suspension or not. Therefore, the decisions at issue were not covered by Article 4a(1):

> 67. It follows from the above that Article 4a(1) of Framework Decision 2002/584 must be interpreted as meaning that the concept of 'decision' referred to therein relates to the judicial decision or decisions concerning the criminal conviction of the interested person, namely the decision or decisions that definitively rule, after an assessment of the case in fact and in law, on the guilt of that person and, where relevant, on the custodial sentence imposed on him.
>
> 68. In the present case, it must be determined whether a decision to revoke suspension of execution of a custodial sentence previously imposed is of such a nature that it can be equated, for the purposes of applying that provision, to a decision such as that defined in the preceding paragraph.
>
> 69. In that regard, it should be pointed out that Framework Decision 2002/584 seeks, by the establishment of a simplified and effective system for the surrender of persons convicted or accused of having infringed criminal law, to facilitate and accelerate judicial cooperation with a view to contributing to the objective set for the European Union to become an area of freedom, security and justice, founded on the high level of trust which should exist between the Member

22 ECJ, judgment of 22 December 2017, *Samet Ardic*, C-571/17 PPU, ECLI:EU:C:2017:1026, para. 76 (emphasis added).

23 ECJ, judgment of 10 August 2017, *Openbaar Ministerie v. Sławomir Andrzej Zdziaszek*, C-271/17 PPU, ECLI:EU:C:2017:629, paras. 75-77.

States in accordance with the principle of mutual recognition (see, to that effect, judgments of 26 February 2013, Melloni, C-399/11, EU:C:2013:107, paragraphs. 36 and 37, and of 5 April 2016, Aranyosi and Căldăraru, C-404/15 and C-659/15 PPU, EU:C:2016:198, paragraphs. 75 and 76).

70. To that end, Article 1(2) of the Framework Decision lays down the rule that Member States are required to execute any European arrest warrant on the basis of the principle of mutual recognition and in accordance with the provisions of that Framework Decision. Except in exceptional circumstances, the executing judicial authorities may therefore refuse to execute such a warrant only in the exhaustively listed cases of non-execution provided for by Framework Decision 2002/584 and the execution of the European arrest warrant may be made subject only to one of the conditions listed exhaustively therein. Accordingly, while the execution of the European arrest warrant constitutes the rule, the refusal to execute is intended to be an exception which must be interpreted strictly (see judgment of 10 August 2017, Tupikas, C-270/17 PPU, EU:C:2017:628, paragraph 50 and the case-law cited).

71. As regards, more particularly, Article 4a of Framework Decision 2002/584, inserted by Article 2 of Framework Decision 2009/299, this seeks to restrict the possibility of refusing to execute the European arrest warrant by listing, in a precise and uniform manner, the conditions under which the recognition and enforcement of a decision given following a trial in which the person concerned did not appear in person may not be refused (judgment of 10 August 2017, Tupikas, C-270/17 PPU, EU:C:2017:628, paragraph 53 and the case-law cited).

72. Under that provision, the executing judicial authority is obliged to execute a European arrest warrant, notwithstanding the absence of the person concerned at the trial resulting in the decision, where one of the situations referred to in Article 4a(1)(a), (b), (c) or (d) of that Framework Decision is established (judgment of 10 August 2017, Tupikas, C-270/17 PPU, EU:C:2017:628, paragraph 55).

73. Accordingly, that provision seeks to improve judicial cooperation in criminal matters by harmonising the conditions of execution of European arrest warrants issued for the purposes of executing decisions rendered in absentia, which is likely to facilitate mutual recognition of judicial decisions between Member States. At the same time, that provision strengthens the procedural rights of persons subject to criminal proceedings, guaranteeing them a high

level of protection by ensuring full observance of their rights of defence, flowing from the right to a fair trial, enshrined in Article 6 of the ECHR (see, to that effect, judgments of 26 February 2013, Melloni, C-399/11, EU:C:2013:107, paragraph 51, and of 10 August 2017, Tupikas, C-270/17 PPU, EU:C:2017:628, paragraphs 58 to 60).

74. To that end, the Court ensures that Article 4a(1) of Framework Decision 2002/584 is interpreted and applied in accordance with the requirements of Article 6 of the ECHR and the relevant case-law of the European Court of Human Rights (see, to that effect, judgments of 10 August 2017, Tupikas, C-270/17 PPU, EU:C:2017:628, paragraphs 78 to 80, and of 10 August 2017, Zdziaszek, C-271/17 PPU, EU:C:2017:629, paragraphs 87 to 89).

75. While the final judicial decision convicting the person concerned, including the decision determining the custodial sentence to be served, falls fully within Article 6 of the ECHR, it is apparent from the case-law of the European Court of Human Rights that that provision does not apply, however, to questions relating to the detailed rules for the execution or application of such a custodial sentence (see, to that effect, ECtHR, 3 April 2012, *Boulois v. Luxembourg*, CE:ECHR:2012:0403JUD003757504, § 87; 25 November 2014, *Vasilescu v. Belgium*, CE:ECHR:2014:1125JUD006468212, § 121, and 2 June 2015, *Pacula v. Belgium*, CE:ECHR:2015:0602DEC006849512, § 47).

76. The position is different only where, following a finding of guilt of the person concerned and having imposed a custodial sentence on him, a new judicial decision modifies either the nature or the quantum of sentence previously imposed, as is the case when a prison sentence is replaced by an expulsion measure (ECtHR, 15 December 2009, *Gurguchiani v. Spain*, CE:ECHR:2009:1215JUD001601206, §§ 40, 47 and 48) or where the duration of the detention previously imposed is increased (ECtHR, 9 October 2003, *Ezeh and Connors v. United Kingdom*, CE:ECHR:2003:1009JUD003966598).

77. In the light of the foregoing, it must therefore be considered that, for the purposes of Article 4a(1) of Framework Decision 2002/584, the concept of 'decision' referred to therein does not cover a decision relating to the execution or application of a custodial sentence previously imposed, except where the purpose or effect of that decision is to modify either the nature or quantum of that sentence and the authority which adopted it enjoyed some discretion in that regard (see, to that effect, judgments of 10 August 2017, Tupikas, C-270/17

PPU, EU:C:2017:628, paragraphs 78 to 80, and of 10 August 2017, Zdziaszek, C-271/17 PPU, EU:C:2017:629, paragraphs 85, 90 and 96).

78. As regards, in particular, decisions to revoke the suspension of the execution of previously imposed custodial sentences, such as those at issue in the main proceedings, it is apparent from the case file before the Court that, in the present case, those decisions did not affect the nature or the quantum of custodial sentences imposed by final conviction judgments of the person concerned, which form the basis of the European arrest warrant which the German authorities are seeking to execute in the Netherlands.

79. Since the proceedings leading to those revocation decisions were not intended to review the merits of the cases, but only concerned the consequences which, from the point of view of the application of the penalties initially imposed and whose execution had, subsequently, been partially suspended subject to compliance with certain conditions, it was necessary to consider the fact that the convicted person had not complied with those conditions during the probationary period.

80. In that context, under the relevant national rules, the competent court only had to determine if such a circumstance justified requiring the convicted person to serve, in part or in full, the custodial sentences that had been initially imposed and the execution of which, subsequently, had been partially suspended. As the Advocate General pointed out in point 71 of his Opinion, while that court enjoyed a margin of discretion in that regard, that margin did not concern the level or the nature of the sentences imposed on the person concerned, but only whether the suspensions should be revoked or could be maintained, with additional conditions if necessary.

81. Accordingly, the only effect of suspension revocation decisions, such as those in the main proceedings, is that the person concerned must at most serve the remainder of the sentence initially imposed. Where, as in the main proceedings, the suspension is revoked in its entirety, the sentence once again produces all its effects and the determination of the quantum of the sentence still remaining to be served is derived from a purely arithmetic operation, with the number of days already served in custody being simply deducted from the total sentence imposed by the final criminal conviction.

> 82. In those circumstances, and in the light of what was stated in paragraph 77 of the present judgment, suspension revocation decisions, such as those at issue in the main proceedings, are not covered by Article 4a(1) of Framework Decision 2002/584, since those decisions leave unchanged the sentences imposed by the final conviction decisions with regard to both their nature and level.[24]

4.2 The General Requirements of 'a Waiver of the Right to Take Part in the Trial' under Article 6 of the ECHR and under Article 4a of FD 2002/584/JHA

Pursuant to the well-established case-law of the ECtHR, the right to participate in the hearing in a criminal case is a significant element of the general right to a fair trial guaranteed by Article 6 of the ECHR. The Court underlines that although this is not expressly mentioned in paragraph 1 of Article 6, the object and purpose of the Article show that a person 'charged with a criminal offence' is entitled to take part in the hearing. Moreover, it would be difficult to see how the applicant could exercise the rights enshrined in Article 6(3) of the ECHR without being present at the hearing.[25]

However, the right to attend the hearing is not an absolute one. This right may be waived by the defendant either expressly or tacitly. In accordance with the general concept of 'waiver', if it is to be effective for the Convention purposes, such a waiver of rights must: 1) be established in an unequivocal manner; 2) be attended by minimum safeguards commensurate with its importance and shall not run counter to any important public interest.[26]

With reference to the right to attend the hearing the requirements of effective waiver are even higher and are defined in the leading case of *Sejdovic v. Italy*. Although there is no requirement that a person charged with a criminal offence be notified of the date of the hearing in person, if this is not the case, the national authorities cannot simply presume that an absent defendant had waived his/her right to appear at the trial. Moreover, an accused should be aware of the consequences of the waiver. As was underlined by the ECtHR:

24 ECJ, judgment of 22 December 2017, *Samet Ardic*, C-571/17 PPU, ECLI:EU:C:2017:1026, paras. 67-82.

25 *See*, ECtHR, judgment of 1 March 2006, *Sejdovic v. Italy* [GC], ECLI:CE:ECHR:2006:0301JUD005658100, para. 81.

26 ECtHR, judgment of 20 October 2015, *Dvorski v. Croatia*, ECLI:CE:ECHR:2015:1020JUD002570311, para. 100.

> ... where a person charged with a criminal offence had not been notified in person, it could not be inferred merely from his status as a "fugitive" [...], which was founded on a presumption with an insufficient factual basis, that he had waived his right to appear at the trial and defend himself.[27]

Furthermore, it is stated that:

> ... before an accused can be said to have implicitly, through his conduct, waived an important right under Article 6 of the Convention, it must be shown that he could reasonably have foreseen what the consequences of his conduct would be.[28]

Additionally:

> ... a person charged with a criminal offence must not be left with the burden of proving that he was not seeking to evade justice or that his absence was due to force majeure [...]. At the same time, it is open to the national authorities to assess whether the accused showed good cause for his absence or whether there was anything in the case file to warrant finding that he had been absent for reasons beyond his control.[29]

In case of an effective waiver of the right to attend the hearing, a trial may be conducted *in absentia* and there is no need to provide the accused with the right to retrial. However, the refusal to re-open proceedings conducted *in absentia*, without any indication that the accused has waived his/her right to be present during the trial, shall be assessed as a 'flagrant denial of justice' rendering the proceedings "manifestly contrary to the provisions of Article 6 or the principles embodied therein".[30]

The ECtHR recognises the right of the State-Parties to the Convention to take measures which would discourage unjustified absences. However, such measures cannot undermine the fairness of the criminal proceedings. Thus, the waiver of the right to attend the hearing

27 ECtHR, judgment of 1 March 2006, *Sejdovic v. Italy* [GC], ECLI:CE:ECHR:2006:0301JUD005658100, para. 87.

28 ECtHR, judgment of 1 March 2006, *Sejdovic v. Italy* [GC], ECLI:CE:ECHR:2006:0301JUD005658100, para. 87.

29 ECtHR, judgment of 1 March 2006, *Sejdovic v. Italy* [GC], ECLI:CE:ECHR:2006:0301JUD005658100, para. 88.

30 ECtHR, judgment of 24 March 2005, *Stoichkov v. Bulgaria*, ECLI:CE:ECHR:2005:0324JUD000980802, para. 56; ECtHR, judgment of 12 February 2015, *Sanader v. Croatia*, ECLI:CE:ECHR:2015:0212JUD006640812, para. 71.

should not deprive the accused of his right to be defended by counsel.[31] The ECtHR stresses the following:

> [...] the right of everyone charged with a criminal offence to be defended effectively by a lawyer is one of the basic features of a fair trial. An accused does not lose this right merely on account of not attending a court hearing. Even if the legislature must be able to discourage unjustified absences, it cannot penalise them by creating exceptions to the right to legal assistance. The legitimate requirement that defendants must attend court hearings can be satisfied by means other than deprivation of the right to be defended (see Van Geyseghem, cited above, § 34; Van Pelt, cited above, § 67; Kari-Pekka Pietiläinen, cited above, § 32; and Neziraj, cited above, § 51).[32]

As was stated in Chapter 2.2. of this Guide, Article 4a(1) of FD 2002/584/JHA was drafted with due respect of the requirements of Article 6 of the ECHR and the relevant case-law of the ECtHR. This provision reflects the main requirements of a fair trial conducted *in absentia*. Thus, in order to strengthen the procedural rights of persons subject to criminal proceedings, Article 4a(1) of FD 2002/584/JHA provides for an optional ground of refusal of execution of the EAW issued for the purpose of executing a custodial sentence or a detention order issued *in absentia*. Such an EAW shall be executed if it states that the person, in accordance with further procedural requirements defined in the national law of the issuing Member State:

> (a) in due time:
> (i) either was summoned in person and thereby informed of the scheduled date and place of the trial which resulted in the decision, or by other means actually received official information of the scheduled date and place of that trial in such a manner that it was unequivocally established that he or she was aware of the scheduled trial;
> and
> (ii) was informed that a decision may be handed down if he or she does not appear for the trial;
> or

31 ECtHR, judgment of 22 September 2009, *Kari-pekka Pietiläinen v. Finland*, ECLI:CE:ECHR:2009:0922JUD001356606, paras. 31-32.

32 ECtHR, judgment of 9 July 2015, *Tolmachev v. Estonia*, ECLI:CE:ECHR:2015:0709JUD007374813, para. 48.

> (b) being aware of the scheduled trial, had given a mandate to a legal counsellor, who was either appointed by the person concerned or by the State, to defend him or her at the trial, and was indeed defended by that counsellor at the trial;
> or
> (c) after being served with the decision and being expressly informed about the right to a retrial, or an appeal, in which the person has the right to participate and which allows the merits of the case, including fresh evidence, to be re-examined, and which may lead to the original decision being reversed:
> (i) expressly stated that he or she does not contest the decision;
> or
> (ii) did not request a retrial or appeal within the applicable time frame;
> or
> (d) was not personally served with the decision but:
> (i) will be personally served with it without delay after the surrender and will be expressly informed of his or her right to a retrial, or an appeal, in which the person has the right to participate and which allows the merits of the case, including fresh evidence, to be re-examined, and which may lead to the original decision being reversed;
> and
> (ii) will be informed of the time frame within which he or she has to request such a retrial or appeal, as mentioned in the relevant European arrest warrant.

Thus, while deciding on the execution of EAW, the executing authority may assume that a defendant had waived his/her right to participate in the trial if at least one out of the above-mentioned three prerequisites is fulfilled. Hence, it is enough that: 1) a defendant was informed in person about the date and place of the trial and was informed that a decision/judgment may be rendered in his absence, or 2) a defendant by other means actually received official information of the scheduled date and place of the trial and was informed that a decision/judgment may be rendered in his/her absence, or 3) a defendant being aware of the date of the trial had given a mandate to a legal counsellor to defend him or her at the trial and he/she was indeed defended by that counsellor at the trial. In addition, the executing judicial authority is not allowed to refuse the execution of EAW if it states that the person concerned either did not ask for a retrial or that s/he will be expressly informed of his/her right to a retrial and will have a right to full retrial or full appeal (both on point of law and facts) after surrender.[33]

33 *See*, ECJ, judgment of 26 February 2013, *Stefano Melloni v. Ministerio Fiscal*, C-399/11, ECLI:EU:C:2013:107, para. 52.

In general, the above-mentioned conditions correspond to the requirements of an effective waiver of the right to participate in the trial, as established in the case-law of the ECtHR. However, there are certain differences which make the FD's standard higher than the ECHR's standard. This issue will be discussed in the following chapters of the Guide.

4.3 Requirements Concerning Knowledge about the Trial and Summoning of a Defendant

4.3.1 *Under the Case-Law of the ECtHR*

As was stated earlier, the effective waiver of the right to participate in the trial shall be accompanied by safeguards commensurate with the importance of this right and shall not run counter to any important public interest. First of all, a defendant must be aware of the criminal charges brought against him. Being aware of criminal charges, he/she is at the same time aware of the criminal proceedings conducted against him/her. The ECtHR underlines that:

> 89. Under the terms of paragraph 3 (a) of Article 6 of the Convention, everyone charged with a criminal offence has the right "to be informed promptly, in a language which he understands and in detail, of the nature and cause of the accusation against him". This provision points to the need for special attention to be paid to the notification of the "accusation" to the defendant. An indictment plays a crucial role in the criminal process, in that it is from the moment of its service that the defendant is formally put on notice of the factual and legal basis of the charges against him (see *Kamasinski v. Austria*, 19 December 1989, § 79, Series A no. 168).
>
> 90. The scope of the above provision must in particular be assessed in the light of the more general right to a fair hearing guaranteed by Article 6 § 1 of the Convention. In criminal matters the provision of full, detailed information concerning the charges against a defendant, and consequently the legal characterisation that the court might adopt in the matter, is an essential prerequisite for ensuring that the proceedings are fair.[34]

34 ECtHR, judgment of 1 March 2006, *Sejdovic v. Italy* [GC], ECLI:CE:ECHR:2006:0301JUD005658100, paras. 89-90; see also: ECtHR, judgment of 24 April 2012, *Haralampiev v. Bulgaria*, ECLI:CE:ECHR:2012:0424JUD002964803, paras. 33-34.

Hence, no valid waiver of the right to take part in the trial can take place if the defendant did not have knowledge of the criminal proceedings against him/her.[35]

If a suspect left the country before institution of criminal proceedings against him/her, the authorities shall act diligently and make sufficient efforts to trace him/her and to establish his/her whereabouts, so that they might notify him/her of the criminal proceedings. In *Coniac v. Romania* case the ECtHR underlined the following:

> 51. The Court observes in this connection that the first question is whether the applicant was officially notified of the criminal proceedings against him. The Court has already held that informing someone that a prosecution is being brought against him is a legal act of such importance that it must be carried out in accordance with procedural and substantive requirements capable of guaranteeing the effective exercise of the accused's rights; vague and informal knowledge cannot suffice (see Sejdovic, cited above, § 99; *Stoyanov v. Bulgaria*, no. 39206/07, § 34, 31 January 2012; and *Kounov v. Bulgaria*, no. 24379/02, § 47, 23 May 2006).[36]

The requirements indicated earlier are not fulfilled if there is no evidence that the applicant was served with a summons at his/her last place of residence or at any other address after institution of criminal proceedings against him/her. In this case (*Coniac v. Romania*) the applicant did not receive any official notification of the institution of criminal proceedings against him or the date of his trial. It appears that each time the police officers went to the applicant's last place of residence they tried to obtain information about his whereabouts, but they did not leave any summons or documents.[37]

Criminal courts should show due diligence in the efforts to locate the accused and to inform him/her about the criminal proceedings. In the *M.T.B. v. Turkey* case the ECtHR stated that notification about the date of the hearing to the address of the accused's company, without any efforts to send a summons to his home address, was not satisfactory. The ECtHR stressed that the applicant's home address was available for the national authorities in the context of other criminal proceedings. Moreover, the police were able to locate this place and arrest the applicant at his home address. Having regard to the above-described circumstances of the case, the Court stated:

---

35 ECtHR, judgment of 12 June 2018, *M.T.B. v. Turkey*, ECLI:CE:ECHR:2018:0612JUD004708106, para. 49; *see*, recently: ECtHR, judgment of 25 September 2018, *Karemani v. Albania*, ECLI:CE:ECHR:2018:0925JUD004871708, paras. 28-34.

36 ECtHR, judgment of 6 October 2015, *Coniac v. Romania*, ECLI:CE:ECHR:2015:1006JUD000494107, para. 52.

37 ECtHR, judgment of 6 October 2015, *Coniac v. Romania*, ECLI:CE:ECHR:2015:1006JUD000494107, para. 53.

> [...] the Court is unable to subscribe to the Government's argument that the trial court showed the requisite due diligence in its efforts to locate the applicant (see, mutatis mutandis, *Davran v. Turkey*, no. 18342/03, § 45, 3 November 2009, and *Büyükdağ v. Turkey*, no. 28340/95, § 67 in fine, 21 December 2000). In such a case, the submission that the national courts served the decision in accordance with the domestic legal provisions, a fact that is disputed between the parties in the present case, is not sufficient of itself to relieve the State of its obligations under Article 6 of the Convention.[38]

In *Dridi v. Germany* the ECtHR found that in the circumstances of this case serving a summons to appear before the court via public notification (it was displayed on the court's noticeboard for two weeks) was not sufficient to enable the applicant to attend the appeal hearing before the court. The ECtHR stressed that the address of the accused in Spain was known to the court. Furthermore, there had been no unsuccessful attempts to serve court documents on the applicant at that address. The applicant was also not informed about the fact of serving a summons by public notification. Moreover, at the time that the summons was served, the applicant was not represented by his lawyer, whose authorisation had been withdrawn by a court. The applicant's lawyer thus learned of the date of the hearing only the day before it was scheduled, and his application for an adjournment was refused.[39]

To the contrary, if a suspect, being aware of charges, leaves the country acting in violation of the obligation not to leave his/her village, the authorities are entitled to assume that s/he effectively waived his right to participate in the trial.[40]

If a defendant was informed in person about the date and place of the hearing and he/she does not appear at that hearing, one can assume that the right to participate was waived by him/her in an unequivocal manner. However, in case of indirect notification (notification by other means than in person) the ECtHR stresses that:

> ... it cannot be inferred merely from the fact that he has been declared latitante (that is to say, wilfully evading the execution of a warrant issued by a court), relying on a presumption with an insufficient factual basis, that he has waived his right to appear at the trial and defend himself [...].[41]

38 ECtHR, judgment of 12 June 2018, *M.T.B. v. Turkey*, ECLI:CE:ECHR:2018:0612JUD004708106, para. 53.

39 ECtHR, judgment of 26 July 2018, *Dridi v. Germany*, ECLI:CE:ECHR:2018:0726JUD003577811, paras. 31-33.

40 ECtHR, decision of 4 December 2018, *Andrei Năstase v. Moldova*, ECLI:CE:ECHR:2018:1204DEC007444411.

41 ECtHR, judgment of 1 March 2006, *Sejdovic v. Italy* [GC], ECLI:CE:ECHR:2006:0301JUD005658100, para. 87.

> However, "at the same time, it is open to the national authorities to assess whether the accused showed good cause for his absence or whether there was anything in the case file to warrant finding that he had been absent for reasons beyond his control".[42]

Article 6 of the ECHR does not determine the manner of summoning to the hearing. In particular, this provision does not guarantee the right to obtain a specific form of service of court documents, such as by registered post. Nonetheless:

> ... the Court considers that in the interests of the administration of justice a litigant should be notified of a court hearing in such a way as to not only have knowledge of the date, time and place of the hearing, but also to have enough time to prepare his or her case and to attend the court hearing (see Kolegovy, cited above, § 40, and the cases cited therein, and *Aždajić v. Slovenia*, no. 71872/12, § 48, 8 October 2015).[43]

The effectiveness of a notification of the date of the hearing must always be assessed in the circumstances of the particular case. Sometimes other documents or information than a confirmation of serving a summons may show that the accused was aware of the criminal proceedings conducted against him. In *Shkalla v. Albania* case the ECtHR stated:

> 70. In previous cases concerning convictions in absentia, the Court has held that to inform someone of a prosecution brought against him is a legal act of such importance that it must be carried out in accordance with procedural and substantive requirements capable of guaranteeing the effective exercise of the accused's rights; vague and informal knowledge cannot suffice (see *T. v. Italy*, cited above, § 28, and *Somogyi v. Italy*, no.67972/01, § 75, ECHR 2004-IV). The Court cannot, however, rule out the possibility that certain established facts might provide an unequivocal indication that the accused is aware of the existence of the criminal proceedings against him and of the nature and the cause of the accusation and does not intend to take part in the trial or wishes to avoid prosecution. This may be the case, for example, where the accused states publicly or in writing that he does not intend to respond to summonses of which he has become aware through sources other than the authorities, or succeeds in

---

42 ECtHR, judgment of 1 March 2006, *Sejdovic v. Italy* [GC], ECLI:CE:ECHR:2006:0301JUD005658100, para. 88.

43 ECtHR, judgment of 28 August 2018, *Vyacheslav Korchagin v. Russia*, ECLI:CE:ECHR:2018:0828JUD001230716, para. 65.

evading an attempted arrest (see, among other authorities, *Iavarazzo v. Italy* (dec.), no. 50489/99, 4 December 2001), or when materials are brought to the attention of the authorities which unequivocally show that he is aware of the proceedings pending against him and of the charges he faces.[44]

4.3.2 *Under the Case-Law of the Court of Justice Concerning Article 4a of FD 2002/584/JHA*

The wording of Article 4a(1)(a)(i) of FD 2002/584/JHA was interpreted by the Court of Justice in the framework of preliminary ruling proceedings initiated by the Amsterdam Court in case C-108/16 PPU, *Dworzecki*. The question concerned the meaning of the term "by other means actually received official information of the scheduled date and place of that trial in such a manner that it was unequivocally established that he or she was aware of the scheduled trial". In particular, the Amsterdam Court wanted to know whether the summons served at the address of the requested person, on an adult resident of the household who undertook to hand the summons over to the requested person, could be considered as fulfilling the requirements of Article 4a(1)(a)(i), while: 1) it was not clear from the EAW whether and when that resident actually handed the summons over to the requested person, and 2) it could not be inferred from the statement which the requested person made at the hearing before the referring court that he was – in due time – aware of the date and place of the scheduled trial.

The Court of Justice stated that:

1. Article 4a(1)(a)(i) [...] must be interpreted as meaning that the expressions 'summoned in person' and 'by other means actually received official information of the scheduled date and place of that trial in such a manner that it was unequivocally established that he or she was aware of the scheduled trial' in that provision constitute autonomous concepts of EU law and must be interpreted uniformly throughout the European Union.
2. Article 4a(1)(a)(i) [...] must be interpreted as meaning that a summons, such as that at issue in the main proceedings, which was not served directly on the person concerned but was handed over, at the latter's address, to an adult belonging to that household who undertook to pass it on to him, when it cannot be ascertained from the European arrest warrant whether and, if so, when that adult actually passed that summons on to the person concerned, does not in itself satisfy the conditions set out in that provision.

44 ECtHR, judgment of 10 May 2011, *Shkalla v. Albania*, ECLI:CE:ECHR:2011:0510JUD002686605, para. 70.

The Court of Justice provided the following reasons for the above interpretation.

> 42. [...] although the right of the accused to appear in person at his trial is an essential component of the right to a fair trial, that requirement is not absolute. The accused may waive that right of his own free will, either expressly or tacitly, provided that the waiver is established in an unequivocal manner, is attended by minimum safeguards commensurate to the gravity of the criminal offence with which the accused is charged and does not run counter to any important public interest. In particular, breach of the right to a fair trial has not been established, even where the accused did not appear in person, if he was informed of the date and place of the trial or was defended by a legal counsellor whom he had instructed to defend him (see, to that effect, judgment of 26 February 2013 in Melloni, C-399/11, EU:C:2013:107, paragraph 49).
>
> 43. The right to a fair trial enjoyed by a person summoned to appear before a criminal court thus requires that he has been informed in such a way as to allow him to organise his defence effectively. [...]
>
> 44. In that regard, as stated in recital 4 of Framework Decision 2009/299, that framework decision is not designed to regulate, at EU level, the forms and methods that are used by the competent authorities in the context of the surrender procedure, including the procedural requirements applicable according to the law of the Member State concerned.
>
> 45. The purpose of Article 4a(1)(a)(i) of Framework Decision 2002/584 referred to in paragraph 43 of this judgment is necessarily achieved by a summons 'in person', as referred to in the first part of that provision, as such a method of service ensures that the person concerned has himself received the summons and, accordingly, has been informed of the date and place of his trial.
>
> 46. As regards the conditions set out in the second part of that provision, they are designed to achieve the same high level of protection of the person summoned, by ensuring that he has the information relating to the date and place of his trial.
>
> 47. Regard being had, in particular, to the wording of Article 4a(1)(a)(i) of Framework Decision 2002/584, which states that it must be unequivocally established that the person concerned 'was aware of the scheduled trial', the fact that the summons was handed over to a third party who undertook to pass

it on to the person concerned, whether or not that third party belonged to the household of the person concerned, cannot in itself satisfy those requirements. Such a method of service does not allow it to be unequivocally established either that the person concerned 'actually' received the information relating to the date and place of his trial or, where appropriate, the precise time when that information was received.

48. Admittedly, as the Commission has observed, it cannot, in principle, be precluded that handing a summons over to a third party satisfies the requirements of Article 4a(1)(a)(i) of Framework Decision 2002/584. In order to achieve the objective referred to in that provision, however, it must be unequivocally established that that third party actually passed the summons on to the person concerned.

49. In that regard, it is for the issuing judicial authority to indicate in the European arrest warrant the evidence on the basis of which it found that the person concerned actually received official information relating to the date and place of his trial. When the executing judicial authority ensures that the conditions set out in Article 4a(1)(a) of Framework Decision 2002/584 are satisfied, it may also rely on other evidence, including circumstances of which it became aware when hearing the person concerned.

4.4 Representation by a Lawyer as a Condition of a Fair Trial Conducted *In Absentia*

4.4.1 *Under the Case-Law of the ECtHR*

Participation of a defence counsel in a trial constitutes one of the important conditions of fairness concerning criminal proceedings conducted *in absentia*. In accordance with the well-established case-law, a person charged with a criminal offence does not lose his/her right to be defended by a lawyer merely on account of not being present at the trial. Nevertheless, the legislature must be able to discourage unjustified absences, provided that any sanctions used are not disproportionate in the circumstances of the case and the defendant is not deprived of his/her right to be defended by counsel.[45]

In the leading case of *Sejdovic v. Italy* the ECtHR emphasised the following.

45 ECtHR, judgment of 21 January 1999, *Van Geyseghem v. Belgium*, ECLI:CE:ECHR:1999:0121JUD002610395, para. 34.

> 93. It is for the courts to ensure that a trial was fair and, accordingly, that counsel who attends trial for the apparent purpose of defending the accused in his absence is given the opportunity of doing so (see Van Geyseghem, cited above, § 33; Lala, cited above, § 34; and Pelladoah, cited above, § 41).
>
> 94. While it confers on everyone charged with a criminal offence the right to "defend himself in person or through legal assistance ...", Article 6 § 3 (c) does not specify the manner of exercising this right. It thus leaves to the Contracting States the choice of the means of ensuring that it is secured in their judicial systems, the Court's task being to ascertain whether the method they have chosen is consistent with the requirements of a fair trial (see *Quaranta v. Switzerland*, 24 May 1991, § 30, Series A no. 205). In this connection, it must be remembered that the Convention is designed to "guarantee not rights that are theoretical or illusory but rights that are practical and effective" and that assigning counsel does not in itself ensure the effectiveness of the assistance he may afford an accused (see *Imbrioscia v. Switzerland*, 24 November 1993, § 38, Series A no. 275, and *Artico v. Italy*, 13 May 1980, § 33, Series A no. 37).
>
> 95. Nevertheless, a State cannot be held responsible for every shortcoming on the part of a lawyer appointed for legal aid purposes or by the accused. It follows from the independence of the legal profession from the State that the conduct of the defence is essentially a matter between the defendant and his counsel, whether appointed under a legal aid scheme or privately financed (*see Cuscani v. the United Kingdom*, no. 32271/96, § 39, 24 September 2002). The competent national authorities are required under Article 6 § 3 (c) to intervene only if a failure by legal aid counsel to provide effective representation is manifest or is sufficiently brought to their attention in some other way (see *Daud v. Portugal*, 21 April 1998, § 38, Reports 1998-II).[46]

A defendant who evaded criminal proceedings by leaving a country is not entitled to a retrial if s/he had employed a lawyer who represented him/her both during the investigation stage and during the court proceedings and with whom s/he kept contact, being thus aware of the progress of the proceedings.[47] In this case the applicant's lawyer acted on his behalf and obtained a reduction of the sentence by the Court of Appeal from ten years to seven years' imprisonment.

46 ECtHR, judgment of 1 March 2006, *Sejdovic v. Italy* [GC], ECLI:CE:ECHR:2006:0301JUD005658100, paras. 93-95.

47 ECtHR, decision of 4 December 2018, *Andrei Năstase v. Moldova*, ECLI:CE:ECHR:2018:1204DEC007444411.

4.4.2 Under the Case-Law of the Court of Justice Concerning Article 4a of FD 2002/584/JHA

The execution of an EAW concerning a judgment/decision rendered *in absentia* cannot be refused if the defendant (Article 4a(1)):

> (b) being aware of the scheduled trial, had given a mandate to a legal counsellor, who was either appointed by the person concerned or by the State, to defend him or her at the trial, and was indeed defended by that counsellor at the trial.

In the *Melloni case*, the Court of Justice found that Article 4a(1) of the FD

> must be interpreted as precluding the executing judicial authorities, in the circumstances specified in that provision, from making the execution of a European arrest warrant issued for the purposes of executing a sentence conditional upon the conviction rendered *in absentia* being open to review in the issuing Member State.

The Court of Justice stated that:

> 49 [...] The accused may waive that right [the right to appeal in person at the trial] of his own free will, either expressly or tacitly, provided that the waiver is established in an unequivocal manner, is attended by minimum safeguards commensurate to its importance and does not run counter to any important public interest. In particular, violation of the right to a fair trial has not been established, even where the accused did not appear in person, if he was informed of the date and place of the trial or was defended by a legal counsellor to whom he had given a mandate to do so.

The above interpretation of Article 4a(1) of FD corresponds to the standard of the ECtHR case-law presented in Section 3.4.1.

The Court of Justice found Article 4a (1) to be compatible with *the requirements under Articles 47 and 48(2) of the Charter of Fundamental Rights of the European Union for the following reasons:*

> 50. This interpretation of Articles 47 and 48(2) of the Charter is in keeping with the scope that has been recognised for the rights guaranteed by Article 6(1) and (3) of the ECHR by the case-law of the European Court of Human Rights (see, inter alia, ECtHR, *Medenica v. Switzerland*, no. 20491/92, § 56 to

59, ECHR 2001-VI; *Sejdovic v. Italy* [GC], no. 56581/00, § 84, 86 and 98, ECHR 2006-II; and *Haralampiev v. Bulgaria*, no. 29648/03, § 32 and 33, 24 April 2012).

51. Furthermore, as indicated by Article 1 of Framework Decision 2009/299, the objective of the harmonisation of the conditions of execution of European arrest warrants issued for the purposes of executing decisions rendered at the end of trials at which the person concerned has not appeared in person, effected by that framework decision, is to enhance the procedural rights of persons subject to criminal proceedings whilst improving mutual recognition of judicial decisions between Member States.

52. Accordingly, Article 4a(1)(a) and (b) of Framework Decision 2002/584 lays down the circumstances in which the person concerned must be deemed to have waived, voluntarily and unambiguously, his right to be present at his trial, with the result that the execution of a European arrest warrant issued for the purposes of executing the sentence of a person convicted in absentia cannot be made subject to the condition that that person may claim the benefit of a retrial at which he is present in the issuing Member State. This is so either where, as referred to in Article 4a(1)(a), the person did not appear in person at the trial despite having been summoned in person or officially informed of the scheduled date and place of the trial or, as referred to in Article 4a(1)(b), the person, being aware of the scheduled trial, deliberately chose to be represented by a legal counsellor instead of appearing in person. Article 4a(1)(c) and (d) refers to circumstances where the executing judicial authority is required to execute the European arrest warrant, even though the person concerned is entitled to a retrial, because the arrest warrant states that the person concerned either did not ask for a retrial or that he will be expressly informed of his right to a retrial.

53. In the light of the foregoing, Article 4a(1) of Framework Decision 2002/584 does not disregard either the right to an effective judicial remedy and to a fair trial or the rights of the defence guaranteed by Articles 47 and 48(2) of the Charter respectively.

4.5 Serving a Judgment on a Defendant as a Condition of Fair *In Absentia* Proceedings

4.5.1 *Under the Case-Law of the ECtHR*

Article 6 of the ECHR does not provide for specific forms of service of court documents, such as judgments.

However, the way in which a judgment is served on a defendant may raise an issue under the right to access to a court. If a legal recourse to a judgment is declared inadmissible because the defendant did not respect the formalities and/or the time frame for lodging that legal recourse and if the defendant was not informed of those formalities and that time frame at the time of serving the judgment, the right to access to a court will be breached.[48]

The object of informing the defendant of the right to a legal recourse is to enable him/her to exercise that right in accordance with the law of the issuing Member State.[49] When serving a judgment of conviction on the defendant, particularly when at the moment of service s/he is detained or not represented by a legal counsellor, s/he must be informed in a reliable and official manner of the possible recourses against that judgment and the time frame within which to exercise those recourses.[50]

The object of informing the defendant of his/her rights could be achieved by providing him/her with a document which indicates the formalities and the time frame to be respected when exercising the right to legal recourse in such a way that it does not require the interpretation of the applicable legislation or the advice of a legal counsellor.[51]

4.5.2 *Under the Case-Law of the Court of Justice Concerning Article 4a of FD 2002/584/JHA*

Article 4a(1)(c) of FD 2002/584/JHA has not been subject to interpretation by the Court of Justice, apart from the general remarks made in the *Melloni* case cited earlier. However, the wording of this provision is quite clear and should not bring considerable difficulties.

48 ECtHR, decision of 5 February 2004, *Bogonos v. Russia*, ECLI:CE:ECHR:2004:0205DEC006879801, with regard to providing the person concerned with a copy of the judgment on appeal.

49 ECtHR, decision of 5 February 2004, *Bogonos v. Russia*, ECLI:CE:ECHR:2004:0205DEC006879801, with regard to providing the person concerned with a copy of the judgment on appeal.

50 ECtHR, judgment of 1 March 2011, *Faniel v. Belgium*, ECLI:CE:ECHR:2011:0301JUD001189208, § 30. ECtHR, judgment of 29 June 2010, *Hakimi v. Belgium*, ECLI:CE:ECHR:2010:0629JUD000066508, § 36.

51 ECtHR, judgment of 24 May 2007, *Da Luz Domingues Ferreira v. Belgium*, ECLI:CE:ECHR:2007:0524JUD005004999, § 58.

If a decision/judgment was served on a defendant and, being informed of the right to retrial or an appeal, he/she decided not to contest a decision/judgment, there is no optional ground for refusal to execute such EAW under Article 4a(1) of FD 2002/584/JHA. It seems reasonable to argue that the way of serving a decision/judgment is not decisive for the purpose of this provision. What matters is whether a defendant is actually aware of the content of a decision/judgment and of his/her right to apply for retrial or an appeal. It is worth stressing that Article 4a(1)(c) of FD 2002/584/JHA does not require *expressis verbis* that a decision be served 'personally' on a defendant. However, such requirement may be derived from the wording of Article 4a(1)(d) of FD 2002/584/JHA.

The general right of a defendant to get access to information is regulated by the Directive 2012/13/EU of the European Parliament and of the Council of 22 May 2012 on the right to information in criminal proceedings (OJ 2012 L 142, p. 1).

In the *Covaci* case the Court of Justice was faced with the problem whether Articles 2, 3(1)(c) and 6(1) and (3) of Directive 2012/13 (concerning the obligation to provide a defendant with certain information in criminal proceedings) must be interpreted as precluding legislation of a Member State, such as that at issue in the main proceedings, which, in criminal proceedings, makes it mandatory for an accused person not residing in that Member State to appoint a person authorised to accept service of a penalty order concerning him/her, with the period for lodging an objection against that order running from the service of that order on that authorised person.

The Court of Justice decided as follows:

> Articles 2, 3(1)(c) and 6(1) and (3) of Directive 2012/13/EU [...] must be Interpreted as not precluding legislation of a Member State, such as that at issue in the main proceedings, which, in criminal proceedings, makes it mandatory for an accused person not residing in that Member State to appoint a person authorised to accept service of a penalty order concerning him, provided that that accused person does in fact have the benefit of the whole of the prescribed period for lodging an objection against that order.

And provided the following reasoning for its interpretative decision:

> 60. While it is true that, because of the summary and simplified nature of the proceedings at issue, the service of a penalty order such as that at issue in the main proceedings is effected only after the court has ruled on the merits of the accusation, the fact remains that, in that order, the court rules only provisionally and that the service of that order represents the first opportunity for the accused person to be informed of the accusation against him. That is confirmed, moreover, by the fact that that person is entitled to bring not an appeal against

that order before another court, but an objection making him eligible, before the same court, for the ordinary inter partes procedure, in which he can fully exercise his rights of defence, before that court rules again on the merits of the accusation against him.

61. Consequently, in accordance with Article 6 of Directive 2012/13, the service of a penalty order must be considered to be a form of communication of the accusation against the person concerned, with the result that it must comply with the requirements set out in that article.

62. It is true that, as the Advocate General observed at point 105 of his Opinion, Directive 2012/13 does not regulate the procedures whereby information about the accusation, provided for in Article 6 of that directive, must be provided to that person.

63. However, those procedures cannot undermine the objective referred to inter alia in Article 6 of Directive 2012/13, which, as is also apparent from recital 27 in the preamble to that directive, consists in enabling suspects or persons accused of having committed a criminal offence to prepare their defence and in safeguarding the fairness of the proceedings.

64. It is apparent from the order for reference that the national legislation at issue in the main proceedings provides that the penalty order is to be served on the person authorised by the accused person and that the latter has a period of two weeks to lodge an objection against that order, with that period running from the service of that order on that authorised person. Upon expiry of that period, the order is to acquire the force of res judicata.

65. Though it is not relevant, in order to answer the question asked by the referring court, to rule on the appropriateness of such a limitation period of two weeks, it is important to observe that both the objective of enabling the accused person to prepare his defence and the need to avoid any kind of discrimination between (i) accused persons with a residence within the jurisdiction of the national law concerned and (ii) accused persons whose residence does not fall within that jurisdiction, who alone are required to appoint a person authorised to accept service of judicial decisions, require the whole of that period to be available to the accused person.

66. If the period of two weeks at issue in the main proceedings began to run from the time when the accused person actually became aware of the penalty order, that order providing information on the accusation within the meaning of Article 6 of Directive 2012/13, it would be certain that the whole of that period is available to that person.

67. By contrast, if, as in the present case, that period begins to run from the service of the penalty order on the person authorised by the accused person, the latter can effectively exercise his right of defence and the trial is fair only if he has the benefit of that period in its entirety, that is to say without the duration of that period being reduced by the time needed by the authorised person to transmit the penalty order to its addressee.[52]

The above interpretation of Directive 2012/13 was further developed in *Tranca and Reiter* case concerning service of a penal order on a person authorised by a defendant not residing in the Member State. The Court of Justice stated that:

47. [...] Member States must ensure that persons accused or suspects in the context of criminal proceedings, who, in circumstances such as those at issue in the main proceedings, are not notified of the charge against them at the stage of execution of the final decision on conviction, nevertheless retain the right to exercise fully their rights of defence. To that end, once an accused person has actually been informed of a criminal decision concerning him, he must be placed in the same situation as if that decision had been served on him personally and he must, in particular, have the benefit of the whole of the prescribed period for lodging an objection.

48. As the referring courts makes clear, although national law provides that a penalty order becomes final on expiry of the period for lodging an objection, which begins to run from service of the order on the agent of the accused person, it also allows that person to apply to have his position restored to the status quo ante and therefore to benefit accordingly from a period of the same duration to lodge an objection to that order, from the time when the accused person became aware of the penalty order.

49. It is thus for the referring courts to interpret national law, in particular the procedure for a person's position being restored to the status quo ante and the

52 ECJ, judgment of 15 October 2015, *Covaci*, C-216/14, ECLI:EU:C:2015:686.

conditions to which the exercise of that procedure is subject, in accordance with the requirements laid down in Article 6 of Directive 2012/13.

50. Having regard to the foregoing considerations, the answer to the questions referred is that Article 2, Article 3(1)(c), and Article 6(1) and (3) of Directive 2012/13 must be interpreted as not precluding legislation of a Member State, such as that at issue in the main proceedings, which, in criminal proceedings, provides that the accused person who neither resides in that Member State nor has a fixed place of residence in that State or in his Member State of origin is required to appoint an agent for the purposes of service of a penalty order concerning him, and that the period for lodging an objection to that order, before it becomes enforceable, runs from service of that order on that agent.

51. Article 6 of Directive 2012/13, however, requires that, when the penalty order is enforced, as soon as the person concerned has actually become aware of the order, he should be placed in the same situation as if that order had been served on him personally and, in particular, that he have the whole of the prescribed period for lodging an objection, where necessary, benefiting from having his position restored to the status quo ante.

52. It is for the referring court to ensure that the national procedure for the accused person's position being restored to the status quo ante and the conditions to which the exercise of that procedure is subject are applied in a manner consistent with those requirements and that that procedure thus permits the effective exercise of the rights provided for in Article 6.[53]

4.6 The Right to Retrial as a Guarantee of Fairness of Proceedings Conducted *In Absentia*

4.6.1 *Under the Case-Law of the ECtHR*

As transpires from the case-law of the ECtHR, proceedings conducted *in absentia* are not in and of themselves incompatible with Article 6 of the Convention. However, a denial of justice nevertheless undoubtedly occurs where a person convicted *in absentia* is unable subsequently to obtain a retrial from a court which has heard him/her, where it has not

53 ECJ, judgment of 22 March 2017, *Tranca* (C-124/16), *Tanja Reiter* (C-213/16), ECLI:EU:C:2017:228.

been established that s/he has waived his/her right to appear and to defend him/herself. Thus, in case of an effective waiver of these rights there is no requirement to guarantee the right to retrial. A 'retrial' means "a fresh determination of the merits of the charge, in respect of both law and fact".[54]

The issues of 'effective waiver' and of minimum safeguards commensurate with such a waiver were at stake in the *M.T.B. v. Turkey* case. The Court underlined the following:

> 62. In the instant case, the Court has already found that the trial court failed to show the requisite due diligence in its efforts to locate the applicant. Nevertheless, both the trial court and the Court of Cassation confined their examination to just that point and dismissed the applicant's application, stating that the decision had been lawfully served on him, that is to say in accordance with the Notifications Act (see, mutatis mutandis, *Kounov v. Bulgaria*, no. 24379/02, § 52 in fine, 23 May 2006). They did not examine whether the applicant had in fact been notified or had unequivocally waived his right to appear and defend himself. Thus, the applicant's applications for a fresh factual and legal determination of his case were rejected, in the absence of any indication that he had waived his right to be present during the trial, a situation previously described by the Court in Sejdovic (cited above, § 84) as a "flagrant denial of justice".[55]

The ECtHR underlines that wide discretion is left to the Contracting States as regards the choice of the means enacted to ensure that their legal systems are in compliance with the requirements of Article 6. However, the Court's task is

> to determine whether the result called for by the Convention has been achieved. In particular, the procedural means offered by domestic law and practice must be shown to be effective where a person charged with a criminal offence has neither waived his right to appear and to defend himself nor sought to escape trial.[56]

54 ECtHR, judgment of 14 June 2001, *Medenica v. Switzerland*, ECLI:CE:ECHR:2001:0614JUD002049192, para. 55; ECtHR, judgment of 1 March 2006, *Sejdovic v. Italy* [GC], ECLI:CE:ECHR:2006:0301JUD005658100, para. 82.

55 ECtHR, judgment of 12 June 2018, *M.T.B. v. Turkey*, ECLI:CE:ECHR:2018:0612JUD004708106, para. 62.

56 ECtHR, judgment of 12 February 2015, *Sanader v. Croatia*, CLI:CE:ECHR:2015:0212JUD006640812, para. 69; ECtHR, judgment of 14 February 2017, *Hokkeling v. the Netherlands*, ECLI:CE:ECHR:2017:0214 JUD003074912, para. 58; ECtHR, judgment of 22 May 2018, *Topi v. Albania*, ECLI:CE:ECHR: 2018:0522JUD001481608, paras. 53-54; ECtHR, judgment of 25 September 2018, *Karemani v. Albania*, ECLI:CE:ECHR:2018:0925JUD004871708, paras. 30-32.

The formal requirements which could be imposed on a defendant seeking to obtain a retrial were summarised in the case of *Sanader v. Croatia.*[57] The ECtHR stated the following.

> 70. [...] there can be no question of an accused being obliged to surrender to custody in order to secure the right to be retried in conditions that comply with Article 6 of the Convention, for that would entail making the exercise of the right to a fair hearing conditional on the accused offering up his or her physical liberty as a form of guarantee (see Krombach, cited above, § 87).
> [...]
> 74. Furthermore, a person charged with a criminal offence must not be left with the burden of proving that he was not seeking to evade justice or that his absence was due to force majeure (see Colozza, cited above, § 30). At the same time, it is open to the national authorities to assess whether the accused showed good cause for his absence or whether there was anything in the case file to warrant a finding that he had been absent for reasons beyond his control (see Medenica, cited above, § 57).

In *Sanader v. Croatia*, the Court found disproportionate the requirement that an individual tried *in absentia*, who had not had unequivocally waived his/her right to appear in court, had to appear before the domestic authorities and provide an address of residence during the criminal proceedings in order to be able to request a retrial. Such requirement impaired the very essence of the right to retrial.[58] This was particularly so because once the defendant is under the jurisdiction of the domestic authorities, s/he would be deprived of liberty on the basis of the conviction *in absentia*. In this regard, the Court stressed that "there can be no question of an accused being obliged to surrender to custody in order to secure the right to be retried in conditions that comply with Article 6 of the Convention".[59] It explained, however, that:

> 88. This does not, of course, call into question whether, in the fresh proceedings, the applicant's presence at the trial would have to be secured by ordering his detention on remand or by the application of other measures envisaged under the relevant domestic law (see, inter alia, Khalfaoui, cited above, § 44). However, if applicable, that would need to have a different legal basis – that of a reasonable

57 ECtHR, judgment of 12 February 2015, *Sanader v. Croatia*, CLI:CE:ECHR:2015:0212JUD006640812, paras. 70-74.

58 ECtHR, judgment of 12 February 2015, *Sanader v. Croatia*, CLI:CE:ECHR:2015:0212JUD006640812, para. 91.

59 ECtHR, judgment of 12 February 2015, *Sanader v. Croatia*, CLI:CE:ECHR:2015:0212JUD006640812, para. 87.

suspicion of the applicant having committed the crime at issue and the existence of "relevant and sufficient reasons" for his detention (see, amongst many others, *Kudła v. Poland* [GC], no. 30210/96, § 111, ECHR 2000 XI; and *Dragin v. Croatia*, no. 75068/12, § 110, 24 July 2014).

4.6.2 *Under the Case-Law of the Court of Justice Concerning Article 4a of FD 2002/584/JHA*

As in the case-law of the ECtHR, under Article 4a(1) of the FD 2002/584/JHA the right to a retrial is also understood as an alternative to an effective waiver of the right to appear at the trial. Thus, if a defendant's presence at the trial was subject to the guarantees indicated in Article 4a(1)(a) to (c) of FD 2002/584/JHA, the EAW should be executed even if no right to a retrial is offered after surrender.

In the *Melloni* case the Court of Justice examined whether Article 4(a)(1) of FD 2002/584/JHA is compatible with the requirements deriving from the right to an effective judicial remedy and to a fair trial, provided in Article 47 of the Charter and from the rights of the defence guaranteed under Article 48(2) of the Charter. The Court of Justice stated:

> 49. Regarding the scope of the right to an effective judicial remedy and to a fair trial provided for in Article 47 of the Charter, and the rights of the defence guaranteed by Article 48(2) thereof, it should be observed that, although the right of the accused to appear in person at his trial is an essential component of the right to a fair trial, that right is not absolute (see, inter alia, Case C-619/10 Trade Agency [2012] ECR, paragraphs 52 and 55). The accused may waive that right of his own free will, either expressly or tacitly, provided that the waiver is established in an unequivocal manner, is attended by minimum safeguards commensurate to its importance and does not run counter to any important public interest. In particular, violation of the right to a fair trial has not been established, even where the accused did not appear in person, if he was informed of the date and place of the trial or was defended by a legal counsellor to whom he had given a mandate to do so.
>
> 50. This interpretation of Articles 47 and 48(2) of the Charter is in keeping with the scope that has been recognised for the rights guaranteed by Article 6(1) and (3) of the ECHR by the case-law of the European Court of Human Rights (see, inter alia, ECtHR, *Medenica v. Switzerland*, no. 20491/92, § 56 to 59, ECHR 2001-VI; *Sejdovic v. Italy* [GC], no. 56581/00, § 84, 86 and 98, ECHR 2006-II; and *Haralampiev v. Bulgaria*, no. 29648/03, § 32 and 33, 24 April 2012).

> 51. Furthermore, as indicated by Article 1 of Framework Decision 2009/299, the objective of the harmonisation of the conditions of execution of European arrest warrants issued for the purposes of executing decisions rendered at the end of trials at which the person concerned has not appeared in person, effected by that framework decision, is to enhance the procedural rights of persons subject to criminal proceedings whilst improving mutual recognition of judicial decisions between Member States.
>
> 52. Accordingly, Article 4a(1)(a) and (b) of Framework Decision 2002/584 lays down the circumstances in which the person concerned must be deemed to have waived, voluntarily and unambiguously, his right to be present at his trial, with the result that the execution of a European arrest warrant issued for the purposes of executing the sentence of a person convicted in absentia cannot be made subject to the condition that that person may claim the benefit of a retrial at which he is present in the issuing Member State. This is so either where, as referred to in Article 4a(1)(a), the person did not appear in person at the trial despite having been summoned in person or officially informed of the scheduled date and place of the trial or, as referred to in Article 4a(1)(b), the person, being aware of the scheduled trial, deliberately chose to be represented by a legal counsellor instead of appearing in person. Article 4a(1)(c) and (d) refers to circumstances where the executing judicial authority is required to execute the European arrest warrant, even though the person concerned is entitled to a retrial, because the arrest warrant states that the person concerned either did not ask for a retrial or that he will be expressly informed of his right to a retrial.
>
> 53. In the light of the foregoing, Article 4a(1) of Framework Decision 2002/584 does not disregard either the right to an effective judicial remedy and to a fair trial or the rights of the defence guaranteed by Articles 47 and 48(2) of the Charter respectively.[60]

Thus far, the Court of Justice has not had an opportunity to interpret the content of 'the right to a retrial or an appeal' used in Article 4a(1)(d) of FD 2002/584/JHA. However, relying on the judgment in *Tupikas* case[61] one may conclude that this notion should be

60 ECJ, judgment of 26 February 2013, *Stefano Melloni v. Ministerio Fiscal*, C-399/11, ECLI:EU:C:2013:107, paras. 49-53.

61 ECJ, judgment of 10 August 2017, *Openbaar Ministerie v. Tadas Tupikas*, C-270/17 PPU, ECLI:EU:C:2017:628.

understood in the same way as the right to retrial under Article 6 of the ECHR. Thus, it should include a fresh determination *of the merits of the charge, in respect of both law and fact.* Such an interpretation also follows from the clear wording of Article 4a(1)(d) of FD 2002/584/JHA.

Although in the *Tupikas* case the Court of Justice defined the notion of a 'trial resulting in the decision', the meaning of this term may be useful for proper understanding of the notion of 'a retrial or an appeal'. The Court of Justice stated as follows:

> 78. As is clear from the case-law of the European Court of Human Rights, the term 'conviction' within the meaning of the ECHR refers to both a finding of guilt after it has been established in accordance with the law that there has been an offence, and the imposition of a penalty or other measure involving deprivation of liberty (see, to that effect, ECtHR, 21 October 2013, *Del Río Prada v. Spain*, CE:ECHR:2013:1021JUD004275009, § 123, and the case-law cited).
>
> 79. Moreover, the European Court of Human Rights has held on several occasions that, where appeal proceedings are provided for, they must comply with the requirements flowing from Article 6 of the ECHR, in particular where the remedy available against the decision given at first instance is a full appeal, the second-instance court having jurisdiction to re-examine the case, by assessing the merits of the accusations in fact and in law, and thus to determine the guilt or innocence of the person concerned on the basis of the evidence presented (see, to that effect, judgments of the ECtHR of 26 May 1988, *Ekbatani v. Sweden*, CE:ECHR:1988:0526JUD001056383, § 24 and 32; 26 October 2000, *Kudła v. Poland*, CE:ECHR:1988:0526JUD001056383, § 122; 18 October 2006, *Hermi v. Italy*, CE:ECHR:2006:1018JUD001811402, § 64 and 65; 25 April 2013, *Zahirović v. Croatia*, CE:ECHR:2013:0425JUD005859011, § 56; and of 14 February 2017, *Hokkeling v. Netherlands*, CE:ECHR:2017:0214JUD 003074912, § 56 and 58).
>
> 80. It is also clear from that case-law of the European Court of Human Rights that where two instances are provided for, the fact that the person concerned was actually able to exercise his rights of defence at first instance does not automatically lead to the conclusion that he necessarily enjoyed the guarantees laid down in Article 6 of the ECHR if the appeal proceedings took place in his absence (see, to that effect, judgment of 14 February 2017, *Hokkeling v. Netherlands*, CE:ECHR:2017:0214JUD003074912, § 57, 58 and 61).

81. Consequently, in the event that proceedings have taken place at several instances which have given rise to successive decisions, at least one of which was given in absentia, it is appropriate to understand by 'trial resulting in the decision', within the meaning of Article 4a(1) of Framework Decision 2002/584, the instance which led to the last of those decisions, provided that the court at issue made a final ruling on the guilt of the person concerned and imposed a penalty on him, such as a custodial sentence, following an assessment, in fact and in law, of the incriminating and exculpatory evidence, including, where appropriate, the taking account of the individual situation of the person concerned.[62]

62 ECtHR, judgment of 12 February 2015, *Sanader v. Croatia*, CLI:CE:ECHR:2015:0212JUD006640812, para. 91.
ECtHR, judgment of 12 February 2015, *Sanader v. Croatia*, CLI:CE:ECHR:2015:0212JUD006640812, para. 87.
ECJ, judgment of 10 August 2017, *Openbaar Ministerie v. Tadas Tupikas*, C-270/17 PPU, ECLI:EU:C:2017:628, paras. 78-81.

5 A Judgment Rendered *In Absentia* as an Optional Ground for Refusal to Execute EAWs

Admissibility of Surrender of a Person Despite That Conditions Indicated in Article 4a(1) of FD 2002/584/JHA Are Not Met

Article 4a(1) of FD 2002/584/JHA provides for an optional ground for refusal of the execution of EAWs. Thus, the executing authorities of the Member States are entitled to surrender a person for the purpose of executing a judgment issued *in absentia* even if none of the conditions indicated in this provision was fulfilled. However, before taking a decision on surrender the executing authorities shall avail themselves of the opportunity to obtain additional information (a procedure provided for in Article 15(2) of FD 2002/584/JHA). The Court of Justice tackled this issue in two judgments: *Dworzecki* and *Zdziaszek*.

In the *Dworzecki* case the Court stated that:

> 50. Furthermore, as the scenarios described in Article 4a(1)(a)(i) of Framework Decision 2002/584 were conceived as exceptions to an optional ground for non-recognition, the executing judicial authority may in any event, even after having found that they did not cover the situation at issue, take into account other circumstances that enable it to be assured that the surrender of the person concerned does not mean a breach of his rights of defence.
>
> 51. In the context of such an assessment of the optional ground for non-recognition, the executing judicial authority may thus have regard to the conduct of the person concerned. It is at this stage of the surrender procedure that particular attention might be paid to any manifest lack of diligence on the part of the person concerned, notably where it transpires that he sought to avoid service of the information addressed to him.
>
> 52. Likewise, the executing judicial authority may also take into account the fact […] that the national law of the issuing Member State in any event affords the person concerned the right to request a retrial, where, as in this instance, service of the summons is deemed to be effected when the summons is handed over to an adult member of the household of the person concerned.

> 53. In any event, the executing judicial authority has the option, pursuant to Article 15(2) of Framework Decision 2002/584, of requesting supplementary information, as a matter of urgency, if it finds that the information communicated by the issuing Member State is insufficient to allow it to decide on surrender.[1]

In the *Zdziaszek* case the referring court asked the Court of Justice whether the FD should be interpreted as allowing the executing judicial authority to refuse to execute the EAW for the sole reason that neither the standard form for an EAW annexed to that Framework Decision nor the additional information obtained from the issuing judicial authority pursuant to Article 15(2) of that Framework Decision provide sufficient information to enable it to establish that one of the situations referred to in Article 4a(1)(a) to (d) of the Framework Decision exists.

The Court stated the following.

> 101. Having regard to the system established by that provision and as is apparent from its very wording, the executing judicial authority is entitled to refuse to execute a European arrest warrant issued for the purpose of executing a custodial sentence or a detention order if the person concerned did not appear in person at the trial resulting in the decision, unless the European arrest warrant indicates that the conditions set out in subparagraphs (a), (b), (c) or (d) of that provision are met.
>
> 102. Thus, where the existence of one of the situations referred to in subparagraphs (a) to (d) is established, the executing judicial authority is under an obligation to carry out the European arrest warrant, notwithstanding the absence of the person concerned at the trial which led to the decision (see, to that effect, today's judgment, Tupikas, C-270/17 PPU, paragraphs 50, 55 and 95).
>
> 103. In the event that that authority takes the view that it does not have sufficient information to enable it to validly decide on the surrender of the person concerned, it is incumbent upon it to apply Article 15(2) of Framework Decision 2002/584, by requesting from the issuing judicial authority the urgent provision of such additional information as it deems necessary before a decision on surrender can be taken.

---

1 ECJ, judgment of 24 May 2016, *Dworzecki*, C-108/16 PPU, ECLI:EU:C:2016:346, paras. 50-53.

104. If, at this stage, it still has not obtained the necessary assurances as regards the rights of defence of the person concerned during the relevant proceedings, the executing judicial authority may refuse to execute the European arrest warrant.

105. That authority not only cannot tolerate a breach of fundamental rights but, as provided for in Article 15(2) of Framework Decision 2002/584, it must also ensure that the time limits laid down in Article 17 thereof for taking the decision on the European arrest warrant are complied with, with the result that it cannot be required to resort to that Article 15(2) again (see, to that effect judgment of 5 April 2016, Aranyosi and Căldăraru, C-404/15 and C-659/15 PPU, EU:C:2016:198, paragraph 97).

106. However, it should be pointed out in that context that Article 4a of Framework Decision 2002/584 provides for an optional ground for non-execution of the European arrest warrant and that the cases referred to in Article 4a(1)(a) to (d) were conceived as exceptions to that optional ground for non-recognition (see, to that effect, today's judgment, Tupikas, C-270/17 PPU, paragraphs. 50 and 96).

107. Accordingly, the Court has already held that the executing judicial authority may, even after it has found that those cases do not cover the situation of the person who is the subject of the European arrest warrant, take account of other circumstances that enable it to ensure that the surrender of the person concerned does not entail a breach of his rights of defence (see, to that effect, judgment of 24 May 2016, Dworzecki, C-108/16 PPU, EU:C:2016:346, paragraphs. 50 and 51).

108. Thus, Framework Decision 2002/584 does not prevent the executing judicial authority from ensuring that the rights of defence of the person concerned are respected by taking due consideration of all the circumstances characterising the case before it, including the information which it may itself obtain.

109. In the light of the foregoing, the answer to the second question is that Framework Decision 2002/584 must be interpreted as meaning that, where the person concerned has not appeared in person in the relevant proceeding or, as the case may be, in the relevant proceedings for the application of Article 4a(1) of that Framework Decision and where neither the information contained

in the standard form for a European arrest warrant annexed to that Framework Decision nor the information obtained pursuant to Article 15(2) of that Framework Decision provide sufficient evidence to establish the existence of one of the situations referred to in Article 4a(1)(a) to (d) of that Framework Decision 2002/584, the executing judicial authority may refuse to execute the European arrest warrant.

110. However, that Framework Decision does not prevent that authority from taking account of all the circumstances characterising the case before it in order to ensure that the rights of the defence of the person concerned are respected during the relevant proceeding or proceedings.[2]

2 ECJ, judgment of 10 August 2017, *Zdziaszek*, C-271/17 PPU, ECLI:EU:C:2017:629, paras. 101-110.

6 Conclusions: Strasbourg and Luxembourg – Difference in Standards

As was stated in Chapter 2.2. of the Guide, Article 4a(1) of FD 2002/584/JHA was drafted with due respect for the requirements of Article 6 of the ECHR and the relevant case-law of the ECtHR. However, FD 2002/548 seems to provide for higher requirements with reference to summoning the accused to the hearing. As transpires from the case-law of the ECtHR, an effective waiver of the right to attend the hearing may be established even if a defendant was not informed in person about the date and place of the hearing. Sending a summons to the address indicated by a defendant, even if there is no proof that this summons has been collected by a defendant, could be assessed as satisfactory, if there are other indications that a defendant is actually aware of the trial being conducted against him. Thus, what matters is a defendant's actual awareness of the proceedings conducted against him/her rather than a particular way of summoning.

A different approach was adopted by the Court of Justice in the *Dworzecki* case. The Court of Justice clearly stated that Article 4a(1)(a)(i) of FD 2002/584 must be interpreted as meaning that a summons which was not served directly on the person concerned but was handed over, at the latter's address, to an adult belonging to that household who undertook to pass it on to him, when it cannot be ascertained from the EAW whether and, if so, when that adult actually passed that summons on to the person concerned, does not in itself satisfy the conditions set out in that provision.

The Report "Improving Mutual Recognition of European Arrest Warrants for the Purpose of Executing Judgments Rendered Following a Trial at which the Person Concerned Did Not Appear in Person" offers a comprehensive analysis of the discrepancies between the higher standard of protection which some elements of Article 4a(1) of FD 2002/584/JHA provide and the case-law of the ECtHR on *in absentia* proceedings.

Table of European Cases

European Commission of Human Rights

ECHR, decision of 5 October 1967, *X. v. the Federal Republic of Germany*, ECLI:CE:ECHR: 1967:1005DEC000242865

ECHR, decision of 6 December 1977, *X. v. Switzerland*, ECLI:CE:ECHR: 1977:1206DEC000764876

ECHR, decision of 9 May 1994, *Sampson v. Cyprus*, ECLI:CE:ECHR: 1994:0509DEC001977492

European Court of Human Rights

ECtHR, judgment of 15 July 1982, *Eckle v. Germany*, ECLI:CE:ECHR: 1982:0715JUD000813078

ECtHR, judgment of 21 January 1999, *Van Geyseghem v. Belgium*, ECLI:CE:ECHR: 1999:0121JUD002610395

ECtHR, judgment of 26 October 2000, *Kudła v. Poland* [GC], ECLI:CE:ECHR: 2000:1026JUD003021096

ECtHR, judgment of 14 June 2001, *Medenica v. Switzerland*, ECLI:CE:ECHR: 2001:0614JUD002049192

ECtHR, judgment of 26 July 2002, *Meftah and Others v. France* [GC], ECLI:CE:ECHR: 2002:0726JUD003291196

ECtHR, decision of 13 May 2003, *Montcornet de Caumont v. France*, ECLI:CE:ECHR: 2003:0513DEC005929000

ECtHR, judgment of 9 October 2003, *Ezeh and Connors v. the United Kingdom* [GC], ECLI:CE:ECHR: 2003:1009JUD003966598

ECtHR, decision of 5 February 2004, *Bogonos v. Russia*, ECLI:CE:ECHR: 2004:0205DEC006879801

ECtHR, judgment of 4 February 2005, *Mamatkulov and Askarov v. Turkey* [GC], ECLI:CE:ECHR: 2005:0204JUD004682799

ECtHR, judgment of 24 March 2005, *Stoichkov v. Bulgaria*, ECLI:CE:ECHR: 2005:0324JUD000980802

ECtHR, judgment of 1 March 2006, *Sejdovic v. Italy* [GC], ECLI:CE:ECHR: 2006:0301JUD005658100

ECtHR, judgment of 24 May 2007, *Da Luz Domingues Ferreira v. Belgium*, ECLI:CE:ECHR: 2007:0524JUD005004999

ECtHR, decision of 7 October 2008, *Monedero Angora v. Spain*, ECLI:CE:ECHR: 2008:1007DEC004113805

ECtHR, judgment of 21 July 2009, *Seliwiak v. Poland*, ECLI:CE:ECHR: 2009:0721JUD000381804

ECtHR, judgment of 17 September 2009, *Enea v. Italy* [GC], ECLI:CE:ECHR: 2009:0917JUD007491201

ECtHR, judgment of 22 September 2009, *Kari-pekka Pietiläinen v. Finland*, ECLI:CE:ECHR: 2009:0922JUD001356606

ECtHR, judgment of 15 December 2009, *Gurguchiani v. Spain*, ECLI:CE:ECHR: 2009:1215JUD001601206

ECtHR, judgment of 29 June 2010, *Hakimi v. Belgium*, ECLI:CE:ECHR: 2010:0629JUD000066508

ECtHR, judgment of 1 March 2011, *Faniel v. Belgium*, ECLI:CE:ECHR: 2011:0301JUD001189208

ECtHR, judgment of 10 May 2011, *Shkalla v. Albania*, ECLI:CE:ECHR: 2011:0510JUD002686605

ECtHR, judgment of 3 April 2012, *Boulouis v. Luxembourg* [GC], ECLI:CE:ECHR:2012:0403JUD003757504

ECtHR, judgment of 24 April 2012, *Haralampiev v. Bulgaria*, ECLI:CE:ECHR:2012:0424JUD002964803

ECtHR, decision of 23 October 2012, *Ciok v. Poland*, ECLI:CE:ECHR:2012:1023DEC000049810

ECtHR, judgment of 28 November 2013, *Aleksandr Dementyev v. Russia*, ECLI:CE:ECHR:2013:1128JUD004309505

ECtHR, judgment of 25 November 2014, *Vasilescu v. Belgium*, ECLI:CE:ECHR:2014:1125JUD006468212

ECtHR, judgment of 12 February 2015, *Sanader v. Croatia*, ECLI:CE:ECHR:2015:0212JUD006640812

ECtHR, decision of 24 March 2015, *Martuzevičius v. the United Kingdom*, ECLI:CE:ECHR:2015:0324DEC001356613

ECtHR, judgment of 9 July 2015, *Tolmachev v. Estonia*, ECLI:CE:ECHR:2015:0709JUD007374813

ECtHR, judgment of 6 October 2015, *Coniac v. Romania*, ECLI:CE:ECHR:2015:1006JUD000494107

ECtHR, judgment of 20 October 2015, *Dvorski v. Croatia*, ECLI:CE:ECHR:2015:1020JUD002570311

ECtHR, judgment of 14 February 2017, *Hokkeling v. the Netherlands*, ECLI:CE:ECHR:2017:0214JUD003074912

ECtHR, judgment of 22 May 2018, *Topi v. Albania*, ECLI:CE:ECHR:2018:0522JUD001481608

ECtHR, judgment of 12 June 2018, *M.T.B. v. Turkey*, ECLI:CE:ECHR:2018:0612JUD004708106

ECtHR, judgment of 26 July 2018, *Dridi v. Germany*, ECLI:CE:ECHR:2018:0726JUD003577811

ECtHR, judgment of 28 August 2018, *Vyacheslav Korchagin v. Russia*, ECLI:CE:ECHR:2018:0828JUD001230716

ECtHR, judgment of 25 September 2018, *Karemani v. Albania*, ECLI:CE:ECHR:2018:0925JUD004871708

ECtHR, decision of 4 December 2018, *Andrei Năstase v. Moldova*, ECLI:CE:ECHR:2018:1204DEC007444411

ECtHR, decision of 25 June 2019, *West v. Hungary*, ECLI:CE:ECHR:2019:0625DEC000538012

Court of Justice of the European Union

ECJ, judgment of 26 February 2013, *Stefano Melloni v Ministerio Fiscal*, C-399/11, ECLI:EU:C:2013:107

ECJ, judgment of 15 October 2015, *Covaci*, C-216/14, ECLI:EU:C:2015:686

ECJ, judgment of 5 April 2016, *Pál Aranyosi and Robert Căldăraru v. Generalstaatsanwaltschaft Bremen*, C-404/125 and C-659/15 PPU, ECLI:EU:C:2016:198

ECJ, judgment of 24 May 2016, *Dworzecki*, C-108/16 PPU, ECLI:EU:C:2016:346

ECJ, judgment of 22 March 2017, *Tranca* (C-124/16), *Tanja Reiter* (C-213/16), ECLI:EU:C:2017:228

ECJ, judgment of 10 August 2017, *Openbaar Ministerie v. Tadas Tupikas*, C-270/17 PPU, ECLI:EU:C:2017:628

ECJ, judgment of 10 August 2017, *Openbaar Ministerie v. Sławomir Andrzej Zdziaszek*, C-271/17 PPU, ECLI:EU:C:2017:629

ECJ, judgment of 22 December 2017, *Samet Ardic*, C-571/17 PPU, ECLI:EU:C:2017:1026

ECJ, judgment of 25 July 2018, *Minister for Justice and Equality (Deficiencies in the system of justice)*, C-216/18 PPU, ECLI:EU:C:2018:586:586

Part IV
Manual for Filling in and Assessing Section (d) of the EAW

1 Introduction

All Member States transposed Article 4a(1) FD 2002/584/JHA,[1] which contains an optional ground for refusal concerning a decision rendered following a trial at which the requested person did not appear in person. Section (d) of the EAW-form[2] gives expression to the requirements of Article 4a(1).

This Manual aims at assisting issuing judicial authorities in filling in section (d) of the EAW and assisting executing judicial authorities in assessing section (d) of the EAW. In addition to the Manual, issuing and executing judicial authorities can also consult the Case-law Guide. This guide provides for systematically arranged summaries of relevant rulings of both the Court of Justice and the ECtHR. These rulings form the bedrock upon which the Manual is built.

The Manual is succinct. It is not an academic treatise. If necessary, the Manual refers to other, easily accessible sources (such as the Case-law Guide).

To ensure user friendliness, the structure of Section 2 closely follows the structure of Article 4a(1) and section (d) of the EAW, guiding the user step by step through the process of filling in or assessing section (d).

In order to apply the national transposition of Article 4a(1) correctly, it is important to understand that this provision contains a number of autonomous concepts of EU law which must be interpreted uniformly throughout the EU and whose definition cannot be left to the discretion of the (authorities of the) Member States. National law transposing Article 4a(1) must be interpreted and applied in accordance with the autonomous EU meaning of that provision, not from the perspective of national criminal procedural law.

Therefore, where there is case-law of the Court of Justice, the Manual shall explicitly refer to it and shall adopt the Court's criterion. If the Court has ruled that a certain concept is an autonomous concept of EU law, the Manual shall stress the autonomous meaning of that concept.

Regardless of whether a concept is autonomous and regardless of whether the meaning of an autonomous concept is clear, when filling in section (d) of the EAW the issuing judicial authority should always describe in a factual way what happened in the proceedings that led to the decision which is at the basis of the EAW. In other words, it should not use

1 This provision was inserted to FD 2002/584/JHA by Framework Decision 2009/299/JHA of 26 February 2009 amending Framework Decisions 2002/584/JHA, 2005/214/JHA, 2006/783/JHA, 2008/909/JHA and 2008/947/JHA, thereby enhancing the procedural rights of persons and fostering the application of the principle of mutual recognition to decisions rendered in the absence of the person concerned at the trial (OJ 2009 L 81, p. 24).

2 As amended by Framework Decision 2009/299/JHA.

legal terms or designations derived from its national law. Quite apart from the issue of autonomous concepts of EU law, using national legal terminology may cause misunderstandings, because that terminology may not have the same meaning in other Member States.

Article 4a(1) of Framework Decision 2002/584/JHA seeks to guarantee a high level of protection and to allow the executing judicial authority to surrender the person concerned despite that person's failure to attend the trial which led to his conviction, while fully respecting his rights of defence.[3]

If an issuing judicial authority issues an EAW for the purpose of enforcing a decision rendered following a trial at which the person concerned did not appear in person, one may assume that it is of the opinion that in reaching that decision the rights of defence were not breached. Therefore, it should be able to explain why, in its opinion, those rights were not breached. A factual description should enable the executing judicial authority to reach the conclusion that surrendering the requested person would not entail a breach of his rights of defence.

3 *See, e.g.*, ECJ, judgment of 24 May 2016, *Openbaar Ministerie v. Paweł Dworzecki*, C-108/16 PPU, ECLI:EU:C:2016:346, para. 37.

2 Roadmap to Section (d)

2.1 Using the Current Version of the Model-EAW

When issuing an EAW, the issuing judicial authority should use the model-EAW, as amended by FD 2009/299/JHA. The consolidated version of the model-EAW in all official languages of the EU is available on the website of the European Judicial Network.[1]

When providing for a translation, the issuing judicial authority should make sure that the consolidated version of the model-EAW in the official or designated language of the executing Member State[2] is used. Only information which the issuing judicial authority added to the model-EAW should be translated. In this way, one avoids potential discrepancies with regard to the standard text of section (d) of the EAW.

2.2 Points 1 and 2: Did the Requested Person Appear in Person at the Trial Resulting in the Decision?

2.2.1 General

According to Article 4a(1) FD 2002/584/JHA, the executing judicial authority may refuse the execution of the EAW, if the person concerned 'did not appear in person' at the 'trial resulting in the decision'.

To enable the executing judicial authority to establish whether this ground for refusal is applicable, the issuing judicial authority must tick either the box of point 1 ("Yes, the person appeared in person at the trial resulting in the decision") or the box of point 2 ("No, the person did not appear in person at the trial resulting in the decision").

If the person concerned appeared in person at the trial resulting in the decision, Article 4a(1) is not applicable. The issuing judicial authority should only tick the box of point 1 of section (d) of the EAW.

If the person concerned did not appear in person at the trial resulting in the decision, Article 4a(1) is applicable. The issuing judicial authority should tick the box of point 2 of

1 https://www.ejn-crimjust.europa.eu/ejn/libcategories/EN/5/-1/0.

2 In accordance with Art. 8(2) of FD 2002/584/JHA, the EAW "must be translated into the official language or one of the official languages of the executing Member State". However, any Member State may make a declaration to the effect "that it will accept a translation in one or more other official languages of the Institutions of the European Communities". Such declarations are published on the website of the European Judicial Network: https://www.ejn-crimjust.europa.eu/ejn/libcategories/EN/4/-1/0.

section (d) of the EAW and also tick one of the boxes of points 3.1-3.4 of section (d) of the EAW (but only if applicable).

If none of the boxes of points 3.1-3.4 of section (d) of the EAW is fully applicable, the issuing judicial should not tick any of them. In such a case, the issuing judicial authority could explain under point 4 of section (d) of the EAW why, in its opinion, surrendering the person concerned would nevertheless not entail a breach of his rights of defence.

2.2.2 Non-appearance 'in Person'

The Court of Justice has not yet defined the concept of '(not) appearing in person'. However, it seems likely that the concept of '(not) appearing in person' refers to situations in which the person concerned was not physically present. Therefore, representation of an absent defendant by his legal counsellor does not constitute appearance 'in person'. In such a case the issuing judicial authority should tick the box of point 2 of section (d) of the EAW.

2.2.3 'Trial Resulting in the Decision'

2.2.3.1 Introduction

The Court of Justice has not yet defined the concept of a 'trial'. However, it seems likely that the concept of a 'trial' does not refer to the 'general prosecution process' (from charge to verdict), but rather to a distinct 'event with a scheduled date and place' which resulted in the decision.[3]

In order to establish whether to tick the box of point 1 or point 2, one must first determine which decision is relevant for Article 4a(1).

The enforceable decision or judgment which is mentioned in section (b)(2) of the EAW is not necessarily the same as the decision referred to in section (d) of the EAW. The enforceability of a judicial decision is decisive in determining when an EAW may be issued[4]: without an enforceable judicial decision no EAW can be issued. However, for the purposes of Article 4a(1) and section (d) of the EAW, the final nature of the decision is determinative: the 'trial resulting in the decision' was defined by the Court of Justice as the "proceeding that led to the judicial decision which finally sentenced" the requested person.[5]

3 Cf. *Cretu v. Local Court of Suceava, Romania* [2016] EWHC 353 (Admin) (26 February 2016), para. 34.
4 ECJ, judgment of 10 August 2017, *Openbaar Ministerie v. Tadas Tupikas*, C-270/17 PPU, ECLI:EU:C:2017:628, para. 71.
5 ECJ, judgment of 10 August 2017, *Openbaar Ministerie v. Tadas Tupikas*, C-270/17 PPU, ECLI:EU:C:2017:628, para. 74 (emphasis added).

While in some cases the enforceable judicial decision and the judicial decision which finally sentenced the person concerned may coincide, it is up to the national laws of the Member States to regulate whether the final decision actually is the enforceable decision.[6]

Depending on the national law of the issuing Member State, therefore, a final decision in the sense of Article 4a(1) and section (d) is not necessarily an enforceable decision. Some examples.

In case of a first instance conviction which was upheld in appeal following an assessment, in fact and in law, of the merits of the case, the law of the issuing Member State may designate the first instance conviction as the enforceable judgment. However, the judgment on appeal, if final, is the decision referred to in Article 4a(1) and section (d) (see Section 2.2.3.2).

If the execution of a sentence was originally suspended, the decision to revoke that suspension may well be the enforceable decision according to the law of the issuing Member State. However, the judgment finally sentencing the person concerned to the custodial sentence or the detention order is the decision referred to in Article 4a(1) and section (d) (see also Section 2.2.3.3).

2.2.3.2 'Trial Resulting in the Decision': Several Instances

If the criminal procedure involves several instances (*e.g.* first instance and appeal) and therefore involves successive decisions, according to the Court of Justice the 'trial resulting in the decision' only refers to the "instance which led to the last of those decisions, provided that the court at issue made a final ruling on the guilt of the person concerned and imposed a penalty on him, such as a custodial sentence, following an assessment, in fact and in law, of the incriminating and exculpatory evidence, including, where appropriate, the taking account of the individual situation of the person concerned".[7]

In such cases, only one proceeding and only one decision are relevant for the purpose of section (d) (the proceeding which led to the last of the decisions, etc.).

Article 4a(1) will, therefore, not be applicable if the person concerned did not appear in person at the trial that led to the first instance decision but did appear in person at the trial on appeal, provided that the appeal court made a final ruling on his guilt and imposed a penalty on him following a full assessment (*i.e.* both in fact and in law) of the merits of the case (*i.e.* of the evidence and, where appropriate, the personal situation of the person concerned). However, Article 4a(1) will be applicable if that person appeared in person at the trial that led to the first instance decision but did not appear in person at the trial on

6 ECJ, judgment of 10 August 2017, *Openbaar Ministerie v. Tadas Tupikas*, C-270/17 PPU, ECLI:EU:C:2017:628, para. 76.

7 ECJ, judgment of 10 August 2017, *Openbaar Ministerie v. Tadas Tupikas*, C-270/17 PPU, ECLI:EU:C:2017:628, para. 81 (emphasis added).

appeal, provided that the appeal court made a final ruling on his guilt and imposed a penalty on him following a full assessment of the merits of the case.

Proceedings concerning questions of law only (such as cassation proceedings) are not relevant for the purpose of section (d). After all, in such proceedings an "assessment, in fact and in law, of the (...) evidence" does not take place.

Appeal proceedings concerning the sentence only are dealt with in Section 2.2.3.3.

2.2.3.3 'Trial Resulting in the Decision': Subsequent Proceeding Amending the Original Penalty

The concept of a 'conviction' has two distinct but related aspects, namely the finding of guilt and the handing down of a sentence. The guarantees laid down in Article 6 of the ECHR apply not only to the finding of guilt, but also to the determination of the sentence.[8]

According to the legal systems of some Member States, the closely related aspects may be dissociated: after the final ruling on guilt and the imposition of a penalty (see Section 2.2.3.4), the *quantum* or the nature of the original penalty may be changed in a subsequent proceeding.[9]

Such a subsequent proceeding resulting in a decision modifying the level or the nature of the original penalty also is relevant for section (d), provided that:

- the authority which adopted the decision enjoyed some discretion with regard to the level or the nature of the penalty "in particular, by taking account of the situation or personality of the person concerned, or of mitigating or aggravating circumstances" AND
- that its decision finally determined the sentence.[10]

It is irrelevant whether the proceeding in question may be favourable to the person concerned, as the level or the nature of the penalty is not determined in advance.[11] Equally, it is irrelevant whether the proceeding in question cannot lead to a heavier penalty.[12]

---

8 ECJ, judgment of 10 August 2017, C-271/17, *Sławomir Andrzej Zdziaszek*, C-271/17 PPU, ECLI:EU:C:2017:629, paras. 77 and 87.

9 ECJ, judgment of 10 August 2017, C-271/17, *Sławomir Andrzej Zdziaszek*, C-271/17 PPU, ECLI:EU:C:2017:629, para. 94.

10 ECJ, judgment of 10 August 2017, C-271/17, *Sławomir Andrzej Zdziaszek*, C-271/17 PPU, ECLI:EU:C:2017:629, paras. 88 and 90; ECJ, judgment of 22 December 2017, *Samet Ardic*, C-571/17 PPU, ECLI:EU:C:2017:1026, paras. 66, 77 and 80.

11 ECJ, judgment of 10 August 2017, C-271/17, *Sławomir Andrzej Zdziaszek*, C-271/17 PPU, ECLI:EU:C:2017:629, para. 92.

12 ECJ, judgment of 10 August 2017, C-271/17, *Sławomir Andrzej Zdziaszek*, C-271/17 PPU, ECLI:EU:C:2017:629, para. 89.

If, however, the subsequent proceeding is 'a purely formal and arithmetic exercise', the competent authority does not enjoy a margin and its decision to modify the level or the nature of the original penalty does not come within the ambit of Article 6 ECHR.

Some examples.

1. A decision on appeal against the sentence only comes within the ambit of Article 4a(1)/section (d), if the court or the judge enjoyed a margin of discretion with regard to the level or the nature of the sentence and if its decision finally determined the sentence.
2. A decision consisting in commuting into a single sentence one or more sentences which were previously imposed on the person concerned comes within the ambit of Article 4a(1)/section(d), if the competent authority of the issuing Member States exercised its discretion as to the level or the nature of the new sentence and if the decision finally determined the sentence. Such a decision is called a 'cumulative judgment'.[13]
3. A decision to revoke the suspension of the execution of a prison sentence does not come within the ambit of Article 4a(1)/section (d), because such a decision does not change the level or the nature of the original penalty.[14] A decision to replace a non-custodial penalty with a custodial sentence does come within the ambit of Article 4a/section (d), if in reaching that decision the competent authority of the issuing Member State enjoyed a margin of discretion with regard to the level and nature of the new sentence.

If a decision changing the level or the nature of the original penalty was taken and if the competent authority enjoyed a margin of discretion with regard to that level or that nature, the question whether the person concerned appeared in person at the 'trial resulting in the decision' must be answered with regard to two sets of proceedings:

1. the proceeding which led to the final ruling on the guilt of the person concerned and to the imposition of a penalty, following an assessment, in fact and in law, of the incriminating and exculpatory evidence, etc. (with respect to the finding of guilt) AND
2. the proceeding which led to the subsequent final decision modifying the level or nature of the original penalty (with respect to the determination of the sentence).[15]

In doing so, one should clearly distinguish both sets of proceedings, *e.g.* by referring to the respective dates on which the decisions were adopted and/or to their respective reference numbers.

13 ECJ, judgment of 10 August 2017, C-271/17, *Sławomir Andrzej Zdziaszek*, C-271/17 PPU, ECLI:EU:C:2017:629, para. 86.

14 ECJ, judgment of 22 December 2017, *Samet Ardic*, C-571/17 PPU, ECLI:EU:C:2017:1026, para. 82.

15 ECJ, judgment of 10 August 2017, C-271/17, *Sławomir Andrzej Zdziaszek*, C-271/17 PPU, ECLI:EU:C:2017:629, para. 94.

2.2.3.4 'Trial Resulting in the Decision': Plea Bargain

In some Member States it is possible to enter into a plea agreement with the public prosecutor. That agreement is reviewed and, if it meets the legal requirements, ratified by a court in proceedings in which no full determination of the merits of the charge against the person concerned takes place.

The executing judicial authorities of some Member States are of the opinion that such decisions come within the ambit of Article 4a(1), while the executing judicial authorities of other Member States deny the applicability of that provision.

As a matter of transparency, the issuing judicial authority is advised to fill in section (d) with regard to that decision and to explain under point 4 that the decision was rendered following plea bargaining. In this regard, it should be recalled that the ECtHR has ruled plea bargaining as to the sentence and pleading *nolo contendere* as to the charge amount to a waiver of the right "to have the criminal case against him examined on the merits".[16] Even if none of points 3.2-3.4 is applicable, it should be possible for the executing judicial authority to conclude that surrendering the person concerned would not breach his rights of defence (see further Section 2.7).

2.2.3.5 'Trial Resulting in the Decision': Trial without a Hearing

In the legal order of some Member States, a court or a judge may impose a penalty without holding a hearing.

The mere fact that no hearing was held does not seem enough to exclude the applicability of Article 4a(1). After all, the purpose of that provision is enabling the executing judicial authority to surrender the person concerned in the knowledge that the rights of defence were fully respected even though the person concerned was not present in person at the trial.[17]

As a matter of transparency, the issuing judicial authority is advised to fill in section (d) with regard to that decision and to explain under point 4 that the decision was rendered following proceedings without a trial.

2.2.3.6 'Trial Resulting in the Decision': Trial Consisting of Multiple Hearings

Neither Article 4a(1) nor points 1 and 2 of section (d) refer to hearing(s). How should the issuing and executing judicial authorities determine whether the person concerned did or did not appear at the trial, when the trial consisted of multiple hearings?

---

16 ECtHR, judgment of 29 April 2014, *Natsvlishvili and Togonidze v. Georgia*, ECLI:CE:ECHR:2014:0429 JUD000904305, § 92.

17 *See, e.g.*, ECJ, judgment of 24 May 2016, *Openbaar Ministerie v. Paweł Dworzecki*, C-108/16 PPU, ECLI:EU:C:2016:346, para. 37.

This issue has not been decided by the Court of Justice. In practice, there are three possible approaches. To exclude the applicability of Article 4a(1): 1) the requested person must have been present at every hearing, 2) he must have been present at least at one hearing or 3) he must have been present at the hearing(s) at which the court examined the merits of the case.

Whatever the approach taken by the issuing judicial authority, when point 1 is ticked, as a matter of transparency it is advised to explain which approach was taken and to describe how many hearings were held, when they were held, at which of the hearings the person concerned was present and what happened at each of the hearings.

2.3 Point 3.1: Was the Requested Person Summoned in Person, etc. in Due Time?

2.3.1 General

According to Article 4a(1)(a) FD 2002/584/JHA, the executing judicial authority may not refuse the execution of the EAW on account of the non-appearance of the person concerned, if the EAW states that the person concerned, in due time:[18]

1)

- either

  was summoned in person and thereby informed of the scheduled date and place of the trial which resulted in the decision,
- or

  by other means actually received official information of the scheduled date and place of that trial in such a manner that it was unequivocally established that he or she was aware of the scheduled trial;

AND

2)

- was informed that a decision may be handed down if he or she does not appear for the trial.

18 The condition of 'in due time' has not been integrated in section (d) of the form of the EAW.

If either of the two alternatives of 1) (personal summons in due time or official notification by other means than a summons in person in due time) is applicable and the condition set out in 2) (being informed of the possibility of a decision be handed down in his absence) is met, the issuing judicial authority must tick the box of either point 3.1a (summons in person) or of point 3.1b (official notification by other means than a summons in person).

If the defendant was either in due time personally summoned or in due time actually officially notified by other means than a summons in person, but the person concerned was not informed that a decision may be handed down if he or she does not appear for the trial, the issuing judicial authority should not tick the box of either point 3.1a or 3.1b.

If the defendant was in due time personally summoned, mention the date on which the person concerned was summoned in person under point 3.1b.

If the defendant was in due time actually officially notified by other means than a summons in person, explain under point 4 in a factual way how and when this condition was met.

If either point 3.1a or point 3.1b is applicable, the executing judicial authority may not refuse to execute the EAW. There is no need to tick any further boxes (if applicable). However, if the issuing judicial authority is of the opinion that multiple points apply, it is free to tick the relevant boxes. Relying on more than one point may enhance the chances of execution of the EAW.

If point 3.1 is not applicable: go to Section 2.4.

2.3.2 *Waiver of the Right to Be Present at the Trial*

Article 4a(1)(a) "lays down the circumstances in which the person concerned must be deemed to have waived, voluntarily and unambiguously, his right to be present at his trial".[19]

2.3.3 *'In Due Time'*

According to recital (7) of the preamble, the meaning of the concept of 'in due time' is that the person concerned should have received the information about the date and the place of the trial "sufficiently in time to allow him or her to participate in the trial and to effectively exercise his or her right of defence".[20]

---

19 ECJ, judgment of 26 February 2013, *Stefano Melloni v. Ministerio Fiscal*, C-399/11, ECLI:EU:C:2013:107, para. 52.

20 Recital (7) of the preamble to FD 2009/299/JHA.

Section (d) of the EAW does not contain a – explicit – reference to the concept of 'in due time'. However, point 3.1a of section (d) (summons in person) requires that the date at which the summons was served is filled in and point 3.1b of section (d) (actual official notification) requires an explanation "how the relevant condition was met" (point 4 of section (d)). Both requirements present an opportunity for the issuing judicial authority to demonstrate and for the executing judicial authority to check that the person concerned was summoned or notified 'in due time'.

2.3.4 *'Summoned in Person, etc.'*

The concept of a 'summons in person' is an autonomous concept of EU law.[21] Such a method of service ensures "that the person concerned has himself received the summons and, accordingly, has been informed of the date and place of his trial".[22] If a particular method of service does not entail that the person concerned himself received the summons, it cannot be considered as a 'summons in person', even though according to national law the person concerned was summoned validly or is even, according to a national legal presumption, considered to have been summoned in person.

2.3.5 *'By Other Means Actually Received Official Information, etc.'*

As with the concept of a 'summons in person', this concept is an autonomous concept of EU law.[23] As with a 'summons in person', this method of service ensures that the person concerned "has the information relating to the date and place of his trial".[24]

For this concept to apply, it must be "unequivocally established (…) that the person concerned 'actually' received the information relating to the date and place of his trial [and], where appropriate, the precise time when that information was received".[25]

21 ECJ, judgment of 24 May 2016, *Openbaar Ministerie v. Paweł Dworzecki*, C-108/16 PPU, ECLI:EU:C:2016:346, para. 32.

22 ECJ, judgment of 24 May 2016, *Openbaar Ministerie v. Paweł Dworzecki*, C-108/16 PPU, ECLI:EU:C:2016:346, para. 45 (emphasis added).

23 ECJ, judgment of 24 May 2016, *Openbaar Ministerie v. Paweł Dworzecki*, C-108/16 PPU, ECLI:EU:C:2016:346, para. 32.

24 ECJ, judgment of 24 May 2016, *Openbaar Ministerie v. Paweł Dworzecki*, C-108/16 PPU, ECLI:EU:C:2016:346, para. 46.

25 ECJ, judgment of 24 May 2016, *Openbaar Ministerie v. Paweł Dworzecki*, C-108/16 PPU, ECLI:EU:C:2016:346, para. 47 (emphasis added).

> The mere fact that the summons was handed over to a third party who undertook to pass it on to the person concerned – whether or not that third party belonged to the household of the person concerned – in itself is not enough.[26]

In the EAW, the issuing judicial authority must mention the "evidence on the basis of which it found that the person concerned actually received official information relating to the date and place of his trial".[27] Such evidence can be mentioned under point 4 of section (d).

> Evidence capable of supporting the conclusion that the requested person actually received the date and the place of the trial might consist of a document originating with the person concerned from which it follows that he was aware of the date and the place of the trial (*e.g.* a written request for an adjournment) or a statement from the third party that s/he actually passed over the information about the date and the place of the trial for and when s/he did so.
> The standard of 'unequivocally established' seems to rule out mere inferences which might reasonably be drawn from the facts, *e.g.* the inference that the partner of the defendant who received the summons at the address given by the defendant and with whom the defendant lived at that address, would have handed over the summons to the defendant.[28] However, for transparency's sake, the issuing judicial authority is advised to mention such inferences under point 4 of section (d). It may well be that the executing judicial authority sees fit to take such inferences under consideration when deciding whether there are 'other circumstances' that enable the executing judicial authority 'to ensure that the surrender of the person concerned does not entail a breach of his rights of defence' (see para. 2.7).

When assessing whether the conditions of Article 4a(1)(a) are met, the executing judicial authority may also rely on other evidence, "including circumstances of which it became aware when hearing the person concerned".[29]

---

26 ECJ, judgment of 24 May 2016, *Openbaar Ministerie v. Paweł Dworzecki*, C-108/16 PPU, ECLI:EU:C:2016:346, para. 47.

27 ECJ, judgment of 24 May 2016, *Openbaar Ministerie v. Paweł Dworzecki*, C-108/16 PPU, ECLI:EU:C:2016:346, para. 49.

28 Compare Cass. (Belgium), judgment of 24 October 2017, Ar nr. P. 17.0666.N (not an EAW-case). See also ECtHR, decision of 6 March 2018, *Nicolae Popa v. Romania*, ECLI:CE:ECHR:2018:0306DEC005524212, § 73; ECtHR, judgment of 2 February 2017, *Ait Abbou v. France*, ECLI:CE:ECHR:2017:0202JUD004492113, § 63-65.

29 ECJ, judgment of 24 May 2016, *Openbaar Ministerie v. Paweł Dworzecki*, C-108/16 PPU, ECLI:EU:C:2016:346, para. 49.

2.3.6 *'Informed That a Decision May Be Handed Down, etc.'*

This requirement will be met, *e.g.*, if the summons was accompanied by a written advisement that a decision may be handed down if the person concerned does not appear in person at the trial. Although a written advisement is preferable, Article 4a(1)(a)(ii) does not seem to exclude that the person concerned is informed verbally of the consequence of non-appearance, provided that it is registered in an official record.

2.4 POINT 3.2: WAS THE REQUESTED PERSON DEFENDED BY A LEGAL COUNSELLOR MANDATED BY HIM?

2.4.1 *General*

According to Article 4a(1)(b) FD 2002/584/JHA, the executing judicial authority may not refuse the execution of the EAW on account of the non-appearance of the person concerned, if the EAW states that the person concerned

- was aware of the scheduled trial, and
- had given a mandate to a legal counsellor (appointed by himself or by the State) to defend him or her at the trial, and
- was indeed defended by that counsellor at the trial.

If applicable, tick the box of point 3.2 and explain under point 4 in a factual way how this condition was met.

If point 3.2 is applicable, the executing judicial authority may not refuse to execute the EAW. There is no need to tick any further boxes (if applicable). However, if the issuing judicial authority is of the opinion that multiple points apply, it is free to tick the relevant boxes. Relying on more than one point may enhance the chances of execution of the EAW.

If point 3.2 is not applicable: go to Section 2.5.

2.4.2 *Waiver of the Right to Be Present at the Trial*

Article 4a(1)(b) "lays down the circumstances in which the person concerned must be deemed to have waived, voluntarily and unambiguously, his right to be present at his trial".[30]

30 ECJ, judgment of 26 February 2013, *Stefano Melloni v. Ministerio Fiscal*, C-399/11, ECLI:EU:C:2013:107, para. 52.

2.4.3 *Legal Counsellor, Appointed by the Defendant or by the State*

Article 4a(1)(b) and point 3.2 do not distinguish between a legal counsellor appointed (and paid) by the defendant (hereafter: a chosen legal counsellor) and a legal counsellor appointed (and paid) by the State (hereafter: an *ex officio* legal counsellor). Both types of legal representation suffice, provided that all the requirements of Article 4a(1)(b) are met.

2.4.4 *'Being Aware of the Scheduled Trial'*

Unlike Article 4a(1)(a), Article 4a(1)(b) does not refer to the date and the place of the trial, but rather to the 'scheduled trial'. The most likely interpretation, therefore, is that awareness of the date and the place of the trial is not required. What is needed is that the defendant knew or could reasonably expect that a trial would take place at some later, yet to be specified date and place (see also Section 2.4.5).

2.4.5 *'Had Given a Mandate to a Legal Counsellor, etc.'*

According to the preamble to FD 2002/584/JHA, the defendant "should deliberately have chosen to be represented by a legal counsellor instead of appearing in person at the trial".[31] A 'mandate', therefore, presupposes a cognitive element ('being aware of the scheduled trial') as well as a volitional element (choosing to be represented by a legal counsellor).

If the defendant or his legal counsellor states that he gave or received a mandate, the issuing judicial authority will have no trouble in establishing that the defendant had mandated his legal counsellor. However, according to the legal system of some Member States, the courts are not allowed to question the relationship between the defendant and his legal counsellor. The question whether the defendant had indeed mandated his legal counsellor may, therefore, be difficult to answer.

If the chosen legal counsellor appears at the trial and mounts a defence on behalf of the absent defendant, as a rule one may safely assume that the defendant had given a mandate to that legal counsellor and that, therefore, the defendant was aware of the scheduled trial.

The same does not necessarily follow for an *ex officio* legal counsellor. If the legal system of a Member State allows for appointment of an *ex officio* legal counsellor in the absence of the defendant, it is possible that the defendant does not know of the appointment, may not have had any contact with the legal counsellor and, consequently, may not have mandated the legal counsellor to defend him. In the absence of indications that the defendant

31 Recital (10) of the preamble to FD 2009/299/JHA.

knew of the appointment of an *ex officio* legal counsellor and accepted being represented by that legal counsellor, it is not advisable to tick point 3.2. Of course, it remains open to mention under point 4 of section (d) that the defendant was defended by an *ex officio* legal counsellor, even if it cannot be established that the defendant had given a mandate to that legal counsellor.

If the issuing judicial authority cannot establish that the person concerned had given a mandate to his or her legal counsellor, it should not tick the box of point 3.2. In such a case, the issuing judicial authority, in the interest of transparency, could mention under point 4 that the person concerned was defended by a legal counsellor, although a mandate by the person concerned could not be established.

2.5 Point 3.3: Did the Requested Person, after Being Served with the Decision (in Person) and Being Expressly Informed about His Right to a Retrial or an Appeal, Acquiesce in the Decision?

2.5.1 *General*

According to Article 4a(1)(c) FD 2002/584/JHA, the executing judicial authority may not refuse the execution of the EAW on account of the non-appearance of the person concerned, if the EAW states that the person concerned:

- was served with the decision and
- was expressly informed about the right to a retrial or an appeal, "in which the person has the right to participate and which allows the merits of the case, including fresh evidence, to be re-examined, and which may lead to the original decision being reversed" and
- either expressly stated that he or she does not contest the decision
- or did not request a retrial or appeal within the applicable time frame.

If Article 4a(1)(c) is applicable: tick the box of point 3.3, fill in the date at which the person concerned was served with the decision and explain under point 4 in a factual manner how the condition was met.

The executing judicial authority may not refuse to execute the EAW. There is no need to tick any further boxes (if applicable). However, if the issuing judicial authority is of the opinion that multiple points apply, it is free to tick the relevant boxes. Relying on more than one point may enhance the chances of execution of the EAW.

If Article 4a(1)(c) is not applicable: go to Section 2.6.

2.5.2 'After Being Served with the Decision'

On the face of it, Article 4a(1)(c) does not require that the decision was served on the person concerned in person. However, the most likely interpretation of this provision is that it requires that the person actually received the decision (see also Section 2.3.5).

If the decision was served on a third party, *e.g.* an adult member of the household of the person concerned, the issuing judicial authority should only tick point 3.3 if it has any evidence that the person concerned actually received the decision. That evidence should then be mentioned under point 4 of section (d).

2.5.3 'After (...) Being Expressly Informed about His Right to a Retrial, or an Appeal'

This requirement will be met, *e.g.*, if the decision was accompanied by written instructions about the right to a retrial or an appeal. Although a written advisement is preferable, Article 4a(1)(c) does not seem to exclude that the person concerned is informed verbally of the consequence of non-appearance, provided that it is registered in an official record.

2.5.4 'In which the Person Has a Right to Participate (...) Being Reversed'

The features of the retrial, or the appeal, described in Article 4a(1)(c)/point 3.3 seem to rule out a number of possible legal remedies.

The phrase 'in which the person has the right to participate' – *i.e.* 'the right to be present'[32] – likely rules out so-called 'written proceedings'.

The phrase 'which allows the merits of the case, including fresh evidence, to be re-examined' likely excludes proceedings in which only questions of law are answered, such as cassation proceedings.

It is not advised to tick the box of point 3.3, if such proceedings were the only legal remedy available against the decision. In the interest of transparency, the issuing judicial authority could mention such proceedings under point 4 of section (d).

2.5.5 Acquiescence in the Decision

The box of either one of the two options – the express statement of non-contest or the failure to request a retrial or an appeal within the applicable time frame – should be ticked. However, this should only be done, if the requested person was indeed served with the

32 Recital (11) of the preamble to FD 2009/299/JHA.

decision and expressly informed about his right to a retrial or an appeal as described above. There is no need to tick one of the boxes just to accentuate that the decision is final. After all, the concept of a 'decision' itself entails that it is final.[33]

If the person concerned stated expressly that he would not contest the decision, the issuing judicial authority should explain under point 4 of section (d) how and when the person concerned made that statement.

The circumstance that the person concerned did not request a retrial or an appeal within the applicable time frame comprises two distinct situations: (1) the person concerned did not request a retrial or an appeal at all and 2) the person concerned did request a retrial or an appeal but not within the applicable time frame. The issuing judicial authority could explain under point 4 which of the two situations applies to the situation at hand.

2.6 Point 3.4: Was the Requested Person Not Served with the Decision in Person, but Will the Decision Be Served on Him in Person after Surrender and Will He Be Expressly Informed about His Right to a Retrial or an Appeal?

2.6.1 General

According to Article 4a(1)(d) FD 2002/584/JHA, the executing judicial authority may not refuse the execution of the EAW on account of the non-appearance of the person concerned, if the EAW states that the person concerned

- was not served with the decision, but will be personally served with the decision without delay after the surrender and
- will be expressly informed about the right to a retrial or an appeal, "in which the person has the right to participate and which allows the merits of the case, including fresh evidence, to be re-examined, and which may lead to the original decision being reversed" and
- will be informed of the applicable time frame, which must be mentioned in the EAW.

If these requirements are met, the issuing judicial authority should tick the box of point 3.4 and fill in the applicable time frame for requesting the retrial or the appeal. The executing judicial authority may not refuse to execute the EAW.

There is no need to explain under point 4 how the condition was met.

33 According to the Court of Justice, the decision referred to in Art. 4a(1) – and in section (d) of the EAW – is the 'judicial decision which finally sentenced' the requested person: ECJ, judgment of 10 August 2017, *Openbaar Ministerie v. Tadas Tupikas*, C-270/17 PPU, ECLI:EU:C:2017:628, para. 74.

If these requirements are not met: do not tick the box of point 3.4 and go to Section 2.7.

2.6.2 *'Personally Served'*

It stands to reason that the concept of 'personally served' must be understood to mean that the person concerned himself actually will receive the decision.

2.6.3 *'Expressly Informed about the Right to a Retrial or an Appeal'*

This requirement will be met, *e.g.*, if the decision is accompanied by written instructions about the right to a retrial, or an appeal. Although a written advisement is preferable, Article 4a(1)(d) does not seem to exclude that the person concerned will be informed verbally of the consequence of non-appearance, provided that it is registered in an official record.

2.6.4 *'In which the Person Has a Right to Participate (...) Being Reversed'*

The features of the retrial, or the appeal, described in Article 4a(1)(d)/point 3.4 seem to rule out a number of possible legal remedies.

The phrase 'in which the person has the right to participate' – *i.e.* 'the right to be present'[34] – most likely rules out so-called 'written proceedings'.

The phrase 'which allows the merits of the case, including fresh evidence, to be re-examined' seems to exclude proceedings in which only questions of law are answered, such as cassation proceedings.

It is not advised to tick the box of point 3.4, if such proceedings are the only legal remedy available against the decision. In the interest of transparency, the issuing judicial authority could mention such proceedings under point 4 of section (d).

34 Recital (11) of the preamble to FD 2009/299/JHA.

2.7 Point 4: If None of the Boxes of Points 3.1-3.4 Can Be Ticked, Are There 'Other Circumstances' That Enable the Executing Judicial Authority 'to Be Assured That the Surrender of the Person Concerned Does Mean a Breach of His Rights of Defence'?

2.7.1 General

Even if none of the situations described in Article 4a(1)(a) to (d) applies – which situations correspond to points 3.1-3.4 of section (d) –, the executing judicial authority may take into account 'other circumstances' that enable it "to be assured that the surrender of the person concerned does not mean a breach of his rights of defence".[35]

This is so, because the ground for refusal is an optional ground for refusal: even if none of the aforementioned situations applies, as a matter of Union law[36] the executing judicial authority is under no duty to refuse to execute the EAW, if it can be established that executing the EAW would not infringe the rights of defence of the person concerned.

The 'other circumstances' may concern "the conduct of the person concerned", in particular "any manifest lack of diligence on the part of the person concerned, notably where it transpires that he sought to avoid service of the information addressed to him".[37]

The issuing judicial authority could bring such other circumstances to the attention of the executing judicial authority in the EAW (*e.g.* under point 4 of section (d)), when answering a request for supplementary information on the basis of Article 15(2) of FD 2002/584/JHA or when forwarding "useful additional information" on the basis of Article 15(3) of FD 2002/584/JHA.

The executing judicial authorities may also rely on such other "circumstances of which it became aware when hearing the person concerned".[38]

2.7.2 What Constitutes 'Other Circumstances'?

Because of the casuistic nature of the case-law of the ECtHR, it is impossible to list exhaustively circumstances other than those enumerated in Article 4a(1) (a-d) which would

35 ECJ, judgment of 24 May 2016, *Openbaar Ministerie v. Paweł Dworzecki*, C-108/16 PPU, ECLI:EU:C:2016:346, para. 50; ECJ, judgment of 10 August 2017, *Openbaar Ministerie v. Tadas Tupikas*, C-270/17 PPU, ECLI:EU:C:2017:628, para. 96; ECJ, judgment of 10 August 2017, *Openbaar Ministerie v. Sławomir Andrzej Zdziaszek*, C-271/17 PPU, ECLI:EU:C:2017:629, paras. 106-107.

36 Some Member States transposed Art. 4a(1) as an imperative ground for refusal.

37 ECJ, judgment of 24 May 2016, *Openbaar Ministerie v. Paweł Dworzecki*, C-108/16 PPU, ECLI:EU:C:2016:346, para. 51.

38 ECJ, judgment of 24 May 2016, *Openbaar Ministerie v. Paweł Dworzecki*, C-108/16 PPU, ECLI:EU:C:2016:346, para. 49.

justify the conclusion that the surrender of the requested person would not entail a breach of his rights of defence.

Such circumstances will most likely occur only in cases in which, although the defendant was not summoned in person or otherwise actually officially informed about the date and the place of the trial, he had sufficient knowledge of the charges against him and the proceedings[39] and

- either unequivocally waived his/her right to attend the trial or
- displayed a lack of diligence in taking proper measures to receive official notifications about the date and the place of the trial.

The case-law of the ECtHR on Article 6 ECHR and *in absentia* convictions provides building blocks which can support a conclusion that the surrender of the requested person would not entail a breach of his rights of defence. This case-law is discussed in the *Case-law Guide.*[40]

2.8 Providing Information in the EAW

Only if the box of points 3.1b, 3.2 or 3.3 is ticked does the issuing judicial authority have to provide information under point 4 of section (d) (see Sections 2.2, 2.3 and 2.4). Under point 4, the issuing judicial authority is asked to "provide information about how the relevant condition has been met". In essence, the issuing judicial authority is requested to mention the information on which it based its conclusion that the particular point is applicable.

The information should be clear, correct and comprehensive and should be presented in such a way that the executing judicial authority will be able to draw the same conclusion. The issuing judicial authority should avoid using legal terms derived from the law of the issuing Member State, but rather use factual terms to describe the relevant situation. Using legal terms derived from the law of the issuing Member State may cause confusion, because these terms may have a different meaning according to the legal system of the executing Member State.

> An example.
> *[X] 3.1b. the person was not summoned in person but by other means actually received official information of the scheduled date and place of the trial which*

39 See ECtHR, judgment of 1 March 2006, *Sejdovic v. Italy* [GC], ECLI:CE:ECHR:2006:0301JUD005658100, § 101.

40 Accessible at www.inabsentieaw.eu.

resulted in the decision, in such a manner that it was unequivocally established that he or she was aware of the scheduled trial, and was informed that a decision may be handed down if he or she does not appear for the trial;
(...)
4. If you have ticked the box under points 3.1b, 3.2 or 3.3 above, please provide information about how the relevant condition has been met:
The summons was handed over to the defendant's wife at the defendant's address on 1 July 2019. Referring to that summons, in a letter of 3 July 2019 the defendant asked for an adjournment of the trial. (...)
The conclusion drawn by the issuing judicial authority that the defendant actually received the summons sometime between 1 and 3 July 2019 follows logically from the fact that the defendant refers to that summons in his letter of 3 July 2019.

Even if none of points 3.1b, 3.2 or 3.3 is applicable and the issuing judicial authority is under no duty to fill in point 4, it may be advisable to do so nonetheless. Explaining the situation under point 4 serves the interest of transparency and may enable the executing judicial authority to draw the conclusion that executing the EAW would not entail a breach of the rights of defence of the person concerned (see Section 2.7).

2.9 Assessing Information Provided by the Issuing Judicial Authority

Where the person concerned did not appear in person at the 'trial resulting in the decision', it is up to the executing judicial authority to "verify whether the situation before it corresponds to one of those described under (a) to (d) [of Article 4a(1)]".[41] The situations described in Article 4a(1)(a) to (d) correspond to points 3.1-3.4 of section (d) of the EAW.

When the issuing judicial authority ticks one or more of the boxes of points 3.1-3.4, in essence it "gives the assurance that the requirements [of Art. 4a(1)] have been or will be met, which should be sufficient for the purpose of the execution of the decision on the basis of the principle of mutual recognition".[42]

The principle of mutual trust dictates that the executing judicial authority should rely on such an assurance. A mere statement of the requested person contesting the veracity of an assurance should not be enough to cast doubt on its trustworthiness. It is up to the requested person to back up his claim with evidence which is capable of demonstrating that an error or mistake has indeed occurred. If and only if such evidence is presented by

41 ECJ, judgment of 10 August 2017, *Openbaar Ministerie v. Tadas Tupikas*, C-270/17 PPU, ECLI:EU:C:2017:628, para. 93.
42 Recital (6) of the preamble to FD 2009/299/JHA.

the requested person should the executing judicial authority enquire with the issuing judicial authority and apply Article 15(2) of FD 2002/584/JHA.

In three distinct situations – *viz.* when the box of points 3.1b, 3.2 or 3.3 is ticked – the issuing judicial authority must explain under point 4 how the relevant condition was met. With regard to the information mentioned under point 4, the previous paragraph applies *mutatis mutandis*.

In these three situations, the executing judicial authority may verify whether the assurance given by the issuing judicial authority is supported by the information presented under point 4. If it is of the opinion that the assurance does not follow from that information and that, therefore, the relevant condition is not met, it should apply Article 15(2) of FD 2002/584/JHA at least once (see Section 2.10).

2.10 More Information Needed?

2.10.1 *General*

The executing judicial authority should bear in mind that requesting supplementary information on the basis of Article 15(2) of FD 2002/584/JHA should be "a last resort in exceptional cases in which the executing judicial authority considers that it does not have the official evidence necessary to adopt a decision on surrender as a matter of urgency".[43]

Therefore, the executing judicial authority must not request 'as a matter of course'[44] general information about the legal system of the issuing Member State.

2.10.2 *The Request*

If the executing judicial authority is of the opinion that it needs supplementary information in order to "validly decide on the execution of the [EAW]", it is under a duty to request the necessary supplementary information.[45]

In requesting supplementary information, the executing judicial authority should not ask open-ended questions, but rather formulate questions which allow for a clear, correct and comprehensive answer by the issuing judicial authority (see Section 2.7). To facilitate such answers, the executing judicial authority should:

43 ECJ, judgment of 23 January 2018, *Dawid Piotrowski*, C-367/16, ECLI:EU:C:2018:27, para. 61.

44 ECJ, judgment of 25 July 2018, *Generalstaatsanwaltschaft (conditions of detention in Hungary)*, C-220/18, ECLI:EU:C:2018:589, para. 61.

45 ECJ, judgment of 10 August 2017, *Sławomir Andrzej Zdziaszek*, C-271/17 PPU, ECLI:EU:C:2017:629, para. 103.

- identify specific parts of section (d) of the EAW which in its view are unclear, insufficient, contradictory or obviously incorrect, and
- indicate what kind of information is needed to remedy the situation.

Moreover, the executing judicial authority should not leave its counterpart guessing as to the reason why a certain piece of information is needed. Explaining the reason behind the request for supplementary information, with reference to relevant case-law of the Court of Justice (if applicable), helps the issuing judicial authority in providing that information and may also afford it an opportunity to clear up any misunderstandings in the initial assessment of the executing judicial authority.

2.10.3 *Time Limits*

In the request for supplementary information, the executing judicial authority may "fix a time limit for the receipt thereof, taking into account the need to observe the time limits set in Article 17" (Article 15(2) of FD 2002/584/JHA).

In the spirit of loyal cooperation, the time limit set for receipt should not be so short as to make answering the request unfeasible.

2.10.4 *Communication Channels*

It is up to the executing judicial authority to choose an appropriate channel for communicating with its counterpart, but given the need to observe the time limits of Article 17 of FD 2002/584/JHA it is advisable to communicate by way of e-mail. Communication by e-mail, rather than, *e.g.*, by telephone, is also in the interest of transparency with regard to the requested person.

2.10.5 *Language*

Insofar as the applicable legal regime permits[46] and taking into account the rights of the person concerned,[47] the need to observe the time limits of Article 17 of FD 2002/584/JHA strongly suggests that the executing issuing judicial authorities communicate with one another in a language which they both understand, thus obviating as far as possible the need for any translation.

46 See Art. 8(2) of FD 2002/584/JHA concerning translation of the EAW.

47 See Art. 3(6) of Directive 2010/64/EU on the right to interpretation and translation in criminal proceedings, concerning translation of the EAW.

2.10.6 *Unsatisfactory Response*

The issuing judicial authority should be aware that a request for supplementary information may be the last chance it gets to convince the executing judicial authority that it should not refuse to execute the EAW on the basis of Article 4a(1) of FD 2002/584/JHA.

After having requested supplementary information once, if the executing judicial authority is of the opinion that it "still has not obtained the necessary assurances as regards the rights of defence of the person concerned during the relevant proceedings", it may refuse to execute the EAW.[48] The executing judicial authority is under no duty to ask for supplementary information again.[49]

2.10.7 *Reasons for Refusal*

According to Article 17(6) of FD 2002/584/JHA, the executing judicial authority must give its reasons for any refusal to execute an EAW. The reasons for a refusal allow the issuing judicial authority to assess whether it can remedy the defect(s) established by the executing judicial authority. If, *e.g.*, the execution of the EAW was refused, because the EAW did not mention the evidence on which the issuing judicial authority based its conclusion that the defendant actually received the summons or the decision, the issuing judicial authority could mention such evidence in a new EAW (see Section 2.11).

2.11 Does a Refusal to Execute the EAW on the Basis of Article 4a(1) of FD 2002/584/JHA Have a ne bis in idem Effect?

If the executing judicial authority refused to execute an EAW on the basis of Article 4a(1) of FD 2002/584/JHA, is the issuing judicial authority prevented from issuing a new EAW with regard to the same person, the same offence and the same judgment?

The Court of Justice has stressed that the executing judicial authority "which does not reply following the issue of an EAW and thus does not communicate any decision to the judicial authority that issued the EAW is in breach of its obligations under those provisions of Framework Decision 2002/584".[50]

---

48 ECJ, judgment of 10 August 2017, *Sławomir Andrzej Zdziaszek*, C-271/17 PPU, ECLI:EU:C:2017:629, para. 104.

49 ECJ, judgment of 10 August 2017, *Sławomir Andrzej Zdziaszek*, C-271/17 PPU, ECLI:EU:C:2017:629, para. 105.

50 ECJ, judgment of 25 July 2018, *AY*, C-268/17, ECLI:EU:C:2018:602, para. 31.

The executing judicial authority, therefore, should take a decision on the execution of an EAW, even though the execution of a previous EAW with regard to the same person, the same offence and the same judgment was refused.

However, it is advisable that the issuing judicial authority should only issue such a new EAW, if it has any information which was not available to the executing judicial authority at the time of the decision on the previous EAW, which might be relevant to Article 4a(1) and which might lead to the execution of the EAW. Of course, the issuing judicial authority should explain all of this in the new EAW.

Maastricht Law Series

The Maastricht Law Series was created in 2018 by Boom juridisch and Eleven International Publishing in association with the Maastricht University Faculty of Law. The Maastricht Law Series publishes books on comparative, European and International law. The series builds upon the tradition of excellence in research at the Maastricht Faculty of Law, its research centres and the Ius Commune Research School. The Maastricht Law Series is a peer-reviewed book series that allows researchers an excellent opportunity to showcase their work.

Published in this series:

Volume 1: Reinhard Zimmermann, Does the Law of Succession Reflect Cultural Differences?, ISBN 978-94-6236-856-9
Volume 2: Anna Berlee, Access to Personal Data in Public Land Registers, ISBN 978-94-6236-841-5
Volume 3: Marcus Meyer, The Position of Dutch Works Councils in Multinational Corporations, ISBN 978-94-6236-848-4
Volume 4: Jaap Hage, Foundations and Building Blocks of Law, ISBN 978-94-6236-860-6
Volume 5: Bastiaan van Zelst, The End of Justice(s)?, ISBN 978-94-6236-881-1
Volume 6: Lars van Vliet & Agustin Parise (eds.), Re- De- Co-dification? New Insights on the Codification of Private Law, ISBN 978-94-6236-900-9
Volume 7: Caroline Rupp, Rafael Ibarra Garza & Bram Akkermans, Property Law Perspectives VI, ISBN 978-94-6236-904-7
Volume 8: Aalt Willem Heringa, Europees Nederlands Staatsrecht, ISBN 978-94-6290-604-4
Volume 9: Symeon C. Symeonides, The 'Private' in Private International Law, ISBN 978-94-6236-949-8
Volume 10: Jaap Hage, European Integration, ISBN 978-94-6236-981-8

Volume 11: Jan M. Smits, Five Uneasy Pieces. Essays on Law and Evolution, ISBN 978-94-6236-982-5
Volume 12: Kei Hannah Brodersen, Vincent Glerum & André Klip, The European Arrest Warrant and *In Absentia* Judgements, ISBN 978-94-6236-985-6
Volume 13: Bram Akkermans & Gijs van Dijck, Sustainability and Private Law, ISBN 978-94-6236-986-3
Volume 14: Antonia Waltermann, David Roef, Jaap Hage & Marko Jelicic, Law, Science, Rationality, ISBN 978-94-6236-989-4

Printed by Libri Plureos GmbH in Hamburg,
Germany

9 789462 369856